The Jacksonians
versus the Banks

The Jacksonians *versus* the Banks

POLITICS IN THE STATES AFTER THE PANIC OF 1837

by JAMES ROGER SHARP

MCMLXX

COLUMBIA UNIVERSITY PRESS

NEW YORK & LONDON

James Roger Sharp is Associate Professor of History
at Syracuse University.

Copyright © 1970 Columbia University Press
ISBN: 0-231-03260-9
Library of Congress Catalog Card Number: 70-127783
Printed in the United States of America

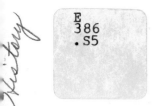
IN MEMORY OF MY MOTHER

SHIRLEY CARLSON SHARP

PREFACE

ALTHOUGH most historians agree that banking was a central issue of the Jacksonian period, there is considerable argument among scholars as to the nature of the relationship between the banking question and the Jacksonians and, thus, as to the nature of Jacksonian Democracy itself.

Almost a quarter of a century ago, Arthur Schlesinger, Jr., in an ambitious reinterpretation of the period, cast the Jacksonians as liberal reformers attempting to impose a check upon a selfish and aggressive business community. He found the theme of politics in the Jacksonian period, as well as throughout American history, to have been "the irrepressible conflict of capitalism: the struggle on the part of the business community to dominate the state, and on the part of the rest of society, under the leadership of the 'liberals,' to check the political ambitions of business." [1]

Since the publication of Schlesinger's ground-breaking work, much of Jacksonian historiography has been a reaction to *The Age of Jackson*. Perhaps the most effective challenge to Schlesinger's work and the interpretation that enjoys the widest currency today is the entrepreneurial thesis, brilliantly argued by Bray Hammond in his *Banks and Politics in America*, published over a decade ago. In contrast to Schles-

---

[1] Arthur M. Schlesinger, Jr., *The Age of Jackson* (Boston, 1945), 514. For an excellent survey of the historiography of the Jacksonian period, see Charles G. Sellers, Jr., "Andrew Jackson versus the Historians," *Mississippi Valley Historical Review*, XLIV (March, 1958), 615–34, and more recently the discussion by Edward Pessen, *Jacksonian America: Society, Personality, and Politics* (Homewood, Ill., 1969), 352–93.

inger, Hammond maintains that the Jacksonian movement was dominated by grasping, acquisitive entrepreneurs and aspiring entrepreneurs, who, in their attack on special privilege, sought impatiently to remove any restrictions upon business. In their battle against the Second Bank of the United States, he contends,

[the] Jacksonians still employed the vocabulary of their agrarian backgrounds. The phraseology of idealism was adapted to money-making, the creed of an earlier generation becoming the cant of its successor. . . . Though their cause was a sophisticated one of enterpriser against capitalist, of banker against regulation, and of Wall Street against Chestnut, the language was the same as if they were all back on the farm. . . . Notwithstanding their language . . . the Jacksonians' destruction of the Bank of the United States was in no sense a blow at capitalism or property or the "money power." It was a blow at an older set of capitalists by a newer, more numerous set. It was incident to the democratization of business, the diffusion of enterprise among the mass of people, and the transfer of economic primacy from an old and conservative merchant class to a newer, more aggressive, and more numerous body of business men and speculators of all sorts.[2]

According to the reasoning of Hammond and other subscribers to the entrepreneurial thesis, the destruction of the Second Bank of the United States was a conscious, well-planned act to open up enterprise. To clinch their case, they point to the rapid increase in numbers of banks throughout the country and the spiraling economic boom after the demise of the national bank as being the direct results of the dominant enterprising spirit within the Jackson movement.

The research of both Hammond and Schlesinger is centered almost entirely on the national level, primarily the destruction of the Second Bank of the United States, with only scant attention paid to state politics, and then only to issues in the northeastern states of New York, Pennsylvania, and Massachusetts.[3] And while there are a number of

[2] Bray Hammond, *Banks and Politics in America: From the Revolution to the Civil War* (Princeton, N.J., 1957), 328–29. Quotations from this work reprinted courtesy of Princeton University Press, copyright © 1957 Princeton University Press.

[3] The same would apply to Marvin Meyers' *The Jacksonian Persuasion: Politics and Belief* (New York, 1960), which is mainly concerned with the intellectual appeal of the Jacksonians, but the persuasion examined is almost exclusively that of New England and New York.

excellent works on individual states,[4] there has as yet been no attempt to bridge the gap between a state focus and a predominantly national one.

The Jacksonians Versus the Banks, then, a nationwide survey of banking and politics on the state level after the Panic of 1837, attempts to add this dimension to the discussion. For the purposes of this inquiry, the country has been divided into four geographic sections—the Southwest, Northwest, Southeast, and Northeast—each of which shared common characteristics and a certain cohesion that made the division useful for analytic purposes. The Northeast was considered in less detail because the banking controversy there was milder and more short-lived than in the nation as a whole, and also because other historians have centered their attention on the Northeast to the exclusion of the other sections.

Since it would have been virtually impossible, and needlessly repetitious, to have undertaken a close study of the political development in all twenty-six states, representative states from each of the sections were singled out for intensive analysis. In each of these states—Mississippi, Ohio, Virginia, and to a lesser degree, New York and Pennsylvania— Democratic rhetoric and action on the state level were studied and a careful analysis made of the positions taken by the party on the bank issue in the state legislatures. In order to determine the basis of the party's grass roots support, constituencies in Mississippi, Ohio, and Virginia were examined. And to help make a more precise determination of constituent support, some statistical methods were employed, particularly rank-difference correlations. Other states in each of the four sections were dealt with in a more summary fashion with the aim of indicating similarities to and deviations from the experience in the representative states.

[4] It is not my intention here to give a comprehensive listing of state studies. However some recent ones are: Lee Benson, *The Concept of Jacksonian Democracy: New York as a Test Case* (New York, 1960); Edwin Arthur Miles, *Jacksonian Democracy in Mississippi* (Chapel Hill, N.C., 1960); William S. Hoffman, *Andrew Jackson and North Carolina Politics* (Chapel Hill, N.C., 1958); and Charles McCool Snyder, *The Jacksonian Heritage, Pennsylvania Politics, 1833–1848* (Harrisburg, Pa., 1958). Benson's book perhaps represents the culmination of this eastern orientation of Jacksonian historiography. He suggests that the New York experience might be a microcosm of Jacksonian politics throughout the country.

There are characteristics that make New York, Pennyslvania, Mississippi, Virginia, and Ohio valuable as analytical entities. New York and Pennsylvania, for example, were both extremely important and influential in national politics, and Philadelphia and New York City were the financial centers of the country. In Mississippi the banking controversy ultimately became a question of whether the state should or should not repudiate state bonds floated to aid in the establishment of the banks. This repudiation issue gave the banking problem there another dimension. In Ohio, politically and economically larger and more important than any other state in the Northwest, the contest between advocates and opponents of the banking system was especially lengthy and virulent. Virginia was one of the leading states in the Democratic coalition, and in the period after 1837 the intraparty feuding over the banking and currency issue took place on both the state and national levels. Because of the importance of the state nationally and the aspirations of some of the leaders within the state, the Independent Treasury question became more divisive to the Democratic party there than in other states.

The Panic of 1837 marks the starting point for this study. The nationwide suspension of specie payments by the banks in that year and the Van Buren Administration's decision to abandon the Deposit Bank System had the effect of atomizing the bank war and thrusting the primary responsibility for the banking issue upon the states. Whereas prior to 1837 men of both parties might hedge on the banking question, afterward the banks became an urgent issue that demanded immediate attention and compelled both parties to take firm stands. And, finally, any judgment as to where the Democratic party stood on the banking issue can be made with more precision after 1837, for the parties in the post-Panic period were more stable and better defined than were the parties of the earlier period, which were more heterogeneous and often, in reality, represented only temporary alliances of shifting coalitions.

ACKNOWLEDGMENTS

THIS STUDY has been a long time in preparation, and the number of people to whom I have become obligated are legion. I am particularly grateful to the skill, patience, and good humor of numerous librarians across the country: John Knowlton and John McDonough at the Library of Congress, Ralph L. Hazeltine at the Wyoming Historical and Geological Society in Wilkes-Barre; Kenneth W. Duckett, previously at the Ohio Historical Society, Mrs. Virginia R. Gray at the Duke University Library, James W. Patton at the Southern Historical Collection at the University of North Carolina Library, James Servies at the William and Mary College Library, Robert L. Brubaker at the Illinois State Historical Library, Mrs. Lee Jordan at the Cincinnati Historical Society, and Mrs. Laura D. S. Harrell at the Mississippi Department of Archives and History. I also want to thank the library staffs at the University of Virginia, the Virginia State Library at Richmond, the New York Public Library, the Pennsylvania Historical and Museum Commission in Harrisburg, the Historical Society of Pennsylvania, the Free Library of Philadelphia, and the Sutro Library in San Francisco. Mrs. Ann Reed and her staff in the newspaper room and the staff of the Interlibrary Loan Department at the University of California Library at Berkeley were marvelously helpful and attentive to my needs. Woodrow W. White of the West Virginia State Auditor's Office and Miss Daphne Gentry of the Virginia State Library provided vitally needed Virginia tax data.

Professor Charles Sellers of the University of California at Berkeley initially suggested the topic to me and guided my work in its early stages. For his help, as a teacher and a friend, I am profoundly in his debt. His insights and perceptive critiques of the manuscript were invaluable in helping me to untangle the knot of Jacksonian politics. Professor Joel Silbey of Cornell University read the entire manuscript and made a number of valuable suggestions, including one that led me to attempt to gain a rudimentary knowledge of useful statistical techniques. I also appreciate the suggestions made by Professor Eric McKitrick of Columbia University. My father-in-law, Professor Edward H. Weatherly of the University of Missouri, proofread the manuscript and saved me from numerous errors of style. I also have profitted from the advice and counsel of a number of friends: Professor Stephen S. Webb of Syracuse University, Professor John McFaul of California State College at Long Beach, and Professor William Stinchcombe of Syracuse University and his wife, Jean. At the outset of the project, Professor Frank Gatell of the University of California at Los Angeles was kind enough to open his bibliography to me. Mrs. Beulah Learnard Levine was untiring in her efforts to tutor me in the use of statistics and invaluable in her help in setting up the statistical appendices and in criticizing the statistical portions of the manuscript. I am grateful to Mrs. Barbara Kawash of Columbia University Press, whose editorial skills improved the text. My typist, Mrs. Diane Wallace, has typed several drafts of the manuscript with unfailing good humor, efficiency, and accuracy. Students at Syracuse University, particularly Miss Gail Ross and Stephen Tober, assisted with the reading of galley proofs.

The graduate school of the University of California at Berkeley, the Appleby Fund at Syracuse University and the American Philosophical Society provided grants to aid me in my research.

And, finally, there is little I could do that would adequately convey my sense of obligation and appreciation to my wife, Nancy. Her work was truly a labor of love. From the beginning, this has been a joint endeavor. She aided me from inception of the work down to the final preparation in proofreading, editing, research, and in mastering rank-difference correlation techniques to save her husband from grievous error. If my argument is clear, logical, and well-organized, much of the credit is due to her. However, in all fairness to all of those who have so generously helped me, I bear the responsibility for any failings of the work.

CONTENTS

GRAPHS AND MAPS

SONG FROM A JACKSON BARBECUE
SEPTEMBER 25, 1839

Hard times, hard times is all the cry,
 The country's in confusion,
The Banks have stop'd, but still they try
 To mistify delusion.
They give us trash and keep our cash,
 To send across the waters,
To pay for things they bought of Kings,
 And gull our sons and daughters.

Then to the Polls, you noble souls;
The Banks they cry for quarters;
But here's their doom, they *shall* resume,
Or forfeit all their charters.

Shall corporations rule the soil
 That Washington defended;
Shall honest people sweat and toil;
 And have their rights suspended;
Shall we be slaves to pampered knaves,
 And Banks still be our masters,
Since all they pay from day to day,
 Is nothing but *Shinplasters?*

Then to the Polls, you noble souls;
The Banks they cry for quarters;
And here's their doom, they *shall* resume,
Or forfeit all their charters.

Brave Jackson fought to set us free—
 He loves his country dearly;
His own metallic currency
 Is not a promise merely.
But little Van's an honest man,
 He'll imitate the Hero.
And lay the Banks that play such pranks
 All just as low as Zero.

Then to the Polls, you noble souls,
The Banks they cry for quarters;
But here's their doom, they *shall* resume,
Or forfeit all their charters.
   Quoted in the Jackson *Mississippian,* October 11, 1839

INTRODUCTION

CHAPTER I

The Democratic Party and the Politics of Agrarianism

I

THE CLOSING DAYS of Andrew Jackson's sometimes tumultuous and always controversial two terms as President came in March of 1837 and were marked by contrasts. As the venerable old military hero prepared to turn the office over to his hand-picked successor, the newly elected Martin Van Buren, he reviewed his eight years in office with satisfaction and happily anticipated his retirement to the Hermitage. The popular Jackson was virtually deluged by gifts from grateful followers. A phaeton constructed entirely of the wood from the frigate *Constitution* was presented to the former general, while another supporter contributed a light wagon made entirely of hickory sticks. A gift enjoyed by many White House visitors was a huge cheese, 4 feet around, 2 feet thick and weighing close to 1,400 pounds.[1]

Amidst the rejoicing and celebrating, however, Jackson expressed grave concern about the development of the banking system, one of the major problems with which the country must deal, he felt. In an address on the eve of his retirement, the chief executive warned, as he had many times before, that the banks posed "serious evils" for American society. The malignant growth of a "paper money system and its natural associates, monopoly and exclusive privileges, have already struck their roots deep in the soil," he reminded his countrymen, "and

[1] James Parton, *Life of Andrew Jackson,* III (New York, 1860), 626.

it will require all your efforts to check its further growth and to eradicate the evil." [2]

The closely allied questions of banking and currency were the most important political issues of the Jacksonian era and were crucial factors in shaping the political history of the entire nineteenth century. But despite Jackson's forebodings, it was not until after he had left the Presidency that the banking issue was thrown into sharp relief by a severe financial panic in the spring of 1837.

Throughout Andrew Jackson's Presidency, and up to the Panic of 1837 itself, there had been within the Democratic party an uneasy ambivalence on the banking problem. On the one hand, a neo-Jeffersonian antagonism to banks was a cornerstone of the Jacksonian credo. But on the other hand, the Age of Jackson was also the Age of Enterprise and was pervaded with an entrepreneurial zeal that deafened the ears of many within the party to Jackson's warnings.

Compounding this ambivalence was the ambiguity of the Jeffersonian legacy. Both James Madison and John Taylor of Caroline were Jeffersonian spokesmen, but they translated the ideology into very different conclusions. Madison's beliefs would encompass a Bank of the United States and an expanded federal government, while Taylor regarded both as anathema.

Furthermore, Jackson's candidacy in the early 1820s had attracted men of widely varying political outlooks, and thus during Jackson's Presidency, especially in the early years, the party had been a heterogeneous group. Former Federalists seeking a fresh political start, Democrats of the Old Republican school, bank men, antibank men, and high- and low-tariff men all had flocked to the banner of the colorful and popular leader. Once the Jackson Administration had assumed power, however, policy decisions had had to be made. And in taking action on public questions, Jackson by necessity lost some of his following. Thus, the veto of the Maysville Road Bill alienated those Jacksonians who had hoped for federal support for internal improvements, while the Old General's strong stand against Nullification offended some of the more militant state rightists within the Democratic coalition.

[2] James D. Richardson, *A Compilation of the Messages and Papers of the Presidents,* II (Washington, D.C., 1911), 1524–25.

Jackson's veto of the bill to recharter the Second Bank of the United States was perhaps the most important action of his two terms.[3] The veto and the subsequent withdrawal of the federal deposits from the bank drove from the party a number of the bank's friends and others who objected to what they considered to be the unlawful use of executive power. The destruction of the national bank did by no means, however, clarify the party's stance and future relationship with the hundreds of other banks in the country. Thus, remaining within the party and forming an uneasy coalition were men opposed in principle to all banks and others who were friendly to the interests of the local banks.

If Jackson's veto message had been analyzed carefully by these friends of banks in the various states, or soft-money men, they would have found it very disquieting. Although directed against the Second Bank of the United States, the message articulated a central antibank theme that could be applied against all banks. To Jackson and his hard-money followers, banks occupied privileged positions in society and exercised tremendous and virtually unchecked power. This power, they concluded, had either to be curtailed and regulated, or destroyed.

In the years between the veto and the Panic of 1837, however, most Americans were caught up in what seemed to be boundless prosperity, and the antibank rhetoric and proposals of the radical wing of the Democratic party did not find an enthusiastic or widespread audience. The hard-money men did, however, fight a rear-guard, and often futile, action during these pre-Panic years in an attempt to slow down bank expansion.

The nationwide bank suspension in 1837 and the following depression acted as a spiritual and political catharsis, purging the party of much of its doubt and making opposition to the banks a test of party

[3] Jean Alexander Wilburn, in her *Biddle's Bank: The Crucial Years* (New York, 1967), argues that there was overwhelming support for the Second Bank of the United States and that the re-election of Jackson in 1832 represented more the triumph of his personal popularity than a successful referendum endorsing his veto. She relies heavily upon memorials, or petitions, sent to Congress, either supporting or attacking the bank. It is open to question, however, as to how correctly such petitions represent public opinion on issues. Rather, it would seem the veto awakened a very deep, but sometimes latent, antibank hostility that pervaded much of American society.

loyalty. The financial collapse raised the most basic economic, political, and moral inquiries about the nature of American society and reinforced the prejudices and anxieties of the Jacksonians about the banking system and the increasing commercialization of the country. In an age dominated by an egalitarian spirit, the banks symbolized aristocratic privilege on the one hand, and the rapid and uncomfortable transition the country was undergoing from an agrarian to a commercial society on the other hand.

Thus the bank issue became the crucible of the Democratic party. It tested and tempered the metal of Jackson's followers and became the mold from which the party was shaped. Beginning with Jackson's veto of the bill to recharter the Second Bank of the United States in 1832, the banking question particularly after 1837 assumed an internal dynamic and logic of its own, pushing the party more and more in the direction of an all-out war against all banks.

Antibank sentiment varied in intensity. Some Jacksonians sought to make the banks safer and more responsible to the public. Others wanted to abolish banking altogether. But it was the hard-money men —either radical or more moderate in feeling—who set the tone, style, and appeal of the Democratic party. They were, however, often frustrated in their efforts by the combined opposition of the Whigs and a small group of soft-money Democrats. Still, the hards were remarkably successful in dominating their party and in imposing restraints upon the banking system.

The Jacksonian attack on the banks was but a single episode in an extended debate over banking, credit, and currency that lasted throughout the nineteenth century. The rhetoric of the Jacksonians and their fears were similar in tone and content to those expressed earlier by John Taylor of Caroline in the early nineteenth century and nearly a century later by Populist leaders. All were representatives of an agrarian society who felt that their moral values were being eroded away by the commercialization of society and the quickening tempo of industry.

Taylor had attacked banks and corporations as the harbingers of a new order, fearing them as powerful, evil influences. Americans, he claimed, after abolishing titles and hierarchies, now were becoming enslaved by patronage and paper. While the American Revolution had exploded the old myth of an immutable social contract, the same worn dogma was reappearing in the guise of the inviolability of modern law charters. There existed, according to Taylor, two sources for the love of wealth. Wealth fostered by honest industry was "an ally of moral rectitude and national happiness," while wealth engendered by "partial laws for enriching corporations and individuals" was akin to immorality and oppression.[4]

The same agrarian ethos is found in the Populist movement at the end of the century. Anticorporate and antibank in nature, the Populist rhetoric echoed the earlier sentiment. At the National Union Conference in Cincinnati in 1891 it was declared that the

right to make and issue money is a sovereign power to be maintained by the people for the common benefit. Hence we demand the abolition of national banks as banks of issue, and as a substitute for national bank notes we demand that legal tender Treasury notes be issued in sufficient volume to transact the business of the country on a cash basis without damage or especial advantage to any class or calling, such notes to be legal tender in payment of all debts, public and private. . . .[5]

This Populist call for an inflationary soft-money policy was not as diametrically opposed as it might seem to be to the deflationary hard-money position of John Taylor of Caroline and the Jacksonians.[6]

---

[4] John Taylor of Caroline, *An Inquiry into the Principles and Policy of the Government of the United States* (New Haven, Conn., 1950), section on Aristocracy; John Taylor of Caroline, *Construction Construed and Constitutions Vindicated* (Richmond, Va., 1820), Section I.

[5] As quoted in John D. Hicks, *The Populist Revolt: A History of the Farmers' Alliance and the People's Party* (Lincoln, Nebr., 1961), 433.

[6] One historian of Reconstruction poses the question of "why the leaders of the old hard-money Jacksonian Democracy, men such as George Pendleton, William Allen, and Francis Preston Blair, Jr., embraced the soft-money philosophy of the post-Civil War period." Answering his own question, he maintains that an "important thread of continuity which linked the pre-war, hard-money Democrats of the age of Jackson and those Democrats, particularly western Democrats of the sixties and seventies, whose proclivities were toward soft money, was a dislike and distrust of banks, bankers, and particularly bank notes. Since the supply of specie in the country was inadequate to sustain a return to coin payments without drastic deflation, it was only natural that western Democrats should prefer greenbacks, the money of the people, to national bank notes which was the money of the banker." Robert P. Sharkey, *Money, Class and Party: An Economic Study of Civil War and Reconstruction* (Baltimore, 1959), 104–107.

Throughout the country there was a fervently held belief that privately issued paper money was an exploitative device by which capitalists and bankers could control prices and the money supply. This, in turn, it was argued, gave these special citizens enormous political and economic power and made a mockery of a society that emphasized equal rights for all and special privileges for none.

2

The Jacksonians' destruction of the Second Bank of the United States had the effect of removing any national control over banking operations in the country. The Philadelphia giant had acted as a great central bank with the financial power to regulate and facilitate the flow of currency and exchange throughout the states.

The federal funds, which had been withdrawn from the Bank of the United States, were subsequently placed in certain selected banks throughout the country. And it was through negotiations with these deposit banks that the Jackson Administration attempted to place some order and control over the anarchic system of banks in the states. This, however, did have the effect of throwing the Democrats into a temporary and unholy alliance with these deposit banks.

Congress was asked to pass laws to regulate these deposit banks to ensure their stability. But until 1836 the legislators refused to do so. In the interim, however, Secretary of the Treasury Levi Woodbury did manage to control these banks rather successfully just through his official dealings with them. And in 1835 a small-note regulation was instituted by the Treasury Department forbidding the deposit banks to accept notes of a lesser value than 5 dollars. A year later Congress prohibited the disbursement of bank notes under 10 dollars, with the provision that the following year the prohibition would be extended to include notes under 20 dollars.

The Deposit Act finally was passed by Congress in 1836, dramatically increasing the number of deposit banks in order that the distribution of federal funds be more widespread. Unfortunately, the expansion of the system had the consequence of weakening it. Another provision of the act, a regulation that no deposit bank could hold federal funds in excess of three fourths of its capital, had an unsettling effect. The result was that there was a large transference of funds between banks. But despite its weaknesses, the Deposit Bank System did provide many of the same important functions the Second Bank of the United States had performed before it had been eliminated as the federal government's fiscal agent.[7]

Also in 1836, trying to put a brake upon the runaway inflation and land speculation, the administration issued the Specie Circular, which provided that only gold and silver [8] could be accepted by government agents in payment for public lands. This action, which was bitterly fought by the Whigs and some members of Jackson's own party, had the effect of increasing the already growing pressure on the state banks by draining their specie holdings.

By the time Jackson retired from the Presidency in 1837, the fiscal storm was about to break. On returning to the Hermitage, he wrote Martin Van Buren, warning his successor of the economic conditions he found in the Southwest. He said he feared for the safety of the deposit banks in that area, for he realized that if any of these banks suspended specie payments, it would shake the new administration "to its center." The planters were heavily obligated, so much so that it would take three good crops "with great economy to meet their debts." [9]

A month and a half later banks across the country had suspended specie payment. This, as Jackson had predicted, put the Van Buren Administration in an untenable position. The Whigs blamed the financial collapse on the Democrats, particularly on the Specie Circular and the destruction of the Second Bank of the United States. Some Democrats countered by charging the Whigs with stimulating the mania of speculation of the 1830s, which they said had led to the ultimate failure of the entire banking system. Other Democratic leaders saw the specter

[7] See John Michael McFaul's excellent dissertation, "The Politics of Jacksonian Finance," unpublished Ph.D. thesis, University of California, Berkeley, 1963. McFaul analyzes the Jackson Administration's attempt to impose tighter regulations on state banks. Also Harry N. Scheiber, "The Pet Banks in Jacksonian Politics and Finance, 1833–1841," *Journal of Economic History,* XXIII (June, 1963), 194–214, and John M. McFaul and Frank Otto Gatell, "The Outcast Insider: Reuben M. Whitney and the Bank War," *Pennsylvania Magazine of History and Biography,* XCI (April, 1967), 115–44.

[8] In certain limited circumstances, land script would be accepted.

[9] Andrew Jackson to Martin Van Buren, March 30, 1837, Martin Van Buren Papers, Library of Congress.

of Nicholas Biddle and the Bank of the United States as being responsible for the ruin. Biddle's motive, it was believed, was to force a new federal charter for his bank.[10]

But behind the charges and countercharges the Van Buren Administration was struggling to work out a financial and banking policy that would answer Whig critics and at the same time satisfy rank-and-file Democrats. Three possibilities were seen. The first, the chartering of another national bank, was an option that would destroy the party and was not seriously entertained. The other two—continuing the Deposit Bank System with some reform and modification, or dissolving all connection between the federal government and banks—were the alternatives that were debated within the party councils during the late spring and early summer of 1837. The third, although it meant relinquishing what measure of control the federal government had over at least the deposit banks, was ultimately settled upon.

John Brockenbrough was an early proponent of the eventual solution, the Independent Treasury System, and he wrote to Van Buren explaining his plan for the federal government's management of its revenue. The federal government should not, argued the Democratic party leader and president of the Bank of Virginia, employ "any corporation to transact its business" but should use "its own agents to collect and disburse the public funds." To implement this plan, which also became known as the Sub-Treasury System, Brockenbrough proposed that a commissioner be appointed in each state for the purpose of handling federal monies.[11]

Van Buren wrote party leaders seeking opinions on Brockenbrough's plan. Silas Wright of New York, an old friend and political ally of Van Buren, approved the idea of separating federal funds from the

[10] Frank P. Blair to Andrew Jackson, May 26, 1837; Andrew Jackson to Moses Dawson, May 26, 1837; Andrew Jackson to Frank P. Blair, July 9 and June 5, 1837; Roger B. Taney to Andrew Jackson, July 3, 1837; Andrew Jackson Papers, Library of Congress. After the Bank of the United States' federal charter expired in 1836, it received a state charter from Pennsylvania and became the United States Bank of Pennsylvania. Unless otherwise noted, the name "Bank of the United States" as used in this book refers to the Second Bank of the United States, chartered in 1816.

[11] John Brockenbrough to William C. Rives, May 20, 1837, William C. Rives Papers, Library of Congress. John Brockenbrough to Martin Van Buren, May 22, 1837, Martin Van Buren Papers.

banks. But he warned Van Buren that the Whigs and many Democrats would bitterly oppose such a scheme. "Have we not," questioned Wright, "cause to fear that so many of our honest friends have accustomed themselves to consider incorporated banks as the richest blessing of modern civil government, . . . that such a proposition would startle them . . . as calculated to diminish to some extent the profits of these institutions . . . ?" [12]

Those Democratic friends of banks were not the only ones who worried Wright. The New Yorker feared what course Missouri Senator Thomas Hart Benton, the champion of the antibank forces, might take but hoped that Benton could be induced "to act wisely and . . . practically and moderately. . . ." [13] Wright had good reason to fear Benton's actions. A long-time critic of the banking system, Benton had decried earlier legislation that had made the notes of the local banks payable for all federal obligations. "I promised," he said, "the currency of the constitution, not the currency of corporations. I did not join in putting down the Bank of the United States to put up a wilderness of local banks. I did not join in putting down the paper currency of a national bank, to put up a national paper currency of a thousand local banks. I did not strike Caesar to make Antony master of Rome." [14]

Disillusionment and a sense of betrayal followed the widespread suspension of specie payments and reinforced the fears and doubts many Democrats had about the banking system. Some complained about the moderate tone that they felt the national party newspaper, the Washington *Globe,* was taking toward the banking system. In portraying banks "as useful or necessary," Gideon Welles of Connecticut wrote, "the editor or editors of the *Globe* are doing the administration an injury," for many Democrats, "constituting some of the most efficient supporters of the administration—men who are tenacious of their principles—are totally and absolutely opposed to the incorporated banking system." [15]

[12] Silas Wright to Martin Van Buren, June 4, 1837, Martin Van Buren Papers.
[13] *Ibid.*
[14] Thomas Hart Benton, *Thirty Years' View; Or a History of the Working of the American Government for Thirty Years, from 1820–1850* (New York, 1860), II, 10.
[15] Gideon Welles to Martin Van Buren, July 24, 1837, and Churchill C. Cambreleng to Abraham Van Buren, August 2, 1837, Martin Van Buren Papers.

Others urged Van Buren to be conciliatory toward the banks. Senator James Buchanan from Pennsylvania proposed that a federal bank,
which would be prohibited from issuing notes or discounting paper, be
established with branches in each state. It was his fear that the radical
hard-money faction within the party might use the opportunity of the
specie suspension to launch an all-out attack against the banking
system.[16] Enos Thompson Throop, former Democratic governor of
New York, shared Buchanan's concern. The suspension of specie payments by the banks, he felt must be defended as "a necessary" and a
"salutary measure." He urged the Van Buren Administration and the
Globe to set a tone of conciliation toward the banks. "Let the war be
carried on against *the* U. States Bank, and a National Bank," he maintained, for it would be "impossible to resist a National Bank, if the
friends of the administration are compelled at the same time to make
war upon the Banking System." Besides, he added, many Democrats
were interested in banks "and with very few exceptions, [they] believe
that they are indispensable." [17]

Some Democrats were not waiting for the administration to make
up its mind, for they saw events leading to the party's taking a position
more radical than they were prepared to support. Senators Nathaniel
P. Tallmadge of New York and William Cabell Rives of Virginia laid
plans to establish a newspaper in Washington to air their views. Tallmadge told Rives that he believed that local banks "properly regulated" were the best substitute for a national bank, and that if the administration had supported the deposit banks properly, there never
would have been a nationwide suspension of specie payment. He
feared that the time had come when every man "should buckle on his
armour," for the "war is now to be carried on against all our banking
institutions, the worst passions of the people are to be appealed to, and
their prejudices operated upon to prostrate our whole credit system,
which has done so much for the prosperity of the country." [18]

In early September, 1837, Van Buren presented his Independent

[16] James Buchanan to Martin Van Buren, June 15, 1837, Martin Van Buren
Papers.

[17] Enos Thompson Throop to Martin Van Buren, May 13, 1837, Martin Van
Buren Papers.

[18] Nathaniel P. Tallmadge to William C. Rives, May 31, 1837, William C.
Rives Papers.

Treasury plan to a special session of Congress. The President told the legislators that the government, in its deposit, transfer, and disbursement of federal funds, had always made use of national and local banks except for "temporary and limited exceptions." But it had become "apparent that the events of the last few months have greatly augmented the desire, long existing among the people of the United States, to separate the fiscal operations of the government from those of individuals or corporations." The history of the connection between banks and the fiscal affairs of the federal government was a most unsatisfactory and melancholy one, he continued. "Should we, then," he argued, again connect the Treasury "with the local banks, it can only be under a conviction that past failures have arisen from accidental, not inherent defects." Thus the separation of government finances from the banks was the only viable alternative. Unfortunately, he concluded, the Constitution did not enable the federal government to exercise any direct control over the banking system. But this was no cause for dismay, for the "whole matter is now under discussion before the proper tribunal—the people of the states," and "never before has the public mind been so thoroughly awakened to a proper sense of its importance; never has the subject in all its bearings, been submitted to so searching an inquiry." The final results of investigation, Van Buren felt, would be "the speedy and efficient adoption of such measures of reform as the public good demands." [19]

To Benton, as well as to other Jacksonians, it was obvious that the proposed Independent Treasury System—which would sever the connection between the federal government and banks—would be only a partial solution. Each state would have to do its part to insure responsible banking and sound currency within its boundaries. The Missouri Senator put the problem into perspective when he several years later advised the legislature in his home state that it could "save the state by excluding all paper money under twenty dollars; (I had much rather say under one hundred); congress can save the general government by establishing the independent treasury system." The local

[19] *Niles' Register,* September 2, 1837. This periodical was published under the name of *Niles' Weekly Register* in Baltimore up to September, 1837. From September, 1837, through April, 1839, it was the *Niles' National Register,* published in Washington, D.C. It returned to Baltimore in May, 1839. In future citations herein, the publication will be referred to as *Niles' Register.*

banks must be "kept in subordination to the laws" and "should be prevented from stopping and suspending when they please, and from inundating the country with small notes, and post notes, and other pestiferous trash." [20]

The advocates of the Independent Treasury were not to see their plans immediately fulfilled. It was not until after the fall of 1839, when the failure of the Second Bank of the United States (now operating under a Pennsylvania charter as the United States Bank of Pennsylvania) triggered a second nationwide bank suspension. What had started in 1837 as a financial panic had become a full-scale economic depression. Thus, in the summer of 1840 Congress, faced with deepening hard times and the second discrediting of the banks, finally passed the Independent Treasury Bill.

3

The decision of the Van Buren Administration to abandon the Deposit System in favor of the Independent Treasury had the effect of atomizing the bank war. Whereas there had been some hope that through the Deposit System the banks might have been regulated, that hope had been abandoned by the fall of 1837. Reform of the banks now became the responsibility of the twenty-six states.

As the country's attention was abruptly focused on the banking issue after the Panic, Jacksonians were forced to reevaluate the role, if any, that banks should play in American society. Just how strong, they had to decide, was their commitment against banks? Was it a fundamental principle of party? Were banks an evil in themselves, or could they be acceptable if reformed? There was an extreme diversity of opinion within party ranks concerning these questions. And as the Democrats labored to work out a more concrete stand on the currency issue, intraparty antagonisms that had been somewhat latent developed into acrimonious battles that, in turn, polarized the party.

The two extreme groups that emerged in the party were the soft-money men and the hard-money men. Occupying the vague and shadow-filled ground between these two major factions were the political brokers, Democratic leaders who were neither soft nor hard in per-

[20] *Ibid.,* July 20, 1839; also, June 8, 1839.

suasion. Sometimes leaning in one direction, sometimes in another, these political brokers put party unity above individual issues and continually maneuvered to keep the party from tearing itself apart over the currency issue.

Soft-money men agreed largely with the Whigs, rejecting any notion of an exclusive metallic currency as visionary and viewing the banks as transforming agents that could supply capital for the building of canals and railroads and provide credit and exchange for transporting goods to distant markets. To these conservatives, then, banks and credit were major creative forces without which society would languish. Unlike the hards, they did not consider the banking issue a matter of principle. Their response, rather, was of a practical and pragmatic nature.

The conservative Democrats, or softs, fell into two categories. Senators Nathaniel P. Tallmadge of New York and William C. Rives of Virginia are representative of the first group. Bitterly against the Independent Treasury, they carried their opposition to the Van Buren Administration to the point where they could not remain within the party. To the others, including Governors David R. Porter of Pennsylvania and Wilson Shannon of Ohio, the Independent Treasury was not the major issue. Porter's and Shannon's conservatism was expressed in efforts to frustrate or weaken reforms sponsored by hard-money Democrats on the state level. Although they aroused considerable antagonism, both governors remained orthodox enough to stay within the party.

The power of the broker and the importance of the broker mentality in American party politics cannot be overemphasized. The brokers performed an immediate service to the two-party system by preventing ideological conflicts from splitting the parties. In rounding the corners and edges of political disputes, however, they sometimes compromised principles in the interest of short-term party harmony and political success. As the brokers created well-organized political institutions, a consensus-minded politics emerged, forcing disappointed radicals and ideologues to leave the ranks of the two major parties and form the third parties of the nineteenth century.

Thomas Ritchie, long-time Democratic editor of the Richmond *Enquirer* and later editor of the Washington *Union,* the national Democratic newspaper under President James K. Polk, is perhaps the best example of the Democratic broker. To Ritchie, as to other broker-politicians, issues took second place to the party, and in Virginia he campaigned to prevent the currency dispute from splitting the Democrats. A broker to the end of his career, in 1850 he worked closely with his old political enemy Henry Clay to work out a compromise on the question of expansion of slavery into the territories.[21]

John Brough, Democratic legislator, auditor, and Unionist governor during the Civil War, was prominent among Ohio broker Democrats. During the late 1830s and early 1840s he and his brother Charles, both of whom later became editors of the Cincinnati *Enquirer,* labored mightily to find common ground upon which the party could build. They reserved their scorn for hards and softs alike, whoever were most guilty at the moment of upsetting the delicate political balance between the factions. Brough temporarily retired from politics in the middle 1840s but emerged from retirement to run for governor of Ohio in 1863 on the Republican-Union ticket and defeated Clement L. Vallandigham.[22]

In Mississippi, the process of party development had not matured to the point it had in Virginia and Ohio. As a result, the political brokers were not disciplined by long-established allegiances to party, and political brokerage became, more often than not, personal opportunism. The politics, as well as the economic development of the state, were open-ended. John Francis Hamtramck Claiborne, Democratic editor and Congressman, and William M. Gwin, Democratic Congressman, managed to direct the antibank sentiment in such a way that the Democratic party remained attractive to hard-money as well as many entrepreneurial-minded men.

While to the softs banks meant the promise of the future, to the hards they symbolized the denial of the past. Within the hard-money group, however, there was some diversity of opinion, which ranged from the more moderate hards generally in the eastern sections who

[21] See Charles Henry Ambler, *Thomas Ritchie, A Study in Virginia Politics* (Richmond, Va., 1913). Also, Holman Hamilton's *Prologue to Conflict: The Crisis and Compromise of 1850* (New York, 1966), 66, 121–22.

[22] Brough and his brother acquired the Cincinnati *Enquirer* in 1841 from Moses Dawson, the venerable Democratic publisher. See Osman Castle Hooper, "John Brough," *Ohio Archaeological and Historical Quarterly,* XIII (January, 1904), 40–70.

grudgingly admitted the necessity of banks and worked for bank reform to the radical hards in some of the western areas who attempted to rid their states of all banks. The hards believed that paper banking caused political, economic, and moral impairment to American society. They regarded the banks, with their charters and special privileges, as bastions of inequality and not unlike cancerous growths, working their profound and corrupting change.

It was this theme of egalitarianism [23] that fused together many of the various positions within the hard-money spectrum. The hard-money Democrats believed that the banks represented power that threatened a free and democratic society, and they responded to this threat in a number of ways. First, reforms were aimed at outlawing the exclusive and monopolistic contracts states made with individual banks in the form of inviolable contracts. This anti-special-charter sentiment usually was manifested in proposals to give states the power to alter, amend, or repeal bank charters at any time deemed in the public interest. Putting an end to the inviolability of charters contravened the Marshall Court's decision in the Dartmouth College Case but was in harmony with the Taney Court's 1837 decision in the Charles River Bridge Case. Ironically, calls for free banking also were sometimes an outgrowth of this antagonism toward special charters. Free banking was simply a device by which any man or group of men could start a bank as long as they met certain general requirements laid down by the state. This, of course, met the hard-money men's criticisms of the special, privileged nature of bank charters but also often opened up a situation in which the number of banks and amount of paper currency would be expanded enormously.

In the Jacksonian Period there was no national paper currency, and in its stead the country's circulating medium consisted of specie (gold and silver) and paper money issued by the hundreds of local banks as well as by the expiring Second Bank of the United States. What this meant was that the nation's private bankers had enormous power over the economy through their ability to expand or contract the amount of

[23] The Virginia Tidewater aristocrats, who subscribed to the doctrine of hard money, were obvious exceptions to this. Nostalgia, rather than egalitarianism, provided the central theme in the hard-money radicalism of the Virginia Tidewater.

paper notes in circulation. Thus, the second major category of hard-money reform was based on a faith in a kind of internal control of the banking system through specie-note ratios and restrictions on the circulation of small notes. A cardinal tenet of the Democratic hard-money doctrine was the belief that specie would act as a kind of perpetual and infallible balance wheel, regulating the workings of the banking system. For example, small notes were to be prohibited, the Democrats argued, so as to force the use of specie in day-to-day monetary exchanges. Specie, they felt, had an intrinsic and independent value of its own and could not depreciate as could paper money. Specie-note ratios were introduced to compel bankers to maintain on hand a certain ratio of specie to back the notes they issued for circulation. Democrats also often urged that bank directors and stockholders be made liable for bank debts. In some instances Democrats proposed to extend the liability to just the amount of stock owned in the banks; in others the liability was to be unlimited. All of these reforms, it was hoped, would provide more stability and responsibility in the banking system.

Some hard-money Democrats concluded that direct state involvement in the banking system was the only way to insure responsible and safe banking. Thus, several states controlled the banks by public ownership. And, finally, some radical Democrats, frustrated at the failure of bank reforms and overwhelmed by what they felt was the total corruption of the banking system, urged that the banks be destroyed. This radical step was generally cloaked in ambiguity and its proponents ranged from those who would eliminate the note-issuing function of banks to those who would close down all banks.

This radical sentiment represented a great deal more than the political and economic position that was manifested on the surface. Although vague and shapeless at the time of the Panic, it developed into a fervid antibank stand, one that eventually gave the party in most states its ethos and identity, and provided the core for a system of values and beliefs that transcended day-to-day politics.

These hard-money Jacksonians occupy a unique place in the history of American politics. Political principles and beliefs meant more to them than they did to their contemporaries or would to most public men of later eras. Intransigent and uncompromising, these Democratic politicians displayed traits more often found in ephemeral third parties dominated by ideology. The faction can, in fact, be described in much the same manner as has been the American socialist movement, whose failure it has been said was

> rooted in its inability to resolve a basic dilemma of ethics and politics: the socialist movement, by the way in which it stated its goal, and by the way in which it rejected the capitalistic order as a whole, could not relate itself to the specific problems of social action in the here-and-now, give-and-take political world. In sum: It was trapped by the unhappy problem of living *in* but not *of* the world; it could only act, and then inadequately as the moral but not the political man in immoral society.[24]

This is not, of course, to argue that the hards rejected the capitalistic order or that they were some kind of agrarian-based levelers. The analogy has meaning when it is recognized that the hard-money men did live more *in* than *of* the world. And they were often hindered from taking effective action, on the banking issue at least, by ethical commitment to an agrarian credo that was daily becoming more archaic and out of touch with the environment.

Considering the nature of the radical Jacksonians' political style, it is not surprising to find some of these men entering the ranks of the Copperheads during the Civil War.[25] In the post-war period, the Greenback and Populist parties also offered attractive ideological and political homes for former hard-money Jacksonians. In all four movements the political style and appeal were similar—nostalgic and populistic, bitter yet hopeful.

Samuel Medary and William Allen were two leading Ohio hard-money Jacksonians who gave their allegiance to Copperheadism during the Civil War. Spokesman for the Democratic party during the banking controversy through his role as editor of the party newspaper,

---

[24] Reprinted with permission of The Macmillan Company from Daniel Bell, *The End of Ideology: On the Exhaustion of Political Ideas in the Fifties* (New York, 1962), 278–79. © by The Free Press, A Corporation, 1960.

[25] Frank L. Klement, in his *The Copperheads in the Middle West* (Chicago, 1960), argues that Copperheadism was the forerunner of the Greenback movement. However, William G. Shade and Ronald P. Formisano have concluded that there was little continuity between the Copperhead and Greenback movements in Illinois. See Ronald P. Formisano and William G. Shade, "The Concept of Agrarian Radicalism," *Mid-America*, LII (January, 1970), 3–30.

the *Ohio Statesman,* Medary later served as editor for a Copperhead paper, *The Crisis.* Called the "dictator"[26] of the Ohio Democratic party, he was a master of political invective. He once condemned banks for presenting

every inducement to attract the confidence of the unwary and seduce into their grasp the most watchful and shrewd, by the convenience and safety they hold out to the public through a thousand pretenses of being the exclusive friends and engines of trade and commerce.

Banks, he went on to explain,

have attempted to seize upon the government of the Union and of the States, and make use of the revenues and loans upon the people's credit to uphold their villainy and grind the people to earth with oppression. In these attempts these corporations have been supported by the powerful array of mercantile wealth—by city and county court lawyers largely in their pay—by the benighted and mercenary portion of the priesthood—by village doctors who love the shade of an awning better than the golden fields of the husbandman or the workshop of the mechanic. . . .[27]

As one of the most extreme pro-peace editors during the Civil War, Medary so infuriated the public that a mob stormed his press and destroyed it. He was said to be the "most bitter and caustic of all of Lincoln's critics," once entitling an editorial, "Abraham Lincoln More of a Traitor than Jefferson Davis."[28]

In a public career spanning four decades, William Allen embraced, in turn, the philosophies of the Jacksonians, the Copperheads, and the Greenbackers. Each commanded a total commitment from this politician who served as United States Senator from Ohio during the banking controversy and as governor of the state after the Civil War. Allen has been depicted as a political opportunist who threw himself into the fray only after he had determined the sentiment of the people.[29] This

---

[26] *Concise Dictionary of American Biography* (New York, 1964), 663. Hereafter cited as *Concise D.A.B.*

[27] Columbus *Ohio Statesman,* July 30, 1839, as quoted in Edgar Allen Holt, "Party Politics in Ohio, 1840–1850," *Ohio Archaeological and Historical Quarterly,* XXXVII (July, 1928), 501–502.

[28] Klement, *Copperheads.* See pages 109–10, 115, 129, 139, 140, 220, 230, and 265.

[29] Reginald Charles McGrane, *William Allen: A Study in Western Democracy* (Columbus, Ohio, 1925).

characterization misses the point. Instead, Allen was a man of intense hatreds and loyalties, his political creed a patchwork of brilliant contrasts rather than muted grays. Allen's biographer described him as a man who:

possessed an innate ability in arousing his hearers to the highest pitch of frenzy as he painted with a bold and firm brush the picture of Whig misrule. He was an orator and master in the art of persuasion. He knew the hypnotic spell of slogans, and he did not hesitate to appeal to the hearts rather than to the minds of listeners. . . . His fearless advocacy of Ohio's claims in the Ohio-Michigan Boundary dispute, his scathing denunciation of France's delinquency in the payment of her debt, his vitriolic analysis of the corrupt influence of banks and corporations in governmental affairs . . . marked him as an acknowledged spokesman of western aspirations.[30]

This man was no politician who made up his mind only after he had determined in what direction his constituents were moving. Rather, Allen was a strong-willed, single-minded leader who was adroit in marshalling support to follow him on his crusades.[31]

The road from Jacksonian to Copperhead was a familiar one to other hard-money men. Besides Allen and Medary, other Ohio hard-money men, including William Medill (member of President James K. Polk's administration) and Clement L. Vallandigham (Copperhead candidate for governor in 1863), reached the same destination. The Jacksonian and Copperhead were both frightened by the slipping away of an old and familiar order and its replacement by a new and alien one. Agrarian in its economic attitudes, which reflected a deep suspicion of banks and the kind of society they represented, Copperheadism, with its Negrophobia, its nostalgia, and its peevishness, became the final stop for many who had been hard-money Jacksonians.[32]

Certainly not all radical Democrats became Copperheads. Benjamin Tappan, one-time Democratic Senator from Ohio, moved in the other direction, joining the Free Soil party. Besides their commitment to

---

[30] *Ibid.,* 260–61.

[31] See *Ibid.,* 262. Allen "became a crusader in behalf of the 'Rag Baby,' an evangelist preaching honesty at a time when ethical ideas seemed lost."

[32] Rather interestingly, of the Democrats classified as brokers, two, David Tod and John Brough, became wartime Republican-Unionist governors of Ohio.

hard money after the Panic, the common denominator uniting Allen, Medary, and Tappan was a certain rigidity of mind and inflexibility of character. Party leaders were constantly worried that Tappan's intransigent hard-money views might upset temporary and uneasy alliances between the hard- and soft-money camps. One leader wrote to Allen that Tappan had arrived at a state Democratic convention and was as "uncompromising upon hard money as the Rock of Gibraltar." [33]

The career of Lyman Trumbull of Illinois, spanning the last two thirds of the nineteenth century, perhaps represents best the evolution of the hard-money ethos. Born in Connecticut, Trumbull was a descendant of the Mather family. "His moderation and abhorrence of excessive drinking, his austere and outwardly cold demeanor, his deep religious beliefs and his life-long devotion to honesty and integrity in public life were part of his Puritan heritage." [34] Trumbull was a hard-money Democrat but left the party over the slavery issue and was elected to the United States Senate as a Free Soiler in 1854. He became a Republican and during Reconstruction supported the radicals. He broke with the radicals, however, over the impeachment of President Andrew Johnson and supported the Liberal Republican ticket in 1872.[35] He ran for governor of Illinois as a Democrat in 1880 and was a Populist supporter in the 1890s.

In the early 1840s Trumbull was sharply critical of the Democratic governor's plan to wind up the banks in Illinois gradually. For Trumbull the bank issue was not one for which gradualist or moderate policies were acceptable, and he advocated the immediate revocation of the banks' charters. Trumbull's opposition to the Democratic administration was politically disastrous; he was forced to resign his state office.[36]

During his candidacy for governor in 1880, the Democratic state convention called for a "constitutional currency of gold and silver and of paper convertible into coin." Defeated for governor, Trumbull, fourteen years later, near the close of his life, addressed the Populist convention in Chicago, denouncing the increasing wealth of the few while

---

[33] Mathias Martin to William Allen, January 5, 1846, William Allen Papers, Library of Congress.

[34] Mark M. Krug, *Lyman Trumbull: Conservative Radical* (New York, 1965), 20.

[35] *Concise D.A.B.*, 1083.

[36] Krug, *Trumbull*, Chapter II.

many were living in grinding poverty. He recommended laws that would prohibit anyone from bequeathing more than 500,000 dollars worth of property. Any amount over that figure would go to the state. Condemning government aid to corporations, Trumbull charged that for many generations "laws have been framed for the protection of property rather than to protect the rights of man." [37]

A Tidewater Virginian, Peter Vivian Daniel had the same political style as did his northern colleagues. The hard-money Jacksonian was active in Virginia politics and a member of the influential Richmond Junto, an informal group of Democratic leaders who directed party affairs in the Old Dominion. Appointed to the United States Supreme Court in 1841 by Van Buren, Daniel served on the bench until 1860.

Daniel's biographer was so taken by the radical independence of the testy and intransigent associate justice that he entitled his book *Justice Daniel Dissenting*.[38] An inflexible and doctrinaire man, Daniel had a violent and passionate hatred and suspicion of the banks and the commercialized society they represented. The Virginia jurist in 1841, according to the biography, was the

embodiment of the Virginia and Kentucky Resolutions of 1798, of a spirit of earliest vintage Jeffersonianism, of the philosophy of John Taylor. To Daniel the economy of the eighteenth century Stafford County or of the pre-1812 Richmond represented the highest possible economic order. Resistance to the Bank of the United States had been for him the simplest kind of act of faith because he was opposed to all banks, and all the more to a federal one. Indeed, in his view, the entire form of corporate business enterprise was subject to the sharpest suspicion, and a class of merchants of greater substance than a grocer or a haberdasher was of distinctly marginal economic utility.[39]

The last years of Daniel's life had a nightmarish quality. The old man, who had always seen things in stark contrasts, now perceived in even more violent and brilliant hues. Personal tragedy and the increasing sectional bitterness led him to blame "even the bad weather on the North" and to be "severely offended that respectful funeral rights should be given to antislavery former President John Quincy Adams."

[37] *Ibid.*, 349–50. Also, Chester McArthur Destler, *American Radicalism, 1865–1901* (Chicago, 1966), 196–97.

[38] John P. Frank, *Justice Daniel Dissenting: A Biography of Peter V. Daniel, 1784–1860* (Cambridge, Mass., 1964).

[39] *Ibid.*, 161.

Daniel refused to go north of the Delaware River ever again, and when "some oranges were sent to him from the Deep South, he was triumphant at this evidence of southern accomplishment, wondering 'when *The North* . . . would ever produce anything . . . that is good and decent.' " [40]

Daniel was the reformer turned fanatic. As a reformer, he had a temperament that was super-sensitive to his environment, perceiving ugliness and unjustice long before those who were less sensitive. But Daniel was a prophet unheeded, and his sensitivity became a curse. The qualities that made him a reformer led him to a frustrated fanaticism in which social evils became personified and assumed exaggerated proportions.

It should not be concluded that such men as Daniel, Trumbull, Medary, Allen, and Tappan were failures as politicians. Obviously they were not. All of them rose to the high councils of their party. But as hard-money Jacksonians, they found it extremely difficult to translate their anxieties about the direction in which society was moving into realistic and meaningful reforms. Petulant and eccentric, the supporters of the hard-money orthodoxy left a political legacy that significantly influenced the Greenbackers and the Populists.

[40] *Ibid.,* 246.

CHAPTER II

Banking Before the Panic

I

A DISTINGUISHED economic historian has singled out the years from 1823 to 1843 as constituting a "critical period" in the country's economic development. "If one were to date the beginning of acceleration in the economy's growth and the years when industrialization began," he contends, "it would be this period." [1]

The banks of this early ante-bellum era, unchallenged as the largest and most important corporate and financial institutions in the emerging nation, were both products and producers of this growth.[2] As late as 1831, the New York Stock Exchange listed no industrial corporations whatsoever, and by 1835 the list included only "eight coal and mining companies, three gas-lighting companies, and four others. . . ."[3] In 1838, a Georgian rather accurately stated that society was in-

---

[1] Douglass C. North, *The Economic Growth of the United States, 1790–1860* (Englewood Cliffs, N.J., 1961), 189. More controversial than the timing of the acceleration of the United States' economic growth are the causal factors. For the latest statement concerning economic growth in this country, see Stuart Bruchey, *The Roots of American Economic Growth, 1607–1861: An Essay in Social Causation* (New York, 1965). Bruchey argues that economic growth cannot be analyzed in quantitative terms. "How does one measure the effects of an increase in vertical social mobility upon incentives to produce," he asks. See Chapter I.

[2] See the review by Arthur Schlesinger, Jr., of Walter B. Smith's *Economic Aspects of the Second Bank of the United States*, in *American Historical Review*, LIX (October, 1953), 140–41. Schlesinger shows that although banking operations of the times were highly inflationary, the growth rate of the country far outstripped the rising prices. In the twenty years before the Panic, prices rose by less than one fifth, while the national income increased by two thirds.

[3] Bruchey, *Roots of Economic Growth*, 152.

debted to the banks for "our canals, our railroads, [and] our steam vessels," and that without them "one half of our national wealth would never have existed" and "the wilds of the South and Southeast would not have been cultivated, as they now are, for a century to come." [4] At about the same time the governor of Ohio declared that bank credit "has given us one of the most enterprising and active set of businessmen that have lived in any age or any country." Credit, he went on, "has bought our land, made our canals, improved our rivers, opened our roads, built our cities, cleared our fields, founded our churches, [and] erected our colleges and schools." [5]

By the middle of the nineteenth century, however, the banks were to become overshadowed by the rise of giant industrial, transportation, and insurance corporations.[6] A century later the largest bank in the country would have only half the assets of the largest utility, and the total assets of the five largest banks would amount to only about two thirds of the total assets of the five largest insurance companies.[7]

The Panic of 1837 was a major milestone in the history of American banking. On the one hand, it dramatically checked the frantic growth of the American economy and the boom times of the preceding half decade. On the other, it signified the eclipse of the mercantilist banking tradition, in which most banks, at least outside of the more commercial Northeast, had been chartered "not because capital was seeking investment nor because places with established commerce and manufacturing needed bank accommodations, but because men without capital and credit wanted loans." [8] Thus these banks in the more rural sections tended to be "land banks which issued their notes on the basis of land and personal estates," in contrast to the banks of the highly

---

[4] Macon *Georgia Messenger,* September 20, 1838, as quoted in Thomas Payne Govan's, "Banking and the Credit System in Georgia, 1810–1860," unpublished Ph.D. thesis, Vanderbilt University, 1938, 1.

[5] As quoted in Carter H. Golembe's "State Banks and the Economic Development of the West, 1830–1844," unpublished Ph.D. thesis, Columbia University, 1952, 196.

[6] William Graham Sumner, *A History of Banking in the United States* (New York, 1896), 414–15.

[7] *Information Please Almanac Atlas and Yearbook, 1962* (New York, 1961), 581.

[8] Fritz Redlich, *The Molding of American Banking: Men and Ideas* (New York, 1951), Vol. II, Part I, 43.

commercialized areas that were money banks and "issued notes on the basis of obligations of merchants and manufacturers."[9]

The Panic and depression had been preceded by an era of economic growth unparalleled before that time. Expansion of industry and internal-improvement systems, increasing public land sales, and the mushrooming of banks reflected the exuberant optimism of the times. In 1830 there had been 329 banks in the country, with a cumulative capital of slightly more than 110 million dollars and with a total note circulation of 61 million dollars. By 1835 the number had more than doubled, increasing to 704 banks with a capitalization of 231 million dollars and almost 104 million dollars worth of notes in circulation. Notes reached a high in 1837, when 788 banks had 149 million dollars in circulation. But the actual high point in number of banks and amount of capital did not come until 1840, when 901 banks had a capital of 358 million dollars.[10]

The depression that followed, "one of the most severe in our history,"[11] reduced the number of banks and bank-note circulation drastically. By 1843 the number of banks had declined to a low of 691, and in the same year the amount of notes in circulation had dropped almost two thirds, from the 1837 high to 58 million dollars. The boom figures were not reached again until the decade of the 1850s. Notes in circulation did not equal the previous record-high until 1851, and it was not until 1854 that the number of banks surpassed the 1840 high. The amount of banking capital authorized by the states did not break the record set in 1840 until seventeen years later.[12]

The mercantilist tradition in banking died a lingering death. It was first laid to rest in the more highly commercialized Northeast. But in

[9] *Ibid.*, 6–7.

[10] *United States Comptroller of the Currency Annual Report for 1876,* 85, 94–95. Accurate banking figures are difficult if not impossible to find for the ante-bellum period. But despite the shortcomings of this document, the statistics give a fairly reliable general outline of banking development. See Joseph Van Fenstermaker, *The Development of American Commercial Banking: 1782–1837* (Kent, Ohio, 1965), 102, for a discussion of the Comptroller's report. See also, chart in George Rogers Taylor's *The Transportation Revolution, 1815–1860* (New York, 1958), 325. He says that in 1830 there were 330 banks. All financial sums are rounded off to the nearest million.

[11] North, *Economic Growth,* 190.

[12] *Comptroller's Report, 1876,* 94–95.

the West the tradition was strong and slow to disappear. As late as 1836 the Arkansas constitution provided that the state might incorporate a bank, "which shall become the repository of the funds belonging to, or under the control of the State, and shall be required to loan them out throughout the State, and in each county, in proportion to representation." The state was also authorized to incorporate another bank "to aid and promote the great agricultural interests of the country; and the faith and credit of the State may be pledged to raise the funds necessary to carry into operation the two banks. . . ." [13]

The period after 1837 was characterized by an increasing interest in the liquidity of banks. It was recognized that the older mercantilist ideas of a capital–circulation ratio or a bond-backed circulation were not adequate to insure a bank's solvency and liquidity. Thus, in the years after the depression, banking became more and more based upon specie, with some states requiring each bank to maintain a certain ratio between specie on hand and notes in circulation.[14]

2

The stages of economic development in the Northeast, Southeast, Southwest, and Northwest [15] in the 1830s and the extent to which each was affected by the boom, Panic, and depression were important determinants influencing banking and politics. Within each section there were similarities in banking practices and problems, bank structure, and degree of commercialization. And this became even more pronounced after 1837.

[13] Redlich, *Molding of American Banking,* Vol. II, Part I, 43. Also, Sumner, *History of Banking,* 331–34.

[14] Redlich, *Molding of American Banking,* Vol. II, Part II, 1–10. Also, Harry Edward Miller, *Banking Theories in the United States Before 1860* (Cambridge, Mass., 1927), 109–20, who discusses the nature of bank deposits. The Louisiana Banking Act of 1842 was a landmark in bank legislation in that it required a fixed ratio between cash liabilities, which included both notes *and deposits,* and specie. See Vol. II, Part II, 32–37, of Redlich's fine study.

[15] The following states are included in the northeastern section: Maine, New Hampshire, Vermont, Massachusetts, Connecticut, Rhode Island, New York, Pennsylvania, and New Jersey. The southeastern states are: Delaware, Maryland, Virginia, North Carolina, South Carolina, and Georgia. The southwestern states are: Alabama, Mississippi, Louisiana, and Arkansas. The northwestern states are: Kentucky, Tennessee, Ohio, Indiana, Illinois, Michigan, and Missouri.

Of the four sections, the Northeast was the most highly commercialized and was, therefore, financially the most sophisticated. Already the major terminus for the country's trade, the Northeast developed a flourishing manufacturing industry in the years before the Civil War. The Southeast and Southwest were "characterized by production for the market of a number of agricultural staples in which slave labor was both the major capital investment and an important intermediate product." [16] But there were significant differences between the two southern sections. The Southeast was past its economic prime and was being rapidly outstripped by the young, vigorous giant to the west. The Northwest was agricultural, like the two southern sections, but had a far more diversified economy.[17] Furthermore, the absence of a slave labor force in most states and the predominance of smaller agricultural production units in the Northwest were important factors in developing its political economy along different lines. The two eastern sections were the oldest and most settled areas of the country, with many banks dating from the late eighteenth century. Neither, consequently, experienced the tremendous rate of growth the two western sections did during the boom times prior to 1837.

Population statistics for the decade of the 1830s give a graphic illustration of the dynamic expansion of the Southwest and Northwest, especially when compared to the slower growth in the East. (See Graph 1.) The Northeast's population increased by 21.8 per cent (from 5.5 million to 6.7 million), while in the Southeast the expansion was only 8.3 per cent (from 3.6 million to 3.9 million). It was a different story in the West. The Southwest registered a 100-per-cent increase in number of residents (growing from almost 700,000 to 1.4 million). The Northwest did almost as well, the population rising by 68.9 per cent (from 2.9 million to 4.9 million).[18]

A comparison of the increase in banking facilities in each section for the same decade again demonstrates the rapid growth of the two western sections. (See Graph 2.) In the Southwest the number of banking institutions leaped 1,328 per cent (from 7 to 100), while in the Northwest the banks were augmented by 769.2 per cent (from 13 to 113).

[16] North, *Economic Growth*, 122.   [17] *Ibid.*, 135.
[18] United States Bureau of the Census, *Historical Statistics of the United States, Colonial Times to 1957*, 13. See Graph 1.

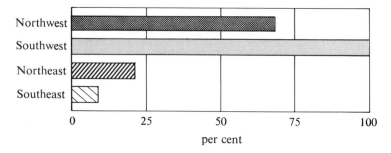

GRAPH 1. INCREASE IN POPULATION BY SECTION, 1830–1840

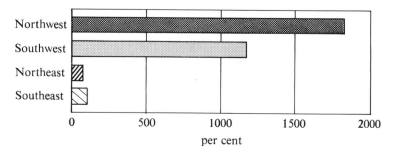

GRAPH 2. INCREASE IN BANKING CAPITAL BY SECTION, 1830–1840

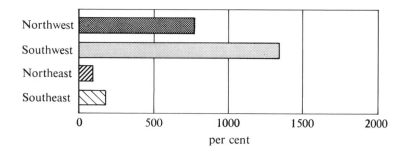

GRAPH 3. INCREASE IN BANKING FACILITIES BY SECTION, 1830–1840

There was a 162.5-per-cent increase in banks (from 48 to 126) in the Southeast, and an 81.5-per-cent increase (from 260 to 472) in the Northeast.[19]

The amount of banking capital rose phenomenally during the same decade. (See Graph 3.) In the Southwest it grew by 1,185 per cent (rising from a little over 7 million dollars in 1830 to almost 90 million dollars in 1840), while at the same time in the Northwest banking capital was expanded by 1,850 per cent (from 2 million dollars to 39 million dollars). The Southeast increased its capital by 100 per cent (from 28 million dollars to 56 million dollars), and a 75-per-cent increment was registered in the Northeast (from 72 million dollars to 126 million dollars).[20]

Thus it is clear that while the 1830s was a decade of expansion everywhere, the Southwest and Northwest were completely outstripping the rest of the country. But, as it is with youth, after a sudden spurt of growth the body becomes strange and alien and the movements awkward; and so, the two western sections (especially the Southwest, which had stretched its economy far beyond the limit of its elasticity), when the contraction came, fell in a shapeless heap.

3

Two questions are central to any discussion of banking before the Civil War. What was the reason for the rapid growth of banking facilities before the Panic? And where was the enormous sum of additional bank capital being invested?

One of the major reasons that there was such a large expansion of banking facilities and capital was that as the population moved west, better means of transportation were needed to extend the market econ-

---

[19] *Comptroller's Report, 1876,* 85. See Graph 2. It should be pointed out that one reason for the vigorous expansion of bank capital in the western sections was that the Panic of 1819 and the following depression had closed a great number of western banks. Thus, there was a dearth of banking capital in the West.

[20] *Ibid.,* 85, 96–121. The number of banks in Mississippi for the year 1840 is unavailable, so the chart in John Jay Knox, *A History of Banking in the United States* (New York, 1900), 610, was used. All figures are rounded to the nearest thousand. See Graph 3.

omy. Enormous sums were raised, partly through the aid of banks, to finance railroad and canal construction. Once these more efficient means of transportation were completed, freight rates dropped, and this had the effect of bringing vast new areas of land into the market economy. Bank capital was needed to finance the buying and cultivating of these new lands and to help move the crops to market. Also, the failure of the Second Bank of the United States to receive a new charter in the early 1830s was a factor that stimulated many states to charter more banks to replace the Philadelphia bank's withdrawn capital.

It is more difficult to answer the second question, to determine the types of loans banks made in the 1830s and who received the loanable funds.[21] In the late eighteenth and early nineteenth centuries, when the first banks in this country were chartered, they were mainly commercial ones specializing in short-term, self-liquidating credit. The commercial economies of the seaboard states were adequately served by bank loans that ran from thirty to ninety days. As the economy of the country began to develop and diversify and the need for credit for capital improvements increased, unbearable pressure was brought upon the commercial banks to make long-term loans. Recognizing the need for this type of credit, many states required their banks to extend these nonliquid loans. This meant that such banks were, in general, in precarious financial positions, and when a squeeze came, their assets were frozen in nonliquid loans, such as on slaves, land, or other capital improvements.

From 1802 to 1816 in Massachusetts, practically every banking charter required a certain percentage of the bank's loans to be made to the agricultural interests of the state. These loans, to be secured by mortgages, normally would run at least for one year.[22]

In Georgia the failure or inability of the commercial banks to furnish long-term loans gave impetus to the state to charter the Central Bank in 1828. The Central Bank was entirely owned by the state and it was to afford relief to persons unable to get loans from existing

[21] Data of this kind are almost nonexistent as few studies analyzing bank loans have been made.

[22] Bray Hammond, "Long and Short Term Credit in Early American Banking," *Quarterly Journal of Economics,* XLIX (November, 1934), 79–87.

banks. Consequently, the Central Bank only ". . . had a small part of its funds in bills of exchange and other short-term paper. Most of its loans were made on a long-time basis, repayable over the course of five years, and to a large extent, were made for the purpose of purchasing land." [23]

In the Southwest, however, as a general rule, the commercial banks were called upon to furnish the long-term loans as well as to handle the short-term commercial paper, such as bills of exchange. In Louisiana it was estimated that 87 per cent of the loans and discounts were of a long-term nature.[24] In 1833 the state of Mississippi chartered the Agricultural Bank of Mississippi on the condition that one half of the capital would be loaned for not less than a year. And in 1837 the charter of the Union Bank of Mississippi provided that two thirds of the bank's capital should be loaned on real estate and that borrowers on mortgages could pay one eighth annually on their notes.[25]

The Northwest was economically a more heterogeneous region than the Southwest, and it is difficult to assess the nature of Northwestern bank loans. One historian confessed that because under "the heading 'loans and discounts' in bank statements of the period there were included all varieties of paper from short-term notes arising from a shipment of hogs . . . to notes based perhaps on the construction of a sawmill," a breakdown of the different types of loans would be impossible to attain.[26]

Loans for internal-improvement projects took up a considerable part of some banks' capital and had little effect on others. By 1840 the State Bank of Indiana had 16 per cent of its total loans and discounts invested in internal-improvement projects, while the State Bank of Illinois had more than one half of its capital "in the form of depreciating state bonds." [27]

Loans for internal improvements were on the whole less important than business loans or loans for the purpose of land speculation. It is estimated that at least one fifth of the loans and discounts of the banks in the Northwest were

[23] Govan, "Banking in Georgia" (thesis), 119–25.
[24] Stephen A. Caldwell, *A Banking History of Louisiana* (Baton Rouge, La., 1935), 55.
[25] Sumner, *History of Banking,* 248–52.   [26] Golembe, "State Banks," 81–82.
[27] *Ibid.,* 187, 187a.

in the form of advances to the business community for purposes other than land speculation. This is most probably a minimum estimate and, further, obscures the fact that for a number of banks, particularly those located in commercial centers, the percentage was much higher.[28]

Loans for land speculation "defy any estimate as to their quantity" but "probably constituted a large percentage of total assets during the entire period—larger than the percentage assigned to business loans," and in "the years 1834–39, they possibly exeeded in amount all other loans combined." [29]

There are indications that the banks in the Northeast, especially in cities, had been highly commercial institutions almost from their inception. In the New England textile mills and the capital markets from 1840–1860 commercial banks handled only 3.5 per cent of the loans of a year and longer. Savings banks and trust companies, on the other hand, made 68.8 per cent of the long-term loans. Nearly 87 per cent of the loans of a duration of thirty days to six months were made by commercial banks as well as 63 per cent of the six-month to one-year loans.[30]

Insurance companies, which later became important capital-accumulating agencies, were not, until the end of the ante-bellum period, able to command large amounts of capital to make the kind of long-term, nonliquid loans that were in such demand. In 1840 there were only fifteen companies with 4.7 million dollars in assets, while a decade later the number had increased to forty-eight with 97.1 million dollars.[31]

Thus, there is evidence that banks in the commercial centers of the country were beginning to be able to concentrate on short-term commercial loans, while other capital-accumulating institutions provided the long-term loans. In the less economically developed sections of the country, mainly the Northwest and Southwest, banks were called upon to furnish both long-term and short-term capital.

[28] *Ibid.,* 237a and 237b.   [29] *Ibid.*

[30] Lance E. Davis, "The New England Textile Mills and the Capital Markets: A Study of Industrial Borrowing 1840–1860," *Journal of Economic History,* XX (March, 1960), chart on page 6. Davis warns that the chart does not include renewals, which "might alter the conclusions markedly." He does feel, however, that "the inclusion of renewals would have increased the proportion of savings banks and trust companies in the long term totals. . . ." See his footnote, page 5.

[31] *Historical Statistics,* 672.

4

Throughout the ante-bellum period it was customary for states to own bank stock. Sometimes this meant that the entire stock of a bank was owned by the state, and in other cases small amounts of stock in a number of banks were state owned. By the end of the second decade of the nineteenth century, the Northeastern states ceased to make further investments in banks, but many continued to hold their stock. In the other three sections, the states continued to hold and accumulate bank stock until the Civil War.

In 1812 Massachusetts owned 1 million dollars out of a total of 8 million dollars of bank stock. After 1820, however, the state did not invest any more capital in the banking business. The high return on bank stock caused private investors to resist the idea of the state's monopolizing blocks of stock.[32] Connecticut owned only 400,000 dollars out of a paid-in bank capital of 7.36 million dollars in 1835.[33] Pennsylvania liquidated its rather large stockholdings in various banks in 1837.[34]

In the Southeast two states, South Carolina and Georgia, had banks that were entirely owned by the state. Before 1811 in Maryland, bank charters generally provided for one third to one tenth of a bank's stock to be saved for state subscription. After that date, the state purchased no more bank stock, although from 1830 to 1833 there was active discussion of a plan to establish a state-controlled bank. The legislature, however, failed to charter such a bank.[35]

From 1804, when the Bank of Virginia was chartered, to 1851, Virginia subscribed to stock in every bank chartered in the state. Several reasons were given for state partnership. First, it was felt that through ownership of stock the state would have a voice in management and

[32] Knox, *History of Banking*, 360–61. Also, Oscar Handlin and Mary Handlin, *Commonwealth, A Study of the Role of Government in the American Economy: Massachusetts, 1774–1861* (New York, 1947), 174–75.

[33] *Niles' Register*, January 3, 1835.

[34] Louis Hartz, *Economic Policy and Democratic Thought: Pennsylvania, 1776–1860* (Cambridge, Mass., 1948), 53.

[35] Alfred Cookman Bryan, *History of State Banking in Maryland* (Baltimore, 1899), 30, 81–84. The objectives of this bank's proponents were: to increase the circulating medium, to provide a repository for the public deposits, to make improvements, to support public education, and to avoid taxation.

thus be able to restrain banks from actions contrary to the public interest. Second, it was desired that the state should share in large profits arising from banking. And third, state investment was needed since
there was a lack of private capital.[36]

In 1812 South Carolina chartered the Bank of the State of South
Carolina because it was "deemed expedient and beneficial, both to the
State and the citizens thereof, to establish a bank on the funds of the
State, for the purpose of discounting paper and making loans for
longer periods than have heretofore been customary, and on security
different from what has hitherto been required." [37] The bank was to
receive all the United States stock, bonds, and bank stock owned by
the state and would also serve as a depository for taxes collected in the
state. The faith of the state was pledged to support the bank and stand
behind any deficiencies.[38] The Central Bank of Georgia, chartered in
1828, was solely owned by the state. Its capital consisted of bonds,
notes, stock in other banks, and other certificates of indebtedness.[39]

Banking in the four states of the Southwest was dominated by the
"plantation bank" system, under which banks could start business on
100 per cent borrowed capital. Plantation owners would mortgage all
or part of their plantations to the banks. In return for this they received stock in the banks and, as stockholders, the first opportunity to
borrow. The state government then, on the security of these mortgages,
would issue bonds to the banks. The banks would sell the bonds on the
international market, using the money raised to provide specie to back
up their banking operations. A student of American banking has characterized the system as a "failure as a type" but "an attempt which de-
serves admiration." These banks could have succeeded only with "a
very high net-profit rate" that would have "permitted them to earn the
whole capital in the period during which the bonds matured." Unfortunately, most of the plantation banks were chartered in the decade
preceding the Panic, and as a result almost all failed. The states that

---

[36] George T. Starnes, *Sixty Years of Branch Banking in Virginia* (New York,
1913), 33–34.

[37] As quoted in Sumner, *History of Banking,* 86.

[38] *Ibid.,* and Knox, *History of Banking,* 564. In 1830 the charter of the bank
was renewed until 1856.

[39] Govan, "Banking in Georgia" (thesis), 119. Also, Knox, *History of Banking,*
575.

had pledged their bonds to the banks were left with bankrupt banks and large debts.[40]

The Union Bank of Louisiana, chartered by the state legislature in 1832, was the first bank set up along the lines of the plantation scheme and was copied elsewhere in the Southwest. It must be emphasized that while the state was the underwriter, these banks were not owned and controlled by the state. The Union Bank of Louisiana's foundation was

laid in a capital of eight millions dollars, in shares of one hundred dollars to be subscribed by citizens of the state, holders of real property only, and secured by bond without interest, and mortgages on such property, of at least equal value with the amount of stock subscribed. Four millions are to be secured on property in the city of New Orleans. Slaves are not to be taken as security, except in the proportion of one-third to two-thirds on land in the case of each subscriber. Brick buildings are only to be taken as security for one-half their value, and frame buildings for one-third, and there are restrictions about unimproved land.[41]

The active capital of the bank was raised through a 7-million-dollar loan. "For this purpose, the state pledges its faith, and issues a five per cent stock for the amount in bonds of one thousand dollars each, one-fourth of which is payable in twelve, one-fourth in fifteen, one-fourth in eighteen and one-fourth in twenty years." Stockholders were "entitled to loans on their own bonds, with the security of their stock, for sums not exceeding in all, one-half their amount of stock," payable in equal installments "for twenty years. . . ." The state of Louisiana was entitled to a loan of 500,000 dollars and to appoint six of the twelve directors.[42] The need for the state to serve as underwriter was demonstrated by the failure of foreign bond houses to accept the 12 million dollars in bonds issued by the Citizens' Bank of Louisiana. Despite the fact that these bonds were secured by 14.4 million dollars in mortgages, the bank could not raise a working capital until the state agreed to issue state bonds with the bank bonds as security.[43]

Arkansas organized both a state bank, in which the state owned the

[40] Redlich, *Molding of American Banking,* Vol. II, Part I, 205–208.
[41] *Niles' Register,* October 6, 1832.
[42] *Ibid.* Also, Caldwell, *Banking History of Louisiana,* 47–48.
[43] Caldwell, *Banking History of Louisiana,* 48–50.

entire capital and appointed all the directors, and a plantation bank.[44] Between 1823, the time of the creation of the state bank, and 1837 Alabama issued over 15.5 million dollars in bonds to increase the banking capital within the state.[45] Mississippi had a plantation bank, which was founded in 1837, and various other banking institutions in which the state had investments. In 1830 the Planters' Bank was chartered to stimulate the economy by increasing the circulating medium, to ease taxation by creating a state-owned revenue-producing bank and to enable the people "to realize the blessings of a correct system of internal improvements." The state owned two thirds of the capital and appointed seven of the thirteen directors.[46]

In the Northwest the constitutions of Missouri, Illinois, and Indiana provided that banks in those states should be state banks only, with branches. There was some question over just what the term "state bank" meant. Did this mean the bank must be owned entirely by the state, or would partial state participation satisfy the state constitutional requirement? Furthermore, if the state owned the bank exclusively, would this violate the federal Constitution, which forbade the states to "coin Money; emit Bills of Credit; [or] make any Thing but gold and silver Coin a Tender in Payment of Debts?"

By 1837 none of the northwestern states had state banks that were entirely state owned and controlled. Missouri owned one half of the capital stock in its state bank and the legislature appointed a majority of the directors.[47] The state of Indiana owned one half of the capital stock in the state bank chartered in 1834 but exercised less control over

[44] Sumner, *History of Banking,* 331–34.

[45] William O. Scroggs, "Pioneer Banking in Alabama," in *Facts and Factors in Economic History, Articles by Former Students of Edwin Francis Gay* (Cambridge, Mass., 1932), 406–16. Also, Leonard C. Helderman, *National and State Banks: A Study of their Origins* (Boston, 1931), 84–87, and Knox, *History of Banking,* 595–96.

[46] The Preamble of the Planters' Bank charter, as quoted in Sumner, *History of Banking,* 248–52. See also, Knox, *History of Banking,* 602–603, and Charles Hillman Brough, "The History of Banking in Mississippi," Mississippi Historical Society *Publications,* III (1900), 320.

[47] James Neal Primm, *Economic Policy in the Development of a Western State, Missouri, 1820–1860* (Cambridge, Mass., 1954), Chapter II. See also, Knox, *History of Banking,* 782–83, and J. R. Cable, *The Bank of the State of Missouri* (New York, 1923), Chapters VI, VII, and VIII.

its operations.[48] In the 1820s the state of Illinois had chartered a state bank and empowered it to issue 300,000 dollars worth of notes backed only by the faith of the state. The bank was liquidated by the early 1830s, and until just before the Panic the state's investment in banks was minimal. In the spring of 1837 the legislature floated a loan of 3 million dollars to invest in the state's banks.[49] A scheme for a state bank in Ohio was proposed in the early 1830s but never adopted. The bank would have been organized similarly to the Second Bank of the United States, with the state owning one fifth of the stock and appointing that proportion of the directors.[50]

Kentucky and Tennessee both had entirely state-owned banks in the 1820s, but these banks were liquidated in the early 1830s.[51] In 1834 Kentucky incorporated the Bank of Kentucky with a capital of 5 million dollars. The state was to subscribe to 1 million dollars raised through 5-per-cent bonds and another million paid by the accumulation of annual dividends. In return for this the state would appoint three out of the eleven directors. Other banks received state investment as well.[52] In 1832 Tennessee chartered the Union Bank of the State of Tennessee with a capital of 3 million dollars. The state appointed five of the fifteen directors and held a minority of the stock.[53]

By 1837 public-private partnership in supplying bank capital was fairly common, especially in the Southeast, Southwest, and Northwest. Exclusive ownership and control of banking by the states had been more common in the 1820s, but by the time of the Panic few states

[48] W. F. Harding, "The State Bank of Indiana," *Journal of Political Economy,* IV (December, 1895), 1–36. Also, Logan Esarey, *State Banking in Indiana, 1814–1873* (Bloomington, Ind., 1912), 251–57. See also, reports in the following documents, which were critical of the state's inability to control the banks: United States Senate *Executive Document No. 471,* 25th Congress, 2nd Session, 279–89; United States House of Representatives, *Executive Document No. 172,* 26th Congress, 1st Session, 893–908.

[49] George William Dowrie, *The Development of Banking in Illinois, 1817–1863* (Urbana, Ill., 1913), 27–32, 61–80.

[50] Charles Clifford Huntington, *A History of Banking and Currency in Ohio Before the Civil War* (Columbus, Ohio, 1915), 135–39.

[51] Claude A. Campbell, *The Development of Banking in Tennessee* (Nashville, Tenn., 1932), 49; also, Knox, *History of Banking,* 633–35.

[52] Knox, *History of Banking,* 634–35 and Sumner, *History of Banking,* 254.

[53] Campbell, *Banking in Tennessee,* 65–66.

were able to exercise more than a minority control of banks in which public investments were placed.

In the older states, both in the Northeast and Southeast, state investment was prompted mainly because it was profitable and would increase the revenue of the state.[54] In the Northwest there were additional reasons. Bank accommodations were needed for the commercial classes as well as for the farmers, and there was a pressing demand for a circulating medium. Even in this section, however, as well as in the two eastern sections, the large profit to be earned by the banking business "was an important, if not the most important, motive which led the States to invest in these industries."[55] It was through liberal dividends from bank-stock investment that many northwestern states hoped to help finance extensive internal-improvement systems.

There was more difficulty in raising capital in the Southwest than in any other section of the country. Although there were no major internal-improvement schemes undertaken in this part of the country, the plantation system required great amounts of capital to enable the planter to buy, clear, and cultivate the land, purchase slaves, and market the crop. In the years before the Panic the four states of the Southwest issued almost 50 million dollars worth of bonds for banking purposes.[56] Much of this was invested in plantation-type banks, which were established for the benefit of the landowner. The landowner's mortgage-investment afforded him special consideration when borrowing money from the bank. The more land he had mortgaged for investment in the bank, the more he was allowed to borrow, and the state underwrote the entire enterprise, guaranteeing the mortgages by issuing state bonds.

5

On the eve of the Panic of 1837 state banking laws were a crazy quilt of restrictiveness and permissiveness. Even to call the banking network a "system" is somewhat misleading, as the word "system"

[54] Guy S. Callender, "The Early Transportation and Banking Enterprises of the States in Relation to the Growth of Corporations," *Quarterly Journal of Economics,* XVII (November, 1902), 160.

[55] *Ibid.*

[56] *Ibid.,* 114, 161–62.

connotes order or rational organization, two qualities that American ante-bellum banking did not possess.

The earliest banks had special charters. That is, individual banks had separate and often widely different contractual arrangements with the state. It was not until the second quarter of the nineteenth century that some states began to standardize their banking regulations by passing general laws. Stockholder liability, compulsory inspection of bank books by legislative committees or bank commissioners, indebtedness–capital ratios, specie–note ratios, and laws prohibiting small notes all were means by which it was hoped that the banks would be forced to exercise public responsibility and restrict notes to the extent that there would be an adequate specie basis for their issues.

The nationwide suspension tragically demonstrated, however, that these reforms and restrictions provided no guarantee that banks would be able to withstand widespread financial pressure of the sort generated in the spring of 1837. Certainly few, if any, of the regulations were as effective in practice as they appeared to be on paper. Perhaps Michigan's experience was not unusual. There, a provision enabling commissioners to inspect the specie holdings of banks was sidetracked by a clever bit of chicanery. On more than a few occasions a single bundle of the required specie was transported from one bank to the next, arriving just ahead of the commissioners so that all would seem to be in order. On one occasion a Michigan inspecting party was not deceived and reported a rather startling discovery:

Gold coin exhibited loose in a drawer, which, being counted, amounted to the sum of one thousand and thirty-seven dollars and seventy-eight cents; about one hundred and fifty dollars in loose silver, was also counted. Beneath the counter of the bank, nine boxes were pointed out by the teller, as containing one thousand dollars each. The teller selected one of these boxes, and opened it; this was examined, and appeared to be a full box of American half dollars. One of the commissioners then selected a box, which he opened, and found the same to contain a superficies only of silver, while the remaining portion consisted of lead and tenpenny nails. The commissioner then proceeded to open the remaining seven boxes; they presented the same contents precisely, with a single exception, in which the substratum was window-glass broken into small pieces.[57]

[57] House *Executive Document No. 172,* 1109–10. See also H. M. Utley, "The

General laws were first passed by states in the Northeast to bring order to a banking system that had its origin in the late eighteenth or early nineteenth century. Because of the large number of banks in existence in these states, the need for uniformity became obvious earlier than in newer states with fewer banks. For example, New England had 47 per cent of the nation's banks in 1837.[58]

In 1827 New York passed a general banking law that sought to abolish the existing evils of the banking system through a general statute rather than through dependence upon individual charters. By this law banks were prohibited from: paying dividends except from profits, reducing capital stock, extending loans and discounts beyond three times the paid-up capital, and loaning or discounting to directors. If a director violated any portion of the law, he was made liable to the creditors and stockholders of the bank for the full extent of the loss. In the case of fraudulent insolvency, the directors' liability was to be exhausted first, then stockholders were liable up to, but not exceeding, the amount of their investment. Notes under a dollar were forbidden, and banks were required to submit annual reports to the state comptroller. This law, applicable to charters granted or renewed after January 1, 1828, lasted only until 1829, when it was superseded by the Safety Fund Law, which provided a common fund to extinguish the debts of broken banks.[59] (See pp. 47–48.)

In 1829 Massachusetts passed a comprehensive banking law, setting down provisions for all new charters and renewals of charters. Stockholders were forbidden loans until they had paid their entire subscription, and bank notes were limited to 25 per cent more than paid-in capital. Furthermore, the banks were not allowed to open for business until 50 per cent of the capital had been paid in specie.[60] This act was, at least in part, a response to the demand of the commercial community for bank reform. Businessmen, however, were not willing to go a step further and sanction the establishment of a safety-fund system like

---

Wild Cat Banking System of Michigan," *Report of the Pioneer Society of the State of Michigan,* V (1884), 209–22.

[58] Van Fenstermaker, *American Commercial Banking,* 77–78.

[59] Robert E. Chaddock, *The Safety Fund Banking System in New York, 1829–1866* (Washington, D.C., 1910), 253–57.

[60] Knox, *History of Banking,* 362.

that in New York, arguing that it was unfair for the well-managed banks to be taxed and responsible for the poorly managed banks.[61]

An act modeled on the New York Safety Fund Law was passed by the Vermont legislature in 1832. Besides creating a fund by which creditors of insolvent banks might be paid, it prohibited a bank from opening its doors until one half of the capital had been paid in. Furthermore, banks were compelled to pay an annual tax on dividends.[62] Four years later, Rhode Island passed a general law that restrained banks from beginning business until one half of the capital had been paid in and this had been certified by bank commissioners.[63]

The Pennsylvania legislature, in renewing a number of bank charters in 1824, brought all banks under uniform regulations. The act specified that the directors were "not to issue notes and incur debts beyond double the amount of stock, actually paid in, and if they do so, they are to become liable for the debts, in their private property." They were further required "to present the stockholders with a statement of the affairs of the bank, on the first Tuesday of November in each year" and "not to make any dividends exceeding the net profits which have accrued. . . ." Each bank was required to give the legislature an annual report on its condition, and in the event of suspension of specie payments the offending bank was to forfeit its charter and pay 6 per cent interest on the protested notes.[64]

Maryland and Virginia legislatures brought banks in the two states under general laws during the two years before the Panic. In 1835 Maryland laid down uniform regulations for city banks, and the following year the country banks were put on a common footing.[65] The Virginia legislature passed a general banking law less than two months before the bank suspension. The most noteworthy feature of the Virginia legislation was the establishment of a minimum specie-note ratio to be maintained by the banks, a forerunner of later proposals and provisions in many other states. Each Virginia bank was prohibited from having "in circulation at any one time a total amount of notes or bills exceeding five times its reserve of gold and silver coin of the legal money of the

---

[61] Handlin and Handlin, *Commonwealth,* 180.

[62] Knox, *History of Banking,* 355–56.

[63] *Ibid.,* 371–73, and Davis R. Dewey, *State Banking Before the Civil War* (Washington, D.C., 1910), 12–13.

[64] *Niles' Register,* April 10, 1824. [65] Bryan, *State Banking in Maryland,* 85–87.

United States," and in the "case of any sudden increase of notes above this ratio the bank could make no more loans nor discounts until . . . the required proportions of one to five had been recovered." The Virginia bill also continued the system of state participation in all banks. Each central, or mother, bank would have nine directors, with the state appointing four of them. The state would appoint three of the seven directors of each branch bank. And the right was reserved for the legislature at any time to increase the number of state-appointed directors to five in the mother banks and four in branch banks, thus giving the state effective directorial control. Furthermore, banks were required to furnish a quarterly statement to the governor and were forbidden to issue notes less than 10 dollars in value; after 1840 notes less than 20 dollars in value were not to be issued.[66]

Prohibition of small bank notes was a reform measure and restrictive device that was spasmodically used and enforced by the states from the time of the earliest banks in the late eighteenth century down to the Civil War. Seldom effective because of the lack of uniform application by all the states, the measure's objective was to increase the amount of specie in circulation and to protect the poor, who would be the most affected by worthless small bills. In the early 1830s William M. Gouge reported that in "Virginia, Pennsylvania, and Maryland, payments of a less amount than five dollars are made in real money: but in the other states, dollar notes circulate, so that payments in specie are made for only fractional parts of the dollar." Furthermore, in "North Carolina, South Carolina, and some other parts of the Union, notes for 25 cents, 12½ cents, and even 6¼ cents are current." [67]

During the years immediately prior to the Panic of 1837 and after Gouge's report, there was a rash of legislation aimed at abolishing small notes. The decision of the British in 1829 to limit the Bank of England to a five-pound-note minimum probably had considerable influence.[68] Maine, New Hampshire, and Connecticut all passed laws in the 1830s prohibiting small bills.[69] In 1835 the New York legislature

[66] Starnes, *Branch Banking in Virginia*, 80–84.

[67] William M. Gouge, *A Short History of Paper Money and Banking in the United States* (Philadelphia, 1833), 56–57.

[68] Miller, *Banking Theories*, 142.

[69] Knox, *History of Banking*, 332–33, 338, and John Gurley Woodward, "Currency and Banking in Connecticut," in *The New England States, Their Con-*

forbade the circulation of bills under 5 dollars.[70] Seven years earlier Pennsylvania had banned the circulation of small notes from other states, and in the 1836 charter of the United States Bank of Pennsylvania notes under 10 dollars were not to be issued.[71] Maryland, as indicated by Gouge, was relatively free of the scourge of small notes and from the earliest bank charter had generally outlawed notes under 5 dollars.[72] The issuance of notes under 5 dollars was prohibited by the Georgia legislature in 1832. To do so subjected the offender to a fine of 100 dollars. The difficulty in enforcing the law was indicated by the fact that in 1835 the fine was raised to 500 dollars.[73]

States in the Southwest and Northwest also made attempts to suppress small notes in the 1830s. Mississippi and Arkansas included provisions in several bank charters that authorized only notes 5 dollars and above.[74] The Alabama legislature forbade the circulation of notes under 5 dollars from out-of-state banks.[75] The Bank of the State of Missouri, although allowed to issue notes as low as 10 dollars, did not in fact issue notes under 20 dollars.[76] In Indiana and Illinois the state banks were forbidden to circulate notes under 5 dollars.[77] The 1832 charter of the Union Bank of Tennessee prohibited notes under 5 dollars.[78] In 1835 the Ohio state senate requested the auditor to determine how many notes under 5 dollars were in circulation in that state and to ask banks if they would be willing to sacrifice their charter right to circulate notes under 5 dollars. The banks were unenthusiastic about the call for sacrifice, but in 1836 the legislature required each bank to pay a 20 per cent tax on their dividends unless they agreed to

stitutional, Judicial, Educational, Commercial, Professional and Industrial History (Boston, 1897), edited by William T. Davis, II, 667.

[70] Chaddock, *Safety Fund System*, 278.

[71] *Niles' Register*, January 24, 1835, and Dewey, *State Banking*, 64–65. A year earlier it had been proposed to limit Pennsylvania bank issues to notes of 20 dollars and above. This proposal, however, was indefinitely postponed by the legislature.

[72] Bryan, *State Banking in Maryland*, 26–29.

[73] Govan, "Banking in Georgia" (thesis), 28–29.

[74] Sumner, *History of Banking*, 248–52, 333.

[75] *Niles' Register*, February 21, 1835.   [76] Cable, *Bank of Missouri*, 165.

[77] Harding, "State Bank of Indiana," 3–6; Esarey, *State Banking in Indiana*, 251–57; Dowrie, *Banking in Illinois*, 61–62.

[78] *Niles' Register*, November 10, 1832.

refrain from issuing notes under 3 dollars; in 1837 the minimum was raised to 5 dollars.[79]

6

The Suffolk System of New England and the Safety Fund System of New York were the most progressive reforms undertaken to establish bank responsibility before the Panic. One privately initiated and the other state imposed, these measures sought to stabilize the currency and insure note-holder security.

In 1819 the directors of the Suffolk Bank in Boston decided that "they might add to the profits of the bank by buying country bank-notes at a discount and sending them home for redemption." A committee was appointed to look into this matter, and it was decided that "if any bank will deposit with the Suffolk Bank five thousand dollars as a permanent deposit, with such further sums as shall be sufficient from time to time to redeem its bills taken by this bank, such bank shall have the privilege of receiving its own bills at the same discount at which they are purchased." [80] By 1824, however, Boston was flooded with the paper of country banks. Although the city had more than 50 per cent of New England's banking capital, the city banks supplied only 4 per cent of the notes in circulation.

The Suffolk Bank then proposed a second plan to the other Boston banks for "checking the enormous issues of country . . . paper" and "securing to the bills of the Boston banks a just proportion of the circulation. . . ." The directors of the Suffolk Bank contended that New England country banks had a circulation representing 75 per cent of their capital and furnishing 7.5 million dollars worth of notes, while the banks in the city, with a capital of 10.2 million dollars, circulated only 300,000 dollars in notes. This large country circulation, it was explained, was not due "to any superior confidence in the stability of these institutions, or in their ability to redeem their promises in gold and silver, but may be attributed to a discount founded on the very difficulty and uncertainty of means of enforcing this payment." Thus, it was proposed that country banks limit themselves to "the discount of

[79] Huntington, *Banking and Currency in Ohio,* 153–55.
[80] David R. Whitney, *The Suffolk Bank* (Cambridge, Mass., 1878), 7.

country notes and the convenience of country traders." If they did this, their "bills would then circulate only in their own immediate vicinity" and "farmers, who had come to this city to dispose of their produce, would take back Boston bills, which the traders would in their turn bring down to pay for foreign or domestic merchandise." As it was, country banks were making a large number of their discounts in Boston. "Loans to an immense amount," it was argued, "are made by their agents here at reduced rates of interest, payable in three or five days after demand, so that they can be in funds at very short notice, and in this manner necessarily deprive us of much valuable business." [81]

The Suffolk Bank became the agent for the associated Boston banks in redeeming country bank notes. Each country bank was to deposit 2,000 dollars as an interest-free, permanent deposit in the Suffolk Bank, along with other funds to take care of the day-to-day redemption of country notes. If at any time the amount of notes redeemed at the Suffolk Bank exceeded a country bank's redemption fund, interest would be charged. And if at any time the excess became greater than the permanent deposit, the Suffolk Bank was authorized to send the notes directly to the country banks for specie redemption. [82]

New York's Safety Fund System was developed a few years after the Suffolk System had been established. Following the passage of the general bank law in 1827 in New York, objections had been raised as to its severity, particularly with regard to the principle of personal liability. So in 1829 the legislature enacted the Safety Fund Law, a banking plan designed to avoid personal liability and still protect the note holder from bank failures. [83] According to the regulation, each new bank charter or bank-charter renewal would require that a small percentage of the bank's capital be pooled with that of other banks in the state to form a common fund "for the payment of all the debts of an insolvent bank." The payments were not to exceed .5 per cent of a bank's capital per year and would continue only until a bank had contributed 3 per cent of its capital to the fund. The act further provided that no bank could begin business until all its capital stock was paid in and that all note issues be restricted to double the paid-up capital. Loans and discounts were limited to two and one half times the capi-

[81] *Ibid.*, 13.   [82] *Ibid.*, 19–20.   [83] Chaddock, *Safety Fund System*, 260–61.

tal, which was a holdover from mercantilist banking theory. A three-man bank commission was established, with one member appointed by the governor and two by the banks. The commissioners, who were given the power to question bank officers under oath, were expected to visit the banks at least once a quarter.[84]

The Safety Fund, in contrast to the Suffolk System, which had been sponsored by the city banks in opposition to the country banks, was vigorously attacked by the New York City banks. The antagonism stemmed largely from the fact that city bankers felt that the provisions of the measure gave country banks the upper hand, taxing the large capitals of the city banks to back the large circulations of the country banks. City banks had four times the capital of country banks, while note issues in city and country were about the same. Furthermore, city banks held about five times as much specie and four times the deposits of the country banks. The profits of the country banks depended mainly on circulation, while the city banks extended discounts through their larger deposits and consequently did not emit as many notes. While the Safety Fund allowed banks to issue notes valued at twice the paid-up capital, this was of little advantage to the city banks, whose circulations amounted to less than one third of their capital. In short, in the opinion of the city bankers, the law was unfair in that its assessment was against bank capital rather than the amount of notes issued.[85]

7

By the time of the Panic, then, some attempts had been made to make banking more responsive to the public welfare and to give the note holder some security. The more commercialized states on the eastern seaboard initiated most of the reforms. In the less commercial western states, efforts were generally limited to restricting small-note issues. New York and Massachusetts sought to introduce an element of financial sophistication and public safety with the Safety Fund and Suffolk systems.

Thus, many banks in the Northeast, supported by judicious reforms, developed into sound, conservative institutions. Although concrete

[84] *Ibid.*, 261–63.   [85] *Ibid.*, 236, 238–42, 267.

evidence is scanty, it would appear that the banks in the Northeast, certainly the ones at the large commercial centers, were able to concentrate their business in short-term, highly liquid, commercial loans. Consequently, the notes of the northeastern banks, especially the New England ones, showed remarkable stability and were discounted close to par value at Philadelphia in the decade and a half before the Panic.[86]

Banks in the other three sections suffered from their remoteness from major financial centers, which in itself made their notes less valuable in that it was more difficult for them to be redeemed. These banks were further handicapped by high percentages of the long-term, nonliquid-type loans. Also, due to naivete or criminal negligence on the part of the state legislatures, many of the banks outside the Northeast had been given virtually a free hand with little or no restriction or supervision of their activities. There were, of course, exceptions. The banks in Virginia and South Carolina were old, responsible, and conservative. In New Orleans, the most important commercial center in the West, the banks were, on the whole, stable institutions.

Despite the attempts of some states to ensure a safe and conservative banking system, the Panic of 1837 proved these efforts to be feeble ones. With the destructive force of a tidal wave, the financial storm destroyed the flimsily constructed banking institutions and put such a strain and stress on the stronger ones that structural weaknesses appeared.

The Panic forced both political parties to focus their attention upon the banking issue and made bank reform the first order of business for the Democrats in the states in the years after 1837.

[86] Van Fenstermaker, *American Commercial Banking,* charts on pages 79 and 83.

THE WEST

IN THE YEARS immediately preceding the Panic of 1837, the western states were caught up in a feverish economic boom. Easterners seeking their fortunes were coming west in ever-increasing numbers. Land sales were at record levels.[1] Vast internal-improvement schemes were planned, and entire communities were laid out by real-estate speculators long before the first settler even appeared. The only limit to this frenetic expansion seems to have been in the fertile imaginations of the most daring of the entrepreneurs.

The northwestern states of Ohio, Indiana, Illinois, Michigan, Missouri, Kentucky, and Tennessee[2] were caught up in the boom to a far greater degree than their neighbors to the east. Nevertheless, in this they were far outstripped by the southwestern states of Mississippi, Alabama, Arkansas, and, to a lesser extent, Louisiana, where everything was exaggerated. The experience in the Southwest provides almost a caricature for what happened to the West as a whole. The psychology of enterprise was all pervasive, and few would have challenged the wonderous alchemic magic the banks seemed to be working in providing the main source of energy for the growth. A contemporary author, Joseph Baldwin, colorfully described the atmosphere:

[1] In 1832 public land sales in the four southwestern states plus Florida totaled about 1 million dollars. By the middle 1830s this had shot up to over 7 million dollars. See North, *Economic Growth*, 124.

[2] The slave states of Missouri, Kentucky, and Tennessee have been somewhat arbitrarily included as part of the Northwest. The latter two were older states and did not experience the kind of growth the states in the Southwest did.

This country was just settling up. Marvellous accounts had gone forth of the fertility of its virgin lands; and the productions of the soil were commanding a price remunerating to slave labor as it had never been remunerated before. Emigrants came flocking in from all quarters of the Union, especially from the slaveholding States. The new country seemed to be a reservoir, and every road leading to it a vagrant stream of enterprise and adventure. Money, or what passed for money, was the only cheap thing to be had. Every crossroad and every avocation presented an opening—through which a fortune was seen by the adventurer. . . .

. . . prices rose like smoke. Lots in obscure villages were held at city prices; lands, bought at the minimum cost of government, were sold at from thirty to forty dollars per acre, and considered dirt cheap at that.[3]

The rapid growth of the 1830s had been accompanied by an orgy of speculation, resulting in a spectacular and uncontrolled expansion of bank capital. By the late 1830s the Southwest, with its sparse and rural population, was second only to the populous and urbanized Northeast in the amount of bank capital authorized.[4] Baldwin also gives a picture of Southwestern finance during those restless days:

Credit was a thing of course. To refuse it—if the thing was ever done—were an insult for which a bowieknife were not a too summary or exemplary means of redress. The State banks were issuing their bills by the sheet, like a patent steam printing-press *its* issues; and no other showing was asked of its applicant for the loan than an authentication of his great distress for money. . . . Banks, chartered on a specie basis, did a very flourishing business on the promisory notes of the individual stockholders ingeniously substituted in lieu of cash. They issued ten for one, the *one* being ficticious. . . . The stampede towards the golden temple became general: the delusion prevailed far and wide that this thing was not a burlesque on commerce and finance.[5]

The tragic result of this heady and exhilarating growth was that both western sections suffered the most when the boom ended abruptly in 1837. The Panic that year, and the depression that followed, severely struck the fast-growing and awkwardly expanding states of the West.

[3] Joseph G. Baldwin, *The Flush Times of Alabama and Mississippi: A Series of Sketches* (San Francisco, 1889), 82–84.

[4] Van Fenstermaker, *American Commercial Banking,* 77–95.

[5] Baldwin, *Flush Times,* 83, 87.

The price index for New Orleans and Cincinnati shows prices falling gradually each year through 1839, after reaching a high in 1836. A sharp dip was registered in 1840, and by 1842–1843 this decline had reduced the price level of 1836 by almost one half.[6]

While there were many similarities between the two western sections, such as their overwhelming rural character and market-oriented agricultural economy, there were also a number of striking differences.[7] The plantation-slave economy of the Southwest, of course, was the crucial factor in distinguishing that section from the Northwest. And although both sections produced and marketed agricultural staple products, this process in the Northwest fostered the growth of a locally oriented industry, while in the Southwest it did not. Furthermore, the development of large, nearly self-sufficient, agricultural units in the Southwest inhibited the growth of small trading towns. "Even in retail trade," one historian has commented, "the most rudimentary of the residentiary industries, the area was conspicuously deficient."[8] A traveler in ante-bellum Alabama comments on the rural and isolated nature of the country he passed through:

During two days' sail on the Alabama River from Mobile to Montgomery, I did not see so many houses standing together in any one spot as could be dignified with the appelation of village. . . . There were many places where cotton was shipped and provisions were landed; still there were no signs of enterprise to indicate that we were in the heart of a rich cotton region. . . . In fact, the more fertile the land the more destitute is the country of villages and towns. And how can it be other wise? The system of management, which is recommended as the most economical and profitable, is to raise and to manufacture on the plantations every thing the slaves require. Of such articles as are in daily use among the rural inhabitants in the poorest districts of the Free States, the slaves are a non-consuming class. An element so essential to rural prosperity is in great measure wanting in the Slave States, and thus few villages are seen. The planters supply themselves with their own necessaries and luxuries of life directly

[6] *Historical Statistics*, 121–22.

[7] For my discussion of the similarities and differences between the two sections, I am heavily indebted to North's *Economic Growth of the United States*, Chapters X and XI. However, I divide the South into two separate sections, the Southwest and Southeast, while North treats both as a single section.

[8] *Ibid.*, 132.

through agents in the large towns, and comparatively little of the money drawn for the cotton crop is spent in the Southern States.[9]

The northwestern states displayed a heterogeneity not found in the Southwest. By 1840, for example, Ohio was well on the way to developing a highly commercial and industrial economy, while Illinois was virtually still in the frontier stage of development. Small urban trading centers were scattered throughout the Northwest to serve the economy, which was considerably more diverse than that of the Southwest, and various trades and services developed in these "urban areas in response to regional consumer demand." [10] And unlike the Southwest, where large agricultural units produced only one or two major crops for direct export, small farmers of the Northwest raised wheat and corn for export and also took advantage of the derivative products of these two cereals, such as "flour, meal, livestock products, and whiskey." [11]

Mississippi and Ohio illustrate the two extremes of the western sections. Mississippi is perhaps the best example of a state totally absorbed in the boom psychology of the middle 1830s only to find dreams of "flush times" turn to nightmares of bankruptcy. And in contrast to Mississippi, a state close to the frontier in time and development, was Ohio, the most economically advanced state of the two western sections. But despite the economic and political differences, Democrats in both states came to similar hard-money, antibank conclusions.

[9] Robert Russell, *North America, Its Agriculture and Climate* as quoted in *Ibid.*, 131–32.

[10] *Ibid.*, 154.   [11] *Ibid.*, 135.

CHAPTER III

Mississippi

I

THE ATMOSPHERE in Mississippi in the 1830s before the Panic was charged with an entrepreneurial exuberance that pervaded and influenced every aspect of life. Joseph Baldwin,[1] for all his exaggerations, probably managed to capture the essential spirit of the times:

The condition of society may be imagined:—vulgarity—ignorance—fussy and arrogant pretension—unmitigated rowdyism—bullying insolence, if they did not rule the hour seemed to wield unchecked dominion. The workings of these choice spirits were patent upon the face of society; and the modest, unobtrusive, retiring men of worth and character (for there were many, perhaps a large majority of such) were almost lost sight of in the hurly-burly of those strange and shifting scenes.[2]

Baldwin's "modest, unobtrusive, retiring men of worth and character" were the genteel Virginians who had come unprepared for "the new era" in Mississippi, ". . . the era of the second great experiment of independence, namely, of credit without capital, and enterprise without honesty."[3] Old and established business rules were cast aside while swindling was "raised to the dignity of the fine arts" and larceny "grew not only respectable, but genteel, and ruffled in all the pomp and purple of fine linen."[4] The newly arrived Virginian,[5] a vulnerable target, was appalled to find that a "stuttering, grammarless Georgian,

---

[1] Baldwin, *Flush Times.*   [2] *Ibid.,* 88–89.   [3] *Ibid.,* 81.   [4] *Ibid.,* 85.
[5] See James McDowell's letters to his wife during his trip to the Southwest. James McDowell to Mrs. Susanna S. McDowell, April 4, 12, and 26, 1837, and March 29, 1839, James McDowell, Jr., Papers, Southern Historical Collection, University of North Carolina.

who had never heard of the resolutions of '98, could beat him in a land trade." For the Virginian

knew nothing of the elaborate machinery of ingenious chicane,—such as feigning bankruptcy—fraudulent conveyances—making over to his wife— running property—and had never heard of such tricks of trade as sending out coffins to the graveyard, with negroes inside, carried off by sudden spells of imaginary disease, to be "resurrected," in due time, grinning, on the banks of the Brazos.[6]

The future or the past had little meaning to Mississippians in the tumultuous years before the Panic, and this had a profound influence on the kind and style of politics in the state. Party lines were extremely fluid. Not altogether atypical was one politician who called himself a Democrat in 1834, a Whig in 1835, a Democrat in 1836, a Whig in 1837, and a Democrat again in 1840. In the process he earned the nickname, "General Weathercock." [7]

Parties were loosely organized, often representing no more than loose coalitions of public men representing various sectional interests. Electioneering and organization were crude. Conventions were held irregularly, and the nominations made at them were often bitterly disputed.[8] There was little or no party discipline. During a political canvass itself, political runners were sent out much as advance men for a circus "to make appointments, circulate documents and make crossroad and bar-room speeches." [9] Then came the opposing candidates, who more often than not were traveling companions, debating one another at each stop on their campaign itinerary.[10]

The crude and open-ended style of Mississippi politics made the parties fertile ground for exploitation by a few political entrepreneurs.

[6] Baldwin, *Flush Times,* 93.

[7] Miles, *Jacksonian Democracy in Mississippi,* 164.

[8] One Mississippian felt that the combined Democratic and State Rights parties' convention in 1839 signified that Mississippi politics was becoming as highly organized as New York's. See John Stewart to Duncan McLaurin, December 25, 1838, Duncan McLaurin Papers, Duke University.

[9] J. F. H. Claiborne, *Mississippi, as a Province, Territory and State, with Biographical Notices of Eminent Citizens* (Jackson, Miss., 1880), footnote page 417.

[10] See J. F. H. Claiborne, "A Trip Through the Piney Woods," Mississippi Historical Society *Publications,* IX (1906), 487–538, for a delightful account of a journey through that area during the campaign of 1841.

There is always the danger that a political party will fall under the control of a small group. But when there exists a formalized structure, responsibility can more easily be assessed and, through regular and frequent meetings, challenges to statewide authority can be generated by those outside the power structure.[11] But in Mississippi, where this formal party structure had not yet evolved, political power rested in the hands of those who had demonstrated a vote-drawing capacity, newspaper editors, and recipients of federal patronage. Political principle did not seem to exert an overriding influence in determining the actions of most Mississippi politicians. Yet they were aggressively vocal in defending their honor. Duels were fought at the slightest provocation. Challenge a man's integrity and an invitation for "coffee and pistols for two" would be swiftly forthcoming.

John Francis Hamtramck Claiborne's career as legislator, congressman, speculator, newspaper editor, and historian is symbolic of the political style in the turbulent Mississippi environment. Born in Natchez, the son of an early settler and political leader, Claiborne had served a full public career by the time he was in his early thirties. In 1838, embittered after his bid for another term in Congress had been denied,[12] the Mississippi broker retired from official public life to devote his energies full time to newspaper work, behind-the-scenes political manipulation, and financial speculations.

"I am at this moment," Claiborne wrote to Levi Woodbury in 1838, "the strongest man in the state; I am a native of Mississippi, and out of my own means, I have established more than half of the public journals that support the administration. Two thirds of the leading political editorials that appear in them are from my pen."[13]

---

[11] There is, of course, an equal danger that once a party becomes highly organized it may become unresponsive to grassroots sentiment. Thus, no matter how democratic in structure a party may be, there is a constant danger that the lines of communication between the leadership and the followers will become fossilized.

[12] In the winter of 1838 the United States House of Representatives decided against seating Claiborne and his Democratic colleague because of the confusion arising as to whether they had been elected only for the special session of Congress meeting in September, 1837, or for both the special session and the regular session. See Chapter V of Dallas C. Dickey's *Seargent S. Prentiss: Whig Orator of the Old South* (Baton Rouge, La., 1945), for a complete account.

[13] J. F. H. Claiborne to Levi Woodbury, November 11, 1838, Levi Woodbury

If Claiborne had any strong conviction, it would have to have been to the doctrine of expediency. He was not the paragon of virtue that he was portrayed to be by at least one contemporary, who described him as "an exemplary model of temperance and moral rectitude," who although not a saint or puritan, yet was a person who

never attends places of amusement; has never been at a public dinner or a political convention; never entered a gambling-house or race course; never played a game of billiards, chess, or backgammon; never carried a bowie-knife or pistol; never smokes or chews tobacco; never uses an oath; is strictly temperate; never was a witness in court, and never had a lawsuit.[14]

During the congressional campaign of 1837, for instance, Claiborne attempted to satisfy everyone on the issue of a national bank. Charged by his enemies with "inconsistency and deception on the bank question," Claiborne neatly and forthrightly redefined his stand—astraddle the issue. He was, he said, "opposed in every shape and form to the late bank of the U. States" and, furthermore, considered it unconstitutional. "No human power," he stoutly declared, would induce him "to vote for the recharter of *that* bank under any circumstances. . . ." Yet, he quickly assured the voters, he was no ultraist and would approve of a limited national bank for relief purposes if the Constitution were amended to satisfy his delicate scruples. Later, Claiborne himself admitted that he had erred when "in a moment of excitement and sympathy for the general distress, I yielded with many of my own party to the belief that a bank, of a certain character, was necessary." [15]

The ambivalence toward banks exhibited by Claiborne was typical of the attitude of many other Mississippi Democrats prior to 1837 and even up to 1839. But by 1839 and 1840 things were changing, and even some soft-money Democrats were beginning to echo the merits of the hard-money doctrine.

Papers, Series 2, Library of Congress. In the early 1840s Claiborne edited the Natchez *Free Trader,* and in 1844 he moved to New Orleans, where he edited a Democratic paper for several years. Returning to Mississippi before the Civil War, he lived until 1884, writing both a history of the state and a biography of his colleague, John Quitman.

[14] James D. Lynch, *Bench and Bar of Mississippi* (place and date of publication unknown), 523–24.

[15] Jackson *Mississippian,* August 4, 1837. See also, Claiborne's letter to the *Mississippian,* October 27, 1837.

These radical notions, which were becoming increasingly widespread, undoubtedly made Claiborne uneasy. And perhaps this, along with his resentment over the refusal of Congress to seat him as the Mississippi representative, accounts for the remarkable proposal he made in the spring of 1840 to the renegade Virginia Democrat, Senator William C. Rives. In a letter, the supremely ambitious Claiborne offered to betray the Mississippi Democratic party to the Whigs. He explained that since he had been defeated for Congress through the "perfidy of leading *democrats*," he was now refusing to take an active role in the party affairs and considered himself only "nominally a member of the Van Buren party." In fact, he confided, he had *"come to the conclusion to abandon the party, but this . . . will be till I hear from you, confined to my own bosom."* Meanwhile, he said, he was "scattering dissension through the ranks," which would, he believed, "break the party down." [16] There is no evidence that anything came of Claiborne's intrigue. He remained within the Democratic party and, although he never again held public office, continued as an important newspaper editor on intimate terms with the leaders of the party.

Politics was not the only area in which Claiborne speculated. He, his friend William M. Gwin, and others had grandiose plans for capitalizing on their neighbors' misfortunes by acquiring lands and slaves thrown on the market at greatly reduced prices by bankrupt owners. Raising a working capital in the East, Gwin and Claiborne acquired lists of lands mortgaged for stock in the Mississippi banks. Apparently they believed that the owners of these lands were potential bankrupts, and the two partners hoped to hasten foreclosures by urging the federal government to put financial pressure upon the Mississippi banks by withdrawing federal funds. [17] The scheme failed, and the partnership eventually ended in a bitter feud, with Claiborne having little compassion for the financially insolvent Gwin. [18]

[16] J. F. H. Claiborne to William C. Rives, May 31, 1840, William C. Rives Papers, Library of Congress.

[17] Robert J. Walker to J. F. H. Claiborne, October 7, 1839; William M. Gwin to J. F. H. Claiborne, October 9, 1839; C. W. Cliffton to unknown, October 10 or 16, 1839; William M. Gwin to Dwight J. Freeman, October 26, 1839; Partnership Contract between William M. Gwin, J. F. H. Claiborne, and John D. Freeman, October 14, 1839; J. F. H. Claiborne Papers, Library of Congress.

[18] In 1845, Claiborne threatened Gwin that he would publish all his letters in pamphlet form and distribute them to every member of Congress unless

2

The entrepreneurial dreams of Mississippians died a hard and lingering death, and for that reason banking failed to become the overriding issue in Mississippi politics until the campaign of 1839. As Claiborne's career illustrates, even as late as two years after the initial financial shock, many still were caught up in the boom psychology and were trying to take advantage of the widespread misfortunes of others. There had been little opposition to the increase in numbers of banks from one in 1830, with a capital of 950,000 dollars, to eighteen in 1837, with a combined capital of 13 million dollars.[19]

In 1837 and 1838, when few would risk opposing the popular tide in favor of banks, there was at least one voice of warning. The editor of the influential Democratic Jackson *Mississippian*, Volney E. Howard,[20] repeatedly cautioned his readers about the evils of the state's banking system and the folly of depending upon the banks for relief from the financial squeeze. He called for a "radical reform" of the banking system. "Quacks may rail as much as they please at hard money," Howard argued, but "no currency can be safe without a sound specie basis." Only the belief "that paper can be converted into gold and silver at the will of the holder [gives] it the least value with the public." [21]

During the campaign of 1837, Howard attempted to define the Democratic position as one unalterably opposed to a national bank and in favor of a radical reform of the state institutions. But, unwilling to risk the displeasure of those Democrats who viewed the state banks as

---

Gwin paid back at least one half of the 30,000 dollars he owed Claiborne's wife. See J. F. H. Claiborne to William M. Gwin, January 16, 1845, J. F. H. Claiborne Papers, Library of Congress.

[19] *Comptroller's Report, 1876*, 32.

[20] Howard was a New Englander who had come from his native Maine to Mississippi in the early 1830s. Although one of the first Democrats to warn publicly against the excesses of banking, Howard broke with the majority of his party in the early 1840s when feelings against banks were so high that the Democratic party successfully advocated the repudiation of the state's obligations to pay the Union Bank bonds. In fact, he was instrumental in organizing the bond-paying Democrats, who competed with the regular ticket in 1843. See sketch of Howard in Lynch, *Bench and Bar of Mississippi*, 250–51.

[21] Jackson *Mississippian*, May 5 and 19, June 9 and 13, and August 18, 1837.

indispensable, he carefully disavowed any intention of returning to an exclusive hard-money currency. Charging that a majority of the state senate during the previous legislative session had held offices and directorships "in the different banks in the State" and that "a great many of the members of the lower house were either officers or stockholders in these institutions," he called upon the public to scrutinize carefully the candidates before them. The "most important business which will come before the next legislature," he predicted, "will be the regulation of the banks," and no man should be elected "who is either an officer, director, or stockholder in these institutions." [22]

Howard threw the support of his paper to Alexander G. McNutt, Democratic gubernatorial candidate from wealthy Warren County. McNutt had been, Howard said, "one of the few men who endeavored in the State Legislature to prevent the evils of our present corrupt system of banking . . . and had the amendments which he proposed to the different bank charters been adopted, both the citizens and the banks would be in a better situation than they now are." Howard urged that the currency issue be made the test of a candidate, for the people had "a right to know who are, and who are not the advocates of a rotten, paper money system." [23]

McNutt succeeded in his bid for the governorship and served in the office until 1842. Thus his administrations caught the brunt of Mississippi's economic and fiscal hardships. A native Virginian who had come to Mississippi in 1822, settled in Vicksburg, and established a law practice, McNutt had not been uniformly opposed to bank charters when he was in the legislature prior to becoming governor. He had voted for chartering a number of banks, but it was explained by the *Mississippian* that he had been instructed to do so by his Vicksburg constituents. Furthermore, while in the legislature he had been the author of a provision that forced the banks to pay 12.5 per cent interest on notes that were not redeemed in specie, a law repealed in 1838 by the Whigs and soft-money Democrats.[24]

---

[22] *Ibid.,* July 14, 1837. [23] *Ibid.,* June 23, 1837.

[24] *Ibid.,* September 20, 1839. See also, Lynch, *Bench and Bar in Mississippi,* 133–35. A Whig campaign tract published in 1847 said of Governor McNutt: "Almost beyond comparison, the most intellectual and efficient man of his party in the State, Alexander G. McNutt may justly be said to be one of those few rulers, on this side of the Atlantic, who have proved that they possessed the

McNutt's career represents the evolution of genuine antibank sentiment within the party. As governor he made an honest, determined effort to reform the banks. This failing, he attempted to rid the state of banks, evoking the animosity of the Whigs and soft-money advocates in his own party. The banks themselves displayed an insulting arrogance in thwarting every attempted reform, refusing to permit state-appointed directors to take their rightful places on the banks' directories, closing their doors to state-appointed investigators, and violating their charters with impunity.

When McNutt assumed office in January, 1838, there were several countercurrents at work. In many Democrats a latent distrust of banks was being aroused by stories about the unsound condition and in some cases fraudulent mismanagement of the banks. At the same time there was a widespread desire for relief from the economic crisis, and to many, penalizing the already prostrate banks would only prolong and widen the distress.

In his first address as governor, McNutt showed that he understood the feelings within the state. "The Banking System is so interwoven with our habits, business and contracts," he said, that it "has . . . become a necessary evil, and cannot speedily be eradicated, without involving the whole State in utter ruin." The Governor advocated a general law to regulate the banks, and since all the banks in Mississippi had violated their charters by suspending specie payment, McNutt suggested that the "present is an auspicious period for placing them under salutary control." [25] A short time later he made specific

---

power to impress for a time upon a *people,* whether for good or for evil, Jackson-like, the character and views of an individual mind.

"Seizing upon the financial crisis of the day as a means of fixing himself in power . . . Alexander G. McNutt appeared, a potent but an evil genius, with new views and new principles, [and he] gathered about him a crowd of crooked political disciples, whose public words and deeds have continuously, up to the present day, proclaimed . . . as the cherished motto of the State *'get all you can and keep all you get;'* subscribing . . . to the new morality that 'creditors are the natural enemies of debtors,' and inculcating the doctrine that creditors ought to be abused, as well as fleeced, as a matter of patriotism. . . ." See Anonymous, *Nine Years of Democratic Rule in Mississippi: Being Notes upon the Political History of the State, from the Beginning of the Year 1838, to the Present Time* (Jackson, Miss., 1847), 23–24.

[25] Jackson *Mississippian,* January 19, 1838.

proposals in a scathing attack on bank abuses, which one irate Whig condemned as libelous to the banks.[26] The Governor recommended that the legislature "should retain by express provision, the power of altering, amending or repealing bank charters at pleasure." Furthermore, he asked the legislature to force the banks to resume by November 1, 1838, or to wind up their affairs.[27] His suggestions were not enacted into law.

There was one major issue involving banks that the Mississippi legislature could not avoid. The Union Bank, capitalized at 15.5 million dollars, had been first authorized by the 1836 legislature. But since the faith of the state had been pledged to raise the money for the capital, the following legislature also had to approve.[28] McNutt had been one of the few to vote against the bank, whose enormous capitalization would more than double the capital in the state, while he was still a senator. But before his election as governor he had pledged not to veto the bill if it were to be passed by the legislature for the second and final time.[29] The 1838 legislature did pass the bill, but there was a sizeable opposition. In the senate, ten Whigs and seven Democrats were

---

[26] *Ibid.*

[27] McNutt also pointed out that the directors of the Planters' Bank had refused both to allow a director commissioned by the state to sit on the board of directors and to permit officers to investigate the condition of the bank. This course of action, he noted, had been persisted in by the directors representing the private stockholders despite the fact that all the state's revenue was deposited in the bank and the state was the bank's largest stockholder. The Agricultural Bank was equally guilty of abusing its charter, he said. Aiming a salvo at his Whig predecessor, McNutt pointed out that no one had been appointed by the Governor for the past two years to inspect the books of the Agricultural Bank, whereas its charter specifically called for such an inspection. *Ibid.,* January 26, 1838. McNutt attempted to enforce the charters of the banks. On February 14, 1838, he appointed John B. Nevill to be the state's representative on the board of directors of the Planters' Bank. He urged Nevill to demand his seat. Alexander McNutt to John B. Nevill, February 14, 1838, Executive Journal, Mississippi Department of Archives and History. See also, Alexander McNutt to William Cannon, June 14, 1838, Executive Journal. In a letter to the president and directors of the Planters' Bank, McNutt warned them against paying their creditors in depreciated paper. Alexander McNutt to President and Board of Directors of Planters' Bank, September 13, 1838, Executive Journal.

[28] Brough, "Banking in Mississippi," 327; Helderman, *National and State Banks,* 69–83; Knox, *History of Banking,* 604–605.

[29] Jackson *Mississippian,* October 13, 1837.

in favor, while two Whigs and ten Democrats were opposed. In the house, thirty-six Whigs and seventeen Democrats approved the bank, and twenty-nine Democrats and four Whigs were against it.[30] Despite the fact that a majority in his party cast negative votes, McNutt kept his campaign promise and did not veto the bill. This 1838 balloting proved to be a foreshadowing of events to come. The Union Bank would remain at the center of the banking controversy, which would rage in Mississippi until 1843, when the state would repudiate its obligation to redeem the bank's bonds.

The 1838 legislature took further action on banking matters. A law assessing damages on non-specie-paying banks was repealed.[31] The chartering of several other banks also was authorized,[32] but in these instances the Governor, not tied to campaign promises, cast his veto. Showing a surprising amount of financial sophistication in his veto message, McNutt argued that the "circulation and value of paper money depends mainly on its convertibility into specie—not entirely on the ultimate solvency of the corporation issuing it, as it is generally supposed." Moreover, he told the legislators,

[30] See the Jackson *Mississippian*, July 19, 1839, for a long discussion of the votes of Whigs and Democrats on a number of bank bills. Miles claims a different vote total in the House of Representatives: eighteen Democrats and thirty-five Whigs in favor, and twenty-seven Democrats and six Whigs opposed. *Jacksonian Democracy in Mississippi*, 142. The future Democratic governor, Tilghman Tucker, and a colleague led a losing battle against the passage of the bill in the senate. They opposed the bill because it would raise the banking capital of the state "far beyond what the wildest advocate of the banking system would consider the wants of the country." And, furthermore, the charter discriminated against those who did not own land because it prevented them from becoming stockholders. See Jackson *Mississippian*, February 9, 1838.

[31] The Governor claimed that this bill removed the only barrier to an issue of over 100 million dollars worth of bank notes. Massachusetts, Pennsylvania, and other states, he pointed out, forced their banks to pay interest as high as 24 per cent on unredeemed bills. The Jackson *Mississippian* blamed the passage of the bill on the fact that it was passed over the Governor's veto the last day of the session, when many Democrats had left for home. See issues of February 16 and 23, 1838.

[32] The Yalobusha and Tallahatchie Railroad and Banking Company was chartered by a vote of twenty-three Whigs and eight Democrats in the house, while twelve Democrats and six Whigs opposed it. The Yazoo Railroad Company was chartered and given banking privileges by a vote of eleven Whigs and six Democrats for and seven Democrats and six Whigs against. Jackson *Mississippian*, July 19, 1839.

These are times to be met—not followed. I cannot co-operate with the Legislature in chartering more banks, more especially when they are based upon principles evidently calculated to depreciate still more the currency, procrastinate for years the resumption of specie payments, destroy confidence, break up the standard of value—and weigh down the planting and commercial interests, by the intolerable evils of a fluctuating depreciated paper currency.[33]

The legislative session of 1839 was practically a repeat performance of that of the previous year. Since all the banks in the state by then had forfeited their charters by issuing excessive amounts of notes and suspending specie payment, McNutt recommended a strict general banking law that would limit circulation and dividends and require publication of bank reports. The banks would be given the choice of accepting the law or facing legal action.[34] The legislature refused to accept McNutt's proposals and instead authorized the Union Bank to issue one- and two-year post notes.[35] The Governor's veto of this provision raised a storm of protest, some critics claiming that McNutt's goal was "to crush the Union Bank."[36]

Soft-money Democrats as well as Whigs were alarmed by McNutt's actions. There were rumors that he would not be the party's candidate for governor in 1839. But, although it was said that he was supported only by the "ultras" in his party,[37] he was renominated. Nevertheless, throughout the spring of 1839 efforts were being made by the more conservative Democrats to remove him from the ticket. The *Mississippian* warned against replacing McNutt with "some pliant tool of the banks" and declared that only *"shin plaster"* Democrats opposed McNutt's re-election. These misguided men were advised to "desert to the Whigs," for they were a "disgrace to any cause."[38] McNutt, it was argued, was not opposed to all banks but favored well-regulated specie-paying banks, forbidden to issue more than 3 dollars in paper for

---

[33] *Ibid.*, February 23, 1838.   [34] House *Executive Document No. 172*, 471–79.
[35] *Niles' Register*, March 16, 1839.

[36] Paulding, Miss., *Clarion* as quoted in the Jackson *Mississippian*, March 22, 1839. Also see *Mississippian*, March 15, 1839, for more editorials supporting McNutt's action.

[37] John Stewart to Duncan McLaurin, December 25, 1838, Duncan McLaurin Papers.

[38] Jackson *Mississippian*, April 26, 1839.

every dollar of specie in their vaults. And this, the editor of the *Mississippian* concluded, "was not near ultra enough." [39]

There are several reasons that the legislature was in no mood to follow the Governor's lead and reform the state's banks. Few Mississippians realized that the depression would be so lengthy and severe. Some were even optimistically predicting that the banks would be able to resume specie payments by the next fall. Furthermore, the financial squeeze paradoxically stimulated a demand for more banks and credit. Bank credit and boom times had seduced many Mississippians to overextend themselves financially. Therefore, any economic readjustment would fall heavily upon them, and they felt that the only solution would be to keep the boom going by creating even more banks.

3

The campaign and election of 1839 took place in an atmosphere of deepening depression and gloom. The rosy optimism about the future, which had resulted in the chartering of so many banks, was turning more and more to disenchantment, and compounding the bitterness was the evidence on every hand of a richly productive land. One 1839 traveler reported that Mississippi was "fine country" and possessed "every agricultural advantage that any country could enjoy" but had been "more abused than any thing . . . imagination can conceive." "They have," he claimed, "a bank for every 30 miles square all over the state," and all "the inhabitants of the state almost are swallowed up in debt." [40] How could a state so favored by nature with rich lands and a mild climate suffer such an economic dislocation? The only satisfactory answer to many was that unscrupulous men had tried to create artificial wealth by chartering banks. Therefore, the actions of some in sinning against the natural laws of economics had forced the entire community to do penance.

The year 1839 was a transitional one for the Mississippi Democratic party. After a series of county meetings throughout 1838, the Demo-

[39] *Ibid.,* June 28, 1839; see also issue of June 7, 1839.
[40] J. C. Claiborne to Richard B. Robinson, June 26, 1839. George Coke Dromgoole and Richard B. Robinson Papers, Duke University.

cratic and State Rights [41] parties held a joint state convention to combine forces against the Whigs. The basis for cooperation was agreement on support for the Van Buren Administration's Independent Treasury scheme and on the need for a thorough reform of the state's banking system. The *Mississippian* claimed that both Whig and Democratic parties were in a "state of purification," with the "Federalists of the Democratic as well as of the States Rights party" joining the Whigs in "advocating a National Bank, as well as the whole legion of pet banks." [42]

The antibank sentiment within the Democratic party increased steadily, and in the fall of 1839 candidates ran on a militant hard-money platform. Even Senator Robert J. Walker, who earlier never could, by any stretch of the imagination, have been called a hard-money man, now decried "the whole paper system . . . as destructive to the morals, dangerous to the liberties, and ruinous to the true interests of the American people." He demanded that the paper of all non-specie-paying banks be outlawed and called for the abolition of all bank notes under 20 dollars and eventually, perhaps, all notes under 100 dollars. [43]

Walker's early career, however, shows little antipathy toward the banks. A critic of Benton and his hard-money notions while in the Senate, Walker enjoyed the patronage of the leading Natchez stockholders in the Planters' Bank and the Bank of Mississippi. By the time the financial squeeze came, he was heavily in debt for both a considerable amount of land and numerous gangs of black slaves. To stave off financial insolvency temporarily, Walker, through his connections, was able to borrow from the sinking fund of the Planters' Bank. [44] Claiborne claimed that Walker's "extraordinary change of opinion on the

[41] In 1833–1834 the State Rights party was organized as an opposition response to President Jackson's strong stand against Nullification. In 1839 the State Rights party held the balance in the legislature. See Miles, *Jacksonian Democracy in Mississippi*, 62–69, and Chapter XI.

[42] Jackson *Mississippian*, August 10, 1838. Discussion of the movement to combine the Democratic and State Rights parties was in the following issues of the *Mississippian*: May 11, June 29, August 10 and 24, November 9, and December 7, 1838.

[43] Letter from Walker to his constituents, *Niles' Register*, August 24, 1839.

[44] Claiborne, *Mississippi*, 409, 415–20. See also, James B. Shenton, *Robert John Walker: A Politician From Jackson to Lincoln* (New York, 1961), Chapter 2.

currency question" was due to his ambition and jealousy of Rives. Evidently Walker saw Rives as blocking his way to a place of national prominence as a conservative Democrat and decided that his best opportunity was with the Sub-Treasury and hard-money wing of the party. Walker's plan, Claiborne wrote, was to support Senator James Buchanan of Pennsylvania as Van Buren's successor "and to have himself nominated on the ticket for Vice President. . . ."[45]

In the 1839 campaign each party blamed the other for creating the banks. Democrats chided the Whigs for abruptly changing the nature of their political attack. Earlier, it was pointed out, the Whigs had denounced as "agrarians and levelers" those Democrats who advocated "an exclusive metalic currency," but now that it was becoming obvious that the banks had lost their popularity, the Democrats were charged with being the bank party.[46]

Seargent S. Prentiss, Mississippi Whig leader, argued that the Democrats had destroyed the soundest bank in the country when they attacked the Second Bank of the United States. In its place they had substituted a bloated paper currency issued by Democratic state banks. Upon the realization of the unpopularity of the institutions of their creation, Prentiss maintained, the Democrats repudiated all "bank paper currency . . . and banks, no matter how honestly conducted, [were] denounced in the most unmeasured terms. . . ." The Whigs, on the other hand, were "desirous of *reforming,* not of *destroying,* the paper money system," for they believed "the plan of an exclusive gold and silver currency not only absurd, but . . . impracticable."[47]

---

[45] J. F. H. Claiborne to William C. Rives, May 31, 1840, William C. Rives Papers, Library of Congress.

[46] Jackson *Mississippian,* July 19, 1839. One Whig paper cited a vote in the house of representatives on a motion to table the Brandon Bank Bill as evidence of the Democrats' culpability. Of the thirteen members voting in favor of the tabling motion eleven were Democrats and two were Whigs. Twenty-seven of the forty-seven voting against the motion were Democrats. The Whig editor, from this rather poor evidence, concluded that the Brandon Bank was "a democratic bank" and "was set on foot by democrats, voted for by one-third more democrats than Whigs in both branches of a Democratic Legislature." Port Gibson, Miss., *Correspondent,* October 25, 1839. See also, issue of November 1, 1839, in which the paper endorsed the local Whig candidates who were "opposed to all manner of shin-plaster banks."

[47] *Niles' Register,* September 28, 1839; also Vicksburg *Tri-Weekly Whig,* August 15, 1839, in Robert J. Walker Papers, Library of Congress.

The *Mississippian* ran a long documented article attempting to refute the Whig charges and insisting it was the Whigs "from the river counties" who "poured like so many Goths and Vandals into the halls and lobbies of the legislature, clamoring for banks." The Democratic editor admitted that "a portion of the democrats have been led off by the whigs in support of banks; but the opposition to these corporations, whether feeble or strong, has come from, and been led on by democrats, while the whigs have gone for the banks in a mass, almost without an exception." [48]

There is no doubt that during the campaign the Democrats exaggerated their previous opposition to the banking system. The truth was that banks chartered during the boom times of the middle 1830s had encountered little hostility, but it also is clear that as a party the Whigs almost always had been united in their support of chartering additional banks, while the Democrats normally had been split. There had been and still were in 1839 many Democrats, both large stockholders and debtors, who were sympathetic to the state's banks. The dream of quick riches faded slowly, dying only when it was realized that the bank stoppage in 1837 had been only the prelude to a deep depression.

The Democratic bank-reform platform proved attractive. McNutt was re-elected, and the Democrats were given an overwhelming majority in the legislature. At the opening of the legislative session in January, 1840, the Whigs challenged the Democrats to make good their campaign pledges,[49] undoubtedly sensing that the Democrats themselves were not absolutely confident that they could maintain party harmony and effect the promised bank reforms.[50]

McNutt tried to galvanize the antibank forces into action and early in 1840 opened what he hoped would be the final battle against the

---

[48] The article pointed out that in the legislative session of May, 1837, the Whig governor recommended the passage of a post-note law. His recommendation was passed by the house, 30 to 23, with twelve Democrats voting for the bill and twenty Democrats opposing it. The story was the same in the senate, as the bill passed 9 to 6, with four Democrats voting in favor and six voting against. The Jackson *Mississippian* article continued, giving numerous examples from the house and senate journals of votes on granting various bank charters, with the results generally following the lines of division of the post-note law. Jackson *Mississippian*, July 19, 1839.

[49] Port Gibson *Correspondent*, January 4, 1840.

[50] Jackson *Mississippian*, January 3, 1840.

banks. "The existing banks," he charged, "cannot be bolstered up, destitute as they are of credit and available means. . . ." Bank reform, therefore, was hopeless because "it would be folly . . . to attempt to infuse vigor and stability into their lifeless forms. . . ." The Union Bank was no exception and could "never . . . be made useful." Therefore, either the bank should be liquidated or that portion of the charter that gave "to private individuals stock in the bank and privileged loans" should be repealed. He recommended that 5 million dollars of state bonds be called in and cancelled, because an examination of the rolls of stockholders of the banks indicated that not one voter out of thirty owned stock. It was not fair "to render the property and persons of forty thousand freemen liable to be assessed to raise money for the especial use of thirteen hundred citizens, many of them men of great wealth. . . ." The legislature had adequate power to bring relief to the citizens of Mississippi, he argued, for as the body that created the banking corporations it was "competent to repeal them." [51]

The legislature, unwilling to accept McNutt's radical solution, decided to give the banks one last opportunity to serve the public welfare, restating at the same time the right of the legislature to repeal bank charters. By an almost strict party vote, the house instructed the committee on banking to bring in a bill to require the banks to resume specie payments by April 1, 1840, or forfeit their charters. One Whig and forty-six Democrats voted for the proposal, while twenty-nine Whigs and five Democrats opposed it. The Whigs viewed the action "with loathing and disgust." Although they were in favor of bank reform and were not apologists for the banks, the Whigs claimed that the legislature's action was an attempt to subvert "the law and the constitution of the country." [52]

Despite the Whigs forebodings the original intent of the legislature was watered down and a law was adopted giving the banks until January 1, 1841, to resume specie payment. The act also prohibited banks from issuing post notes, from circulating more than three times the

---

[51] House *Executive Document No. 172*, 605–11. A committee appointed to investigate the Union Bank reported that the directors had monopolized one twelfth of the whole capital and were liable as endorsees for more than one fifth of the whole capital. See the Jackson *Mississippian*, February 28, 1840.

[52] Port Gibson *Correspondent*, February 1, 1840.

amount of their specie, and from loaning more than 20,000 dollars to a single individual or firm.[53] The bill passed 50 to 33, with four Democrats against it and four Whigs voting in favor of it.[54]

The Governor and other more radical Democrats were not satisfied. McNutt lamented that he had exerted his "best endeavors to correct the abuses of the Banking system," but that the "Whig party in the mass and a portion of my own party have failed to sustain me." [55] Another Mississippi Democrat reported that despite the heavy Democratic majority, it "dwindled away . . . towards the close of the session," because of the "corrupt influence" of the banks.[56] Among other measures considered, the legislature defeated both a scheme that would have made the issuance of small notes punishable by fine and imprisonment and a bill to repeal the charter of the Union Bank.[57]

Although the radicals had had to settle for less than they had hoped for, some of the more conservative Democrats feared the trend that seemed to be developing in the party. John A. Quitman, resident of wealthy Adams County and president of the Mississippi Railroad Bank, who was to become Democratic governor of the state a decade later, wrote to his wife that his presence in Jackson during the legislative session of 1840 prevented more radical measures from being taken against the banks.[58] One of Quitman's correspondents feared the Democratic party was "a little too *rabid* in *spirit,* and a little too *agrarian* in *principle.*" [59]

Earlier in the 1830s, Quitman had been a member of the State Rights party and had supported Judge Hugh L. White for President in 1836. At the end of 1838 he disavowed any support for the Whigs,

[53] Sumner, *History of Banking,* 378–87. Also, House *Executive Document No. 172,* 686–90.

[54] Jackson *Mississippian,* February 7, 1840.

[55] Alexander McNutt to C. L. Aiken, March 5, 1840, Executive Journal.

[56] Edward Walmough (or could be Watmough) to Levi Woodbury, March 5, 1840, Levi Woodbury Papers, Series I.

[57] *Niles' Register,* March 7, 1840. Also Lorenzo A. Besancon to J. F. H. Claiborne, February 20, 1840, J. F. H. Claiborne Papers, Mississippi Department of Archives and History.

[58] John Quitman to Eliza Quitman, February 11, 1840, John A. Quitman Papers, Southern Historical Collection, University of North Carolina.

[59] Thomas Harney to John Quitman, February 6, 1840, J. F. H. Claiborne Papers, Mississippi Department of Archives and History.

claiming that he differed "entirely and radically from Messrs. Clay, Harrison, and Webster in every essential political tenet. . . ." Therefore, he announced, he would "co-operate freely and boldly with all genuine Republicans, be they Democrats or Nullifiers. . . ." [60] His business dealings were extensive, and in 1839 he traveled to Europe, armed with numerous letters of introduction, [61] to attempt to sell bonds for the Mississippi Railroad Bank. As the depression deepened, Quitman found himself heavily in debt:

I owe $95,000, over $40,000 of which I have had to assume for others. I am likewise indorser for our unfortunate friend ———— for $24,000 and for various others whose circumstances are very doubtful, for over $20,000. All this, it is probable, will fall on me. I have 160 slaves. My other property is worth, perhaps, $200,000. [62]

Debt was a humbling experience for Quitman and he vowed "when once free" he would "never be a slave again." When he met his creditors on the street, Quitman said that he was forced "to acknowledge the superiority which the look of *'you owe me, and can't pay',* gives them." [63]

A former Democratic governor, Hiram G. Runnels, the president of the Union Bank, also bitterly fought the growing radical tendencies of the party. At one point his antagonism became so great that he fought a duel with Volney Howard. After Runnels heard that McNutt, on the eve of the duel, had drunk a toast wishing Howard good luck against "the prince of Bank thieves," Runnels gave McNutt "a severe caning in the streets of Jackson." A month later, the president of the Union Bank declared his support for William Henry Harrison. The *Mississippian* said that the Democrats had no regrets and reported that Runnels had "not acted with the Democratic party for two years past," and that his "course at the head of the Union Bank had been opposed by

---

[60] John Quitman to T. Bole and S. Schakelford, December 13, 1838, in *Life and Correspondence of John A. Quitman* edited by J. F. H. Claiborne, I (New York, 1860), 165–68.

[61] J. A. Cartwright to Andrew Stevenson, April 25, 1839; Robert J. Walker to Andrew Stevenson, April 27, 1839; and Robert Y. Hayne to Andrew Stevenson, May 12, 1839; Andrew Stevenson Papers, Library of Congress.

[62] John Quitman to J. F. H. Claiborne, January 27, 1840, in *Life and Correspondence of John A. Quitman,* I, 186–87.

[63] *Ibid.*

the whole Democratic party in the State, and applauded by the Whigs. . . ." [64]

4

The smoldering embers of the bank war were fanned into full flame in 1841 by the decision of some members of the Democratic party to press for the repudiation of the Union Bank bonds. The Union Bank had become hopelessly insolvent. Interest on the bonds that the state had floated to raise money for its capital was overdue. The state itself was practically bankrupt and would not be able to meet the payments to the bondholders.[65] The directors of the bank, however, refused to abide by the Governor's decree to forfeit its charter, insisting that the state had not the power to interfere with the business of the bank, despite the fact that the bank was operating almost entirely on capital raised by the state.[66]

The issue split the Democratic party as no other had before. A large majority of the Democrats, led by McNutt, supported repudiation of the Union Bank bonds as a punitive measure against the bank. Later, in 1843, some were willing to follow McNutt and seek to repudiate the Planters' Bank bonds as well. Other Democrats, led by William M. Gwin, supported the repudiation of the Union Bank bonds but only reluctantly and as a tactical measure. The soft-money Democrats and a few hards favored paying all bonds and in 1843 were to split from the party and run on an independent bondpaying ticket. The issue did not divide the Whigs, who almost unanimously supported paying the bonds.

The legislature that assembled in Jackson in January, 1841, was

[64] John Stewart to Duncan McLaurin, July 30, 1840, Duncan McLaurin Papers; Jackson *Mississippian,* July 31 and August 7, 1840; and *Niles' Register,* August 15, 1840.

[65] It was reported by the state treasurer in November, 1842, that there was "a balance in the Treasury of $302,956, consisting of the Attorney General's receipts for claims on the . . . Brandon and other broken banks for the sum of $238,102, the notes of the insolvent Mississippi Railroad Company for $63,030, the notes of the Mississippi Union Bank for $1,800, the notes of the Hernando Railroad Company for $20, Jackson corporation tickets $3.65, and specie in the sum of 34 cents! At the same time there existed claims against the State exceeding $8,000,000." From Brough, "Banking in Mississippi," 338.

[66] Jackson *Mississippian,* July 24, 1840.

closely divided, with the Whigs holding a slight edge in the house. William Henry Harrison had proved to be a popular candidate the preceding fall; in fact the election of 1840 was the only one in the ante-bellum period that the Mississippi Democrats failed to carry for their presidential candidate.

In his message to the legislature, McNutt declared that the state was not legally responsible for the Union Bank bonds since the bonds had been sold for less than par value, in violation of the legislative act of incorporation. Furthermore, the legislature had no power "to release the private stockholders from their obligations. . . ." [67] In defiance of the Governor's call for repudiation, a legislative committee reported a resolution that "Mississippi is bound to the holders of the bonds . . . for the amount of the principal and interest due. . . ." The Democrats sought to amend the resolution by requiring that assets of the Union Bank, along with those of the Planters' Bank and the Railroad Bank, be used to redeem the circulation and that the balance be put in the hands of trustees for the benefit of the bondholders. After these assets were exhausted, "and also the liabilities of the stockholders . . . exhausted, then the question . . . [would] come before the people" who, it was believed, would "meet their legal and moral liabilities." The amendment was defeated by a strict party vote, with Democrats favoring it and the Whigs opposing it. The committee's original resolution was then passed. Seven Democrats changed

[67] In a letter to Hope and Co., Dutch financiers, McNutt elaborated. Besides the fact that the bonds were sold below par value, they were sold on credit, which resulted in the loss of a considerable sum to the state. Furthermore, Nicholas Biddle as an agent for the Bank of the United States was involved in the transaction. This made the sale illegal because the charter of that institution prohibited it from purchasing stock directly or indirectly. The Dutch financiers were also told that the Mississippi constitution forbade the legislature from pledging the faith of the state until two successive legislatures had approved. Although the original charter of the Union Bank had met this stipulation, a supplemental act passed in 1838 changed the relationship between the state and the Union Bank. Whereas under the original charter the state simply pledged its faith to back the bonds, the supplemental act provided that the state should subscribe for 50,000 shares of stock, and 5 million dollars worth of bonds were floated to pay for them. *Ibid.,* January 8, 1841. Also Alexander McNutt to Hope and Company, July 13, 1841, Executive Journal, and Reginald C. McGrane, *Foreign Bondholders and American State Debts* (New York, 1935), Chapter X.

sides and voted with the Whig majority in favor of redeeming the bonds. The opposition was exclusively Democratic.[68]

The Governor vetoed the resolution, and in a demagogic style, which was to be echoed a half a century later by the Populists, denounced one of the bondholders, Baron Rothschild, as one "in whose veins 'the blood of Judas and Shylock' flowed." It was for the people to decide whether the banker "who had a mortgage on 'the sepulchre of our Savior,' shall have a mortgage on our cotton fields and make serfs of our children." [69]

The apparent Democratic harmony in the legislature was no indication of the true state of affairs within the party. Even prior to the controversy over the bonds, disorganizing factors had been present. The disastrous defeat in the fall of 1840 had had the effect of magnifying differences. Some of the conservatives, unhappy over the antibank course McNutt had charted, split from the party in 1840 and joined the Whigs. Others remained but were unenthusiastic in their support. Robert J. Walker, for example, reacted to Van Buren's defeat that year with "amused indifference." [70]

To the broker William M. Gwin, business and political partner of Claiborne, this apathy and disunion within the party offered both an opportunity and a challenge. The repudiation of the Union Bank bonds was the issue that he and other broker Democrats hoped to use to revitalize and rebuild the Mississippi Democracy. Gwin, who was elected to Congress in 1841, and his colleagues were not fundamentally hostile to banks, but they saw the political value in the repudiation issue. On the one hand, the antibank men would be attracted to repudiation as a measure to punish the bank, while on the other hand, some soft-money men who were large bank debtors might also see that it would be to their economic interest for the state to declare the

[68] Jackson, Miss., *Southron,* January 30, 1841.

[69] As quoted in Dunbar Rowland, editor, *Mississippi: Comprising Sketches of Counties, Towns, Events, Institutions, and Persons, Arranged in Cyclopedic Form* (Atlanta, Ga., 1907), I, 200, and McGrane, *Foreign Bondholders,* 201.

[70] Shenton, *Robert John Walker,* 29–30. Although Shenton claims that Walker was "firmly attached to the hard money politics of Van Buren" and mainly was alienated from the administration over the question of territorial expansion, it is doubtful whether Walker ever was really converted to the hard-money orthodoxy.

charter of the bank illegal. In that eventuality, the debtors could argue that they were not legally bound for their debts.

Gwin originally had been raised to prominence in Mississippi in 1833, when President Jackson appointed him United States Marshal for the District of Mississippi. A lucrative position, Gwin used it to good advantage to build his personal wealth and political influence. He became a large speculator in public lands, and in 1839 combined with Claiborne to buy up the lands and slaves of bankrupt planters.[71]

In later years Claiborne was to compare his former partner with Robert J. Walker. The latter, Claiborne said, was "thoroughly unscrupulous when he had an object to accomplish." Nevertheless, he "had a master" in William M. Gwin. Gwin was not Walker's "equal as a scholar or an orator; not versed . . . in the learning and strategy of the law," but Gwin was "far more practical and resolute; blending a rare combination of sagacity, energy and firmness, with courage equal to any emergency. . . ."[72]

A major problem confronting Gwin, however, was the threat to party unity by such hard-money Democratic leaders as Governor McNutt, who was for taking more extreme measures against the banks and opposed relieving bank stockholders from their obligations, arguing that these had been the men who had controlled the banks and had benefited from the majority of the loans. Fortunately for the brokers, the Constitution of 1832 forbade any man from holding the governor's post for more than four years out of any six. This meant that McNutt, who was finishing his second two-year term, was ineligible for re-election, and thus the leader of the hards was removed from active politics and political power.[73]

[71] Later Gwin moved to California, helped draw up the state's first constitution, and was elected twice to the United States Senate. At the beginning of the Civil War he was arrested as a southern sympathizer. Released, he went to France and interested Napoleon III in a scheme to colonize the Sonora area of Mexico with southerners. This plan, however, failed to materialize, and after a short imprisonment upon his re-entering the United States, Gwin died in obscurity in 1885.

[72] For sketch of Gwin see Claiborne, *Mississippi*, 419–20, 427–34. For further information see the Papers of William M. Gwin, Bancroft Library, University of California.

[73] Miles, *Jacksonian Democracy in Mississippi*, 39. McNutt attempted to regain his power in the Democratic party by running for the United States Senate

At the party convention in January of 1841, Gwin found that there was "an absence of harmony, co-operation and confidence" and that the "ticket presented did not seem acceptable." Thus, he asked Tilghman Tucker to run for governor in place of the candidate who had been nominated by the convention. By the end of April, the *Mississippian* had placed Tucker's name on the masthead. Two weeks later, the paper announced that Tucker had consented to run.[74]

It became obvious by the time the Democrats had organized their ticket in the spring of 1841 that the main campaign issue would be the Union Bank bond question, with the Democrats running on a militant antibond platform. A campaign journal, *The Old Soldier and Anti-Bondsman,* was established, pledged to oppose "the wild system of borrowing, banking, and bonding." [75] Claiborne was uneasy about the bond question and wished the party had not decided to wage a campaign on it. "Whether the Bond question is *really* aiding us or not, I cannot tell," Claiborne wrote Walker:

In the *East* I *know* it makes us stronger, but we shall lose by it in the river region. Gwin and Freeman write me from the north, that antibondism is carrying everything before it and they claim 7 or 8000 majority. But this is too sanguine. I regret that the question was raised, but when I took the Free Trader it was evident that we had to fight *on* the question or divide the party into factions, and fall an easy prey to our enemies.[76]

The bond payers were as motley and incongruous a group as the anti-bond payers, being made up of both Whigs, who, of course, were virtually unanimous in their opposition to repudiation, and Democrats. And, ironically, although the bond-paying faction within the Democratic party was dominated by conservatives, led by John A. Quitman,

---

in 1845. McNutt, however, was so unpopular with the softs and brokers that Gwin and Quitman, both of whom had announced their candidacy for the office, threw their support to Henry S. Foote in order to assure McNutt's defeat. Claiborne reported that McNutt in his campaign "made war not only on his competitors, but on Tucker . . . and other leaders of the Democratic party, and traveled through the State like an Ishmaelite." The brokers were again successful and Foote was elected. Claiborne, *Mississippi,* 439.

[74] Claiborne, *Mississippi,* 433, and Jackson *Mississippian,* April 30 and May 14, 1841.

[75] Prospectus for the new paper in *Ibid.,* April 30, 1841.

[76] J. F. H. Claiborne to Robert J. Walker, October 13, 1841, Robert J. Walker Papers.

there were also a few hard-money advocates, such as Volney Howard, within the ranks. To the Whigs and soft-money Democrats, repudiation meant that the state's credit would be ruined and that projects such as the railroad Quitman dreamed of would be impossible to finance. Howard, on the other hand, opposed repudiation because he thought it was simply a device to relieve the speculators and bank debtors who had monopolized the bank's capital in the first place. Of concern to both Howard and Quitman was the effect that repudiation might have on state rights. If state debts were not paid, Howard feared, then perhaps the federal government would assume them, and this "would reduce the States to the merest petty corporations." Thus, he considered it the duty of the state to wind up the banks and apply their assets and those of "the stockholders, if liable, to the payment of the interest and the principal of these bonds." [77]

The opposition of the bond payers to the main body of the Democratic party failed to develop into more than a verbal battle.[78] And, despite the schism, the Democrats handily won the election of 1841. In the ensuing legislative session, they carried out their popular mandate by repudiating the bonds. Of the fifty-four voting in favor of repudiation, fifty were Democrats, and of the thirty-seven voting against repudiation, twenty-nine were Whigs.[79]

The antibond issue began as a logical extension of the increasing antibank sentiment within the state. Small farmers and planters, who had

[77] Jackson *Mississippian*, January 15, 1841. Robert J. Walker joined Howard and Quitman in favoring payment of bonds. He thought the money could be "made out of the bank debtors and stockholders." See Robert J. Walker to J. F. H. Claiborne, August 21, 1841, J. F. H. Claiborne Papers, Mississippi Department of Archives and History.

[78] The *Mississippian* attempted to play down the differences among the Democrats. The paper contended that all agreed the state was not *legally* bound to pay the bonds, and the only difference between the Democratic bond payers and anti-bond payers was that the bond payers felt the state had a moral obligation to pay the debt. It was pointed out that during the past legislative session *all* Democrats had supported efforts to pass a bill winding up the bank and placing all the assets of the bank at the disposal of the bond holders. The Whigs had defeated the measure because the bill did not release the stockholders from liability. Jackson *Mississippian*, June 18, 1841.

[79] Jackson *Southron*, February 24, 1842. See also, Mississippi House of Representatives *Journal*, 1842, 897–98. Party affiliations are listed in the Natchez *Free Trader*, November 24, 1841.

received few if any favors from the Union Bank or other banks and had been bombarded by reports of charter violations and of bank directors' monopolizing the loans, rallied to McNutt's banner of repudiation. One Whig claimed that "all the large tax payers were almost universally in favour of the payment," and "those persons and counties that pay no tax were almost unanimously opposed to it." [80]

5

Mississippi in the 1840s must have appeared to have been the victim of a mysterious but deadly plague. Once-flourishing plantations stood deserted, their owners having escaped a crushing debt by taking their slaves and moving out of the country to Texas. One traveler described the procedure:

. . . on the evening before abandonment those plantations would present no unusual appearance. The stock would be in the stables, properly attended to; the cows would be in the cowpen; the hogs would be called and fed; the sheep would be herded; the plantation negroes would be in their proper places, and over all the hush of evening and the stillness of night would fall. On the morning following the smoke would curl from the chimneys, from residence and quarters, the cows would be lowing in the pen, the sheep bleating in the fold, the hogs in their place; not a wagon gone, not a vehicle missing; the meat left in the smokehouse, the poultry raising their usual disturbance—and not a human being, nor horse, nor mule, nor saddle, nor bridle on the whole place. Every negro, every horse, every mule spirited away in the darkness of the night . . . all, all in a double quick march for Texas. . . . The first object was to get across the county line, the next to cross the Mississippi River, and the next to cross the line of the Republic of Texas. All this had to be done before the executions would . . . be placed in the hands of the sheriffs of the different counties.[81]

What the depression meant to the town of Lafayette was explained by a man from Choctaw County. During the boom times, he recalled, an advertisement had been "set up announcing the sale of lots . . .

---

[80] John Stewart to Duncan McLaurin, March 24, 1842, Duncan McLaurin Papers.

[81] J. A. Orr, "A Trip from Houston to Jackson, Miss., in 1845," in *Publications of the Mississippi Historical Society,* IX (1906), 175-76.

and on the appointed day the lots were disposed of at high prices, on credit. A grog shop and a store, with something more than two hundred dollars worth of goods, marked the spot where stood this famous city." Now, in 1841, in place of a city stood a farm that one man purchased for 15 dollars.[82]

A planter from Franklin County in the southwestern part of the state reported in 1842 that Mississippi currency was at a discount of 30 to 40 per cent. "I have never known money to be any thing like as scarce in this section of the country as it is now," he said. "There has been a cry of *hard* times for the last five years but they are harder now than ever and appear to be worse coming."[83]

The broker-Democrats had a major job to keep the party together in 1843. Tucker, a rather lackluster governor, wished to seek a second term, but the brokers wanted to replace him with Albert Gallatin Brown, a candidate whom they felt would unite the party since he had not been involved in the bitter bond dispute.[84] It was hoped that the bond issue would be accepted as settled. But many of the bond payers, humiliated by the legislature's action, were trying to organize support for overturning the legislature's decision. Furthermore, McNutt and other hard-money men, constituting a second threat to party harmony, were pushing their hard-money logic a step further and now advocating the repudiation of the Planters' Bank bonds as well. This undoubtedly was a great worry to Gwin, who had once cautioned Claiborne that "if the group opposed to the Planters' Bank bonds" ever got "a foothold they will ruin the Democratic party now and forever. . . ."[85]

Joining with McNutt in this crusade was James Hogan, vitriolic editor of the Vicksburg *Sentinel,* who in 1840, as a member of the bank commission, had asked why "should a few rich men be allowed the privilege of drawing interest on three dollars for every one they possess?"[86] Master of an acid and vindictive pen, Hogan was de-

[82] Jackson *Mississippian,* February 12, 1841.

[83] John Stewart to Duncan McLaurin, March 24, 1842, Duncan McLaurin Papers.

[84] James Byrne Ranck, *Albert Gallatin Brown: Radical Southern Nationalist* (New York, 1937), 28.

[85] William M. Gwin to J. F. H. Claiborne, March 10, 1842, J. F. H. Claiborne Papers, Library of Congress.

[86] Rowland, *Mississippi,* I, 200.

scribed by an enemy as "famous for attacking, without scruple, the characters of the oldest and most respectable citizens of the country, as though they were the mere mushrooms of the hour. . . ."[87] Hogan's unrestrained newspaper columns made too many enemies. In the spring of 1843 he was challenged and shot down in the streets of Vicksburg. His death and the growing strength of the brokers eliminated as a threat to Democratic unity those who would repudiate the Planters' Bank bonds. The majority of the Democrats evidently agreed with Brown, who felt that the issue was "not a legitimate party question," and that it would "be madness to abandon" the high ground to follow the fortunes of this *"will o the wisp."* [88]

Brown was nominated in the February, 1843, convention. But such an uproar was created by Tucker's supporters in the northern part of the state, who felt their candidate lost because some of their counties were not represented at the convention, that Brown withdrew. A new convention was called for the summer of 1843 to make nominations and try again to resolve the bond question, which the winter convention had ignored.[89] The convention reconvened in the summer of 1843. Brown again was chosen to be the candidate for governor, while Tucker received the nomination for congressman in order to conciliate him and his followers. There was, however, no meeting of the minds between those who stood behind the legislature's action in repudiating the Union Bank bonds and those who protested the action.

The Whigs taunted the feuding Democrats, ridiculing Brown, who tried to sidestep the issue by announcing that during the campaign "he would not be drawn into a discussion of State policy. . . ." The Whig *Southron* reacted to this by suggesting that it would not be surprising

---

[87] Anonymous, *Nine Years of Democratic Rule in Mississippi,* 143.

[88] Albert G. Brown to J. F. H. Claiborne, February 6, 1843; William M. Gwin to J. F. H. Claiborne, June 10, 1843; J. F. H. Claiborne Papers, Library of Congress. See also Rowland, *Mississippi,* I, 830–31.

[89] The course of the brokers may be traced in the following letters: Albert G. Brown to J. F. H. Claiborne, January 4 and 23, 1843; C. M. Price to J. F. H. Claiborne, February 7, 1843; J. F. H. Claiborne to C. M. Price, February 9, 1843; A. A. Kincannon to J. F. H. Claiborne, March 2 and 7, 1843; J. F. H. Claiborne Papers, Mississippi Department of Archives and History. See also, John D. Freeman to J. F. H. Claiborne, February 3, 1843; R. E. Harris to J. F. H. Claiborne, February 11, 1843; William M. Gwin to J. F. H. Claiborne, June 4, 1843; J. F. H. Claiborne Papers, Library of Congress.

if Gen. Brown, before the canvass is over, should be dilating in his mellowest strains of oratory, upon the right of search, the right of visit, the proper policy to be used by his Celestial Highness towards the English, or the cutting of a canal through the Isthmus of Panama. And why not? The great democracy certainly can find "common ground" upon which to stand to fight their battles against a powerful enemy, without touching on matters of State policy! What does Mississippi democracy care about her internal and domestic affairs when the whole world is to be attended to? [90]

The bond payers had made tentative plans months before the summer Democratic convention to run a separate ticket in the fall of 1843. In a letter urging Quitman to head a list of bond-paying candidates by running for governor, Volney Howard put forward his views on how the bond-paying Democrats should conduct their campaign. The faction, he argued, should cooperate with the Whigs to the extent that Whigs and bond payers do not run for the same office, because if this were not done, "the question cannot then be bond and anti bond." [91] Another bond payer suggested similar strategy, regretting that a third party might give the state to the Whigs. But then, he added, he could not say that he had "a principle in common with the apparently dominant part of the *Democratick* party in Miss." [92]

Nothing more was done that spring. But the failure of the summer convention to conciliate the warring factions brought the bond payers out in full and open opposition to the main body of the party. Volney Howard's brother, B. D. Howard, established a bond-paying Democratic newspaper, the *Statesman,* in Jackson. Quitman, although declining to run for office, gave the movement his support, and a partial ticket was organized.

The *Statesman* hit the anti-bond payers on an unprotected flank by constantly pointing out that many of the large debtors of the Union Bank had become important members of the antibond party. Howard explained that:

men who had been the pets of the banks, their loudest advocates, and of course obtained the largest loans from them—who, by refusing to pay the

[90] Jackson *Southron,* July 12, 1843.

[91] Volney Howard to John A. Quitman, March 1, 1843, J. F. H. Claiborne Papers, Mississippi Department of Archives and History.

[92] Samuel J. Gholson to John A. Quitman, March 7, 1843, J. F. H. Claiborne Papers, Mississippi Department of Archives and History.

bank, had rendered it unable to pay its honest and deluded creditors—these very pet borrowers raised such a cry against bank frauds, that they concealed their own frauds, from the people. . . .[93]

If these debtors only had been compelled to pay back their debts in the first place, Howard contended, "the blight of repudiation would not now have rested upon us."[94] Among those who owed large sums to the Union Bank were William M. Gwin, who had borrowed for his own use and endorsed loans for others to the amount of more than 311,000 dollars, and Brown, who owed over 50,000 dollars.[95]

Howard continued to heap scorn on the hypocrisy of some of the antibondsmen. But he made a distinction between "the special repudiators, who oppose the Union Bank bonds on technical grounds alone, and the repudiators of all national debts, who place the right on the broad ground of the want of authority in any government to tax for any other than governmental purposes. . . ." Former Governor McNutt belonged to the latter group and was "a man of more intellect than all the half-way anti-bonders, and possessing as much heart as the best of them. For, the *Statesman* declared, if

we are to bear the disgrace of repudiation, give us the repudiation of all state debts, such as ours, because that will establish some principle of extended national advantage; but this repudiation of one debt on merely technical grounds is disgrace without arriving at any thing, but a refusal to pay one single pecuniary claim.[96]

Governor McNutt's "scheme of repudiation," while "improper and unjust," at least "had the merit of offering a deceptive relief to the whole people."[97]

In contrast to the *Statesman's* treatment of McNutt, which was cleverly devised to attract the hard-money faction of the antibond party, Howard was unmerciful in his denunciation of Tucker, Brown, and Gwin. "And who is Dr. Gwin," he asked:

A gentleman whom Gen. Jackson imported into this state to load with the most lucrative office in his gift; and who has always been a dead weight upon the party. A man destitute of all generous bearing, without any claim to learning and information. A man who never read a book through in

---

[93] Jackson *Statesman,* August 5, 1843.   [94] *Ibid.*
[95] *Ibid.,* August 19, 1843.   [96] *Ibid.,* July 22, 1843.
[97] *Ibid.,* October 21, 1843.

his life, since Pike's Arithmetic, and the "treaty of Dancing Rabbitt Creek;" but who, by the influuence [*sic*] of money, has obtained dominion over the press, and dictates to the party.[98]

And as for Tucker, the newspaper bluntly suggested, "you may, without any further preface, 'write him down Ass!!' We use the term with all respect, and only because no other can adequately describe him." [99]

The rebellion was short lived. The election of 1843 resulted in an overwhelming victory for the Democratic antibond payers. The bond payers in the party failed to carry a single county. This ended, for the most part, the controversy over the payment of the Union Bank bonds, and Quitman and other leaders of the faction rejoined the party. And despite the harshness of the language that accompanied the party split, the brokers had been busily working to pave the way for the bond payers to return to the party after the election. Claiborne assured Quitman that he had tried to prevent the bond issue from becoming a party question and that the *Free Trader* would "never recognize any distinction in national politics between democratic bond-paying and democratic anti-bonders. . . ." [100]

6

Although the election of 1843 ended the open rebellion of the bond payers, there was another issue, closely allied with the repudiation question, that required the maintenance of the uneasy alliance between the hard-money and broker Democrats. Controversy over the Briscoe Bill, a proposal to establish stringent legal procedures for winding up the broken banks, strained this relationship from 1842, when it was introduced by a Whig-turned-Democrat, until 1846, when it was finally passed in its original form. Among other things, it provided that forfeited charters would revert to the state and that banks would be prohibited from collecting debts due them, thus allowing bank debtors to escape their obligations.

In general, those who had supported paying the Union Bank bonds,

[98] *Ibid.,* August 13, 1843.　　　　　[99] *Ibid.*

[100] J. F. H. Claiborne to John A. Quitman (letter not dated but obviously written sometime in fall of 1843), J. F. H. Claiborne Papers, Mississippi Department of Archives and History.

the Whigs and the bond-paying Democrats, also joined forces to oppose the Briscoe Bill. Such a bill, Quitman was told by an associate, was *"not* for the benefit of the Banks," and his help would be needed to defeat the measure.[101] The bond-paying *Statesman* labeled it "a measure exclusively for the benefit of those indebted to the banks . . . adventurers, speculators, and bank directors." [102] The Jackson *Southron* pointed out the strong motive of self-interest of the bill's advocates. It was alleged that its author, General Parmenas Briscoe from Claiborne County, owed the banks "a sum not less than $30,000," while the Democratic speaker of the house had a similar debit, with his son indebted to the banks for about 150,000 dollars.[103]

The Democrats engaged in considerable demagogy in defending the Briscoe measure. They played upon the unpopularity of the banks, and, in arguments that were to be used repeatedly throughout the remainder of the nineteenth century, they explained that the bank debts were pegged at inflated prices. Therefore, they argued, it would be grossly unfair to force the "poor laborer" to pay back the debt he had incurred when he had purchased a "little farm for himself and family" at a highly inflated price.[104] To allow the broken banks to collect their debts, the Democrats concluded, would only "fatten bank attorneys, bank assignees, [and] brokers. . . ." [105]

Actually, the bill did pass in 1843, but its intent was nullified by a Whig amendment that permitted the banks to collect the debts due them.[106] And so after that the cry of the Democrats was for the *original* Briscoe Bill, and in 1845 it became a party measure. Democrats were urged to purge those members who were "sailing under false colours" because the "bank advocates" had not yet been "conquered." "By the side of Repudiation, and opposition to unjust taxation," the Democrats "must engrave the 'Briscoe Bill' " on their banner.[107]

---

[101] J. D. Tyler to John A. Quitman, January 25, 1842, J. F. H. Claiborne Papers, Mississippi Department of Archives and History.

[102] Jackson *Statesman*, July 22, 1843.

[103] Jackson *Southron*, August 23, 1843.

[104] Jackson *Mississippian*, September 24, 1845.

[105] *Ibid.*, December 6, 1843; see also August 17, 1843; March 5, April 30 and June 4, 1845; and February 25, 1846.

[106] Jackson *Southron*, July 26, 1843.

[107] Jackson *Mississippian*, June 11, 1845.

Although by 1845 many of the bond-paying Democrats had rejoined the party, the agitation over the original Briscoe Bill threatened to split the party again but along somewhat different lines. A correspondent of Claiborne reported that

> upon the matter of the adoption by the next Legislature of the *Original Briscoe Bill*, a want of unanimity is growing up in the Party. Many of the Northern Democratic Counties whose people have happily never been tempted to burden themselves in Bank Debts, seem desirous to retain the present shape of the Bill to insure a collection of the Bank debt for Some one's use, while our region, the West and South, insist upon the utter and absolute annihilation of the now gasping monsters.[108]

Jefferson Davis,[109] a Democrat running for Congress from Warren County on the Mississippi River, maintained that Mississippians were divided into three camps. Members of the first (exponents of the *original* Briscoe Bill) believed that when a bank's charter was forfeited "all debts to and from it . . . [should] be expunged. . . ." The second group believed that when a bank forfeited its charter, all debts of the bank should be collected for the benefit of the state. Others, including Davis, held that after the forfeiture of a charter, trustees should be appointed "to collect the assets and dispose of the property of the corporation for the benefit of the creditors and stockholders." It was, Davis said, "Anti-American to seize the property of individuals."[110]

The opponents of the amendment were successful during the legislative session of 1846, and the original bill was made the law of the state. A majority of the Democrats voted in favor of the original bill, with a majority of the Whigs voting in opposition.[111]

The Whig author of an 1847 book attacking the past nine years of Democratic "mis-rule" of Mississippi contended that the passage of the

108 J. S. B. Thacher to J. F. H. Claiborne, July 31, 1845, J. F. H. Claiborne Papers, Mississippi Department of Archives and History.

109 On the issue of repudiation of the Union Bank bonds Davis had hedged, contending that the bonds had been issued illegally but that the state might be sued for recovery of the bondholder's investment. See Rowland, *Mississippi*, I, 612–13.

110 Jefferson Davis to John Jenkins, July 5, 1845, in Jefferson Davis, *Jefferson Davis, Constitutionalist, His Letters, Papers, Speeches*, edited by Dunbar Rowland (Jackson, Miss., 1923), I, 13–17.

111 Mississippi House *Journal*, 1846, 684–87.

original Briscoe Bill in 1846 was accomplished by a pact between Democrats of the northern and the southern counties. The northern counties of the state had opposed the Briscoe Bill but supported it in exchange for southern votes to apportion the state in favor of the North. The South got the Briscoe Bill passed, but the apportionment bill was so "prejudicial to the Southwestern section," which was the "most heavily taxed" in the state, "that the secession of that portion of the State from the rest . . . has been seriously entertained. . . ." [112]

In 1845, at the height of the Briscoe Bill controversy, one Mississippian had observed that the "fruitful and long agitated question of the banks never excited more feeling than just now." [113] However, by 1847 there was evidence that the antibank fever was on the wane. A constitutional amendment, which would have prohibited the legislature from chartering any banks, was submitted to the people. But it failed to arouse much enthusiastic backing, despite the fact that the action was hailed by the *Mississippian.* "Louisiana moved first, by incorporating an anti-bank provision in her new constitution," the newspaper said optimistically, and Mississippi would continue the movement, which was "becoming popular in all the states of the union. . . ." Even the Whig *Southron,* it was noted, had thrown its support behind the amendment. So, the *Mississippian* predicted, the "tree will not only be hewed down, but its very roots will be plucked up and consumed." [114]

The amendment failed to win an absolute majority of those casting ballots, so it was not adopted. Few banks had survived the collapse, and the ones that had were small and did a very restricted business. Several other banks that confined their activities to the exchange and brokerage business withstood the pressure and continued in operation. Thus, by 1847 banking was no longer the inflammatory issue it had been. For example, in wealthy Adams County, which had been the headquarters for a number of banks, few persons felt that the issue was a pressing one, for fewer than half of those voting for governor that year bothered to cast a vote either for or against the antibank amend-

[112] Anonymous, *Nine Years of Democratic Rule in Mississippi,* 282–83.
[113] J. S. B. Thacher to J. F. H. Claiborne, July 31, 1845, J. F. H. Claiborne Papers, Mississippi Department of Archives and History.
[114] Jackson *Mississippian,* October 8, 1845.

ment. Actually, the fate of the amendment was of little importance, for no more banks of issue were chartered in the state until the Civil War.[115]

Thus, in Mississippi during the decade following the Panic of 1837 the brokers had been remarkably successful in imposing order and unity on a divided Democratic party that had been threatened with disintegration over the banking controversy. As political issues are created both by men and circumstances, it had been their job to exploit the banking question in such a way as to retain the loyal followers and yet also attract as many of the marginal voters as possible. The Democrats moved from bank reform to state repudiation of debt to repudiation of personal debt. These positions were shrewdly calculated to extend the attractiveness of the party from those who had few dealings with banks but were vehemently antibank to those planters who were suffering under the burden of large personal debts to the banks. These shifts by the party managers, although successful, strained the loyalty of Democrats residing in the small-farm areas of northeastern Mississippi and the Piney Woods region in the southeast. They had received few if any bank favors and looked upon the state-sponsored banking system as aristocratic, as it favored the large planter of the Delta who was able to mortgage his improved lands to the bank in exchange for stock and loan preferences. The Briscoe Bill was attractive to the hard-money Democrats in that it provided a legal method and remedy for getting rid of the banks. But the sections of the bill that allowed debtors to escape the burden of their debts were extremely unpopular, and it required the utmost brokerage ability of the Democratic leaders to keep the party united.

[115] Rowland, *Mississippi*, I, 204; Miles, *Jacksonian Democracy in Mississippi*, 157; and Natchez *Free Trader*, November 4, 1847.

CHAPTER IV

Mississippi Constituencies

I

VIEWING A political party and its leaders in action in a state legislature or constitutional convention is similar to looking at the exposed portion of an iceberg. In both cases the foundation, broader than its visible manifestations, lies hidden beneath the surface. Whereas on the national or state level a party comprises a hopeless jumble of competing and contradictory interests and principles, its character on the county level is only as complicated or simple as the county's economic and social structure. The local constituency is, then, the vital heart and soul of a party, the bedrock of its strength.

Material influences such as the wealth of a county and the extent of its participation in the commercial market are major factors affecting political inclination. The quality and ambition of the local political leadership are also of considerable importance in forming an area's political climate, as are the heritage and traditions of the people. Habits, especially political ones, are difficult to break or change, and it is probably such long-term factors rather than more immediate ones that are most important in determining political conduct. This partially explains why certain constituencies continued to be hard money in sympathy even after it became obvious that it was contrary to their economic interests.

Cotton was king in ante-bellum Mississippi, and political, social, and economic institutions in the state were organized in such a way as to maximize its production. Economic conflicts between urban-commercial and agricultural areas, prevalent in many parts of the country during the ante-bellum years, were not found in Mississippi, which was overwhelmingly rural, having no large commercial center approaching the size and importance of Mobile and New Orleans in the neighboring states of Alabama and Louisiana. Even the small but commercially and politically influential county seats, typical in most other states, were not common in Mississippi, and this circumstance stunted the state's political growth. The lack of small, county-oriented trading towns resulted in a corresponding scarcity of avenues of local communication. There was little or no opportunity for planters and farmers of a single political constituency to gather informally and discuss common problems. Newspapers, for instance, were published in only twenty of the more than fifty counties in 1838.[1] Thus, it was difficult for a constituency to develop any sense of cohesion and identity. Even a century later, Mississippi was the "most rural of southern states," with only twelve towns having a population in excess of ten thousand. This has led one scholar to conclude that the state's "small urban centers—supply-points for the surrounding agricultural regions—do not bulk large enough to temper the robust tone of a rural politics."[2]

Despite the fact that Mississippi was uniformly rural, there was great diversity within the state, especially with respect to the wealth of the soil in the various sections. Roughly, the state can be divided into four general regions: the Delta-Loess, the Black Prairie, the Eastern Hills, and the Piney Woods.[3]

[1] Compiled from data in Lorenzo Augustus Besancon, *Besancon's Annual Register of the State of Mississippi* (Natchez, Miss., 1838), 217–20.

[2] V. O. Key, Jr., *Southern Politics in State and Nation* (New York, 1949), 230. I am particularly grateful for the insights Stanley Elkins and Eric McKitrick made in comparing various frontier communities in their "A Meaning for Turner's Frontier," *Political Science Quarterly,* LXIX (September and December, 1954), 321–53 and 565–602.

[3] See Map 1. For greater clarity in analyzing the Mississippi constituencies, I have arbitrarily divided the state into the four above-mentioned sections. There are ten different soil areas within the state, ranging in fertility from the rich Delta region to the Piney Woods. However, to use ten classifications would result in a hopeless jumble with parts of counties represented in several different soil types. Thus I have tried to divide the state into the four sections, retaining county boundaries while still remaining as faithful as possible to soil classifications. For example, the Delta-Loess section includes all the counties within two soil areas: the Yazoo-Mississippi Basin and the Brown Loam and Loess. The Black Prairie is a narrow belt of soil coming into the state in the center of its eastern boundary running west and then north, narrowing as it comes to the Tennessee border. Although this fertile Black Prairie belt cuts through or touches

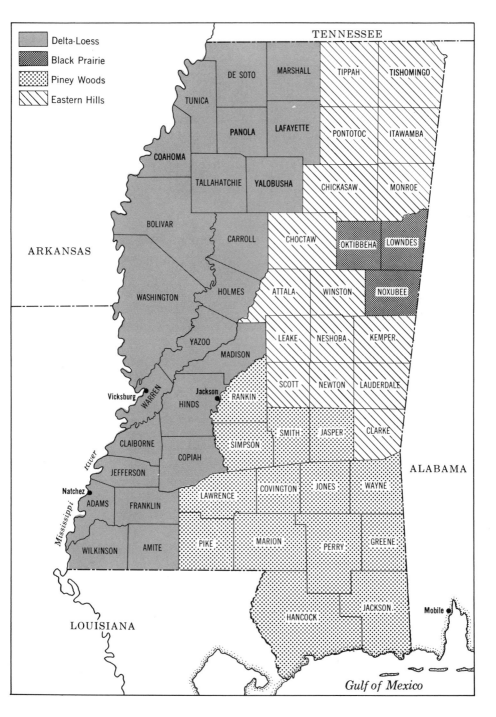

Legend:
- Delta-Loess
- Black Prairie
- Piney Woods
- Eastern Hills

TENNESSEE

ARKANSAS

DE SOTO
MARSHALL
TIPPAH
TISHOMINGO
TUNICA
PANOLA
LAFAYETTE
PONTOTOC
ITAWAMBA
COAHOMA
TALLAHATCHIE
YALOBUSHA
CHICKASAW
MONROE
BOLIVAR
CARROLL
CHOCTAW
OKTIBBEHA
LOWNDES
WASHINGTON
HOLMES
ATTALA
WINSTON
NOXUBEE
YAZOO
LEAKE
NESHOBA
KEMPER
MADISON
SCOTT
NEWTON
LAUDERDALE
Vicksburg
WARREN
Jackson
RANKIN
HINDS
SMITH
JASPER
CLARKE
CLAIBORNE
COPIAH
SIMPSON
ALABAMA
JEFFERSON
LAWRENCE
COVINGTON
JONES
WAYNE
Natchez
ADAMS
FRANKLIN
WILKINSON
AMITE
PIKE
MARION
PERRY
GREENE
Mississippi River
JACKSON
Mobile
LOUISIANA
HANCOCK
Gulf of Mexico

MAP I. MISSISSIPPI GEOGRAPHIC SECTIONS

The western Delta-Loess counties,[4] many of which bordered on the Mississippi and Yazoo rivers, had the richest soils in the state and, according to one geologist at least, "among the most fertile on earth."[5] So, as might be expected, this section contained the wealthiest and largest slave-holding plantations, where the bulk of the state's cotton crop was produced. A second area of fertile soil in Mississippi was the Black Prairie,[6] a small section along the east-central border. Counties there were wealthier than the average in the state but still less well off than those in the Delta-Loess. The poorest sections of the state were the Eastern Hills[7] in the northeast, where the soil was not too productive and the terrain sometimes very rugged, with a few hills reaching an altitude of 650 feet, and the Piney Woods[8] in the southeast, which was sparsely inhabited and heavily forested. Both regions, with their mean and inhospitable soils, were characterized by subsistence agriculture. The farms were small and there were few slaves.

---

ten counties, I have defined it as a three-county area since Noxubee, Lowndes, and Oktibbeha seem to have been the main counties influenced by the wealth of the soil, at least by 1840. The Eastern Hills includes a number of soil areas, among them the Short-Leaf Pine, Flat Woods, Pontotoc Ridge, Northeast Highland, and the Central Prairie. The Piney Woods includes two soil areas: the Long-Leaf Pine and the Gulf Coastal Meadows. My information on the soils of Mississippi comes from E. N. Lowe, *A Preliminary Study of Soils of Mississippi* (Nashville, Tenn., 1911), 60–67; Charles S. Sydnor, *Slavery in Mississippi* (Baton Rouge, La., 1966), soil map across from title page; and Albert D. Kirwan, *Revolt of the Rednecks: Mississippi Politics, 1876–1925* (Lexington, Ky., 1951), soil map between pages 40 and 41.

[4] Included in this section are the following counties: Adams, Amite, Bolivar, Carroll, Claiborne, Coahoma, Copiah, De Soto, Franklin, Hinds, Holmes, Jefferson, Lafayette, Madison, Marshall, Panola, Talahatchie, Tunica, Warren, Washington, Wilkinson, Yalobusha, and Yazoo.

[5] Lowe, *Soils of Mississippi*, 66–67.

[6] Included in this section are the following counties: Lowndes, Noxubee, and Oktibbeha.

[7] Included in this section are the following counties: Attala, Choctaw, Clarke, Itawamba, Kemper, Lauderdale, Leake, Neshoba, Newton, Pontotoc, Scott, Tippah, Tishomingo, and Winston.

[8] Included in this section are the following counties: Covington, Greene, Hancock, Jackson, Jasper, Jones, Lawrence, Marion, Perry, Pike, Rankin, Simpson, Smith, and Wayne.

2

Contrasts between the more prosperous and poorer counties in Mississippi were more than purely economic in nature. They were political as well. The wealthier a county was, the more likely were its residents to give a higher percentage of their votes to Whig presidential aspirants. And conversely, the poorer the county, the more likely it was to vote strongly Democratic. This assertion can be proved statistically through the use of the rank-difference correlation formula. When Mississippi counties are ranked according to wealth (specifically, the per capita real-estate and personal taxes paid in 1845) and also according to politics (specifically, how residents voted in three presidential elections: 1836, 1840, and 1844) and the two lists compared, the result is a striking statistical correlation.[9]

Furthermore, since the sections of Mississippi varied radically in wealth, the political-economic divisions also were geographic. The Delta-Loess was a Whig stronghold, and the Piney Woods was a bastion for the Democracy. While voters in the Eastern Hills leaned heavily toward the Democrats, there were signs that Democratic strength in the Black Prairie was ebbing.

For the purposes of this discussion, Mississippi counties not only have been ranked but also have been divided into seven political categories, according to a system worked out by historian Lee Benson. The categories range from Very Strong Democratic to Very Strong Whig, with Strong Democratic, Moderate Democratic, Neutral, Moderate Whig, and Strong Whig in between.[10] In Mississippi, all nine of the

[9] See Map 2. The resulting coefficient of correlation was a very high and significant .769. See Mississippi in Appendix A, which explains the method and gives the rankings.

[10] The categories are taken from Benson's *Concept of Jacksonian Democracy,* 138, with the one exception that his label "anti-Democratic" has been changed to "Whig" because from 1836 to 1844 in Mississippi the Whigs comprised the opposition to the Democrats. The categories, based on the percentage of the total vote that went to the Democrats, are as follows: Very Strong Democratic (65 to 100 per cent), Strong Democratic (57.5 to 64.9 per cent), Moderate Democratic (52.5 to 57.4 per cent), Neutral (47.5 to 52.4 per cent), Moderate Whig (42.5 to 47.4 per cent), Strong Whig (35 to 42.4 per cent) and Very Strong Whig (0 to 34.9 per cent).

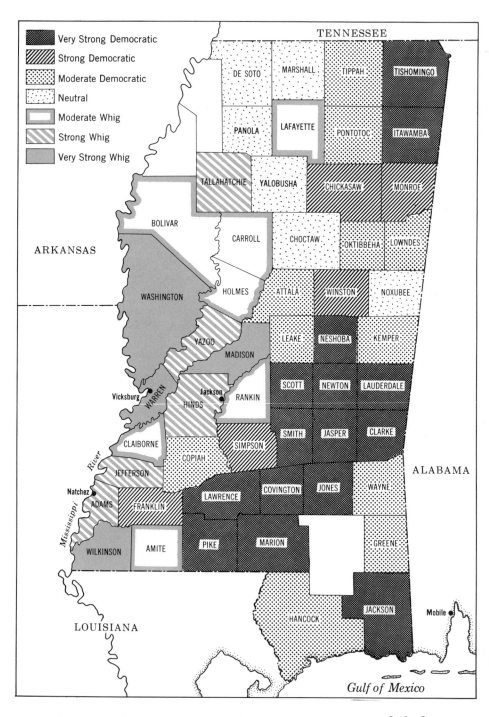

MAP 2. DEMOCRATIC AND WHIG STRENGTH IN MISSISSIPPI, 1836–1844

(*Data not available for unlabeled counties—Tunica, Coahoma, and Perry*)

counties that fall into the Very Strong Whig and Strong Whig categories were from the Delta-Loess, while all fifteen Very Strong Democratic counties were from either the Piney Woods or the Eastern Hills.

Whig constituencies also were likely to be ones of heavy slaveholding. All of the ten counties with the highest percentages of slaves in the overall population were in the Whig camp.[11] Also, the distribution of newspapers and periodicals around the state clearly indicates that Whig strength came from relatively more cosmopolitan and better-informed areas. If a county had a town large and prosperous enough to support the publication of a newspaper or periodical, there was a good chance the county would be Whig rather than Democratic. Of the thirty-three newspapers in Mississippi in 1838, twenty-two of them were published in the sixteen Whig counties and only seven in the thirty-one Democratic counties. Four were published in the six Neutral counties.[12]

One of the most useful insights in comparing Whig and Democratic constituencies is gained by contrasting the pattern of land and slaveholding in the various counties. Information of this type ordinarily is difficult, if not impossible, to find, but for Mississippi a study has been made of twelve sample counties for the decade of the 1850s. An analysis of the data points to the unmistakable conclusion that there was a significantly higher concentration of large land and slave holdings in Whig constituencies than in Democratic ones, where the farms were much smaller and the great majority of farmers owned no slaves. Of the sample counties used in the study, four were Whig, five Democratic, one Neutral, and two had not yet been organized in the

[11] On this list were all of the four Very Strong Whig counties, four of the five Strong Whig counties, and two of the seven Moderate Whig counties. The remaining Strong Whig county ranked eleventh in slaveholding. Per-capita slaveholding figures were compiled from data in the 1840 Census as published by the Department of State in its *Compendium of the Enumeration of the Inhabitants and Statistics of the United States, as Obtained at the Department of State, From the Returns of the Sixth Census* (Washington, D.C., 1841), 56–59. My manuscript was in the final stages of publication when David Nathaniel Young's "The Mississippi Whigs, 1834–1860" (unpublished Ph.D. thesis, University of Alabama, 1968) became available to me. Young relies heavily on statistical analyses of social and economic factors, and, in general, his findings substantiate my own conclusions. The Whig party, he maintains, was more attractive to voters in wealthier areas of the state.

[12] Compiled from data in Besancon, *Annual Register of Mississippi,* 217–20.

1836–1844 time period. In the Whig counties of Adams, Bolivar, Hinds, and Jefferson, 46.84 per cent of the farmers worked from 1 to 199 acres of improved land and 17.81 per cent owned over 500 acres, while in the Democratic counties of Jones, Lowndes, Scott, Tishomingo, and Wayne, 82.96 per cent owned from 1 to 199 acres and only 3.07 per cent possessed over 500 acres. A comparison of slaveholding indicates much the same sort of pattern. A total of 26.75 per cent of the farmers in the Whig counties owned no slaves and 16.81 per cent had over 50, while 63.69 per cent of the farmers in Democratic counties owned no slaves and only 1.84 per cent held over 50.[13]

The five strongest Whig counties in the years 1836–1844—Wilkinson, Warren, Washington, Madison, and Adams, in that order—were among the eight wealthiest in the state and were heavy areas of slaveholding and cotton production. In 1840, average slaveholding per person in the free population in these five counties was 2.91 slaves, more than double the statewide average of 1.08 and more than six times the average of .44 in the five strongest Democratic counties. In 1840, an average of 4,413 pounds of cotton per member of the free population was gathered in these Whig counties, well above the state average of 1,048 pounds, and far outstripping the 265-pound average for the five strongest Democratic counties.[14]

All five of the leading Whig counties were in the Delta-Loess region,

[13] The above discussion is based on the tables in Herbert Weaver's *Mississippi Farmers, 1850–1860* (Nashville, Tenn., 1945), 39, 74. See also pages 47 to 62 for a discussion of the social and economic classes of the state. The two counties that were not organized in 1840 and that were not used were Issaquena and Harrison. Marshall was the politically neutral constituency. The percentages that were used in the above discussion of the Whig and Democratic constituencies were compiled by averaging Weaver's data. I have used the term "farmers" to include both yeoman farmers and planters in lieu of Weaver's "agricultural operators." Finally, I realize that Weaver's data is for 1850 and not 1840, which would have been more relevant to my study. Despite this limitation, however, I feel that it can be used to indicate meaningful differences between Whig and Democratic constituencies as long as it is realized that the conclusions are used only to indicate a general tendency. In other words, I am assuming that if data on the distribution of land and slaves *were available* for 1840, it would differ from the 1850 figures only on specifics, not in the general outline.

[14] Statistics compiled from data in Department of State, *Returns of the Sixth Census*, 56–59, 227–37. Also see rankings in Appendix A. The five strongest Democratic counties were Jackson, Lawrence, Clarke, Lauderdale, and Covington.

and four of them were bounded on the west by the Mississippi River, which gave planters an excellent means for transporting their cotton to market in New Orleans. The one exception was Madison County, described by one ante-bellum Mississippian as presenting "an almost unbroken body of the most fertile cotton land any where to be found in the cotton region of the Union." [15] There planters shipped their crop to market via the Big Black and Pearl rivers.

The only two cities large enough to be listed separately by the 1840 census, Natchez and Vicksburg, were located in the heavily Whig counties of Adams and Warren, respectively. Natchez, the larger of the two, with a population in 1840 of 4,800, was a city of stately and expensive homes and a place where the myth of the Old South tended to be a living reality. John Quitman described it when he arrived in 1822:

Natchez is a bustling place. The streets are lined with carriages, drays, and wagons. The rush to the river is incessant. Every hour we hear the roar of cannon, announcing the arrival and departure of steamers. Hundreds of arks, or flat-boats, loaded with the produce of the Western States, even from the interior of Pennsylvania, here line the landing for half a mile, often lying five tier deep!

In the city proper, and the surrounding country, there is genteel and well-regulated society. . . . The planters are the prominent feature. They ride fine horses, are followed by well-dressed and very aristocratic servants, but affect great simplicity of costume themselves. . . . They live profusely, drink costly Port, Madeira, and sherry, after the English fashion, and are exceedingly hospitable.[16]

By 1838 the town had three banks and nearly a dozen hotels among its more than six hundred buildings. Natchez also had three periodicals and some industry, including two cotton presses and two steam saw mills.[17]

---

[15] Besancon, *Annual Register of Mississippi*, I, 169.

[16] John Quitman to his father, January 16, 1822, in *John A. Quitman*, I, 70–73.

[17] Besancon, *Annual Register of Mississippi*, I, 117–22. D. Clayton James in his *Antebellum Natchez* (Baton Rouge, La., 1968) concludes that "Natchez was not a center of Federalist-Whig predominance," and that "no Natchez political clique can justly be considered aggressive in the sense of being militant, domineering, or assertive." Natchez citizens, however, "usually favored Republican-Democratic candidates, while the county voters generally supported Federalists and Whigs." See page 135. I believe, however, that the evidence mar-

Further north on the Mississippi River was Vicksburg, which had a population of 3,104 in 1840 and was "the second city in the state in wealth and population." [18] It was the seat of the wealthy Warren County, which was bounded by three rivers, the Mississippi and two main tributaries, the Yazoo, and the Big Black. A traveler described his impression of the city in 1835, concluding that there was no town in the Southwest more flourishing. "It contains," he said,

nearly two thousand inhabitants. Thirty thousand bales of cotton, about one eighth of the whole quantity shipped by the state at large, are annually shipped from this place. In this respect it is inferior only to Natchez and Grand Gulf, the first of which ships fifty thousand. There is a weekly paper published here . . . and another in contemplation. There are also a bank, with two or three churches, and a handsome brick court-house. . . .[19]

The densest slave population in the entire state was found in Washington County, where in 1840 the 660 free residents were greatly outnumbered by their 6,627 slaves. It was also the county of the greatest wealth per capita in the free population. But unlike Adams and Warren counties, and even Madison County with its county seat of Canton,[20] Washington County was almost entirely rural. Although its

---

shaled to support this thesis still leaves the politics of Natchez open to question. The author points out that Van Buren carried Natchez in 1836 by a vote of 171 to 143. The next presidential election for which he has separate voting returns for Natchez is 1852, when the Whig, Scott, received the city's vote, 366 to 334. Furthermore, since detailed election data on the state elections is not available, James points to the men from Natchez who were elected to territorial, state, and national offices and concludes that the majority of these men were Republicans and Democrats. For example, after 1833 eleven Natchez Democrats and only eight Natchez Whigs served as state representatives (see discussion 128–35). It is questionable, however, just what this proves. It might prove, for example, that the Whigs preferred to draw their candidates from the county in order to attract the out-of-city vote, knowing that the Natchez vote was theirs anyway. Furthermore, it might prove that the Democratic party in Adams County and Natchez was basically conservative and often appealed to Whiggish voters. This would certainly be true as far as the banking issue was concerned and in the period after 1837 until the middle 1840s.

[18] Besancon, *Annual Register of Mississippi*, I, 207.

[19] Joseph Holt Ingraham, *The South-West: By a Yankee* (New York, 1835), II, 169–70.

[20] With a population of three hundred whites and one hundred slaves, Canton had two banks, two hotels, ten dry goods stores, one drug store, three groceries, one bakery, one tin shop, three tailor shops and two watchmaker shops. See Besancon, *Annual Register of Mississippi*, I, 169–71.

land area in 1838 was greater than that of any other Mississippi county, it did not have a single retail store within its boundaries.

There was some sign of Whig strength in the Black Prairie region. Noxubee County, although classified as Neutral in its presidential voting from 1836–1844, did, however, lean in the direction of Whigs in balloting for gubernatorial candidates in 1841 and 1843. A relatively new, rapidly growing, and wealthy county, Noxubee was watered by the navigable Noxubee River. Macon, which in 1838 had a branch of the Union Bank and two weekly newspapers, was the flourishing county seat.[21]

Any attempt to impose a strict economic determinism in interpreting Mississippi politics is belied by the experience in Perry County,[22] which offers the greatest contrast to the typical Whig constituency in the Delta-Loess area. One of the poorest of the Piney Woods counties, Perry gave Whig presidential candidates substantial majorities (averaging 59 per cent) in the elections of 1840 and 1844 and also supported Whig gubernatorial candidates in 1841 and 1843. There were only two villages in the remote county in 1838—Augusta, the county seat with three families, and Monroe, with six or seven families. In earlier years, around 1820, it was reported that Augusta had been in a

prosperous and thriving condition; and it was confidently anticipated that it would be a town of some importance in the eastern part of the state. Its dilapidated and untenanted houses give evidence, however, that those anticipations, then apparently well founded, have been doomed to disappointment. It now presents to the eye of the traveller all the appearances of a deserted village. . . .[23]

Frequent flooding of the low lands, plus the attraction of more congenial lands in northern Mississippi, had turned away many earlier settlers.[24]

3

The Eastern Hills and sparsely populated Piney Woods counties were strongholds of Democratic strength. All fifteen of the Very

---

[21] *Ibid.*, 177–78.

[22] Perry County is not included in the rank-difference correlations (in Appendix A) because data for the 1836 presidential election were not available.

[23] Besancon, *Annual Register of Mississippi*, I, 186.   [24] *Ibid.*, 190.

Strong Democratic counties for the years 1836–1844 came from these two areas, which, for the most part, were settled by small farmers, who "tended toward self-sufficiency" and had few slaves. Most of the land under cultivation was devoted to "subsistence crops," especially in the Piney Woods, where the soil was so unproductive that many farmers used the land only for grazing livestock sold once a year at market towns. The small income received was then used to purchase articles that could not be produced locally, such as sugar and salt.[25]

These residents of eastern Mississippi were described by a traveler several years before the Panic. They formed, he said, a

peculiar class, and include the majority of the inhabitants on the east part of this state. With the awkwardness of the Yankee countryman, they are destitute of his morals, education, and reverence for religion. With the rude and bold qualities of the chivalrous Kentuckian, they are destitute of his intelligence, and the humour which tempers and renders amusing his very vices. They are in general uneducated, and their apparel consists of a coarse linsey-woolsey, of a dingy yellow or blue, with broad-brimmed hats; though they usually follow their teams barefooted and bareheaded, with their long locks hanging over their eyes and shoulders, giving them a wild appearance. Accost them as they pass you . . . and their replies will generally be sullen or insulting. . . . They have a decided aversion to a broad-cloth coat, and this antipathy is transferred to the wearer. . . . At home they live in log-houses on partially cleared lands, labour hard in their fields, sometimes owning a few slaves, but more generally with but one or none.[26]

Eastern Mississippi politicians also developed their own inimitable style, as is shown by the career of Franklin Plummer, one of the state's most colorful campaigners. A native of Massachusetts who settled in the Piney Woods, he was a master at translating the mood and unarticulated desires of his backwoods constituency into political capital. He had little formal education, but "could read, write and cipher up to the Rule of Three" and had "push, shrewdness and the 'gift of gab,' and was considered at that time, and in those new settlements as a walking encyclopedia." [27] Powhatan Ellis—later a U.S. Senator and minister to

[25] Weaver, *Mississippi Farmers,* 56–61.

[26] Ingraham, *The South-West,* II, 171–72.

[27] Claiborne, *Mississippi,* 424. For a sketch of Plummer's career, see pp. 411–12, 415–16, 423–27. Plummer began his career as a Jackson man, but later left the

Mexico—learned, much to his sorrow, how skilled Plummer was in the practical politics of southeastern Mississippi. During one campaign when Ellis was opposing Plummer, the former lost his portmanteau while he was fording a stream. This led the irrepressible Plummer to publish the following newspaper advertisement:

Lost by Hon. Powhatan Ellis, in crossing Tallahala, the following articles: six lawn handkerchiefs; six cambric shirts; two night do; one nightcap; one pair stays; four pair silk stockings; hairbrush; flesh-brush, nail-brush, clothes brush, razors and dressing-glass, pomatum, perfume. . . .

Needless to say, Ellis' appeal to the rough frontiersmen was considerably dampened, for "such a sample of 'swelled head' effeminacy, and Natchez dandyism, was not wanted in the Piney Woods." [28]

Life in the Piney Woods was hard and simple, and Mississippians from the more civilized Delta regarded it as a barbarous area. Claiborne had held this view and was pleasantly surprised during his trip to find that it had been exaggerated. Despite this, in his reports to his readers in the Natchez *Free Trader,* it is clear that the plainness of life shocked him. He described a meal he shared with residents of the area:

The repast was abundant, excellent and scrupulously neat—but almost every dish was composed of *potatoes* dressed in many various ways. There were baked potatoes and fried potatoes—bacon and potatoes boiled together—a fine loin of beef was flanked round with potatoes nicely browned and swimming in gravy. A hash of wild turkey was garnished with potatoes mixed up in it. A roast fowl was stuffed with potatoes, beside us stood a plate of potato biscuit, as light as sponge; the *coffee,* which was strong and well flavored, was made of *potatoes,* and one of the girls drew from the corner cupboard a rich potato pie. In about an hour a charming blue-eyed girl brought us a tumbler of potato beer that sparkled like champagne and rather archly intimated that there were hot potatoes in the ashes if we felt like eating one. The beer was admirable, and we were told that good whiskey, molasses and vinegar were sometimes made of potatoes.[29]

---

party. His career does illustrate the robust political style of backwoods Mississippi.

[28] The above story may be found in Claiborne, *Mississippi,* 426.

[29] Claiborne, "A Trip Through the Piney Woods," 533–34.

All fifteen of the Piney Woods counties were solidly Democratic, except the wealthiest county in the region—the Moderate Whig Rankin County on the Pearl River—and the aforementioned Perry County. Among the most isolated and rural backwoods counties was the strongest Democratic county in the state, Jackson, which from 1836 to 1844 gave 93 per cent of its votes to Democratic presidential candidates. Its county seat was "situated near the center of the county, on a small stream," and, one traveler noted, there was nothing at the "place to distinguish it from the ordinary farms of the country: it contains no public buildings whatever; the courts are usually held in a room of the dwelling house of the only family residing at the place." [30]

Jones County in the Piney Woods was the poorest county in the state and remained isolated and sparsely populated up to the Civil War. The early settlers raised corn, potatoes, and cotton, mainly for family use. Some wool and cotton were taken along to market when turkeys, sheep, and cattle were driven to Mobile, a trip of more than 100 miles and one requiring three weeks time.[31] Claiborne described the county when he visited there in 1841:

This county is thinly settled and adapted chiefly to grazing. . . . Much of it is covered exclusively with the long leaf pines; not broken, but rolling like the waves in the middle of the great ocean. . . . Thousands of cattle are grazed here for market. The unbroken forests abound with game. The red deer troop along by dozens; for miles the wild turkeys run before you in the road. . . . But for this panorama of life, the solitude of a ride through this region would be painful. The houses of the road stand from ten to twenty miles apart. . . .[32]

During the secession crisis the county elected an opponent of secession to the state convention, and during the Civil War it raised a company of men to fight against the local Confederate forces.[33]

Wayne County in the Piney Woods had at one time been among the leading counties in the state, but after land in northern Mississippi was opened for settlement in the early 1830s many left for more hospitable

[30] Besancon, *Annual Register of Mississippi*, I, 149.

[31] Works Projects Administration, "Jones County, Mississippi," (manuscript, Mississippi Department of Archives and History, Jackson, 1937), 1–6.

[32] Claiborne, "A Trip Through the Piney Woods," 514–15.

[33] Rowland, *Mississippi*, I, 974–76.

soil. "Next to Lawrence," Claiborne wrote, "Wayne has given the larg-est number of settlers to the new counties."[34] While in the county in 1841, he found "neither a *lawyer, judge, justice, sheriff, clerk nor con-stable in the county,* and but for the contemplation of several mar-riages and the necessity of obtaining licenses, it is not supposed that any of these respectable functionaries would ever again have appeared in that county."[35]

After 1838 there was little concentrated soft-money strength within the Mississippi Democratic party, but there was one county, Oktibbeha, which gave consistent support to the soft-money position. Legislators from that Moderate Democratic County in the rich Black Prairie re-gion defied the majority in their party both in 1838, by voting in favor of the Union Bank Bill, and in 1841, by opposing the repudiation of its bonds. In 1843, after faithfully supporting Democratic gubernatorial nominees in 1837, 1839, and 1841, the county gave the majority of its votes to the Whig candidate for governor in preference to the antibond Democrat.[36]

Oktibbeha was located in the midst of the area in northern Missis-sippi that had been Indian lands until the early 1830s, when treaties with the Choctaws and Chickasaws opened the area up for settlement. During the "flush times" of the 1830s, newcomers poured into the new counties and quickly made them the most populous in the state.[37] The destination for many of the settlers was the fertile Black Prairie, and by 1840 Oktibbeha and its neighbor to the east, Lowndes County, were the two most prosperous Democratic counties in the state and were two of the three leading Democratic counties in slaveholding. In 1834 and 1835 the town of Columbus in Lowndes had the busiest land office in the entire country.[38]

The transformation that took place in the Black Prairie undoubtedly was similar to that in another of the new counties, Marshall, where the

[34] Claiborne, "A Trip Through the Piney Woods," 529.
[35] *Ibid.*, 529–30.
[36] Data for vote on Union Bank Bill in 1838 from Mississippi House *Journal,* 1838, 137–38, and Jackson *Mississippian,* December 1, 1837, for party affiliations. Data for vote in 1841 from Jackson *Southron,* January 30, 1841, and the Jackson *Mississippian,* January 21, 1841.
[37] Weaver, *Mississippi Farmers,* 38–40.
[38] Miles, *Jacksonian Democracy in Mississippi,* 118.

community of Holly Springs was described as being "one of those towns in the vast West, which seems to have sprung into existence as if by magic. Three years previous . . . it was an open cotton plantation; it now numbers its inhabitants by thousands, and spreads its habitations over several miles square." [39]

The opening up of the new lands for settlement stirred the imaginations of men living on less favored terrain. In the poorer Piney Woods section, for example, many counties were practically stripped of their inhabitants, as residents deserted their homes for a promise of a better life. These transplanted farmers, perhaps, retained a sense of loyalty to the Democratic party, which had a strong hold in the Piney Woods. But they also quickly became caught up in the boom psychology and the limitless opportunities they found in their new homes, and this exuberance of enterprise had the effect of undermining old beliefs and allegiances.

Oktibbeha became a county in 1833, and by 1840 the population had increased from a few hundred to 4,276. In the brief period between settlement and the financial panic, the county enjoyed prosperity.

From the organization of the county, the farmers had been rapidly clearing and developing their lands; and now many of them were increasing the number of their slaves. . . . The merchants were bringing in large stocks of goods; it is said that one of the stores in Starkville carried goods of almost every description—groceries, hardware, drugs, drygoods. Some of the general stores carried even the finer liquors, including champagne. . . . People generally were engaging in extravagance.

Credit—everybody had credit—the county was full of money. Nearly all transactions were on a credit basis. The merchants sold on credit. One Starkville store sold on credit more than fifty dollars worth of goods a day through a period of several months. And the credit sales of another was about a hundred dollars a day, sometimes more.[40]

Transportation proved to be a problem to Oktibbeha planters. Not having the advantages of the Yazoo and Mississippi rivers, as did the planters in the Delta, or the Tombigbee River, as did the planters in the counties to the east, cotton growers in Oktibbeha had to haul the

[39] Bishop Leonidas Polk as quoted in *ibid.,* 118.
[40] Thomas Battle Carroll, *Historical Sketches of Oktibbeha County Mississippi* (Gulfport, Miss., 1931), 40–41.

bulky cotton many miles overland before reaching navigable water to take their crop to market in Mobile. By 1840, however, several landings had been built on Tibbee Creek, which flowed into the Tombigbee. One or more planters then built or purchased barges to take their cotton either to Lowndes County river ports or all the way to Mobile.

Oktibbeha's prosperity was short lived. The financial panic hit hard, and it was said that "the sheriff sold more property in the three years following 1837 than any other sheriff has ever sold in the same length of time." The financial dislocation retarded Starkville's growth, and the county seat "decreased in size and importance between 1838 and 1848." [41]

4

It has been shown that in Mississippi the greatest support for the Democratic party came from the poorest counties and those with the fewest slaves. It must be mentioned here, however, that recent studies by Thomas B. Alexander and associates [42] lead to quite different conclusions about politics in the adjacent state of Alabama. Alexander uses a number of quantifying techniques to analyze the basis of support of the Alabama Whig party and concludes that the traditional view of the Whig party as the party of the planter and large slaveholder is at best misleading and probably incorrect. Using a number of rank-difference correlations to test the relationship between politics and geographic, economic, and social data, he finds that the "strongest evidence for the traditional view in so far as it associates Whiggery with planting and slavery is found in the significant correlation between Whig voting strength and percentages of Negro population." Yet he immediately discounts this by asserting "that the Black Belt counties

---

[41] *Ibid.*, 47 and 59. For a general discussion of Oktibbeha see Chapters III, IV, and VI.

[42] Thomas B. Alexander, Kit C. Carter, Jack R. Lister, Jerry C. Oldshue, and Winfred G. Sandlin, "Who Were the Alabama Whigs?" *The Alabama Review,* XVI (January, 1963), 5-19, and Thomas B. Alexander, Peggy Duckworth Elmore, Frank M. Lowrey, and Mary Jane Pickens Skinner, "The Basis of Alabama's Ante-Bellum Two-Party System," *The Alabama Review,* XIX (October, 1966), 243-76.

were not the strongest Whig counties—were, in fact, frequently closely divided." [43]

Alexander's use of only one presidential election to determine a county's politics and especially the election of 1840 raises some questions. William Henry Harrison's victory has been categorized as a "surge" election and thus might not be the most appropriate choice of data to reflect traditional political allegiances. A "surge" election has been defined as one in which:

(1) there was a sharp upturn in voter participation, bringing to the polls a large number of infrequent voters having weak or non-existent party identifications; (2) since such voters are mainly moved by short-term forces, there was an unusually heavy majority for the party that was temporarily advantaged as to circumstances, issues, and candidate personality; and (3) the underlying pattern of party identifications was not significantly affected, reasserting itself in subsequent state and congressional elections when the ephemeral voters stayed home.[44]

Alexander also analyzes scattered voting data from "beats," or local election districts, to strengthen his findings. In Tuscaloosa County, data from the 1844 and 1848 elections "tended to bear out in limited measure the economic association of Whiggery with plantation economy." However, he continues, the 1857 and 1860 elections do "not so clearly sustain the economic interpretation." [45] In the Black Belt county of Lowndes, beat returns were analyzed for the years 1836, 1851, 1855, and 1860, and it was concluded that there was "little reason to accept the traditional view that the Whig party was the party of the planting aristocracy, and some reason to believe that in the Black Belt of Alabama the reverse was more often the case." [46] The voting data, again, could be misleading. Traditional lines of division between the Whigs and Democrats were forged in the 1830s at a time when the major questions—the bank, tariff, and internal improvements—were, in the main, economic. By the 1850s, these issues, for the most part, were

[43] Alexander, "Who Were the Alabama Whigs?" 9.

[44] Charles Sellers, "The Equilibrium Cycle in Two-Party Politics," *The Public Opinion Quarterly*, XXIX (spring, 1965), 20–21.

[45] Alexander, "Who Were the Alabama Whigs?" 17–18. For a discussion of the methodology employed in *The Jacksonians Versus the Banks*, see Appendix A, Footnote 1.

[46] *Ibid.*, 18–19.

dead ones. The sectional conflict was in the process of redefining the nature of political divisions and challenging traditional party loyalties. By weighting his research with voting data from the 1850s, Alexander is in danger of obscuring the true nature of the politics of the Jacksonian era. How many Whigs, for example, decided to switch their allegiance to the Democratic party in the 1850s when it became clear that the party of Jackson had become the champion of southern rights and southern interests? A comparison of Alabama presidential election returns shows a dramatic falling off of Whig strength, from 48.3 per cent of the vote in 1848, to 34.0 per cent in 1852, 38.6 per cent in 1856, and 31.1 per cent in 1860. In Mississippi, two poor counties, Jones and Tishomingo, that were categorized as Very Strong Democratic during the Jacksonian era were heavily influenced in their politics by the sectional crisis, and, by the time of the Civil War, both counties were strongly opposed to the Democrats' call for secession. Therefore, to draw conclusions on the entire period of ante-bellum politics, as Alexander does, based mainly on voting data from the decade prior to the war, can only lead to tenuous conclusions.

Despite Alexander's denial of the validity of the traditional view of ante-bellum Whiggery, his conclusions are not drastically revisionist:

In the counties with the more advanced stages of general economic development, with the greater cash cropping and the greater commercial contacts with the outside world, in short, in the counties more nearly in the main stream of the national and world economy, Whig party appeals were more effective to all types of voters regardless of individual economic status. It is not that a planter with many slaves or an affluent merchant was more likely to be a Whig than was a carpenter or small farmer or blacksmith; it is simply that all of these men were more likely to be Whigs if they lived in well-developed economic communities rather than in frontier, or isolated, or more nearly self-sufficient communities.[47]

The Mississippi experience would not, in general, belie this. Obviously, the wealthy Delta-Loess counties were not peopled exclusively by great planters, and for the Whigs to be successful in those constituencies, they had to make a broader appeal. This does not deny the fact, however, that the *raison d'etre* of these counties was the production of cotton, and it was to the interest of the yeoman farmer as well as all those

[47] Alexander, "The Basis of Alabama's Ante-Bellum Two-Party System," 266.

who provided attendant services to see that this production was maximized.

The political divisions of Mississippi during the Jacksonian period were neither superficial nor ephemeral, and although the analysis cannot be pushed too hard and one must be wary of over-simplification, the same basic political dichotomy existed in the state almost a century later. In his study of southern politics, political scientist V. O. Key, Jr., describes a division in twentieth century Mississippi between the Delta and the Hills and says further that the line between the two is

more than economic. The mores, morals, and ways of life of the two groups differ—perhaps not so much as their preachers would have them believe but enough to have political significance. State-wide prohibition, for example, receives least support in the delta. The preachers of the hills fight demon rum and their followers vote for prohibition, while the sinful delta votes for liquor. . . . Prohibition . . . represents an unattainable objective and has a special appeal to the hill people, while the delta planters, less disposed to pursue will-of-the-wisps, take a more realistic view.[48]

Prohibition was not an issue in Mississippi during the 1830s and 1840s, but banking was, and to many Democrats it was not just a political and economic issue, but, like prohibition, it assumed moral overtones. The banks seemed to be privileged institutions erected to aid and to make wealthier the already wealthy men of the community. Their very existence was viewed by many as a denial and contradiction of their conception of how a democratic society should operate.

The life style of men in the Delta differed considerably from that of the hill people and of Piney Woods residents. The planters of the Delta had better communication and transportation resources. Trips to Natchez, Vicksburg, and even New Orleans were considerably easier for them. Furthermore, the inhabitants of the Delta were better informed, at least in the sense that they had a greater opportunity to read current newspapers and were nearer to the main artery to the outside world, the Mississippi River. The large planters in the Whig Delta constituencies needed the banks and the credit they could provide. Deeply conservative, these men resisted bank reform and bank destruc-

---

[48] V. O. Key, Jr., *Southern Politics in State and Nation* (New York, 1949), 233. Quotations from this work reprinted courtesy of Alfred A. Knopf, Inc., copyright © 1949 Alfred A. Knopf.

tion and bitterly fought the Democrats on the repudiation issue. The large planter was nationally and internationally minded. Repudiation was a blot on his state's honor, and, perhaps more important, he feared it would dry up the sources of international credit that had been available to Mississippi.

The hill areas and especially the counties in the Piney Woods were bastions of isolation. Men of the Piney Woods lived meager, narrow, and provincial lives. Vaguely discontented with their hardships in trying to maintain a bare existence, these men regarded the banks as devices by which Delta planters could increase their advantage over them. Furthermore, the banks symbolized outside hostile and threatening forces that were little understood but much hated and feared by Piney Woods residents.

CHAPTER V

The Southwest

I

SOUTHWESTERNERS were reluctant to abandon their hopes for quick riches immediately after the Panic. But in the early 1840s, when they finally had to admit defeat and recognize that the whole inflated economic system had been built on false optimism, Democrats in Mississippi, Louisiana, Arkansas, and Alabama took more drastic steps against the banks than did most of their compatriots elsewhere. By the middle of the decade two states, Louisiana and Arkansas, had succeeded in constitutionally prohibiting banks within their boundaries, and Alabama and Mississippi were in the process of winding up their broken banks by legislative action. So, paradoxically, it was the Democrats in the Southwest who eventually were hailed by hard-money Jacksonians throughout the country as being in the vanguard of the fight against the banks.

If Mississippi was the most representative state in the section, the older and more settled Louisiana was the most atypical. Almost all statistics for the years surrounding the Panic point to Louisiana as being the most stable and mature of the Southwest states. The population there was increasing, but not nearly so rapidly as elsewhere in the Southwest. In the decade of the 1830s the free population in Louisiana increased by 50 per cent and the slave population by a third. At the same time, the slave populations of Alabama, Mississippi, and Arkansas doubled, tripled, and quadrupled, respectively. Arkansas's free population tripled during the decade, while Mississippi's doubled. Alabama registered an increase in free population of 60 per cent.[1]

[1] North, *Economic Growth*, 129.

Also, Louisiana banks, both before and after the Panic, tended to be more responsible than banks in the other states, but this did not protect them from harsh treatment by reformers after specie payments were discontinued. In the fifteen years before the Panic, when the notes of Mississippi and Alabama banks were discounted at from 5 to 25 per cent of par value on the Philadelphia market, Louisiana notes ran at only a 3 to 11 per cent discount.[2]

The ratio of specie to circulation plus deposits is another indicator of the more conservative nature of the Louisiana banks. After the Panic they steadily contracted their liabilities, slowly increasing specie holdings from 16 cents per dollar in 1837 to 96 cents in 1844. In contrast, rather than curtailing their operations following the Panic, Mississippi banks expanded note issues from 7.5 million dollars in 1838 to about 15.2 million dollars in 1840. Two years later the amount of note issue had been reduced to 2.4 million dollars worth. In the years from 1834 to 1842, Mississippi bankers never had more than 13 cents in specie for every dollar in circulation and deposits. This was the high reached in 1837, and five years later the amount of specie had dropped to four tenths of one cent for every dollar of circulation and deposits.[3]

The relative stability of Louisiana banks was undoubtedly due, at least in part, to the influence of New Orleans, the only major commercial center in the entire South. Its importance to Louisiana cannot be overemphasized. As a major national and international market, it was a center of financial activity. In 1840 the Crescent City was one of the five largest cities in the country and ranked first in exports. Even twenty years later, it was the only Southern entry in the list of the country's fifteen largest cities.[4]

The political system of Louisiana was more stable than those of her sister states in the Southwest, which were still in the frontier stage of development in 1837. Rapid population growth and poor communication networks, two characteristics of the frontier, made it extremely difficult for strong party organizations to take root. It was not until about 1840

---

[2] See graph in Van Fenstermaker, *American Commercial Banking,* 89.

[3] All figures from *Comptroller's Report, 1876,* 112–13. See Appendix B, Table 1, for complete ratios of specie to circulation and deposits.

[4] Merl E. Reed, *New Orleans and the Railroads: The Struggle for Commercial Empire, 1830–1860* (Baton Rouge, La., 1966), 5; North, *Economic Growth,* 130.

that a two-party system was in operation in Mississippi and Alabama.
In Louisiana this development came somewhat earlier.[5]

Whereas in Louisiana the parties were nearly balanced in strength,
in Mississippi, Alabama, and Arkansas, Democrats dominated state
politics. In all elections from 1840 to 1856 Democratic presidential nominees carried both Alabama and Arkansas. In Mississippi after a Whig
victory in a close 1840 race, the Democrats won the next four presidential contests. The Whigs received Louisiana's electoral votes in 1840
and 1848, while the Democrats won in 1844, 1852, and 1856.[6] State elections indicate about the same. The Alabama Whigs normally received
about 45 per cent of the vote in the state elections and remained com-
petitive but always in the minority. The Mississippi Whigs, equally unable to obtain the voters' favor, were never able to win a statewide majority. In Louisiana, the Whigs controlled the governor's office down to
1842 but were never able to win a gubernatorial election after that.[7]

2

Democrats in Louisiana, Arkansas, and Alabama reacted to the
Panic in much the same way as did the Jacksonians in Mississippi,
their position evolving from one of bank reform to that of bank abolition. The reforms of the late 1830s and early 1840s failed, the Jacksonians felt, to force the banks to act responsibly and to furnish a sound
currency. The only course open, then, was to let the banking system
gradually die. With its demise, paper currency would be withdrawn
and specie would replace the depreciated and worthless paper.

Ironically, it is the Louisiana Whigs who have normally been given
credit for the most progressive bank law passed by a state legislature in
the ante-bellum period.[8] Their role, however, has been exaggerated. In

---

[5] See Richard P. McCormick, *The Second American Party System: Party
Formation in the Jacksonian Era* (Chapel Hill, N.C., 1964), 269, 293–303,
319–20.

[6] *Historical Statistics*, 689.

[7] Perry H. Howard, *Political Tendencies in Louisiana, 1812–1952* (Baton Rouge,
La., 1957), 48; McCormick, *Second American Party System*, 302–303, 293–94,
318.

[8] Sumner, *History of Banking*, 387–89; Redlich, *Molding of American Banking*, Vol. II, Part II, 32–37; Hammond, *Banking and Politics*, 680–85.

1842 the Louisiana legislature passed a banking act that required the cash liabilities of banks to be liquid at all times. Each bank was compelled to hold in its vaults specie equal to one third of its liabilities in notes and deposits. The remaining two thirds would be covered by short-term commercial paper, running no longer than ninety days.[9]

The Louisiana legislature, which passed the 1842 act, was fairly closely divided politically, the Whigs having the majority in the lower house, and the parties being evenly split in the upper chamber.[10] The bill passed and was signed by a Whig governor. During the debate over the measure, one member of the legislature chided his colleagues for their reluctance to reform the banks:

The question seems to be, who will bell the cat? *Who will bell the cat?* And if any member has the temerity to stand up and say, "I am ready to do it," several good natured legislators start up in their places and say, "You shall not, sir, you shall not. Why, bless your soul, sir, you would not only place your own life or your own interest, which is almost the same thing, in jeopardy, but you would destroy *your* interest—you would annihilate the planting interest—the mercantile interest—you would, in a word, sir, bring ruin to the whole country." Thus the cat is allowed to cut up his "didoes," and the few who have the courage are not permitted to *bell him*.[11]

One historian has suggested that the 1842 bank act was unique in that it represented the triumph of a modern outlook in which specie was made the "regulator of banking, the governor of a well-constructed engine possessing within itself the power of expansion and contraction." [12] This reform principle, however, was not one that was held exclusively by the Whigs, either in Louisiana or elsewhere. The use of specie as a kind of automatic regulator of banking was a cardinal tenet of the Democratic hard-money doctrine.

Four years earlier, for example, the Louisiana legislature had passed a bill very much like the 1842 enactment, but the measure had been

[9] *Ibid.*, for a discussion of this act see also Caldwell, *Banking History of Louisiana,* 71–89.

[10] Irene Neu, "Louisiana Politics and the Bank Act of 1842," unpublished manuscript read at the annual meeting of the American Historical Association, December, 1964.

[11] As quoted in Caldwell, *Banking History of Louisiana,* 65–66.

[12] Redlich, *Molding of American Banking,* Vol. II, Part II, 35–36.

struck down by the veto of the Whig governor.[13] This 1838 bill included the same provision calling for specie in the vaults to cover at least one third of the note circulation and deposits.[14] On the first vote, the bill was approved in the house by the wide margin of 31 to 8, but the legislature was not able to override the veto, the second vote in the house being 21 to 19 against the measure.[15] Whigs and Democrats had joined to pass the bill on the first vote, but with the Governor's veto party discipline was asserted, and the Whigs withdrew a substantial part of their support from the reform measure.[16]

Thus, although the Whigs are usually given credit for the reform measure of 1842, it is fairly certain that they moved only reluctantly in the direction of reform and that bank reform was accomplished only with Democratic encouragement and support. From 1838 to 1842 Democratic criticism of the banks provided the stimulus for the Whigs to help "bell the cat." Indeed, it might be said that they were moved to "bell the cat" only after he had swallowed the canary.

The Democrats, however, did not feel that the 1842 reform act had freed the state from bank abuses. In 1845 a convention assembled to rewrite the Louisiana Constitution, with the banking problem as one of the major points at issue. The Democrats held twice as many seats as the Whigs, and it was at this convention that the more radical, hard-

[13] Edward Douglass White.

[14] Another provision of the bill, deleted in 1842 and not so progressive, would have compelled the banks to make two fifths of their loans outside the cities of New Orleans and Lafayette.

[15] Louisiana House of Representatives *Journal,* 2nd Session of the 13th Legislature, 58; House *Document No.* 227, 518–26 for text of bill, 527–32 for Governor White's veto message; *Niles' Register,* March 17, 1838; New Orleans *Daily Picayune,* March 4 and March 8, 1838; Caldwell, *Banking History of Louisiana,* 62.

[16] Although there is no definite means by which to identify the party affiliation of the legislators of that session, a comparison of votes on several measures allows some generalizations to be made. In the 1838 session a resolution passed by one vote (22 to 21) condemning proposals to establish a new national bank. It is safe to say that the Democrats tended to be opposed to the establishment of a new national bank while Whigs favored it. A comparison of this vote with the vote taken to overturn the Governor's veto of the state-bank bill indicates that the men who voted to sustain the veto were the same ones who had voted against the anti-national-bank resolution. Thus, while the bank-reform bill had Whig support initially, most of this support was withdrawn after the veto.

money, antibank Democrats probably reached the zenith of their strength and success. A Whig newspaper warned:

The dominant party in the Convention are locofocoes. They are in favor of certain measures and a course of general policy, to which the conservative portion of our population are justly hostile. Flushed with their recent triumphs . . . the majority of the Convention will be eager to fasten upon the new Constitution too many offshoots of wild, agrarian and radical theories. They need a check. . . .[17]

The Whigs had reason to be fearful, for the Democrats succeeded in placing in the new constitution an article resolving that no "corporate body shall be hereafter created, renewed or extended, with discounting privileges." [18]

One Whig, who noted that he had never voted for a bank charter during his career in the legislature due to his belief that "there should be but one bank in the country, and that was a bank of the United States," dissented from the antibank provision, maintaining that the problem transcended state boundaries. If Louisiana prohibited "the establishment of banks," he argued, "our State will be flooded with the paper of the banks of other States, over which we can exercise no control. . . ." [19]

In answer to the objection, a Democrat introduced a motion prohibiting any person from circulating or causing "to be circulated, any paper money issued by any corporation or persons existing in any other State or country. . . . If we are to put down banking, let us put it down effectively, and let us return to the good old system of hard money." This motion, however, was tabled,[20] and the convention settled for a policy that prohibited new banks and allowed old ones only to live out their charters.

This Democratic triumph over the banks in Louisiana was, perhaps, the most dramatic and most publicized of the hard-money men's victo-

[17] New Orleans *Bee,* November 26, 1844, as quoted in James K. Greer, "Louisiana Politics, 1845–1861," *Louisiana Historical Quarterly,* XII (July, 1929), 410.

[18] *Proceedings and Debates of the Convention of Louisiana, 1844* (New Orleans, 1845), 849; Howard, *Political Tendencies in Louisiana,* 46–48; Caldwell, *Banking History of Louisiana,* 82–83.

[19] *Proceedings and Debates of the Convention of Louisiana, 1844,* 848.

[20] *Ibid.,* 849.

ries in the Southwest. However, Democrats in other southwestern states were equally successful in putting down the banks. In Alabama, for example, it was eventually accomplished, but only after a serious split in the Democratic party. Extensive state financial support for the banking system and individual indebtedness initially inhibited Alabama Democrats from taking action. The state had issued over 15.5 million dollars worth of bonds to support the banks in the fourteen years preceding 1837, and it was reported that in 1838, of the 55,000 voters in Alabama, over 11,000, including many Alabama legislators, were in debt to the banks.[21] During one session of the legislature it was claimed that of the sixteen members of the committee on banks, twelve owed the banks a total of more than 125,000 dollars.[22] Thus although the Democratic governor, Arthur Pendleton Bagby, urged bank reform, the Alabama legislature was ill disposed to take any steps against the banks.[23]

By the early 1840s, however, the economic situation had deteriorated to the point that Alabama bank currency was discounted at 50 per cent.[24] Many Democrats were becoming dissatisfied with the inaction, and in 1841 William L. Yancey and Benjamin Fitzpatrick led an anti-bank insurgency within the Democratic party, and this faction succeeded in elevating Fitzpatrick to the governorship. The commitment of Fitzpatrick to bank reform caused a number of prominent Democrats to denounce his candidacy and support the Whig gubernatorial aspirant.[25]

During the next four years, despite opposition from Whigs and a small band of Democrats, the Fitzpatrick Administration initiated measures, the effect of which was to put most of Alabama's banks in liquidation. After 1844 only one bank remained in the state.[26]

The split in the Democratic party remained throughout Fitzpatrick's

[21] Helderman, *National and State Banks,* 84–87; Scroggs, "Pioneer Banking in Alabama," 419–20.

[22] Albert B. Moore, *History of Alabama* (University of Alabama, 1935), 308–309.

[23] Bagby advocated that banks be required to maintain a 50-per-cent specie reserve and be prevented from issuing notes under 20 dollars. See *Niles' Register,* December 28, 1839, and November 21, 1840.

[24] William Garrett, *Reminiscences of Public Men in Alabama for Thirty Years* (Atlanta, 1872), 258–59.

[25] Moore, *History of Alabama,* 239–40.

[26] Scroggs, "Pioneer Banking in Alabama," 421–23; Sumner, *History of Bank-*

term of office. At the convention that was to choose his successor, transportation difficulties delayed the arrival of a number of the western delegates. The pro-bank Democrats took advantage of this and nominated Nathaniel Terry, a man who had the dubious distinction of being the largest bank debtor among Democrats in the legislature. Hard-money Democrats refused to accept Terry's nomination and nominated their own candidate, Joshua L. Martin, to run for governor on an antibank platform. The majority of Democrats and a few antibank Whigs supported Martin, who won the election.[27]

The same course, from reform to abolition, was followed by the Arkansas Democracy. The constitution of 1836 had provided for the establishment of two banks, one owned and operated by the state and a plantation bank "to aid and promote the great agricultural interests of the state." When both, unable to withstand the pressure generated by the Panic, suspended,[28] Democratic Governor Archibald Yell called for a legislative investigation. Reflecting the growing conviction that a bond-backed currency was not adequate to ensure responsible banking, he suggested that a specie to circulation ratio be required.[29] Two years later, however, conditions having worsened, Yell advised the legislature to wind up the affairs of the banks,[30] which it subsequently did.

In 1844 another Democratic governor of Arkansas, Thomas Drew, commented on the closing of the banks. "The pursuits of our people, and the condition of our country, just emerging from the wilderness, did not then, and do not now, justify the use of banking facilities, if at all, to the extent provided, and of which we availed ourselves," he said.[31]

Climaxing the antibank reaction, a constitutional amendment was passed in 1846; it provided that "no bank or banking institution shall hereafter be incorporated in this state." [32] The sentiment against banks

---

ing, 433–34; Carlton Jackson, "A History of the Whig Party in Alabama, 1828–1860," unpublished Ph.D. thesis at University of Georgia, 1962, 84–86.

[27] Moore, *History of Alabama,* 243–45.

[28] Sumner, *History of Banking,* 331–34.

[29] United States House of Representatives, *Executive Document No. 111* 26th Congress, 2nd Session, 1082–83.

[30] *Niles' Register,* December 10, 1842.

[31] House *Executive Document No. 226,* 898–901.

[32] Helderman, *National and State Banks,* 122–24.

was so great that the amendment passed both houses of the legislature unanimously.[33]

Both parties in Arkansas had been involved in the speculative mania in the pre-1837 years. Although two Whigs had been instrumental in establishing the state bank and one had become the president of the real-estate or plantation bank, the chartering of the Arkansas banks had been a bipartisan effort. For example, only three out of sixteen senators had voted against the creation of the state bank.[34] Furthermore the officialdom of the banks was bipartisan. Of the managers, supervisors of subscriptions, directors, and trustees, eighty-three claimed allegiance to the Democratic party, while fifty-six were Whigs.[35]

Governor Yell had not been above engaging in speculative enterprises himself. Prior to the business collapse, he had been involved in numerous land deals, which included buying acreage for an old friend, James K. Polk. Yell's biographer is puzzled by the Governor's seemingly contradictory behavior. On the one hand Yell was attracted to speculation and enterprise, while on the other, he sincerely condemned banking and desired "to see a return to the currency based on gold and silver." Yell, it is concluded, was a "venturous conservative" and a man who "honestly desired to preserve the agrarian virtues of the Old Republic, but who also felt himself caught up in the new and pressing temptations of a rapidly developing capitalistic economy." [36]

Although the evidence is sketchy it would appear that Governor Yell and the Arkansas Democrats did not act much differently than other Democrats in the Southwest. Seduced by visions of quick riches, he and his associates reacted with great vehemence against the banks, symbols of speculation and enterprise, once the Panic had dashed their dreams. While the Whigs finally accepted the winding up of the banks out of political as well as practical necessity, the Democrats were

[33] W. B. Worthen, *Early Banking in Arkansas* (Little Rock, Ark., 1906), 94.

[34] Ted R. Worley, "The Arkansas State Bank: Ante-Bellum Period," *Arkansas Historical Quarterly*, XXIII (spring, 1964), 66.

[35] Ted R. Worley, "The Control of the Real Estate Bank of the State of Arkansas, 1836–1855," *Mississippi Valley Historical Review*, XXXVII (December, 1950), 404–405.

[36] Melinda Meek, "The Life of Archibald Yell: Chapter II, The Congressman from Arkansas," *Arkansas Historical Quarterly*, XXVI (summer, 1967), 181–83. Miss Meek, here, accepts Marvin Meyer's central theme in his *Jacksonian Persuasion* to explain Yell's behavior.

driven to such acceptance by the hot fury of men who temporarily had been led astray from their principles. Afterward, the Governor lamented the seduction, and the ruin it caused, but was hopeful for the future:

The industry of our hardy population, and the ample resources of our young State, bid us be of good cheer, and look to the fertile fields of our own rich valleys and beautiful prairies, as a sure indemnity against all the evils which have swept, like "a deadly sirrocco," over this once prosperous and flourishing people. I have full confidence that, if this mode is carried out, we shall have money sufficient to meet all the legitimate wants of the country, without encouraging "the credit system," which is certain to end in loss, and often in ruin, to States as well as individuals.[37]

3

Throughout the Southwest, the number of banks had been reduced drastically by the middle of the 1840s. Of the twenty-six banks in Mississippi in 1838, only one remained by 1851. Seven banks were in business in Alabama in the early 1840s, while only one remained by the end of the decade. During the same time, Louisiana banks were reduced from forty-seven to twenty-eight.[38]

The continued growth of the region plus the shrinkage of banking facilities combined in the decade before the Civil War to create enormous pressure for more bank capital. As a result, Alabama and Louisiana passed free-banking laws in 1850 and 1853, respectively, and in 1854 Mississippi considered but rejected a free-banking scheme.[39]

The constitutional prohibition against creating new banks had caused an acute problem for Louisiana. Concurrent with the drying up of bank capital, there was a general business decline in the state. While in the late 1830s and early 1840s New Orleans had led or at least tied New York City in exports, the city's relative position had deteriorated to the point where by 1850 the value of its exports was only 1 million

---

[37] Worthen, *Early Banking in Arkansas*, 85.

[38] *Comptroller's Report, 1876*, 112–13. Caldwell, in his *Banking History of Louisiana*, claims that only five commercial banks were in operation in 1850. See page 83.

[39] Sumner, *History of Banking*, 433–34.

dollars more than in 1836.[40] The shortage of bank capital drove up interest rates, making the available capital expensive.[41]

In 1851, the Whigs won the state election after a campaign based on condemnation of the Jacksonian 1845 Constitution, which they argued was too restrictive on business enterprise, particularly with regard to the chartering of banks and other corporations. The next year, when the Whig majority met to write a new constitution, one Whig paper jubilantly declared: "We now have it in our power to place Louisiana beyond the reach of Locofocoism and to retain its government in our hands for years to come." [42]

The new constitution was a victory for the commercial forces. Besides empowering the legislature to charter banks by special or general laws, it ended the previous twenty-five year limitation on the lives of corporations and authorized internal-improvement companies to raise money by public subscriptions.[43] In 1853, the same year the new constitution was adopted, the Louisiana legislature passed a free-banking act.[44] This law required only a 33⅓ per cent specie reserve for deposits, since notes were considered adequately backed by bonds. One historian has concluded that its provisions represented a step backward from the 1842 law.[45] By the end of the decade of the 1850s, the amount of banking capital in the state had more than doubled.[46]

On the eve of the Civil War, after a decade of free banking, Alabama had eight banks with a total capital of 4,901,000 dollars. This was only one third of the bank capital the state was reported to have had in the early 1840s. Furthermore, one historian of the state has concluded that these remaining banks were safer and more responsible, for their "charters . . . carried more restraints than the earlier charters, particu-

---

[40] Reed, *New Orleans and the Railroads*, 62–63.

[41] Caldwell, *Banking History of Louisiana*, 82–83.

[42] Baton Rouge *Gazette*, July 10, 1852, as quoted in Roger W. Shugg, *Origins of Class Struggle in Louisiana: A Social History of White Farmers and Laborers During Slavery and After, 1840–1875* (Baton Rouge, La., 1939), 136.

[43] Shugg, *Origins of Class Struggle in Louisiana*, 137.

[44] Caldwell, *Banking History of Louisiana*, 84–86.

[45] Redlich, *Molding of American Banking*, II, Part 2, 10.

[46] In 1853 Louisiana had 10.9 million dollars of banking capital. By 1861 there was 24.6 million dollars of bank capital in the state. See the *Comptroller's Report, 1876*, 112–13.

larly regarding note issues." Alabamians, he claims, "had learned at great cost valuable lessons about banks. . . ."[47]

4

In the Southwest, Democrats as well as Whigs had been caught up in the banking mania of the period before the Panic and depression. However, after 1837, and especially after 1839, most Democrats took the position that the banks had to be reformed or, failing that, destroyed. Many reforms proposed by the Democrats were based on the notion that specie should act as a kind of financial balance wheel, an automatic, internal regulator of banking, and that the amount of specie in each bank's vaults would determine the amount of notes that it would be permitted to circulate. Most of the banks, however, in Mississippi, Alabama, and Arkansas, were beyond reviving and closed their doors in the 1840s as a result of government action and/or economic necessity. As a result, the Democratic party in the Southwest became in the 1840s the envy of the nation's hard-money men. It was hoped that the militant hard-money attack, which had virtually rid the section of banks, would be duplicated in other sections of the country.

Southwestern banks were defended, as a general rule, by a virtually united Whig party and a small group of soft-money Democrats who feared the economic consequences of a bankless society. And although the Whigs denied that they were the bank party, it would have been politically impossible for them to take a militant antibank position and still keep their normal political support.

The victory of the agrarian-minded hard-money Democrats was not as complete or final as they had hoped. Shutting down the banks did not solve the problem. Agitation increased for banking, credit, and exchange facilities as the memory of the depression dimmed and economic conditions returned to normal. And in the early 1850s free-banking laws were passed in Louisiana and Alabama.

Significantly, in the two decades from 1830 to 1850 both Louisiana and Alabama were experiencing a much slower growth in population than Mississippi and Arkansas. Thus, in the two less mature and set-

[47] Moore, *History of Alabama*, 314; *Comptroller's Report, 1876*, 112–13.

tled states of the Southwest the fear of banking remained, and, despite conditions of rapid growth, times often conducive to an easy-money policy, the specter of 1837 and the hard-money reaction provided a deterrent to another period of bank and credit expansion. Also, the large planters of Mississippi and, perhaps, Arkansas, by the very nature of their operations, probably depended almost entirely upon New Orleans and Mobile credit and exchange facilities.

CHAPTER VI

Ohio

I

IF MISSISSIPPI represented the most rural and agricultural state in the two western sections, Ohio was the most industrially and commercially advanced. Ohio was a land of contrasts, where the frontier and commercial ways of life were blended together. The state was as urban as Cincinnati, the most cosmopolitan and industrially active city in the West outside of New Orleans, and as agrarian as the countless farms and hamlets that dotted the verdant and rolling landscape of the interior counties. A few Ohioans were as isolated as the Mississippi Piney Woods countrymen, but, in general, farmers were served by the numerous market centers scattered throughout the state.

The Democratic party was more highly organized in Ohio than in Mississippi, and local and state conventions, meetings, and celebrations were held with regularity. Towns, especially on court days, were rallying points for political speeches, debates, and discussions. As a result, Democratic constituents in Ohio were considerably more active and played a larger role in shaping party policy than their counterparts in Mississippi.

Ohio was older and more mature politically and economically than Mississippi. Consequently, the rate of growth immediately preceding the Panic had not been nearly so strenuous as it had been in Mississippi. In the two decades from 1830 to 1850, Ohio's population a little more than doubled, while Mississippi's increased nearly four and one half times.[1] In 1838 Ohio reported thirty-eight banks with 11.3 million dollars of capital and 17.2 million dollars of loans and discounts. The

[1] *Historical Statistics,* 13.

same year Mississippi had twenty-six banks with 19.2 million dollars in capital and 28.99 million dollars in loans and discounts. The Ohio banks had a specie–note ratio of 26 cents of specie for every dollar of circulation and deposits, while the Mississippi banks had a ratio of only 6 cents of specie to the dollar. The contrast between the banking systems in the two states is further illustrated by the prices of their bank notes in Philadelphia the same year. The notes of the Mississippi banks fluctuated from a discount of 15 to 35 per cent, while the more stable Ohio notes ranged from 4 to 7 per cent.[2]

Ohioans had been less extravagant than Mississippians in participating in the boom times of the middle 1830s, and as a result, when the bubble burst, hard times were not quite as severe in the northwestern state. This was noted by one observer who commented in 1842, near the depth of the depression, that Cincinnati was not in as bad straits as some other places.

The scarcity of money has crippled all business. Little is doing, either in trade or manufactures, and all transactions are for cash. Had not the banks and the business men of Cincinnati been sound, the ruin would have been great, and the distress deplorable. But there has been less of wild speculation here, and far less bloated credit, than at most places, and our city maintains a healthy existence though reduced in wealth and activity.[3]

Despite the differences between Mississippi and Ohio, the Democratic party in both states reacted in much the same way to the Panic and depression. After an initial period of marking time, Democrats in the two states advocated a radical and comprehensive program of bank reform and ultimately supported the winding up and destruction of all banks. In Ohio the banks had more friends in both parties than in Mississippi, and as a consequence the bank war was longer and more bitter there, not reaching a climax until the state's constitutional convention in 1850.

The initial political effect of the Panic in Ohio was to force both parties, and the factions within them, to warily size up one another's positions. What the political consequences of the economic collapse would

[2] *Comptroller's Report, 1876,* 86–87, 113, 119.
[3] Cincinnati, Ohio, *Daily Chronicle,* November 5, 1842, as quoted in Thomas Senior Berry, *Western Prices Before 1861, A Study of the Cincinnati Market* (Cambridge, Mass., 1943), 468–69.

be was not immediately obvious. Amid charges and countercharges, definite lines of cleavage did not emerge for several years. The Democrats were branded bank destructionists; and the label "bank party" was pinned on the Whigs. Both parties were vulnerable, as there was much truth in the partisan rhetoric. But, nonetheless, the Democrats in the early years went to great lengths to deny the Whig allegations, and yet at the same time to assure their followers that the party was fundamentally antibank. The Whigs charged that the whole financial mess was due to Jackson's ruinous policies. In destroying the Bank of the United States and enforcing the Specie Circular, Jackson, they felt, had disrupted the delicate mechanism of "a complicated machine." [4] At the same time, the image of the Whig party as a political entity traditionally had been closely tied to the now discredited banking system. A Whig editor recognized this liability when in the summer of 1837 he advised his party to choose as candidates for the legislature only those "men who are entirely disconnected with *Bank direction,* or *heavy Bank investments.*" [5]

Even in the areas of the state that later became hotbeds of hard-money sentiment, Democratic reaction was tentative. There was no call, as there would be in later years, for sweeping change, no call for an all-metallic currency, no call for the destruction of the banking system. Hamilton County Democrats, for instance, urged bank reforms but insisted that they were not "contending for an exclusive metallic currency, or the abolition of all credit, which the opposition . . . [had] falsely charged. . . ." [6]

To listen merely to the rhetoric of Ohio political leaders in the early months following the Panic, one would have thought the two parties to be in virtual agreement. The banks should be reformed, but not destroyed. Yet, even the early reaction to the Panic belied any consensus. The Whigs quickly introduced a proposal to revoke the Democratically enacted small-note law and, thus, to permit the banks to resume issuing notes in denominations under 5 dollars. All the Democrats in

[4] New York *Journal of Commerce,* as quoted in the Columbus *Ohio State Journal,* July 24, 1837.

[5] *Ibid.*

[6] Resolutions of meeting sent to Martin Van Buren in letter from Moses Dawson, September 29, 1837, in the Martin Van Buren Papers.

the 1837–1838 legislature voted against the proposal to offer some measure of leniency to the banks. They were in the minority, however, and were unable to stop the passage of the bill, with all the Whigs, except one, voting in favor of it.[7]

The election in the fall of 1838, in which the Democrats were successful in elevating Wilson Shannon to the governor's chair and in capturing a majority of the seats in both houses of the legislature, gave the Democrats the power to act on the banking issue for the first time after the Panic.[8] Responsibility for formulating some kind of Democratic policy fell on the shoulders of John Brough, chairman of the committee on banking and currency in the state house of representatives. Reform was the keynote of the committee report, which proposed to enforce limited individual liability upon the stockholders,[9] to appoint three state bank commissioners to oversee banking operations, to limit bank-note issues to three times the amount of specie held, and to require any banks that failed to pay specie for thirty days in any single year to forfeit their charters. This was, according to Brough's committee, "all that the people require. They do not seek here any measure of annihilation of these institutions. . . ."[10]

Again the Whigs stood in opposition to any attempt to curtail or reform bank operations. In this case they aimed their fire against the stockholder-liability provision, which they claimed would necessitate amending existing bank charters. This they believed to be unconstitutional and a device by which the Democrats could force the entire Whig party against the bill so that the people would conclude that Whigs were against bank reform.[11] Earlier, Brough himself had confi-

[7] *Ibid.*, December 8, 1837; Huntington, *Banking and Currency in Ohio,* 161–62; Columbus *Daily Journal and Register,* March 5, 1838.

[8] *Niles' Register,* October 20 and 27, 1838. There were nineteen Democrats and seventeen Whigs in the senate, while the house was made up of thirty-eight Democrats and thirty-four Whigs.

[9] This individual liability proposal applied only when the "banks may owe more than one and a half times the amount of their capital stock, or when they shall have in circulation more than three dollars to one of specie in their vaults. . . ." Furthermore, the stockholders were liable only for the amount of stock owned. House *Executive Document No. 227,* 627–40. Also Huntington, *Banking and Currency in Ohio,* 164.

[10] *Ibid.*

[11] Circlesville, Ohio, *Herald,* as quoted in the Columbus *Daily Journal and Register,* February 4, 1839.

dentially expressed doubts as to whether the judiciary would uphold this tampering with the charters of the banks.[12]

This Bank Commissioner Bill became law despite Whig opposition. The banks were loath to accept its provisions, but the refusal of the state supreme court to prevent the bank commissioners from examining the books of a Cincinnati bank persuaded them to acquiesce to its provisions.[13]

The banks resumed specie payment in the summer of 1838, and so, although there were a few cries for stricter bank regulations, most Democrats probably considered the problem settled. John Brough's report had led to a law radical enough to mollify the majority of the more discontented within the party without destroying the banks. Few would have predicted then that the banking issue would, within even a few months, develop into a bitter and lengthy fight that would threaten the very structure of the party.

2

The second bank suspension hit the country in the fall of 1839.[14] This dampened hopes that the jolt of the Panic of 1837 would result in simply a temporary economic dislocation. Ohioans, as well as other Americans, reluctantly began accepting the fact that there was no end in sight for the hard times and bank instability. The 1839 suspension brought quite contradictory responses from different Democrats. To radicals, such as Moses Dawson, editor of the Cincinnati *Advertiser and Journal,* the suspension served to reinforce the long-held opinion that the banking system was basically defective and that the Bank Commissioner Law, as a moderate reform intended to prop up the existing system, was hopelessly inadequate. On the other hand, soft-money men, such as Thomas Hamer, reacted to the suspension with sympathy and patience for the hard-pressed banks.

A naturalized Irish-American, Dawson was a long-time friend of

[12] John Brough to Benjamin Tappan, November 8, 1838, Benjamin Tappan Papers, Ohio Historical Society.

[13] Huntington, *Banking and Currency in Ohio,* 166.

[14] It is not entirely clear what immediate impact the suspension had upon the Ohio banks. There are indications that some Ohio banks managed to delay a general suspension until 1841. See *Ibid.,* 163–64.

Andrew Jackson and a champion of the cause of the radical Democracy in the Cincinnati area. He was an ardent supporter of Martin Van Buren and in 1837 had immediately hailed the President's Independent Treasury proposal, avowing that it had "raised the confidence of one portion of the democracy and fixed the wavering of another. . . ." [15] Dawson had a fundamental distrust of monopolies and banks. "Those charters that have an evil influence on our people," he wrote, "and such as have conveyed to corporations those exclusive privileges of which that people have had to complain" should be expunged from the statute books. Furthermore, banks "should be regulated by law, and not by the selfish, mercenary dispositions of those men who become rich without labor, who accumulate fortunes at the expense of the producing classes of the community, and who take every opportunity of oppressing those classes. . . ." The testy old radical editor concluded that he rejoiced "to find that the principles of what is by the monopolists and their dupes falsely called agrarianism are spreading through the country with the rapidity of lightning. . . ." [16] By the summer of 1839, several months before the suspension, Dawson appealed to his readers that "a radical reform in the banking system in this state is every day becoming more and more necessary." [17] By the fall of that year he had come to the position that the banks should be given no quarter and that those refusing to pay specie should be treated as delinquent debtors and their property made responsible to their creditors. Although bank officials protested that this would force them to coerce their debtors, Dawson retorted that it would work a hardship only on bank directors and stockholders who had obtained most of the credit. [18]

Thomas L. Hamer, a conservative Democrat from Brown County, on the Ohio River, responded quite differently to the suspension. It is not clear whether Hamer was personally interested in banks, but he had always been a strong supporter of the banking system. In 1839 he wrote to Secretary of the Treasury Levi Woodbury urging him to place government deposits in the Commercial Bank of Cincinnati where the "principal officers . . . are gentlemen of undoubted integrity

---

[15] Moses Dawson to Martin Van Buren, September 9, 1837, Martin Van Buren Papers.

[16] Cincinnati *Advertiser and Journal*, April 5 and 12, 1837.

[17] *Ibid.*, July 31 and August 5, 1839.   [18] *Ibid.*, October 22, 1839.

and warm friends of the administration."[19] One factor pushing Hamer toward the soft position was the extreme shortage of currency in his part of the state. With no specie or Ohio paper, that area was solely dependent upon "Indiana paper, with now and then a straggling Kentucky bank bill." And if the Indiana bank should fail, the counties "would be literally without a currency of any kind."[20]

Born in Pennsylvania and moving to Ohio as a young man, Hamer's career exemplifies the proverbial rags to riches folk myth. It was recounted that Hamer began his quest for fame and fortune "with only one suit of clothes, that of homespun, on his back, and a cash capital of 'one and sixpence.' "[21] Befriended and tutored in law by Thomas Morris (United States Senator from Ohio between 1833 and 1839), Hamer later broke with and denounced his early patron. A critic described Hamer as having a "clear, strong, vigorous, discriminating mind" but also as a person who, "for the sake of gratifying personal ambition, lends himself to base party purposes, whenever, by so doing, he can secure consideration for himself, with his party."[22] The characterization was a telling one. The pragmatic Hamer, although critical of the dominant hard-money faction of the party, always managed to stay within the bounds of political propriety. And despite disputes with the state party on the currency issue, he carefully maintained good relations with the national party. After representing his constituency in Congress from 1833 to 1839, Hamer was appointed Brigadier General by President James K. Polk during the Mexican War. This office was to be his last. He died of fever in Mexico at the age of forty-six.[23]

After the suspension in 1839, Hamer admitted that it had created a

---

[19] Thomas L. Hamer to Levi Woodbury, October 18, 1839, Levi Woodbury Papers, Series II.

[20] *Ohio Eagle,* as quoted in the Columbus *Ohio State Journal,* June 2, 1842.

[21] Henry Howe, *Historical Collections of Ohio, An Encyclopedia of the State* (Cincinnati, 1907), I, 331. Three editions of Howe's work were consulted in the course of this study: the two-volume edition cited above, the two-volume 1896 edition published in Norwalk, Ohio, and the one-volume 1847 edition published in Cincinnati.

[22] As quoted in Frances P. Weisenburger, *The Passing of the Frontier, 1825–1850* (Columbus, Ohio, 1941), 326.

[23] Howe, *Historical Collections of Ohio,* (1907 edition) I, 331. See also B. Franklin Morris, editor, *The Life of Thomas Morris* (Cincinnati, 1856), 398–99.

sensation in his county but argued that public confidence in the banks' "ultimate solvency seems to be but little shaken." The government and the people, he felt, should keep firmly in mind the distinctions between specie-paying and non-specie-paying banks. Some banks in the West, Hamer reported, were strong enough to hold out against suspension. "Shall we not extend aid and comfort to them," he asked, "where it can be done consistently with our principles and with the constitution and laws of the country?" [24]

Wilson Shannon, conservative Democratic governor, stunned Moses Dawson and other radicals by giving public voice to this soft-money sentiment in his message to the legislature in December of 1839. A political acrobat, Shannon had exceptional success in maintaining his balance in the rough and tumble politics of ante-bellum Ohio. The first Ohio governor born in the state, Shannon, like Hamer, was tempered suitably by hardships and economic deprivations in keeping with nineteenth-century political folklore. Losing his father at an early age, he, with the help of his brothers, attended three institutions of higher learning but left school without being graduated to take up the study of law. Shannon was admitted to the bar and served as prosecuting attorney for Belmont County from 1833 to 1837. Little known outside his local area, he was, nevertheless, nominated by the Democrats for governor in 1838 and successfully ran on a bank-reform platform. Defeated for re-election in 1840, Shannon won a second term in 1842. Assailed by the hards for his heretical soft-money notions, Shannon seemingly was completely discredited in the eyes of most Democrats at the end of his second term. Resigning the governorship in 1844, he threw in his lot with President John Tyler and his collection of renegades from both parties and was appointed Minister to Mexico. Recalled for ineptitude, this Ohio Ishmael next led a band of gold seekers to California in 1849. Returning to Ohio, he recouped his political fortunes by being elected to Congress in the early 1850s.[25]

[24] Thomas L. Hamer to Levi Woodbury, October 18, 1839, Levi Woodbury Papers, Series II.

[25] Ultimately, Shannon was appointed by President Franklin Pierce to be governor of the Kansas territory. But this endeavor worked out unsuccessfully, and Shannon finally retired from public life. For short sketches of Shannon's life, see Howe, *Historical Collections of Ohio* (1907 edition), I, 313. Also Ohio Historical Society, *The Governors of Ohio* (Columbus, 1954), 42–45.

In his message of December, 1839, Shannon maintained that banking institutions were necessary and that "a system of independent banks properly restricted and limited in their powers, placed under the supervision of bank commissioners, and being at all times under the control of the legislature, if not the best system that could be adopted, is perhaps the best within our reach, for the present, or for some time to come."[26]

Shannon's message, which apparently accepted the permanency of the existing banking system and paper currency, struck like a bombshell and thrust him into the forefront as a target for antibank Democrats, especially in Hamilton, Butler, and Columbiana counties. One Hamilton County Jacksonian accused him of betraying his party because he had given the impression that he was against the banks, and it was on this ground that he had been elected. His message was labeled an "unparalleled piece of effrontery and impudence."[27]

Moses Dawson complained that Shannon had simply used the arguments against the impracticability of a specie currency that advocates of a paper credit system had used for years. To accept Shannon's reasoning, the old editor argued, would mean that "banks, and paper banks, too, must be entailed upon the country forever; for surely the longer it continues, the more deeply it will become rooted in the community. . . ."[28]

The revolt proved to be little more than a tempest in a teapot. Brokers were working behind the scenes to put down the rebellion and to keep the party together. One Democratic politician summed up the situation thus:

The governor's message has not met with that cordial reception that could have been desired by his friends. His Bank notions go a little too far and I think I can see some disposition in many of our friends to lay Shannon aside and take a new man but I think . . . to now lay him aside, though they think that he has in some measure deviated from the Democratic channel, would produce . . . disunion in our ranks—and serious consequences would result from it. I cannot go with the Governor in some of his notions but still I think that it will be good policy to "try him

26 Holt, "Party Politics in Ohio," 503.
27 Cincinnati *Advertiser and Journal,* December 10, 12, 13, 14, and 16, 1839.
28 *Ibid.,* December 7, 1839.

again." His policy will not take generally in the state but still in many
parts it is popular.[29]

Another man, calling himself a "radical," maintained that he disap-
proved of many of Shannon's statements on the bank question but, on
second thought, concluded that Shannon's message could be politically
useful, for it would "silence and prevent Whig clamor." Shannon, he
predicted, would take a more cautious path in the future.[30]

John Brough was concerned about the uproar against Shannon. But
as the renomination showdown neared, Brough became more confident
of avoiding a major party split, claiming that the "feeling in relation to
the message is gradually softening down, and will yield readily to the
renomination of Shannon. . . ."[31]

Brough was right. The dominant mood of the convention was conservative and moderate. This was reflected in the resolutions passed,
the election of Thomas L. Hamer as president of the meeting, and the
renomination of Shannon by acclamation. The delegates, in a rather
ambiguous fashion, resolved that the General Assembly should pursue
bank reform "with zeal and energy, until all the rottenness of the present system has been fully exposed, and effectual measures adopted to
secure the people against future frauds and impositions."[32]

Immediately after the convention, Dawson's paper was strangely si-
lent. But within two weeks Shannon's name as candidate for governor
was placed on the masthead along with Martin Van Buren and R. M.
Johnson for President and Vice President.[33] This apparent party harmony, however, was to no avail. The Whigs handed the Democrats a
crushing defeat in the fall of 1840, capturing both the governorship and
a majority in the legislature.

[29] T. Buchanan to William Medill, December 15, 1839, William Medill Papers,
Library of Congress.

[30] C. A. Barker to William Medill, December 13, 1839, William Medill Papers.

[31] John Brough to William Medill, December 7 and 25, 1839, and John Cassell
to William Medill, December 18, 1839; William Medill Papers.

[32] Cincinnati *Advertiser and Journal,* January 11 and 14, 1840; John P. Helfen-
steine to Levi Woodbury, January 9, 1840, Levi Woodbury Papers, Series I.

[33] Cincinnati *Advertiser and Journal,* January 21, 1840.

3

By the time the Democrats recaptured a majority in the legislature in 1841,[34] they were confronted with the impending expiration of most of the state's bank charters in January, 1843. The radicals, who as the depression deepened were becoming increasingly more vocal in their hard-money militancy, were in a key position. They could no longer be stalled, for some action had to be taken on the banking question.

Several options were open to the Democrats: to allow banking in Ohio to die a natural death by the expiration of the bank charters, to extend the charters of the existing banks, or to pass a general law with stringent reforms and force any bank that desired to continue in business to accept its provisions. The third alternative eventually prevailed because it was the only one of the three that both hards and softs would join in supporting. The softs could never have been induced by the hards simply to allow the demise of banking in the state through the expiration of the charters. The hards, for their part, would never have sanctioned the extension of the lives of the existing banks, which they believed to be rotten and broken institutions operating under monopolistic and permissive charters. Still, the general-law compromise was for the hards a shrewdly plotted, deceptive course of action. While allegedly favoring reform of the banks, leaders of this faction were in reality working toward bank destruction by incorporating into the general law provisions so stiff that they were convinced (and rightly so, it was to turn out) that Ohio bankers would not seek charter renewals. In the unlikely event that the new regulations would be accepted, the hards reasoned, the resulting banking system would be more in harmony with the public welfare.

The first issue to be considered by the 1841–1842 legislature, however, was a bill calling for the resumption of specie payment by the banks in March, 1842. The Democrats, even before the session had begun, had resolved in convention that the banks should be forced to resume specie payment at the earliest possible date and that those that failed to

[34] *Niles' Register,* November 13, 1841. Both houses were closely divided. In the senate there were nineteen Democrats and seventeen Whigs, while in the house there were thirty-seven Democrats and thirty-five Whigs.

comply should "surrender their charters and wind up. . . ." "Let the banks pay up or break up!" was the way it had been put in the Cincinnati *Enquirer*,[35] the successor to Dawson's old *Advertiser and Journal,* which had passed into the hands of John Brough and his brother, Charles.

When the bill came before the legislature, three conservative Democrats joined the Whigs in the senate and supported an amendment that would have given the banks additional time to resume specie payments, defending their action by arguing that requiring the banks to resume by March was tantamount to destroying the banks.[36] The amendment failed by a vote of 17 to 17,[37] and two of the renegade Democrats withdrew their support for a more gradual resumption and voted with their party to set the resumption date for March 4.[38]

The second bill passed during the session was the controversial general banking act, named Latham's Law after its author, Allen Latham. Basically, it required that all capital be paid in specie, that banks be inspected by commissioners, that a bank's liabilities (with the exception of deposits) be limited to one and one half times capital, that one third of the circulation be held in specie, that taxes be fixed at one half of one per cent on paid-up capital, and that officers be made liable for mismanagement or loss of capital.[39]

The Whigs accused the Democrats of deception, dubbing the bill, "Latham's humbug." They were, in general, correct in their analysis that the real motive of the Democratic radicals was to use the general bank bill to eliminate banking in Ohio. But it was not until the next year, that C. J. McNulty, a radical Democrat, admitted publicly that the Latham Bill had been a humbug and had been passed only as a highly political electioneering device.[40] Through it the hards had hoped to retain as wide support as possible by giving lip service to the idea of reform while in actuality presuming that the bill would sound the death knell to banking in Ohio.

Most of the more conservative Democrats accepted the bill uneasily,

---

[35] Cincinnati *Enquirer,* January 10 and 11, February 2, 1842.

[36] Columbus *Ohio State Journal,* February 9, 1842.

[37] *Ibid.,* February 15, 1842.   [38] *Ibid.; Niles' Register,* February 19, 1842.

[39] Sumner, *History of Banking,* 400–403; Knox, *History of Banking,* 673–74; Huntington, *Banking and Currency in Ohio,* 177–78.

[40] Cincinnati *Enquirer,* January 11 and 16, 1843.

realizing that it was probably all they could get. However two softs in the house refused to vote with their party on the final passage,[41] and Latham (a wealthy man and a stockholder in the Bank of Scioto) did not vote for his own bill during the final vote in the senate. It came back from the house with so many amendments, he later explained, that it became "impracticable and a humbug." [42]

During the entire session, the hard-money men had been hard pressed to hold the support of the conservative Democrats. One hard had attacked the wavering of some of his colleagues:

. . . there were men smiling around this Legislature—hovering about members, who were exerting a baneful and dangerous influence. It did seem almost impossible for the people to secure a faithful representative of their principles and wishes in the halls of the Legislature. You may send men here, culled fresh from the ranks of the people . . . devoted in their professions and promises, but in five or six weeks they began to fall off, to become pliant and yielding, to swerve from their duty, the victims of the seductions of bank officers with the corruption of hell, who hovered round the Legislature, to defeat by their sinister appliances the wants and wishes of the people.[43]

Less than a month after the passage of the 1842 general banking act, a group of conservative Democrats met in West Union in Adams County to denounce the tack the Democratic party was taking. Prominent among this group was Thomas Hamer, who moved for the adoption of resolutions that called for the establishment of a "well regulated Banking system" in Ohio, offering "safety to the bill holders, a fair profit to the bankers" and, at the same time, a "currency convertible into specie at the will of the holder." It was regrettable, the resolutions stated, that a radical hard-money faction opposed to all banks of circulation was growing in Ohio and "steadily . . . preparing for a war of extermination upon all paper currency. . . ." [44]

The West Union resolutions, according to Hamer, represented the true position of the Democratic party on the banking question. Although Samuel Medary, radical editor of the *Ohio Statesman*, and the

[41] Columbus *Ohio State Journal*, February 26, 1842.

[42] *Ibid.*, January 20 and 21, 1843; Cincinnati *Enquirer*, January 23, 1843.

[43] Columbus *Ohio State Journal*, February 15, 1842.

[44] Columbus *Ohio State Journal* and Cincinnati *Republican*, as quoted in the Cincinnati *Enquirer*, April 16, 1842.

hard-money clique represented only 10 per cent of the party, Hamer charged, the general bank law was the work of this group and calculated to rid the state of banks. The vast majority of the people of Ohio wanted a well-regulated system of banking, and if the Democrats would not provide it, the people would turn to the Whigs. Hamer challenged any Democrats who wanted "to prohibit banking altogether" to "come out like men and say so, and make the issue, '*Bank or no Bank*'—and not be guilty of the meanness and cowardice of pretending to be bank men, whilst they are inducing the confiding, inexperienced and unwary portion of the democracy to agree to restrictions. . . ." To Hamer's disdain, the theories of John Taylor of Caroline appeared to be the "polar star" by which Medary and other hards were "steering." This worn-out dogma, "after a profound sleep of nearly thirty years," Hamer complained, had "been raked up from the rubbish of a past generation and made the standard for the Ohio Democracy. . . ." [45]

The West Union apostasy brought an immediate response from the hards. Medary attacked Hamer as a bank attorney and debtor who had become the banks' "most obsequious defender and apologist." [46] Another Democrat, defending the general banking law, said that if the bankers would not submit to regulations and restrictions and conduct their business upon the "same principle of individual responsibility, which regulates the business transactions of all our private citizens . . . then . . . I shall be proud to know that I am classed with your 'hard money faction.' " [47] There was considerable discussion within Democratic circles as to what Hamer's motives had been. One speculated that Hamer hoped to "throw into the next legislature enough . . . doubtful democrats to hold the balance of power" and to thwart the reelection of Senator William Allen, a radical. [48] A Cincinnati Democratic newspaper appealed to the Democrats of Highland and Brown counties to forsake the leadership of Hamer. "Will you," the paper asked, "be made the plaything of any man's caprice or ambition?" [49]

[45] *Ohio Eagle*, as quoted in Columbus *Ohio State Journal*, June 2, 1842; Georgetown, Ohio, *Standard*, as quoted in Columbus *Ohio State Journal*, July 23, 1842, and August 10, 1842.

[46] Cincinnati *Enquirer*, July 12, 1842.   [47] *Ibid.*, April 22, 1842.

[48] M. Birchard to Benjamin Tappan, May 23, 1842, Benjamin Tappan Papers, Library of Congress.

[49] Cincinnati *Enquirer*, May 30, 1842.

Some of the hard-money Democrats were in no mood for compromise. Edwin M. Stanton, from his home in Steubenville in Jefferson County, wrote to his law partner Benjamin Tappan, in the United States Senate, that Hamer's resolutions were "a very lucky move" for the Democratic party, for "the Bank men will now form a distinct organization and we shall get rid of them." [50]

The public discussion between the warring factions in the Democratic party did little to clarify the issue. The question remained: was it true, as some were now charging, that the Democratic party had attempted by subterfuge to eliminate all banks of issue? Or was the bank act of 1842 a legitimate attempt to reform the system? And if the banks refused the terms offered in the general law, thus bringing about (whether intentionally or not) the elimination of banks from the state, what should the next move of the party be?

The answer was not clear. What was clear, however, was that any answer or solution would further split the party. Cautious ambiguity seemed to be the watchword. One Democratic meeting resolved

. . . that although we repudiate and repel with indignant contempt the epithet of *"a hard money faction"* which the demagogues and federalists attempt to fix upon us, we will hail the day which will restore to us a gold and silver currency, for all ordinary transactions, as only less glorious than that which made us an independent nation and a free people.[51]

The Democrats increased their margin in the legislature in the election of 1842.[52] This victory, however, did not alleviate the feuding within the party. A hard-money Democrat from Henry County, J. B. Steedman,[53] worried whether the balloting represented a "triumph of

[50] Edwin M. Stanton to Tappan, April 22, 1842, Benjamin Tappan Papers, Library of Congress. For information on pro-bank sentiment near Steubenville see: Cincinnati *Enquirer*, May 13, 1842; Edwin M. Stanton to Benjamin Tappan, April 20, 1842, and July 17, 1842, Benjamin Tappan Papers, Ohio Historical Society; Edwin M. Stanton to Unknown (presumably Benjamin Tappan), May 31, 1842, Edwin M. Stanton Papers, Library of Congress. A faction led by J. Means and closely tied by stock ownership to the Farmers' and Mechanics' Bank in Steubenville had become alienated from the party because it had failed to extend the bank's charter. But with Stanton's leadership and support, the Means faction had been read out of the party by the summer of 1842.

[51] Cincinnati *Enquirer*, June 13, 1842. See also issue of June 7, 1842.

[52] The 1842–1843 legislature had twenty-two Democrats and fourteen Whigs in the senate, while there were forty-two Democrats and thirty Whigs in the house. *Niles' Register*, November 12, 1842.

[53] Originally from Louisville, Ky., Steedman moved to the Maumee Valley in

the pure anti-bank democracy, or, have we only succeeded in displacing one set of bank swindlers to make room for another set who go in for a more moderate system of robbery?" If the Democratic party had run on a hard-money platform throughout the state, as they had in Steedman's district, he was confident that they would have won an even more overwhelming victory.[54]

Steedman's fears proved valid. When the legislature met for the 1842–1843 session, it soon became obvious that a majority of the Democrats had become convinced that some modification of the 1842 law was necessary. It was reported that conservative Wilson Shannon, who had been re-elected governor, believed that unless the Democratic legislature would "incorporate the *solvent banks* whose charters expire this winter, with *reasonable restrictions,* we will be driven into a hopeless minority at the next election." [55] Thus, the hards were faced with a revolt by the softs and even a few moderate hards unless a new bank law, more palatable to bankers, was passed.

As a temporary expedient aimed at buying time until a more nearly permanent solution could be worked out, the Democrats introduced a bill to give short extensions to the expiring bank charters. It was not intended as a reform measure, but it did contain an individual liability clause.

Ironically, the measure was defeated by the bedrock hards and the Whigs.[56] These hards claimed that they refused to go along with the majority of their party either because they were against the entire paper system or because the banks whose charters would be extended were insolvent and "had been seven times condemned by the voice of the people." The Whigs rejected the measure on the grounds that its

---

1837, becoming a canal contractor. He served in the state house of representatives in the early 1840s and as a member of the state board of public works in the early 1850s. See H. S. Knapp, *History of the Maumee Valley* (Toledo, 1877), 651.

[54] J. B. Steedman to Unknown (presumably Benjamin Tappan), October 25, 1842, Benjamin Tappan Papers, Library of Congress.

[55] George M. McCook to Benjamin Tappan, December 15, 1842, Benjamin Tappan Papers, Library of Congress.

[56] The vote was ten Democrats and twenty-eight Whigs opposed, thirty Democrats and two Whigs in favor. See Cincinnati *Enquirer,* December 29, 1842. See also issues of December 28, 1842, January 2 and 10, 1843; and Columbus *Ohio State Journal,* January 3, 1843.

provisions were too strict. Particularly obnoxious to them was the individual liability clause. Many Whigs also realized that the longer the bank issue could be kept alive, the better the chance for the Democratic party to be rendered politically impotent by factional feuding.[57]

Hard-money Democrats contributing to the defeat of the bill were soundly denounced. Two of them, C. J. McNulty and Legrand Byington, were ridiculed by the Tuscarawas *Democrat* as "a couple of demagogues in the Legislature . . . that should be . . . hungup by their heels a little while, for their downright knavery." [58]

In a party caucus, or "tinpan," the Democrats agreed upon a new compromise bank bill. A description of it by Stanton indicates that, as had been the case the previous year, the Democrats had little intention of allowing banking under it. This new proposal, Stanton wrote, "will not . . . do any other harm than always follows the taking [of] untenable ground, for no banking will be done under it and if adopted, it cannot bring along with it the power the old system possesses." The bank men, Stanton continued, "have already flinched, and it may be that our folks becoming provoked will kick over the whole concern." [59]

In the middle of February, 1843, the new banking bill was passed, amending and slightly relaxing the restrictions of 1842. The most important concession in the new law was the modification of the individual liability clause whereby the banks were released from liability for all claims except on their circulations. Not one bank, however, was to accept a new charter under this law.[60]

The new banking bill passed the lower house, 37 to 30, by a fairly strict party vote. Four Democrats joined the Whigs in an unsuccessful

[57] Cincinnati *Enquirer,* December 28 and 30, 1842. See also Edwin M. Stanton to Unknown (probably Benjamin Tappan), December 24, 1842, Edwin M. Stanton Papers.

[58] Tuscarawas, Ohio, *Democrat* as quoted in Cincinnati *Enquirer,* January 9, 1843.

[59] Edwin M. Stanton to Unknown (presumably Benjamin Tappan), Benjamin Tappan Papers, Ohio Historical Society, February 8, 1843.

[60] The bill provided that when a bank's assets were insufficient to meet its note liabilities, the creditors could "proceed against the Directors until their property is exhausted, and as a last resort . . . proceed against the Stockholders." Cincinnati *Enquirer,* February 25, 1843. Also see *Enquirer* issue of February 7, 1843; Huntington, *Banking and Currency in Ohio,* 177–78; Knox, *History of Banking,* 678; and Sumner, *History of Banking,* 402.

attempt to defeat the bill. Two of them were McNulty and Byington, who felt it was too lenient with the banks. Byington, however, subsequently changed his vote. In the senate, Latham and one other Democrat voted with the Whigs against the bill, which passed 19 to 12.[61]

The Democratic Zanesville *Aurora* probably reflected the sentiment of most Democrats when it claimed it was "glad this vexed question is settled." The paper warned the bankers not to follow the urgings of Whigs to refuse to participate under the general law, because "we will plant ourselves on the bill which has just been passed, and if bankers don't try it, why then let's try the alternative—hard money." [62]

4

The years 1844 and 1845 were discouraging ones for hard-money Democrats. The bank bill hammered out in 1842 and modified the following year was being ignored by bankers who, in an attempt to force its overthrow, were stubbornly refusing to do business under its provisions. And despite radical hopes that their refusal would bring an end to Ohio banking, it was the evasive strategy of the bankers that proved successful instead.

There was increasing popular sentiment for the banking services which had been drastically curtailed as a result of the general laws. While in 1842 there had been twenty-three banks with a combined capital of more than 7 million dollars in assets, by January, 1844, the number had dwindled to eight with a capital slightly in excess of 2.3 million dollars. H. C. Whitman, radical Democratic lawyer from Lancaster in Fairfield County, worriedly described the climate of opinion:

Taxes are very high—business dull and all the circumstances of business in Ohio tend to make all . . . jacket pocket arguments . . . weigh . . . with the people. . . . A feverish energy, partaking somewhat of desperation in its character, manifests itself in political, social, religious and business life—instability, impatience, and aversion to reflection, characterises our people. The maxims of Franklin, as of sound political economy, fall with

---

[61] Cincinnati *Enquirer*, February 16, 1843; Columbus *Ohio State Journal*, February 15, 1843; and *Niles' Register*, March 4, 1843.

[62] Zanesville, Ohio, *Aurora* as quoted in Cincinnati *Enquirer*, February 25, 1843.

cold effect on a people struggling to throw off in a moment, the incubus of debt and embarrassment caused by the ruinous policy of a paper money system continued for years. To preach economy, industry, and contentment with the results of the natural laws of Trade as the only remedies for the financial difficulties of the State, meets small favor, at present, while they are characterised as "Hard Money doctrines". . . . I consider our nation and especially a part of Ohio *sick* on the currency question . . . and like an individual who is sick, the nostrums of quack doctors promising immediate relief are often resorted to, in preference to the slow prescriptions of a regular Physician.[63]

William Medill observed a similar situation in his county, where he found a "cry for Banks-Banks." [64]

Thus, by late 1843 considerable pressure was being exerted upon the Democratic party to relax its opposition to the banks. Governor Shannon evidently was sensitive to the building sentiment, for the errant conservative Democrat shocked many in his party with his annual address to the legislature,[65] in which he seemed to reject the general banking laws of 1842 and 1843 as the settled policy toward the banks.[66] Democratic hards denounced him and predicted that his message would be used to good advantage by the Whigs and softs in overturning the settlement. Whitman wrote to Allen that there were "several soft Demos in the Senate who only waited for Shannon to lead on the currency question to show their hands." To discipline them, the Democrats would have to wait until after the close of the campaign of 1844, Whitman said. But then he hoped "the guillotine . . . [would] be put in operation in Ohio." [67]

[63] H. C. Whitman to William Allen, January 4, 1844, William Allen Papers.

[64] William Medill to William Allen, January 11, 1844, William Allen Papers; William Medill to Benjamin Tappan, January 12, 1844, Benjamin Tappan Papers, Library of Congress.

[65] The Democrats had a slight edge in the senate and the Whigs had a majority in the house in the 1843–1844 legislature. The approximate division was 20 to 16 in favor of the Democrats in the senate and 37 to 30 in favor of the Whigs in the house. *Niles' Register,* October 28, 1843.

[66] Cincinnati *Enquirer,* December 5, 1843; Columbus *Ohio State Journal,* December 6, 1843; House *Executive Document No. 226,* 1140–41.

[67] H. C. Whitman to William Allen, December 15, 1843, William Allen Papers; William Medill to Benjamin Tappan, December 14, 1843, Benjamin Tappan Papers, Library of Congress. Cincinnati *Enquirer,* December 8, 1843.

The worst fears of the hards were justified. Whigs and soft-money Democrats banded together to pass the Wooster Bank Bill, extending the charters of the Wooster and four other banks and exempting them from complying with the provisions of the general law. The vote in the Democratically controlled senate was 20 to 16 in favor of passage of the measure. Four Democrats deserted their party to vote with the Whigs, who were unanimous in their support. In the house, thirty Whigs, thirteen Democrats, two who called themselves Independent Democrats, and two of unknown party affiliation voted in favor. Negative ballots were cast by sixteen Democrats, five Whigs, and one unknown.[68]

The main body of Democrats opposed the Wooster Bill for a number of reasons. First, it opened up a subject that many assumed had been settled by the general laws of 1842 and 1843. Second, although on the surface at least the bill embraced the doctrine of individual liability, many felt that the specific clause was a mere sham and would be practically unenforceable. Third, the bill abolished the tax on capital (which Democrats considered to be more equitable and more in line with the taxes paid by individual citizens) and placed it on profits. And last, the Wooster Bill did away with the general-law provision requiring banks to register their notes and pay for the expense of the bank commissioners.[69]

The Democrats who voted for the Wooster Bank Bill held a meeting afterward in Columbus and resolved that the legislation embodied all the principles the party had fought for in 1838, 1840, and 1842. Of the forty-eight Democrats in the Ohio legislature that session, only sixteen signed the conservative manifesto, four of them in the senate and twelve in the house.[70]

---

[68] Cincinnati *Enquirer*, February 8, 13, and 15, 1844; Columbus *Ohio State Journal*, February 15, 1844; Holt, "Party Politics in Ohio," 550–51. The other four banks were the Lafayette Bank of Cincinnati, the Bank of Xenia, the Bank of Sandusky, and the Bank of Norwalk. See *Niles' Register*, October 28, 1843, for party affiliations. *Niles'* lists three legislators as Independent Democrats, which probably means conservative Democrats.

[69] Cincinnati *Enquirer*, February 2 and 17, 1844; Columbus *Ohio State Journal*, February 16, 1844.

[70] In a vote to organize the senate, a Democrat was elected over a Whig by a vote of 19 to 14. In the house, a Whig was elected, 38 to 29. Columbus *Ohio*

The reaction of the bulk of the party to the passage of the bill was bitter and heated. The four Democratic senators who had voted with the Whigs were particularly excoriated, since it had been expected that the Democratic-controlled senate would defeat any attempt by the Whig-controlled house to upset the banking settlement of 1843. James J. Faran, radical Democrat from Cincinnati and one-time speaker of the house, reported to Senator Allen that the outcome had caused many Democrats to give up politics, for "to be sold by those professing to be Democrats, in the hour of victory, makes them lose all confidence in the purity of men and the final and permanent triumph of democratic principles." [71]

The Wooster Bank Bill was especially significant because the Wooster Bank in Wayne County had been and continued to be the rallying point for conservative Democratic strength in Ohio. Stockholders and officers in the bank included both Whigs and Democrats who, despite their different political affiliations, worked extremely well together when banking matters became political problems. John P. Coulter, president of the bank and a Whig, had been supported in his bid for the state senate by "many bank Democrats. . . ." Benjamin Jones, Joseph S. Lake, and C. Lake, leading stockholders, were active in the conservative faction of the Democratic party. Wilson Shannon's "right hand man," William McMahon, was the bank's attorney. The Cleveland *Plain Dealer* was reportedly owned by Wooster Bank conservatives. And C. Lake, the cashier, was the agent for the *Plain Dealer* in Wayne County. [72]

Samuel Lahm, Democratic senator from Stark County and one of the Democratic senators who defied his party on the bill, was closely tied to the clique around the Wooster Bank. As a political reward for his vote, he was to receive support for a federal appointment to the office of Ohio district attorney. Also, it was reported that in the event the

---

State Journal, December 4, 1843. For the Columbus meeting, see issue of February 17, 1844.

[71] Cincinnati *Enquirer,* February 13, 1844; James J. Faran to William Allen, February 25, 1844, William Allen Papers. See also, J. T. Woodfall to William Allen, February 14, 1844, William Allen Papers.

[72] M. A. Goodfellow to Samuel Medary, April 15, 1845, and J. P. Spencer to William Allen, November 23, 1845, William Allen Papers; J. P. Spencer to William Medill, August 24, 1845, William Medill Papers.

appointment did not come through Lahm was to have the support of the Whigs and Wooster Bank Democrats in a bid for a congressional seat.[73]

A Democratic politician from Wooster, who voted against the Wooster bill and thus had been designated a marked man by the bank clique, claimed that the bank men had the approval of only one fourth of the local Democratic party. The rest supported true principles; "[they] consist of the bone and sinew of the party as we have but one merchant with us, in the town of Wooster, the balance are all softs and Whigs." [74]

In Carroll County, just below Stark, a Democratic editor had a more pessimistic view. Although a hard-money man himself, the journalist feared that the doctrine "would not meet the approbation of the party here," and that to advocate an exclusive metallic currency "would be a death-blow to our party." He concluded that the Democrats would have to wait for "the villanies of the banks themselves to work." [75]

The softs were not without powerful support. Wilson Shannon, long a headache for hards as well as for brokers trying to keep the party together, stated publicly that he would have voted for the Wooster Bank Bill had he been in the legislature and denied that the Democratic party ever had been the party of hard money. In most areas of the state, Shannon argued, the currency situation was critical. In Stark County, the "currency that is now paid out on the canal . . . is composed principally of St. Clair small bills, Pennsylvania relief notes, Rhode Island and Virginia paper." Concluding, the Governor contended that the people of Ohio wanted banks. The general laws of 1842 and 1843 were too strict, preventing bankers from doing business under them. Therefore the Democratic party would have to recognize the impracticability of its position.[76]

In the months following the passage of the Wooster Bank Bill, ru-

[73] William Dunstan and Daniel Gotshall to William Allen, March 14, 1845; M. A. Goodfellow to William Allen, January 20, 1845; and William Dunbar to William Allen, February 25, 1846; William Allen Papers.

[74] Charles Wolcott to William Allen, December 2, 1844, William Allen Papers. See also Wolcott's letter to Benjamin Tappan, September 22, 1844, Benjamin Tappan Papers, Library of Congress.

[75] A. W. Morrison to Benjamin Tappan, March 19, 1844, and April 6, 1844, Benjamin Tappan Papers, Library of Congress.

[76] Columbus *Ohio State Journal*, February 26, 1844.

mors were rife among Democrats as to the extent of Wooster Bank influence within the party. To many it appeared both far-reaching and devious. Adding to the ferment was the election of a Democrat, James K. Polk, as President in 1844, which opened up prospects for appointments to lucrative and politically powerful federal positions. Both hards and softs hoped to receive Polk's favor and thereby influence federal patronage in the state. This intensified intraparty antagonisms and, as Democrats competed for political preference, there were charges and counter-charges of party disloyalty.

The situation was too explosive even for the perennial broker, John Brough, who was distrusted by the hards and condemned by the softs. At one point his name cropped up as being supported for a federal appointment by the conservative faction. Seeming to corroborate these reports that Brough was slipping into the soft camp was the story that he had scotched a federal appointment for Medary.[77] Although it is not clear whether these rumors were correct, Brough, in a frank public letter in the summer of 1845, described his connections with the conservatives. He admitted that he had known Joseph Lake of the Wooster Bank for many years and that he had been asked to aid in getting the Polk Administration to transfer government funds to the bank. Although Brough proclaimed himself a consistent opponent of the Deposit System, he said that he had agreed to recommend the transfer anyway. Despite earlier reservations, he explained, he had determined by the summer of 1844 that the Wooster Bank was "as solvent as any institution in the state" and an admirable one in that it had lent its aid in helping to maintain the state's credit during difficult times. Nevertheless, Brough denied that he had, in fact, ever actually made the recommendation, claiming that the opportunity to do so had never presented itself. Finally, Brough insisted that his interest in the bank did not stem from improper motives. He "never had a dollar of money from the bank," he said, and "never an act of kindness, save the personal friendship of some who are or have been stockholders." [78]

---

[77] Brough had told Polk, so the story went, that the Ohio Democrats could not spare Medary. This Brough was said to have done in response to urgings of conservatives who wanted to punish Medary for his position on the currency question. M. A. Goodfellow to Samuel Medary, April 15, 1845, and M. A. Goodfellow to William Allen, January 20, 1845, William Allen Papers.

[78] Cincinnati *Enquirer,* August 26, 1845.

Scorned by hards and softs alike, Brough thus dropped from active politics, not coming out of retirement until the Civil War, when he was elected governor under the Republican-Unionist banner. Perhaps Brough's fate was inevitable. Trying to satisfy all factions, the broker ultimately failed in his attempt to establish some consensus on the currency issue. Brough was like the one who attempted to ride a tiger and eventually wound up inside.[79]

Whether or not Brough made the recommendation, federal funds were placed in the Bank of Wooster, much to the dismay of the hard-money men. Medary wrote to Medill, who had just received an appointment to the Polk Administration, that "if the Government deposits are not removed from the Wooster Bank, I see no possible way of preventing a general war in our own ranks." The placing of funds in this bank, Medary continued, was particularly obnoxious to Democrats because the Wooster Bank had "been at the bottom of all our troubles in Ohio." [80]

The next year, 1845, the Whigs, now in complete control of the state, passed a comprehensive and more lenient general bank law that provided for the continuation of the remaining old banks as well as two new classes of banks: a loose federation of state banks, apparently without state investment, and independent banks. Notes as small as one dollar were allowed, and the circulation of the state banks was backed

[79] Feuding and suspicion also developed later within the hard-money camp. By the end of 1846 Benjamin Tappan and Samuel Medary were at odds with one another about Medary's decision to resume editorship of the *Ohio Statesman* at Columbus. Medary had in 1845 turned the paper over to a New Englander, Charles C. Hazewell, who steered the paper on a more moderate course than it had followed before. "The permanent ascendancy of the democracy," Hazewell editorialized, "can only be secured through the union of *all* its members." Since union with the Shannon and Wooster Bank clique had become anathema, the hards, under the leadership of Benjamin Tappan, established a rival Democratic paper. Medary, according to the elder Tappan, had given the venture his blessing, promising never to resume publication of the *Ohio Statesman*. Thus, when he did so, Tappan felt he had been betrayed. For details see: Samuel Medary to William Allen, January 22, 1846 (misdated: should be 1845), and Marcus Morton to Benjamin Tappan, August 3, 1845, William Allen Papers; D. A. Robertson to William Medill, August 5, 1845, and Benjamin Tappan to William Medill, November 25, 1846, William Medill Papers; Marcus Morton to Benjamin Tappan, August 25, September 22, and October 1, 1845, Benjamin Tappan Papers, Library of Congress.

[80] Samuel Medary to William Medill, August 11, 1845, William Medill Papers.

by a safety fund system, while the notes of the independent banks were secured by government stock.[81] This measure, which spurred an increase in bank capital, provided the foundation for Ohio banking throughout the next twenty years.

5

The passage of the Whig bank bill and the Democratic failure at the polls in the years following, although hard blows to the Ohio Democracy, did at least have beneficial effects in healing the party's wounds. The next half decade was characterized by a lessening of open antagonism between softs and hards, who could now join together in denouncing the Whigs and their law.

This superficial harmony gave rise to false hopes in the hard-money camp, and there was an increasing willingness to avow hard-money principles openly. These Democrats had concluded that the hedging and deceptive tactics connected with the 1842 and 1843 bank laws had brought only defeat. The true answer, then, was a frank stand for hard money as the sole way to bring about moral and political redemption. A major change in the strategy was worked out. Rather than seek a legislative settlement as in the past, the Ohio Democrats—like their compatriots in the Southwest—would set their aim on a constitutional settlement.

The softs, meanwhile, were quietly content. What little criticism they did offer was only half-hearted. Theirs was an enviable spot. They could derive political gain from denouncing the Whig bill and at the same time enjoy the privileges of a revitalized network of banks. These conservatives, more interested in immediate political objectives, were happy in the prospect that the ultimate confrontation between the two factions could be put off to some indefinite future date. Thus, by being denied the burden of power and responsibility, the Democrats could for a time live with one another.

News that Louisiana had outlawed banks in 1845 in its new constitution was a major factor in bolstering confidence in Ohio that hard-

---

[81] Huntington, *Banking and Currency in Ohio*, 193–98; Helderman, *National and State Banks*, 43–44. Huntington says that the bill passed both houses by a party vote.

money principles would ultimately triumph.[82] The hards found the victory of the Louisiana Democrats over an aroused Whig and bank opposition "one of the most cheering and important ever achieved by the opponents of Whiggism." [83] Here at last "the true principles of political economy have . . . prevailed." [84] Encouraged, some prophesied that Mississippi, Missouri, Indiana, and Illinois would follow suit.[85] And Ohio, they hoped, would not be left behind. For the success of "correct principles" elsewhere was a challenge to members of the Ohio party to rewrite their state's constitution and prohibit "forever hereafter the creation of banking corporations." [86]

The radicals were not impulsive, however, and seemed content to wait for the opportune moment to make their move. One Democratic leader early in 1846 warned that the time had not yet arrived to make banking the "direct issue." Should "we be beaten now in a direct issue on that question," he said, "I fear it would put us back for ten years," and "it is too important a question for us to loose [*sic*] by indiscretion." [87] At the same time, the Cincinnati *Enquirer* urged Democrats in Hamilton and Putnam counties, which were further advanced on the currency question, to be patient and to "continue to agitate and discuss the question, till those *behind* come up with those *before*, so that perfect union of feeling and *action*, as well as perfect union in *principle*, shall pervade our ranks, in every section of the state." [88]

Democratic failures at the polls from 1846 through 1848 did not discourage the hards. There seemed to be an ever increasing sense that ultimate victory on "correct principles" would be theirs. "The currency question so long a rock on which many have foundered . . . no longer distracts our own friends," one hard-money man reported. The worst shortage of specie since 1838 and the flood of bad paper money have "clearly demonstrated to . . . our people that *bank paper* instead of a

[82] T. J. Morgan to Unknown, December 2, 1845, William Allen Papers; Cincinnati *Enquirer*, October 4 and December 13, 1845.

[83] Cincinnati *Enquirer*, February 12, 1846.   [84] *Ibid.*, January 22, 1846.

[85] *Ibid.*, October 4 and December 13, 1845; T. J. Morgan to Unknown, December 2, 1845, William Allen Papers.

[86] Cincinnati *Enquirer*, February 12, 1846.

[87] Mathias Martin to William Allen, January 5, 1846, William Allen Papers.

[88] Cincinnati *Enquirer*, January 5, 1846.

benefit is a curse." All doubts of the *"honest* doubting" have been re-moved and they have become "as *'hard'* as the hardest could desire." [89]

The growing hard-money sentiment evidently worried at least some bankers. In Lancaster, the promoters of a new bank were attempting to persuade "democrats of standing" in every township to take a few shares of stock. It was hinted to one Democrat that he might be given a position with the bank. But the offer and bank were ridiculed and cursed.[90]

As early as 1846 radicals in Hamilton County had supported the idea of calling for a new constitution that would prohibit the legislature from creating additional banks.[91] Despite the fact that there were nu-merous other questions besides that of banks—such as taxation, the debt, and the judiciary—that needed new constitutional guidelines, the Whigs steadfastly refused to support a call for a convention. It was not until 1849, therefore, that the Democrats and Free Soilers in the legisla-ture were able to override Whig objections and submit the question of a constitutional convention to the people. In October of that year the plan for a convention was endorsed by a wide margin.[92]

As the opening of the constitutional convention of 1850–1851 ap-proached, the party seemed, superficially at least, united. But this new enthusiasm for the "hard" was partially generated by some Democrats who actually were only paying lip service to the doctrine. The political course of three broker Democrats during the 1840s is illustrative of this. David T. Disney, Reuben Wood, and David Tod, all with defi-nite soft leanings, were among those forced by political expediency to embrace the antibank credo.

[89] H. H. Robinson to William Medill, October 9, 1847, and A. S. Perrill to William Medill, January 13, 1848, William Medill Papers. For tracing Demo-cratic maneuvering in the campaign of 1846, see H. C. Whitman to William Medill, December 23, 1845; William Ewing to William Medill, November 25, 1845; and D. A. Robertson to William Medill, April 23, 1846; William Medill Papers. Also, Unknown to William Allen, February 8, 1846; George Kesling to William Allen, February 15 and 18, 1846; T. W. Bartley to William Allen, March 2, 1846; Unknown to William Allen, March 19, 1846; W. C. Rayley to William Allen, May 25, 1846; and James Sanger to William Allen, June 20, 1846; William Allen Papers.

[90] D. A. Robertson to William Medill, January 24, 1846, and J. C. Cassell to William Medill, February 13, 1846, William Medill Papers.

[91] Cincinnati *Enquirer*, January 22, 1846.

[92] Weisenburger, *Passing of the Frontier*, 477–79.

David Tod was born in Youngstown, the son of a founder of the Western Reserve Bank in Warren. As entrepreneurial minded as his father, David, in his post as president of the Cleveland and Mahoning Railroad, inaugurated the "steps which led to the development of the vast coal mines of the Mahoning valley." [93]

Nominated by the Democrats for governor in 1844, Tod, in a public letter, endorsed the "old system of banking." Immediate attacks by the hards puzzled Tod, who claimed that his position on banking was based upon the "leading principles of reform" supported by a great majority of the party. He recognized that a Democratic faction was "opposed to all Banks," but he never supposed "that such was the sentiment of our party." [94]

Defending Tod, one of his supporters told Tappan that Tod, although not as sound on the currency issue as Allen and Tappan, would support the principles of the general laws of 1842 and 1843. Tappan cynically replied that there was little difference on the banking question between Tod, Wilson Shannon, and the Whig gubernatorial candidate, Mordecai Bartley. In response, Tod's defender said that Tod had opposed the Wooster Bank Bill while Shannon favored it, and Mordecai Bartley opposed stockholder liability and would give the banks unlimited privileges.[95]

Tod lost the election in 1844 but was given another chance for the nomination in 1846. Radicals still suspicious of Tod's soundness were willing to forgive and forget, but only on his affirmation of hard-money principles. In a letter to the Democratic convention, Tod said that he once had believed that the evils surrounding banking could be corrected by legislative enactment. But recent events had convinced him that no system of banking could be devised that would provide adequate safeguards to the public and not be based upon inequality.

---

[93] Information about Tod and his friend, John Stambaugh, in Howe, *Historical Collections of Ohio* (1907 edition), II, 182; A. B. Coover, "Ohio Banking Institutions, 1803–1866," *Ohio Archaeological and Historical Quarterly,* XXI (April–July, 1912), 318; Harriet Taylor Upton, *History of the Western Reserve* (Chicago, 1910), I, 607.

[94] Columbus *Ohio State Journal,* March 9, 1844; David Tod to William Allen, March 24, 1844, William Allen Papers.

[95] M. Birchard to Benjamin Tappan, March 20, 1844, Benjamin Tappan Papers, Library of Congress.

Concluding, he called for a constitutional amendment to solve the currency problem. This evidently satisfied most hards, for Tod was renominated.[96] However, under the banner of the Democratic party, he was again denied the governorship. Only later, as the Republican candidate in 1861, did Tod reach his goal.

Next to Wilson Shannon, David T. Disney of Cincinnati was probably involved in more political intrigue than any other man in the state. Disney was a director of the Ohio Life Insurance and Trust Company, one of the largest banks in the state. But being a bank director and an aspiring politician in the most radical hard county of the state created a number of problems. A lesser politician might have been stopped. Disney, however, resigned from his position in the bank and pledged to vote against any renewals or extensions of privileges for banks if he were elected to the state senate. He was accepted grudgingly by the hards and won the election.[97] Ironically, several years later both Charles Reemelin, one of the most radical Democrats in the state, and Disney together introduced in the Ohio legislature a bill to repeal the Whig bank law of 1845.[98]

With Polk coming to the Presidency in 1845, some Democrats hoped that Disney might win a federal appointment and thus be eliminated as an intriguer in state politics. One Democrat wrote to Allen that if Disney succeeded, "we may lose a dangerous politician and the Government get a bad minister" and "what would be our gain, would be the nation's loss. . . ."[99]

Reuben Wood,[100] a native of Vermont and resident of Cleveland, was nominated by the Democratic party for governor in 1850 at a convention that declared itself emphatically for hard money. His position on the matter had never been so clear cut. A past state senator and state supreme court jurist, Wood had earlier aroused the ire of the hards when it had been alleged that he felt that a bank charter, once

---

[96] H. C. Whitman to Benjamin Tappan, November 23, 1845, and Benjamin Tappan to David Tod, November 29, 1845, Benjamin Tappan Papers, Library of Congress. H. C. Whitman to William Allen, November 23, 1845, William Allen Papers; Cincinnati *Enquirer,* October 14, 1845, and January 13, 1846.

[97] Cincinnati *Enquirer,* August 23 and 26, and September 29, 1843.

[98] Weisenburger, *The Passing of the Frontier,* 424.

[99] George B. Flood to William Allen, January 16, 1845, William Allen Papers.

[100] For short sketch of Wood, see Upton, *Western Reserve,* 521.

granted by the legislature, was inviolable.[101] When challenged, Wood reacted by condemning the former Bank of the United States as unconstitutional, supporting the Independent Treasury, and claiming that the bank charters were not protected by the contract clause in the Federal Constitution. He passed the party test and the legislature re-elected him to the supreme court. Still, eight Democrats had not been satisfied and had cast blank ballots.[102] Wood's trimming to gain hard-money support evidently did not disenchant the softs. Among others working diligently for Wood's re-election was George Flood, an attorney for the Granville Bank and a close political ally of Thomas Hamer.[103]

Wood, Tod, and Disney would no doubt have been soft-money men if their political aspirations could have been fulfilled in a local office supported by a soft or moderate constituency. But Tod and Wood sought statewide political office, while Disney had to face a predominantly hard-money constituency. This forced the three of them to come to terms with the hard-money men who throughout the decade of the 1840s were increasingly able to make hard money the party's test of principle.

6

The Whigs were aghast at the widespread hard-money clamor that had built up by the eve of the constitutional convention.[104] They desperately tried to awaken fears held by the more moderate hards and softs within the opposition party. The radicals, the Whigs pronounced, were "dreamers, enthusiasts, visionaries" and had "no practical knowledge of the men and things as they actually exist around us." The

[101] Essay for publication in Columbus *Ohio Statesman* signed by "Buckeye," undated, in Edwin M. Stanton Papers.

[102] Reuben Wood to David Tod and others, January 7, 1840, Benjamin Tappan Papers, Library of Congress; Edwin M. Stanton to Benjamin Tappan, January 14, 1839 (misdated: should be 1840), Edwin M. Stanton Papers.

[103] Edwin M. Stanton explained to Benjamin Tappan that "the first application to file an information against that Bank was made in August to Wood in Cleveland under the impression that he being a democrat would grant the leave." The bank sent Flood to Cleveland to talk to Wood, who agreed to refuse to give the leave. As a result, Flood became attached to Wood. See January 22, 1840, letter in the Benjamin Tappan Papers, Ohio Historical Society.

[104] Cincinnati *Enquirer*, July 9, 1850.

moderate-minded men of the Democratic party, according to the Whigs, had in the years when their party was in a minority allowed the hard-money faction to predominate and impose its doctrines upon the party as a whole. Now it was too late, the Whigs despaired, and the entire party was being "impelled onward to this work of self immolation by the zealous, unthinking madcaps in their own ranks." [105]

There was much truth in this characterization. Expectations of the radical Democrats were at a peak as the convention opened. They had waited long and patiently for this day, and now they were anxious to implement their work of bank destruction. Giving rise to the radical optimism was the election of convention delegates—fifty-eight Democrats, forty-one Whigs, and nine Free Soilers [106]—and soon afterward the election of Reuben Wood as the first Democratic governor since the early 1840s. Although Wood was not too sound on the currency question in the eyes of the hards, his victory came after a campaign in which the Whigs tried to make the issue banks or no banks. Thus, Wood's election meant to the hards that the people, at long last, had given their clear-cut endorsement of hard-money principles.

The committee on banks and the currency presented its report to the constitutional convention on July 5, 1850. The four Democratic members stated the party's case in the majority report, while their Whig colleagues registered dissent in a minority report.

The Democrats began by denying the constitutionality of paper money and contending that the Ohio banking system was at once a failure and a great danger. It had failed because it had not relieved the people from hard times, and in "1842 and '43, when the banking system was nearly at an end in Ohio, times were easier, pecuniary difficulties far less, and money apparently more abundant." The banking system represented a grave danger because it was a "political engine of great potency." It bound together by strong ties of "pecuniary interest an extensive and influential class of men from all parts of the State, and . . . [operated] secretly and unseen, with a systematic and concentrative influence, which . . . [penetrated] every county and neighborhood." [107]

[105] Columbus *Ohio State Journal,* July 5, 1850.
[106] Cincinnati *Enquirer,* April 19, 1850.
[107] *Report of the Debates and Proceedings of the Convention for the Revision*

To remedy this situation, the committee urged the convention to adopt their three recommendations, the first of which would forbid the General Assembly to

create or incorporate banks or banking institutions whatever, or to authorize the making, emission, or putting in circulation of any bill of credit, bond, check, ticket, certificate, promissory note, or other paper medium intended or calculated to circulate as money or currency.

The second stipulation would prohibit

any person or persons, associations, company or corporation now in existence, from exercising the privileges of banking or creating, emitting, or putting in circulation any bank notes or papers, of any description whatever, to circulate as money or currency.

And finally, the report demanded that the

business of loaning and dealing in money . . . be left free to all, subject to such restrictions as may be provided by law; but no special privileges or exemptions shall ever be granted to those engaged in, or who may hereafter engage in such business; nor shall any person or persons either natural or artificial, ever be allowed to deal in or issue paper money. . . .[108]

The Whig minority report rejected the Democratic recommendations and urged the convention to adopt a resolution to the effect that it was "inexpedient to confine the people" to a metallic currency. Whig newspapers denounced the majority report and warned that if the Democrats stood fast, their hard-money platform would be "converted into a political gallows."[109]

No action was taken on the currency question immediately, but before much time had elapsed it became obvious that although the Democrats had a clear majority at the convention, their desire for radical reform again would be frustrated by a small group of conservatives within their ranks. The first indication of this occurred not over a currency question, but over the closely allied issue of whether a legislature could repeal or amend a charter once granted. The test occurred December 30, 1850, when, by a vote of 44 to 42, the convention refused to incorporate into the new constitution a provision that would have given

---

of the Constitution of the State of Ohio, 1850–51 (Columbus, Ohio, 1851), I, 707–709.
[108] *Ibid.*   [109] *Ibid.;* Columbus *Ohio State Journal,* July 6, 1850.

the legislature the power "to repeal or revoke any charter of incorporation, now or hereafter granted. . . ." [110] A number of Democrats—including Edward Archbold, J. R. Swan, L. Case and Judge Elijah
Vance—voted with the Whigs in defeating the proposal.

Prominent in this soft-money Democratic faction was Archbold, an
attorney from the backwoods Monroe County who in 1844 had been
among the renegade Democrats voting for the Wooster Bank Bill. At
one point in the debates he had chided a hard-money Democrat from
Cincinnati, charging that he could afford his radical views because he
represented "an immensely rich constituency" of "nabobs and million-
aires." Hamilton County "has already all the improvements of the kind
which it needs: or if it has not, it has wealthy individuals, who are
able to make them. . . ." To limit drastically or make less attractive
the principle of incorporation would "render improvements, in the
newer and less favored counties, impossible." [111]

The Whigs were elated with the result of the vote. Although, they
pointed out, "Mr. Archbold, the old war-horse from Monroe always
did hold Sam Medary . . . in perfect contempt, and has often so declared," he had always before found few Democrats to support him.[112]
The Democrats were stunned. The action of the softs in voting with
the Whigs against a key Democratic principle triggered a statewide
shower of abuse upon the traitors. The *Enquirer* charged that on "every
question that has arisen, or that will arise in this Convention, affecting
corporations on one hand and the Democratic people on the other, Mr.
Case, of Licking, is *rotten—rotten to the core.*" While he was sent to
the convention to "represent the *people*—he is representing *stock interests*—and stock interests have a faithful *proxy.*" [113]

As a result of this rising indignation, a public meeting in Butler
County demanded the resignation of Judge Vance, who subsequently
resigned but reminded his antagonists of his overwhelming election.
The *Enquirer* retorted that it was due only to the fact that Whigs had
campaigned for him.[114] A public letter from Franklin County, Judge

[110] *Report of the Debates,* II, 210.   [111] *Ibid.,* I, 388.
[112] Chillicothe, Ohio, *Scioto Gazette,* January 3, 1851.
[113] Cincinnati *Enquirer,* January 9, 1851. The *Enquirer* ran editorials from
papers all over the state denouncing the Democrats who had voted with the
Whigs. See issues of January 10, 12, and 14, 1851.
[114] Cincinnati *Enquirer,* January 15, 1851.

Swan's constituency, explained that their representative's apostasy was not too surprising. Although Swan was generally regarded as "an anti-bank man, and a radical on the currency question," he had "but little real feeling with the great mass of the Democratic party." [115]

This defeat of the hard-money men on the section to allow the legislature to repeal or amend charters alarmed some of the more moderate Democrats. They feared that the convention would not accept the Democratic majority report on banks and currency and, as a result, offered several compromise alternative proposals, which called for gradual elimination of bank notes from the state and/or the submission of the entire question to the people.[116] One Democrat who claimed to be a hard-money man warned his colleagues that it was "now well understood by every member of the convention, that no hard money proposition can be engrafted into this constitution. . . ." And, attempting to persuade the hards to accept a compromise solution, he offered this analogy:

I have a field of grain, with a poor fence around it, and my neighbor's cattle are in the habit of breaking in, and destroying my crop. My neighbor makes to me the suggestion, that I had better repair my fence, at once, by putting on an additional rail or two. But I reply, no; I shall wait until after the harvest, and then I will make a good fence from the ground up. I wait, and my crop is destroyed.[117]

But all appeals for compromise and moderation fell on deaf ears, and the compromise proposals were turned down decisively.

The hard-money majority report of the banking and currency committee was next voted upon. Each of the three sections was rejected by a coalition of unanimous Whig opposition in combination with negative ballots cast by a few soft-money Democrats. But although the anti-bank hopes of the Democrats were quickly dashed, it is clear that the overwhelming majority of Democratic delegates did want (and voted for) the radical reforms.

The first section of the report, which would have prohibited the legislature from authorizing additional banks or paper money, was defeated by a tie vote, 47 to 47. Voting in favor were forty-three Demo-

[115] *Ibid.*, January 8, 1851.
[116] *Report of the Debates*, II, 344–46, 392–96, 404–405, 418.
[117] *Ibid.*, 419–23.

crats and four Free Soilers, while nine Democrats, four Free Soilers and thirty-four Whigs were opposed. The second provision, more radical because it provided that the legislature should destroy banks already in existence, was voted down by the widest margin, 57 to 38. Favoring the proposition were thirty-six Democrats and two Free Soilers; sixteen Democrats, six Free Soilers, and thirty-five Whigs voted in the negative. The last section, which opened up to all citizens the business of loaning and dealing with money but denied banks special privileges or authority to issue paper money, was rejected by a 51 to 43 vote. The Democrats and Free Soilers gave the measure forty and three votes, respectively, but eleven Democrats, five Free Soilers, and thirty-five Whigs joined to defeat the last section of the report.[118]

The only agreement that could be reached on the currency question, and that only in the waning moments of the convention, was that no further legislative grant of banking powers would take effect until after it had been approved by a majority of the voters in a general election.[119]

At the same time that the fight over banking and currency was raging in the constitutional convention developments were taking place in the legislature, which also was in session. Frightened by the possibility of future constitutional curbs on banking, the Whigs, who dominated the legislature, were attempting to push a free-banking law through the house and senate. Such a law was needed, the Whigs asserted, because it was "a matter of notoriety to all business men that we have *not* enough bank capital in Ohio to do the legitimate annual business of the State." [120]

The Democrats attempted to amend the bill by making stockholders individually liable for a bank's circulation and all other debts. The Whigs claimed that unlimited liability was unnecessary and tended to frighten people from engaging in the banking business. This Democratic attempt to amend the bill failed, as did another to prohibit the free banks from issuing notes under 5 dollars. The bill passed both houses by a strict party vote, the Democrats all against it.[121]

---

[118] *Ibid.*, 423–24.　　　　　[119] *Ibid.*, 850–51.

[120] Columbus *Ohio State Journal*, February 6, 1851.

[121] Although the small-note law and individual-liability clause were rejected, the bill did provide a specie-note ratio, requiring that 30 per cent of the note

The Democrats denounced the free-banking bill as a "scheme to flood the land with shinplasters" and predicted "that the people of Ohio" would speedily demand its repeal.[122] In the next year thirteen new banks were organized under the new act. However, in 1852 the attorney general rendered the decision that the newly adopted constitution prohibited any new banks from being formed under the free-banking law.[123]

Why no Democrat voted with the Whigs remains somewhat of a mystery. There were Democrats representing constituencies that definitely were attracted to a free-banking scheme. The Toledo Democratic paper had declared itself in favor of free banking in 1849.[124] In the constitutional convention, one of the Democratic delegates from Licking County asserted that the people he represented were for a free-banking system. Probably the few Democrats who might have bolted their party on the issue recognized that the bill would pass without their assistance. Thus, they could avoid the censure sure to follow from the dominant hard-money faction of the party. Another factor was the overwhelming desire in the Democratic party to settle the banking question in the constitutional convention. One Democrat-sponsored amendment that the Whigs and Free Soilers rejected would have submitted the free-banking bill to the people. Had this been accepted or had the authors of the bill included an unlimited-liability clause in their bill, it *might* have received some Democratic support.

The defeat of the hard-money Democrats on the free-banking bill marked the end of the banking controversy in Ohio. The growing industry, agriculture, and commerce of the state, and the accompanying needs for banks and credit, made the hard-money notions of the Democrats quaint relics of the past. The fight between the Whigs and Democrats over the banking issue had been a long and fierce one. In the first few years after the Panic, however, the Democrats employed radical rhetoric rather than deeds. Then, when forced into action by

---

circulation be kept in a bank's vaults in specie or a safe equivalent. See *ibid.*, March 1, 3, and 22, 1851; Cincinnati *Enquirer*, February 14, 1851; and Huntington, *Banking and Currency in Ohio*, 209.

[122] Cincinnati *Enquirer*, March 26, 1851.

[123] Huntington, *Banking and Currency in Ohio*, 210.

[124] Columbus *New Constitution*, September 8, 1849.

the impending expiration in 1843 of most of the bank charters in the state, they hoped to abolish the banks by subterfuge in enacting such strict reforms into law that the bankers would not accept them. This alienated the softs, whose antagonism to the party stand caused bitter feuding and, more important, allowed the Whigs to pass their own banking plan in 1845, giving them the ascendancy in the state until the end of the decade. Democrats gained control of the constitutional convention in 1850, but the softs again sided with the Whigs, frustrating attempts to incorporate hard-money provisions in the new document. Nonetheless, despite their failure to attain their antibank objectives, the hard-money Democrats were successful in dominating their party throughout the post-Panic era in Ohio.

CHAPTER VII

Ohio Constituencies

I

THE OHIO ECONOMY at the time of the Panic of 1837 was in a transitional stage. In 1840 the census reported that 76 per cent of all employed Ohioans were engaged in agriculture.[1] But, while Mississippi had a one-crop slave economy, Ohio was developing a diversified agriculture based on free labor and complemented by commercial and industrial growth. Ohio was also among the most urbanized of the western states. In addition to Cincinnati, there were numerous smaller commercial centers scattered throughout the state. To facilitate economic expansion, Ohio by 1840 was completing an important canal system and planning a comprehensive railroad network. In Ohio there was not the sectional dichotomy between wealth and lack of wealth that divided the Delta-Loess from the counties to the east in Mississippi. Except for the poorer, more sparsely populated Maumee Valley on the northwestern frontier, the sections of Ohio—the Miami Valley, Scioto Valley, Hocking Valley, Muskingum Valley, Western Reserve, and the River Counties—all were relatively well settled and were of nearly comparable wealth.[2]

Corn and wheat were the major crops in Ohio. In 1840 the state ranked third in the country in corn growing and first in wheat; by 1850 it had climbed to first in corn and dropped to second in wheat. Counties in the Miami Valley in southwestern Ohio and the Scioto

[1] W. A. Lloyd, J. I. Falconer, and C. E. Thorne, *The Agriculture of Ohio: Bulletin 326 of the Ohio Agricultural Experiment Station* (Wooster, Ohio, 1918), 43.

[2] See Appendix A, Table II. See also Map 3.

MICHIGAN

Lake Erie

WILLIAMS

Toledo
LUCAS

HENRY | WOOD | SANDUSKY

HURON | LORAIN

Cleveland

CUYAHOGA
and
GEAUGA

ASHTABULA

TRUMBULL

PAULDING

SENECA

PUTNAM | HANCOCK

VAN WERT

CRAWFORD

RICHLAND

WAYNE

MEDINA,
PORTAGE
and
STARK

COLUMBIANA

MERCER

ALLEN

HARDIN

MARION

HOLMES

CARROLL

KNOX

TUSCARAWAS

JEFFER-
SON

SHELBY

LOGAN

UNION | DELAWARE

COSHOCTON

HARRISON

DARKE

CHAMPAIGN

FRANKLIN

LICKING

GUERNSEY

BELMONT

MIAMI

CLARK

MADI-
SON

Columbus

MUSKINGUM

MONROE

PREBLE

MONTGOM-
ERY

GREENE

PICKAWAY

FAIRFIELD | PERRY

MORGAN

WASHINGTON

FAYETTE

BUTLER

WARREN

CLINTON

ROSS

HOCKING

ATHENS

Ohio   River

HAMILTON

Cincinnati

CLERMONT

HIGHLAND

PIKE

JACKSON

MEIGS

VIRGINIA

BROWN

ADAMS | SCIOTO

GALLIA

KENTUCKY

LAWRENCE

Maumee Valley

Miami Valley

Scioto Valley

Hocking Valley

Western Reserve

River Counties

Muskingum Valley

MAP 3. OHIO GEOGRAPHIC SECTIONS

Valley in the south-central portion of the state were leaders in corn production, while wheat was the major staple in the east, especially in the Muskingum Valley and the River Counties.[3] Cattle and hog raising also were important elements in Ohio's agricultural economy. The cattle industry was concentrated in the Scioto Valley and Western Reserve. In the latter this gave rise to the development of a dairy industry. By 1849 more than 75 per cent of the 20 million pounds of cheese made that year throughout the state came from the Western Reserve area.[4] The most important and renowned cattle raising area in the state, however, was the Scioto Valley, from which herds of cattle were being shipped to eastern markets as early as 1808. In 1833 the Ohio Importing Company in Ross County imported English Shorthorns or Durhams from England, and this has been hailed by one historian as the "greatest event in the history of the cattle industry of the West." These Shorthorns made the Scioto Valley famous throughout the West, and sales of livestock in Madison County "attracted buyers from all sections of the country."[5]

The raising of hogs and the production of pork was a major industry for the Miami and Muskingum valleys, which included eight of the top ten hog-producing counties in 1840.[6] As a result, Cincinnati won such great renown as a hog market that the city was dubbed "Porkopolis." Numerous travelers recount having seen virtually unending herds of hogs being driven into and through the city. One newspaper reported that on "all the avenues leading to the city, droves of hogs may be seen. . . . There is scarcely an hour in the day in which Broadway is not alive with them."[7] Mrs. Frances Trollope from England was particularly annoyed at the ever-present swine and complained that "if I determined upon a walk up Main-street, the chances were five hundred to one against my reaching the shady side without brushing by a snout fresh dripping from the kennel. . . ."[8]

Although Ohio remained primarily an agricultural state through-

[3] Weisenburger, *Passing of the Frontier*, 58–61.
[4] Lloyd, *Agriculture of Ohio*, 87.
[5] *Ibid.*, 63; Weisenburger, *Passing of the Frontier*, 70.
[6] Department of State, *Compendium of the Sixth Census*, 275.
[7] Alvin Fay Harlow, *The Serene Cincinnatians* (New York, 1950), 81.
[8] Frances Trollope, *Domestic Manners of the Americans* (New York, 1949), 88.

out the period, there were important industrial and commercial developments prior to the Civil War, especially in Cincinnati, which was accurately described by the French traveler, Michel Chevalier, as "the great interior mart of the West." [9] Ideally located on the Ohio River and profiting from an extensive system of canals, the burgeoning Hamilton County metropolis served as the producer, processor, and emporium of a growing quantity and variety of goods shipped to the lower Mississippi Valley. One enthusiastic supporter predicted in the early 1840s that "within one hundred years from this time, Cincinnati will be the greatest city in America; and by the year of our Lord two thousand, the greatest city in the world." [10] At the time of the Panic, Cincinnati had a vigorous local industry that exported a total of 8.1 million dollars worth of goods annually, including: "Pork, $3,000,000; flour, $600,000; whiskey, $750,000; manufacturers of iron, $2,000,000; manufacturers of other articles (chiefly hats, clothing, books, beer, furniture, ship carpentry . . .), $1,350,000; and miscellaneous, $400,000." [11] In 1840 Hamilton led Ohio counties in the amount of capital invested in manufacturing, followed by Summit, Montgomery, Franklin, Muskingum, Columbiana, Licking, and Stark counties. In this respect, however, Hamilton was in a class by itself, having 8 million dollars invested—a total 16 times that of its nearest rival.[12]

Coal, iron, and salt became important factors in the Ohio economy during the 1830s and 1840s. Coal mining was chiefly concentrated in the Hocking and Muskingum valleys and the River Counties. In 1840 Meigs County in the Hocking Valley was the leader, producing twice as much as its closest competitor. The Ohio iron industry was centered in the Scioto and Hocking valleys in an area that came to be known as the Hanging Rock District and included parts of Lawrence, Scioto, Gallia, Jackson, and Hocking counties. In the 1840s the Youngstown area in Mahoning County also was developing a success-

[9] Harlow, *Serene Cincinnatians,* 32–33.
[10] Charles Cist, *Cincinnati in 1841: Its Early Annals and Future Prospects* (Cincinnati, 1841), 275.
[11] Berry, *Western Prices,* footnote on 253.
[12] See Harold E. Davis, "Economic Basis of Ohio Politics, 1820–1840," *Ohio Archaeological and Historical Quarterly,* XLVII (1938), 295–96, for a discussion of industry in the 1830s.

ful iron industry. Salt mining was an important pursuit in Athens, Morgan, and Meigs counties. This trio marketed more than five sixths of all salt produced in the state in 1840.[13]

The development of Ohio's agricultural and mineral resources, however, would have been impossible had it not been for the state's extensive internal improvement system including roads, canals, and, eventually, railroads. Ohio was blessed with the proximity of excellent natural waterways. The completion of the Erie Canal in the 1820s meant that northern Ohioans on Lake Erie could send their goods across the lake to Buffalo and then through the canal to eastern markets. Equally fortunate were those living in the southern and southeastern counties, where the Ohio and Mississippi River systems opened up western, southern, and eastern markets for Ohio goods. Perhaps the most important road in the state was the National Road, which connected Ohio to Wheeling, Virginia, and eastern markets. By 1838 the road had been completed across Ohio as far as Springfield.[14]

The building of the Ohio canals, "one of the greatest systems of internal improvements in the country," [15] however, was the most important development in bringing the interior of the state into the market economy. By the middle of the 1840s the state had built two major canals with extensions linking the Ohio River with Lake Erie. The first, the Ohio Canal, was completed in 1833 and ran from Cleveland on the lake to Portsmouth on the Ohio River. The Miami and Erie Canal between Cincinnati and Toledo was opened the entire way for traffic in 1845.[16] The canals had an enormous impact upon the areas they bisected. In Licking County, for example, one observer noted that before the Ohio Canal had been built "wheat sold at 25 cents per bushel, corn 12½ cents delivered in Lancaster or at distillery,

[13] Emilius O. Randall and Daniel J. Ryan, *History of Ohio: The Rise and Progress of an American State* (New York, 1912), IV, 79–82; Davis, "Economic Basis of Ohio Politics," 297–98; Weisenburger, *Passing of the Frontier*, 76–79; and Department of State, *Compendium of the Sixth Census*, 274–75.

[14] Weisenburger, *Passing of the Frontier*, 108–110.

[15] Taylor, *Transportation Revolution*, 46.

[16] See C. P. McClelland and Charles Clifford Huntington, *History of the Ohio Canals, Their Construction, Cost, Use and Partial Abandonment* (Columbus, 1905), chapters 1–5; Weisenburger, *Passing of the Frontier*, 89–105; Chester Finn, "The Ohio Canals: Public Enterprise on the Frontier," *Ohio Archaeological and Historical Quarterly*, LI (January–March, 1942), 1–28.

oats ten cents." But, he added, even before the southern mileage of the canal had opened,

the North End, from Dresden to Cleveland, was in operation. Then wheat sold on the canal at 75 cents per bushel, and corn rose in proportion, and then the enemies of the canal, all of whom were large landholders or large taxpayers, began to have their eyes opened. . . . And now let me say, as I have lived to see all to this time, the Ohio canal was the beginning of the State's prosperity.[17]

Railroads did not play a leading role in the Ohio transportation network until the 1850s. At mid-century the state had only a little more than 300 miles of railroad trackage in operation. The most important early route linked Sandusky with Cincinnati via the Mad River and Lake Erie Railroad and the Little Miami Railroad.[18]

The population of Ohio was as diverse as the state's geography and economy. In the two decades after 1830 the population increased from just over 900,000 to almost 2 million. Of that latter figure in 1850 about 500,000 had been born in other states and 250,000 had been born outside the United States. Those persons from other states came from Pennsylvania (43 per cent), Virginia (18 per cent), New York (17 per cent), Maryland (8 per cent), New Jersey (5 per cent), Connecticut (5 per cent), and Massachusetts (4 per cent). The quarter of a million foreign born were mainly German and Irish, and about one third of them lived in Hamilton County.[19] In 1830 approximately 5 per cent of Cincinnati's population was of German ancestry, and by 1840 the number had increased to 23 per cent. A year earlier a city directory had listed 10,000 names out of a total population of 40,000, giving among other things the place of nativity. Germany easily ranked first with 1,578 persons listed, followed by Pennsylvania with 1,098 and Ohio with 916.[20] The rest of the state was less cosmopolitan and more culturally homogeneous than Cincinnati. The Western Reserve was largely settled by New Englanders, especially from Massa-

---

[17] Howe, *Historical Collections of Ohio* (1896 edition), II, 72–73.

[18] Finn, "Ohio Canals," 28; and Randall and Ryan, *History of Ohio*, IV, 82–83.

[19] Robert E. Chaddock, *Ohio Before 1850: A Study of the Early Influence of Pennsylvania and Southern Populations in Ohio* (New York, 1908), 40–41.

[20] Also at the top of the list were Ireland and New Jersey, each with 717, and England with 679, New York with 607, Virginia with 521, and Maryland with 487. See Weisenburger, *Passing of the Frontier*, 47 and 52.

chusetts and Connecticut. The southern part of the region, however, in portions of Trumbull, Portage, and Medina counties, had been settled by Pennsylvanians. In eastern Ohio, the River Counties of Jefferson and Columbiana and the Muskingum Valley counties of Carroll and Harrison had been peopled by Scotch-Irish from Pennsylvania as well as a few Pennsylvania Germans, or Pennsylvania Dutch. The Pennsylvania Dutch were the largest element in the backbone counties of Stark, Wayne, and Richland. Southeastern Ohio, including the Scioto Valley, had attracted residents from Virginia, Kentucky, Maryland, and a few from Pennsylvania. The Miami Valley included people from New Jersey, New York, and New England, with the dominant portion of the population coming from Pennsylvania and the south. The southerners included many "Scotch-Irish covenanters" and Quakers who moved to Ohio out of their opposition to slavery. Northwestern Ohio, or the Maumee Valley, was very sparsely settled at the time.[21]

2

Despite Ohio's economic and ethnocultural diversity, there was less political polarity there than in Mississippi. For example, in Ohio only nine of the total seventy-one counties or county group constituencies can be classified as either Very Strong Democratic or Very Strong Whig for the years 1836–1844, while in Mississippi, nineteen of the fifty-three county constituencies were in those categories. And in Mississippi almost 64 percentage points separated the strongest Democratic constituency from the strongest Whig constituency, while in Ohio the extremes were separated only by about 46 percentage points. There was a greater intensity of support for the Democrats in Mississippi and for the Whigs in Ohio, for in Mississippi fifteen of the nineteen Very Strong county constituencies were Democratic, while in Ohio six of the nine Very Strong county or county group constituencies were Whig.[22]

[21] Lloyd, *Agriculture of Ohio,* 43.
[22] For information about political classifications, see Footnote 10 in Chapter IV, Appendix A, and Map 4. A more statistically accurate measure of the greater political diversity in Mississippi than in Ohio can be obtained through the

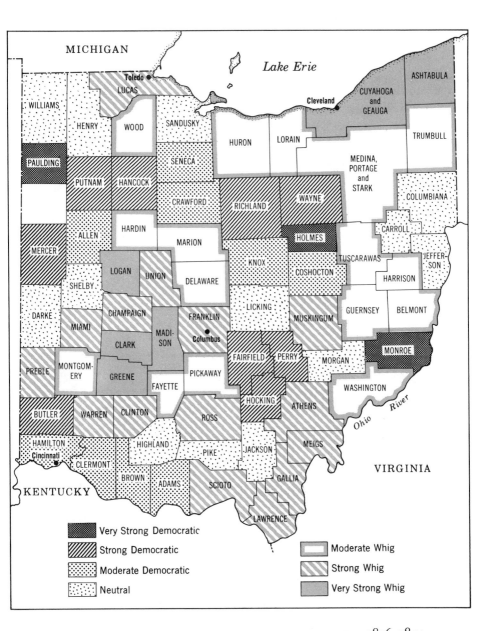

MAP 4. DEMOCRATIC AND WHIG STRENGTH IN OHIO, 1836–1844

(Data not available for unlabeled county—Van Wert)

As in Mississippi, there was in Ohio a high correlation between wealth and Whiggery and lack of wealth and support for the Democrats. Of the wealthiest fifteen constituencies in Ohio, for example, thirteen were Whig. However the correlation in Ohio was not quite as high as in Mississippi. As with politics, there was less polarization of wealth in Ohio than in Mississippi. In Ohio, for instance, the wealthiest constituency was about 10 times as wealthy as the poorest constituency, while in Mississippi there was a difference of 127 times. Thus in Mississippi the high degree of political and economic variation permitted the extremely high correlation between economics and politics that was obtained, while in Ohio the correlation was slightly lower but still highly significant.[23]

This lack of variation in Ohio was a result of the social and economic complexity of the state. There was no planter class in Ohio, nor were there plantations dependent upon slave labor. The family-size farm worked by a single farmer and his family was the typical agricultural unit in Ohio. Whereas in Mississippi only those who lived near natural waterways had easy access to markets, the Ohio government had been more responsive to the needs of the farmer and an elaborate system of canals bisected the state, bringing formerly remote areas into the market economy. The influx of the Irish and the Germans into Ohio, especially of the Germans into wealthy Hamilton County, gave the Democrats a solid base of support in a wealthy commercial constituency that had all the earmarks of a stronghold of Whiggery. And finally, history itself gave an added dimension to Ohio politics. Ohio was an older, more mature political entity than Mississippi and comparatively more stable. As a result of all this, change in Mississippi was often open-ended, erratic, and highly ac-

---

use of the formula to compute the Semi-Interquartile Range $\left(Q = \dfrac{Q_3 - Q_1}{2} \right)$. This shows that in Ohio 50 per cent of the counties fell within 6.94 percentage points of the median county, whereas in Mississippi 50 per cent of the counties fell within 10.25 percentage points of the median county. See Footnote 17, Chapter X. The formula is explained in Henry E. Garrett's *Statistics in Psychology and Education* (New York, 1949), 50–55. In Mississippi all the constituencies considered in this analysis were single counties. However, in Ohio, county boundary changes between 1836 and 1844 necessitated county groupings in several instances.

[23] See information about rank-difference correlations in Chapter IV and Appendix A.

celerated, while in Ohio it tended to be slower and more orderly.

The one single strongest Whig area in Ohio was the Western Reserve, where all six counties or county groups were predominately Whig, none giving the Democratic party an average of more than 44.7 per cent of its vote for the presidential elections of 1836–1844, and Ashtabula County registering only 21.2 per cent for the Democrats. As has been mentioned, this area was populated mainly by New Englanders, who gave it an ethnocultural homogeneity that no other section in the state could match. These transplanted settlers brought their Yankee heritage with them and, according to one observer, were

endowed with the pioneer qualities of energy, self-reliance, and perseverance yet retained the sober and prudent character of Connecticut people. With them they brought Connecticut ideas of religion and education; and almost before the smoke from the first clearings had vanished schoolhouses and meeting-houses began to nestle under the protecting shadows of the forest giants. . . .[24]

In the election of 1824 Andrew Jackson had received only 10 per cent of the Western Reserve's vote, and, although improving himself slightly four years later, he still had been far from the majority candidate. The appeal of a fellow New Englander, John Quincy Adams, an educated and cultivated gentleman, as opposed to the seemingly crude and unlettered Jackson, was a powerful factor in molding political habits in the 1820s. It was reported that in 1833 the founders of Oberlin College found it "almost as necessary to be Whigs as to be Christians." [25]

The emphasis that the Whigs and National Republicans placed on internal improvements and development of transportation facilities undoubtedly also was attractive to the settlers in the Western Reserve, who were in a position to benefit from both the Erie and Ohio canals. There is no better example of the importance of the opening of these

[24] Emerson O. Stevens, "The Western Reserve University," *New England Magazine*, XIV (April, 1899), as quoted in Kenneth V. Lottick, "Culture Transplantation in the Connecticut Reserve," *Bulletin of the Historical and Philosophical Society of Ohio*, XVII (July, 1959), 159.

[25] I am grateful to Donald Ratcliffe for allowing me to read his unpublished manuscript, "Political Divisions in Ohio in the Years of Jacksonian Democracy" (Bachelor of Philosophy Thesis, Oxford University, 1966). Ratcliffe analyzes the years from 1824 to 1840. See pages 37–39.

waterways than the almost spectacular growth of Cleveland. In 1825 it was a city of 500 inhabitants; twenty years later it had grown to a population of 10,135 and was well on its way to becoming Ohio's second city. Having one of the best harbors on Lake Erie, Cleveland by the mid-1840s had become

the great mart of the greatest grain-growing State in the Union, and it is the Ohio and Erie canals that have made it such, though it exports much by way of the Welland canal to Canada. . . . The natural advantages of this place are unsurpassed in the West, to which it has a large access by the lakes and the Ohio canal. But the Erie canal constitutes the principal source of its vast advantages; without that great work, it would have remained in its former insignificance.[26]

The Scioto and Miami valleys also were areas of Whig strength, with seven of the ten strongest Whig constituencies in Ohio coming from these two sections. In the presidential elections from 1836 to 1844, a total of nineteen constituencies in the two sections were Whig, five were Democratic and five Neutral. In the presidential elections of 1828 and 1832, the Democrats had done better, carrying half the constituencies, but they had lost support once Jackson left office.[27] Transportation facilities were good for both sections. The Ohio Canal bisected the Scioto Valley from north to south, and the National Road ran across it from east to west. The road's western terminus was in the Miami Valley, which was also tied to Cincinnati, and later Toledo as well, by the Miami and Erie Canal. Most of the counties in both sections, as has been shown earlier, were devoted to growing corn, grazing cattle, and raising hogs. Eight of the ten leading corn-growing counties in 1840 were in the Miami and Scioto valleys,[28] and of these, six were Whig and two Democratic.

The extensive cattle business in the Miami and Scioto valleys began in the latter, where farmers fattened cattle and then drove them east to market over the National Road. In the early 1830s one observer made the claim, although somewhat exaggerated, that the graziers of Madison County in the Scioto Valley "make money fast at the busi-

[26] Howe, *Historical Collections of Ohio* (1896 edition), I, 498–99.
[27] For voting strength of Ohio counties from 1828 to 1832, see Ratcliffe, "Political Divisions in Ohio," 69–70. For the years 1836–1844, see Appendix A.
[28] Department of State, *Compendium of the Sixth Census,* 276.

ness. . . ." From what he could learn, "they make about fifty per cent clear on their money annually." [29] Cow towns sprung up and served as assembly points for organizing cattle drives. These included London in Madison County and Springfield and South Charleston in Clark County, perhaps the leading cattle county in the Miami Valley.[30] The second strongest Whig constituency in the state, Clark County was described in an 1830s gazetteer:

This county, taking its size and secluded position into consideration, is one of the most productive counties in the state. As yet it has no outlet to market save the common roads of the country; yet such is the fertility of its soil, and the beautiful face of the country, interspersed with durable streams and well watered by springs, that a very large portion is under a high state of cultivation. The whole number of acres within the limits of the county are computed at 263,680, and the number returned for taxation about 245,000, leaving but a small proportion unlocated.[31]

The importance of the cattle-raising industry to the farmers of the Miami and Scioto valleys was not lost upon Whig politicians. During the years after the Panic there were two severe droughts back-to-back in 1838 and 1839, and the Whigs attempted to take advantage of the hard times by telling the cattlemen that the Whig tariff of 1842 must be supported or else the cattle business would find itself squeezed "between high prices for stock cattle and low prices in the eastern markets for fat cattle." [32]

There was also considerable Whig strength in the important coal- and salt-producing counties in the Hocking and Muskingum valleys. Four of the five largest coal-mining counties, Meigs, Tuscarawas, Lawrence, and Muskingum, were Whig, as were two of the three leading salt-mining counties, Meigs and Athens. Meigs County had

[29] As quoted in Paul C. Henlein, *Cattle Kingdom in the Ohio Valley, 1783–1860* (Lexington, Ky., 1959), 60. Henlein says that profits ranged from 25 to 33 per cent.

[30] A number of other Miami Valley counties, including Warren, Greene, and Montgomery, developed flourishing cattle businesses. But unlike the Scioto Valley counties, most beef in the Miami Valley area did not go east to the Pittsburg market, but instead was sent to Cincinnati.

[31] Warren Jenkins, *The Ohio Gazetteer and Traveller's Guide,* rev. ed., (Columbus, 1841), 120–21.

[32] Henlein, *Cattle Kingdom in Ohio Valley,* 49. The information on the cattle business has been drawn from Henlein's third chapter.

been long and steady in its opposition to the Jacksonians, giving them a little less than 35 per cent of the vote in 1828–1832 and an average of only slightly more in the presidential elections of 1836 through 1844. The county was not a wealthy one; in fact in 1840 it was the twelfth poorest Ohio constituency. However the influence of New England settlers and the increasing importance of the coal mines to the county probably were key factors in keeping and retaining the anti-Jackson majority. Furthermore, it is not unlikely that the early entrepreneurs who exploited the mineral resources of the county would have been attracted to the party of enterprise, the Whigs, and they in turn provided both the economic and political leadership in the area. One early businessman was Samuel Pomeroy from Boston, who in the early 1830s began to mine coal in Meigs County. He and his sons purchased a considerable amount of coal land with easy river access, hired a work force, built a company town, and by the middle 1830s had constructed a steamboat to tow coal barges to and from Cincinnati. A decade later they had five steamboats, employed two hundred men, and marketed about 2 million bushels of coal annually.[33]

Lawrence was another incipient industrial county. Besides being a large producer of coal, it was in the center of the state's iron industry, and, like Meigs, a poor county. In 1840 it was the second poorest county in Ohio. But, also like Meigs, it offered great promise for the future. Lawrence had given Jackson about 49 per cent of its vote in 1828 and 1832, but gave Van Buren and Polk only about 37 per cent. In 1838 it was reported that there were eight iron furnaces and two forges in the county.

The number of furnaces is steadily on the increase, several new ones going into operation the present year. . . . Each furnace employs, on an average, about one hundred men, and fifty yoke of oxen—all which are fed from produce grown in this county and those lying higher up the country on the Ohio and Muskingum rivers, affording an extensive home market for large quantities of corn, oats, flour, and bacon, and already nearly as important as that of Cincinnati, to many of the river counties.[34]

[33] Howe, *Historical Collections of Ohio* (1847 edition), 350–51.
[34] *Hildreth's Geological Report,* as quoted in Jenkins, *Ohio Gazetteer,* 254.

There are indications that many of the workingmen at the furnaces were landless, thus contributing to the poor showing in the 1840 list. One observer noted in 1847 that when "the iron works were first established, only about one eighth of the land was entered, since which, the workmen have accumulated means to purchase more." [35]

In the strongly Democratic Maumee Valley, Lucas County was an island of Whig strength. The entire Maumee Valley was a thinly populated region and Lucas was no exception. Lucas, however, on the western end of Lake Erie and the northern terminus of the Miami and Erie Canal completed in the 1840s, was in an enviable position. Many predicted that the county's mushrooming city, Toledo, would become one of the most important commercial centers of the state. At the time of the Panic the city had a population of almost 2,100 and a flourishing business community that, in anticipation of the completion of the canal, included forty-one mercantile establishments, six hotels, thirty-five mechanic shops, two steam saw mills, two brickyards, two weekly newspapers, four lumber yards, and a single iron foundry. In addition, the city enjoyed a brisk lake trade, with 390 steamboats and 211 schooner arrivals in 1836. It was enthusiastically predicted in 1838 that the opening of the Miami and Erie Canal, and others connecting with it, would render it certain that Toledo would become "one of the most important cities of the West. This will not appear unreasonable to any one who will take into consideration the important natural location of Toledo, and the advantage she derives from the railroad already in operation. . . ." [36]

3

The main sources of Democratic strength in Ohio were the Maumee Valley, the backbone counties of the upper Muskingum Valley, and five border counties in the lower Miami and Scioto valleys in the southwestern part of the state: Butler, Hamilton, Clermont, Brown, and Adams. The Democrats also were strong in Hocking, Fairfield,

---

[35] Howe, *Historical Collections of Ohio* (1847 edition), 289.

[36] Jenkins, *Ohio Gazetteer,* 430–31; and Howe, *Historical Collections of Ohio* (1847 edition), 317–32.

and Perry counties in the upper Hocking Valley, and in Monroe, an isolated county on the Ohio River. There was not, as has been indicated, as high a correlation in Ohio as there was in Mississippi between wealth and politics. Although there was a good correlation in Ohio, there are important exceptions, and the data indicate that wealth was more important as an index of politics in some sections than others. For example, in the Maumee Valley, the area closest to the frontier in Ohio, there was a clear correlation between the poorer constituencies and Democratic allegiance. Of the twelve counties, seven were Democratic, three Neutral, and two Whig. All the Democratic counties, except Seneca, were among the poorest third of Ohio's constituencies and the latter was in the poorest half. On the other hand, the two Whig counties, Lucas and Wood, were the second and thirteenth wealthiest constituencies in the state. Wealth does not seem to have been a distinguishing factor in the politics of the Miami Valley or Muskingum Valley. In the latter, Democratic strength appears to have come from constituencies that were heavily populated by persons of German extraction, while Democratic support in the five southwestern counties seems to have been generated both by a large German population and a long-held suspicion of banks.[37]

The Maumee Valley in northwestern Ohio resembled, superficially at least, Mississippi's Piney Woods. Both were sparsely settled, isolated frontier areas that gave solid support to the Democratic party. A large portion of the Maumee Valley was covered by what was called the Black Swamp, a forbidding, inaccessible area about the size of the state of Connecticut. Dense forest growth made the swamp "almost impenetrable to the rays of the sun, and its gloomy silence remained unbroken until disturbed by the restless emigrants of the west. . . ."[38] This was perhaps the most remote section within the Maumee Valley, but until the Miami and Erie Canal was completed in the middle 1840s most of the region was cut off from the rest of the state and commercial markets. As a consequence, most farmers were subsistence farmers, raising only crops that could be used for food or feed for the animals and leaving enough surplus to barter for certain necessities that could not be raised or produced on the farm. One early settler

[37] See Appendix A, Table II.

[38] Howe, *Historical Collections of Ohio* (1847 edition), 245.

in Allen County recalled his boyhood in the town of Lima, where there were no newspapers nor any

outlet or inlet either by rail or earth. . . . Our roads were trails and section lines. . . . The nearest mills were at settlements in adjoining counties, and the labor of [settlers] going thither through the wilderness and the delays on their arrival in getting their grain ground, so great that they had recourse to hand-mills, hominy blocks and corn-crackers; so the labor was largely performed within the family circle.[39]

Despite the isolation, the tranquility of the Maumee Valley was upset in the years immediately preceding the Panic by a frenzy of speculation induced by the prospect of the completion of the canal. One resident gave a colorful and perhaps exaggerated description of the boom times:

During the "flush times" of 1835 and 1836, paper money ruled all values, and everybody was rich in "rags and lamp black," and "water" or "corner" lots. . . . A Spirit, adverse to making money by the old methods, was rife throughout the land. The few who held former ways of accumulation were regarded by the multitude as "old fogies," and "behind the age."

There were very few manufacturing or mechanical establishments. They were not in demand; and if they had been, there were none to operate them. Farmers had mostly deserted their fields; mechanics their shops; physicians and lawyers, to a considerable extent, their offices; and even many clergymen their pulpits—all classes and conditions of people becoming seized with the fever of speculation, and of gathering speedy wealth by means of their wits. . . . Old ideas of obtaining competency and wealth in fields of legitimate industry were banished; and old-fashioned toil was at a discount.[40]

The Panic of 1837 struck just as the Maumee Valley was in the beginning stages of its transition from a subsistence to a commercial agricultural area. Many residents, stimulated by the prospects of the canal ending their isolation, had overextended themselves and were particularly vulnerable. Few places were hit by the crash "as severely as . . . the Maumee Valley."[41] As an underdeveloped area, the structure of the economy had been to a large extent built on shifting sands of speculation, and, when the quake came, the hastily built foundation

[39] Howe, *Historical Collections of Ohio* (1896 edition), I, 243.
[40] Knapp, *History of the Maumee Valley*, 629–31.   [41] *Ibid.*

collapsed. Compounding the economic distress was the great influx of worthless bank paper from Michigan's free banks, imported in hopes of financing continued construction of the canal.

In order to prevent the suspension of the canal work, arrangements were made for loaning this wild-cat money to contractors and for business men of the town to receive it from the workmen in payment for goods and provisions. The remedy was a desperate one, but it did keep the work in many cases from suspension. These bank notes were worthless; but it was supposed or hoped they might possibly have some value. . . . The wild-cat system of course soon exploded, loading the community with piles of broken bank notes, nearly as valueless as so many pieces of blank paper.[42]

Their optimism shattered by the Panic and their plight aggravated by useless paper money, it is little wonder that residents of the Maumee Valley gave strong support to the hard-money Democracy.

Five Democratic counties in the lower Miami and Scioto valleys, Butler, Brown, Clermont, Hamilton, and Adams, offer a vivid contrast to the counties of the Maumee Valley. These southwestern counties were, on the whole, older, more populous, and more accessible to transportation routes than their Democratic counterparts in northwestern Ohio. Furthermore, the southwestern counties were all, with the exception of Adams, wealthier than the average Ohio county and all, with the exception of Hamilton, which is a unique case, gave the Democrats an average of at least 54 per cent of the vote in the presidential elections from 1836 to 1844. In the two preceding presidential elections, the Democrats had done substantially better, receiving at least 65 per cent of the vote.[43]

Butler County was the ninth wealthiest constituency in Ohio and the state's leading hog-raising and corn-growing county in 1840. It was a flat fertile area, and Hamilton, the county seat, was located only 22 miles north of the major market, Cincinnati. Adams County was the poorest of the group, with hilly, broken, and infertile land, especially on its eastern boundary. Much of the hill area was still owned by the government and occupied by squatters who

[erect cabins] towards the head of some ravine, collect the chestnut-oak bark from the neighboring hill tops, drag it on sleds to points accessible by wagons, where they sell it. . . . Besides this common trespass, the

[42] *Ibid.*
[43] See Appendix A, Table II, and Ratcliffe, "Political Divisions in Ohio," 69–70.

squatter helps himself out by hunting deer and coons, and, it is said, occasionally by taking a sheep or a hog. . . .[44]

There is no simple explanation of the politics of this area. The only common denominator seems to have been a firm attachment to the Democratic party. Probably the best explanation has been offered by a historian who suggests that the strong support for the Jacksonians was prompted originally by an intense dislike of Henry Clay.[45] It might seem more logical to expect "Harry of the West" to have been extremely popular in this highly commercialized agricultural area where there was considerable sentiment for a protective tariff and internal improvements. Yet such was not the case. Clay's close association with the Second Bank of the United States ruined his political chances in the area as well as those of the Whig party. The 1819 financial panic and business depression evidently had hit Cincinnati and the surrounding southwestern counties harder than most areas of the country. Making matters worse, the Cincinnati branch of the national bank had closed its doors and had recalled its debts, thus heightening the economic crisis. As an unhappy result, the Bank of the United States "came to own a large part of Cincinnati. Hotels, coffeehouses, stores, stables, warehouses, iron-foundries, residences, and vacant lots were numbered among the bank's holdings. It also owned over 50,000 acres of good farm land in Ohio and Kentucky."[46] Clay became the superintendent for the bank's Ohio and Kentucky legal business and in 1824 represented the bank before the United States Supreme Court in its case against the state of Ohio. Thus, it is not surprising to find that Clay ran third among three presidential candidates in that section of the state in 1824. Jackson benefited from this reaction, and his party continued to win support in the region. The distaste that many had for Clay and the bank was generalized into an opposition to the Whigs and all banks. The Panic of 1837 simply confirmed the prejudice.

The political history of Cincinnati and wealthy Hamilton County [47]

[44] Howe, *Historical Collections of Ohio* (1847 edition), 27–28.

[45] This interpretation has been drawn from Ratcliffe, "Political Divisions in Ohio," 26–33.

[46] Huntington, *Banking and Currency in Ohio,* 94.

[47] Of the seven leading cities in Ohio in 1840, only two, Cincinnati and Steubenville, were in counties that gave the Democrats a majority of their votes in presidential elections from 1836 to 1844. The cities were: Cincinnati,

also tends to substantiate this view. With its wealth and greater degree of urbanization, it might be presumed that Hamilton County would have been a stronghold of Whiggery. On the contrary, the county was a bastion of hard-money Democratic strength. Even Cincinnati, the commercial and industrial center of the state, gave Jackson about 52 per cent of its vote in 1824 and 1828. But as the commercial interests of the city became more important and the memory of the Panic of 1819 dimmed, support for the Old Hero waned, and in 1832 he received only 41 per cent of Cincinnati's vote. The anti-Jackson party continued to do very well in Cincinnati and in 1840 gave the Whig Harrison a 1,500-vote majority in the city, which enabled him to carry Hamilton County. This, however, was only a temporary phenomenon, for a large Democratic vote in the county usually nullified the Whig majority in the city.[48]

The memory of hard times and the corresponding antibank and anti-Clay sentiment only partially explains the Democratic sympathies of Hamilton County. The presence of a large German-American population in Hamilton County and in other areas scattered throughout the state was a crucial factor in producing Democratic majorities.

Although statistical data concerning the nationality and location of Ohio's populace is not available, impressionistic evidence gives some indication where the Germans and Pennsylvania Dutch settled. In the southwestern area, the Germans were politically important mainly in Hamilton County and to a lesser degree in Butler County. Most of the counties in the Miami and Maumee valleys had at least a few pockets of German settlement, but it is difficult to assess their political influence. For example, contemporary as well as later sources

---

with a population of 46,388, in Hamilton County; Cleveland, 6,071 inhabitants, Cuyahoga County; Dayton, 6,067, Montgomery County; Columbus, 6,048, Franklin County; Zanesville, 4,766, Muskingum County; Steubenville, 4,247, Jefferson County; Chillicothe, 3,977, Ross County. Montgomery County, with a sizeable German population, gave the Democrats a fairly high 47 per cent of its vote, while Cuyahoga, Franklin, Muskingum, and Ross Counties gave only 34.07, 40.63, 39.37, and 41.43 per cent of their vote, respectively, to Democratic candidates. The 1840 population figures come from Lloyd, *Agriculture of Ohio,* 41.

[48] Ratcliffe, "Political Divisions in Ohio," 112–14.

indicate that a number of Germans lived in the Democratic counties of Mercer and Clermont as well as in the Neutral county of Shelby and the Whig county of Montgomery.[49] Settlers of German descent were numerous and influential in the backbone counties of Wayne, Stark, Holmes, Tuscarawas, and Richland; the Hocking Valley counties of Hocking, Perry, and Fairfield; and the River county of Columbiana.[50]

The Germans were convinced that the Democratic party was the stalwart defender of the immigrant and his rights. Even the Whigs ruefully recognized this political fact, for in 1842 they attributed their election defeat to the fact that they had failed to attract the German vote. One Whig newspaper in Scioto County advised Whig leaders in Cincinnati to establish a German language newspaper and to treat foreigners with more respect. That same year the Whigs started *Der Deutsche Republicaner* in an attempt to win their share of German support. The state's official Whig newspaper, the *Ohio State Journal,* pointed out the necessity for establishing such a journal and urged all Whigs to give it liberal support.[51]

[49] Howe, *Historical Collections of Ohio* (1896 edition), I, 342; Reverend Emmet H. Rothan, *The German Catholic Immigrant in the United States (1830–1860)* (Washington, D.C., 1946), 33–35; Faust, *German Element in the United States,* I, 426–28; and Jenkins, *Ohio Gazetteer,* 301–302.

[50] Faust, *German Element in the United States,* I, 422–23; Jenkins, *Ohio Gazetteer,* 175–76, 354; Howe, *Historical Collections of Ohio* (1896 edition), I, 435–66, 587–601, 927–33, and II, 382–400. Of the above-mentioned counties, Tuscarawas was the only Whig county. Unfortunately, due to county boundary changes, Stark County for the rank-difference correlations in Appendix A had to be grouped with two Whig counties, Medina and Portage. However, in the three elections Stark County voters gave Democratic candidates an average of 54.3 per cent of their votes. In the 1836 election, however, the county included two northern townships, Franklin and Greene, that in 1840 were taken, along with townships from Medina and Portage counties, to form Summit County.

[51] Carl Wittke, *We Who Built America: The Saga of the Immigrant,* rev. ed. (Cleveland, 1967), 232; and Edgar A. Holt, "Party Politics in Ohio, 1840–1850," *Ohio Archaeological and Historical Quarterly,* XXXVII (July, 1928), 535–36. See also Albert Bernhardt Faust, *The German Element in the United States; With Special Reference to its Political, Moral, Social, and Educational Influence* (New York, 1927), II, 126. Faust states that "Before 1850 the great mass of Germans for good reasons were Jacksonian Democrats." According to Henry A. Ford and Mrs. Kate B. Ford, compilers, *History of Cincinnati, Ohio* (Cleveland, 1881), the Whigs as early as 1836 had established a German language newspaper.

The attachment the Germans had for the Democracy was once explained to Henry Clay by Gustave Koerner, a German-American who was to become an influential Illinois politician. Koerner, a young man at the time, had just arrived in Kentucky to study law when a friend persuaded him to visit Clay's home, Ashland. Despite Koerner's embarrassed reluctance to call upon the famous Clay without a formal introduction, he was graciously ushered into the presence of the "Great Compromiser." Much of the conversation concerned the German-Americans, whom Clay praised as being "very honest people, fine farmers, and very industrious," but concluded that the " 'only thing I do not like . . . is their politics.' " Koerner explained to Clay that the Germans were Democrats because they "were not then used to paper money (1834) in their own country, distrusted all banks, and, besides, having been oppressed by their governments and their nobility, were attracted by the very name of Democracy." [52]

There were cultural characteristics that appear to have given the Germans a certain affinity for the Democrats. Their clannishness, suspicion of speculative enterprise, and hatred of banks all seem to have cemented German support for the Democratic party. Although the Germans tended to settle together in small compact communities throughout the state, there was, perhaps, no better example of their clannishness than Cincinnati's German district. This was a section, north of where the canal entered the city, called "over the Rhine." There life went on not too differently from the way it had in the old country. The well-kept, glistening homes, the German food and clothing, the beer gardens with boisterous German music in the background all were part of life "over the Rhine." [53]

The Ohio Germans were anxious to retain their native language and customs. In Cincinnati, for example, they agitated for several years to introduce the German language into the public schools and were finally successful after convincing the Democratic party that this was the price it would have to pay for continued German support at the polls.[54] Perhaps one reason for the Germans' desire to retain their unity

---

[52] Gustave Koerner, *Memoirs of Gustave Koerner, 1809–1896* (Cedar Rapids, Iowa, 1909), I, 350.

[53] Carl Wittke, "The Germans of Cincinnati," *Bulletin of the Historical and Philosophical Society of Ohio,* XX (January, 1962), 3–14.

[54] Ford and Ford, *History of Cincinnati,* 134.

was their fear of nativism, which they associated more with the Whigs than the Democrats. But their clannishness and insistence upon speaking in the native tongue and retaining old customs had the effect of increasing the hostile suspicions of the nativists. In the period from 1840 to 1842, for example, a number of fires were started, ostensibly by nativists, in the German section of Cincinnati. These outbreaks, in turn, seemed only to make the Germans more unanimous in their support for the Democratic party, which they believed to offer some protection against the antiforeign outbursts. But the Germans were wary lest the Democrats too should become susceptible to nativism, and in 1843 they organized the *Deutscher demokratischer Verein* in Hamilton County. They warned that if "the odious prejudices toward the foreigners should also show themselves in the Democracy, the Germans were to take up the fight against such unworthy members of their party." [55]

There also is evidence that the German population was not receptive to the kind of entrepreneurial spirit that pervaded much of nineteenth-century America. Industrious and frugal, these men of steady habits were not as likely to be caught up in the speculative fever that was so captivating to others. Hard work, rather than luck, was the measure of success for the Germans, as is shown in this description of a German village in the upper Miami Valley.

A marked characteristic of the people is the industry observable on every hand. This German element came here into the woods, and by hard incessant toil cleared away the primeval forest, wringing farms from the wilderness and building a town on the ruins of a forest. In common with the people of the township the inhabitants are almost uniformly Catholics in religion and Democratic in politics. . . . After settlement here the Germans strove to prevent the settlement of Americans in their midst, and by different methods very nearly succeeded.

Throughout the town and township the German characteristics are preserved to such an extent that a stranger would question his senses as to the possibility of a community, no larger than this, maintaining the integrity of all German habits, customs and manners.[56]

[55] William A. Baughin, "The Development of Nativism in Cincinnati," *Bulletin of the Cincinnati Historical Society,* XII (October, 1964), 240–55; and Ford and Ford, *History of Cincinnati,* 138–39.

[56] Howe, *Historical Collections of Ohio* (1896 edition), II, 605.

A traveler on a Lake Erie steamer, after observing the German immi-grants who were her fellow passengers, perceptively compared the traits of the Germans with those of other Americans:

The emigrants from German and Swiss nations are invaluable to us and ought to be warmly received, for in industry, economy and patience, they set a very excellent example to our extravagant people. They always suc-ceed; their settlements and farms present an admirable order and neatness, and yield a rich reward to their patient labor. The restless spirit, the excite-ment, caused by a hope of rising in the world, of seeing no one above him, which animates the American bosom, and many of our transplanted breth-ren, never agitates them. Where they plant themselves they remain, and in labor and social duties, pass the even tenor of their way.[57]

These Germans were not against enterprise; their success belies this. But the German-Americans above all else wanted security, and more limited economic success was preferable to the anxiety-ridden state of their neighbors who pursued the more adventuresome speculative riches.

Considering this suspicion of entrepreneurial excesses, it was only natural for the Germans to become hard-money, antibank Democrats. In 1842 a run on the Cincinnati banks and the suspension of specie payments led to a riot in which the banks were looted and heavily damaged. The Germans were blamed. In a public meeting they denied the accusation but also denounced the banks.[58] Whether or not the Germans were responsible, the fact that they were accused indicates that they had been openly hostile to banks. In Cincinnati it was reported that many Germans, rather than place their money in banks for safe keeping, entrusted it with a number of prominent brewers or with one Catholic bishop who became known as "one of the largest 'bankers' in Cincinnati." [59]

Resolutions passed at a Democratic county convention in the mid-dle 1840s were designed to appeal to the prejudices of the Cincinnati Germans by claiming that both kings and bankers had used similar practices to defraud the people. There was little difference, it was pointed out, between the way tyrants had debased "the currency by clipping or adulterating the coin" and the way bankers were now

[57] Eliza R. Steele, *Summer Journey in the West* (New York, 1841), 82–83.
[58] Holt, "Party Politics in Ohio," 523.
[59] Baughin, "Development of Nativism in Cincinnati," 251.

substituting paper money for gold and silver as "an attempt to make a very cheap material answer to the purposes of a dear one." Both tactics were seen as devices to rob the people, but as the profit "was formerly realized by the king," it was "now . . . obtained by the banker." [60]

The political career of Charles Reemelin illustrates and clarifies the nature of the attraction many Germans had for the hard-money Democracy. Coming to the United States from his native Germany in 1832, Reemelin immediately had been drawn to the Democratic party. A legislator and reformer, Reemelin studied law but never practiced, choosing instead to enter politics.[61] It was said that his "studies and experience at home had already given him an enthusiasm for free trade and a prejudice against paper money and a banking system; and he thought he saw in the Whig party an inclination toward puritanism which was naturally repugnant to the genuine German nature." [62] Reemelin settled in Cincinnati and represented Hamilton County both in the legislature and the constitutional convention, where he was the most vociferous radical democratic leader. His experience in Germany had convinced him that the sole power over the currency should be exercised by the federal government. For each state to retain the power to authorize the issuance of paper money would soon bring the United States to the same condition as Germany, where "after every twenty-five miles travel there is a new currency." Answering the criticism of a soft, Reemelin said that he would like to take the conservative to Europe where

we would then find francs on one side of the Rhine, and guilders on the other. . . . But, going over a little further, into Prussia, for instance, we would there find Rixdollars, and in every place a different gold currency. The money you have, won't go here . . . and if you go to the brokers for exchange, they will shave you a good deal closer than your barber. . . . Shave upon shave meets you. . . . This is not only the case in reference to coin, it is also as to paper money. . . . The only difference there, as here, being that you are shaved a little harder for paper money than for coin.[63]

[60] Cincinnati *Enquirer*, September 2, 1845.

[61] He was a founder of Cincinnati's German newspaper, the *Volksblatt*, and after retiring from politics devoted full time to his farms and writing, publishing books on politics as well as a volume on wine making.

[62] Howe, *Historical Collections of Ohio* (1896 edition), II, 264–68.

[63] *Report of the Debates*, II, 406–10.

Reemelin continued, showing that although similar conditions existed in the United States, a solution was near at hand. The old Whig and soft argument that there was not enough specie in the country to allow elimination of the banks of circulation was no longer valid. Because just "as fast as the golden sands of California shall flow into this country, just so fast will come the triumph of Democratic principles, and just as fast will we return to a constitutional currency." Paper money had been an impediment to the working out of certain economic natural laws. But now the acquisition of California with its enormous gold supply proved that "whenever men plant themselves upon any principle in harmony with the laws of human nature, if they but stand to it, the time will surely come which shall justify them, and show that they are in the right." [64]

To Reemelin and many other Ohio Germans, banking with its special privileges seemed a denial of the promise America had represented. Prices, rather than being subject only to economic natural laws, were controlled by bank directors who could alter the price level by contracting or expanding bank notes. Monopolistic practices were not of course condemned just by the Germans. But it is likely that a newcomer would be particularly sensitive to the difference between what he had expected and what actually existed in his adopted homeland.

Although the majority of Democrats supported the hard-money, antibank position, there was an important minority of softs who often frustrated the wishes of the hard majority. This was especially the case in 1844, when a number of softs voted with the Whigs to overturn the bank settlement of 1843, and again during the constitutional convention, when a small body of conservative Democrats joined with the Whigs to defeat the bank-reform proposals of the Democratic radicals. Soft-money sentiment within the Democratic party is difficult to analyze, because it came from areas that appear to have had little else in common. For example, there was considerable support for the soft position in Licking County,[65] one of the sixteen wealthiest

---

[64] *Ibid.*

[65] A Democrat from Licking, H. S. Manon, said at the constitutional convention that the party's hard-money platform had not even been recognized by the Licking County Democrats and was not even published in the Democratic news-

constituencies in the state, and also in Monroe County, the poorest. One factor does stand out, however. Except for Monroe, predominantly Democratic constituencies were unlikely to elect soft-money representatives. Democratic delegates from only four counties, Delaware, Belmont, Licking, and Morgan, defied the majority in their party by voting with the Whigs against all three proposals advanced by the committee on banks and the currency in the constitutional convention of 1850–1851. They also voted against the attempt to give the legislature the power to alter corporate charters. Democratic representatives of three other counties, Monroe, Highland, and Miami, voted with the Whigs on three of these four measures. In this group of seven, only Monroe can be classified Democratic in terms of its voting in presidential elections from 1836 to 1844. Of the remaining six, Miami was Strong Whig, Delaware and Belmont were Moderate Whig, and Licking, Morgan, and Highland were Neutral. Interestingly enough, representatives of all seven of these counties had voted in favor of the Wooster Bank Bill in 1844. Only four, however, Belmont, Morgan, Delaware, and Monroe, were represented by Democrats at the time. The rest had sent Whigs to the legislature.[66]

The course of Monroe County, a staunchly soft-money constituency and one of the three Very Strong Democratic counties in the state, can perhaps best be explained by the influence of Edward Archbold, its leading Jacksonian politician. Archbold's backwoods constituency was an isolated river county that remained comparatively cut off as late as 1846, when it was described by a traveler:

---

papers in the county. Another delegate pointed out that this was undoubtedly due to the fact that the largest Democratic newspaper there belonged to a bank stockholder. *Report of the Debates,* II, 404–405.

[66] Monroe County voters always sent Democrats to the Ohio house of representatives in the elections for which party affiliations are known: 1839, 1840, 1841, 1842, 1843, 1845, 1846, 1849, and 1850. Licking County usually was represented by Democrats, while the representatives from Belmont and Morgan counties were about evenly divided between the two parties. Delaware, Highland, and Miami almost always sent Whigs to Columbus. For information on the party affiliations of members of the Ohio lower house for the various sessions, see *Niles' Register,* November 23, 1839; October 31, 1840; November 13, 1841; November 12, 1842; and October 28, 1843. See also, Columbus *Ohio State Journal,* December 7, 1850, and Cincinnati *Enquirer,* October 25, 1845; October 26, 1846; and October 14 and 18, 1849.

A steamboat had landed me on the Ohio some 16 miles away, and I came up the hills meeting scarcely a soul or seeing much else than hills and trees. Woodsfield . . . was then much out of the world. Indeed the entire county was quite primitive; its people largely dwelt in cabins.

Monroe county was away from all travel, except on the river fringe. This is 29 miles long and the river hurries by, falling in that distance 20 feet 6½ inches, and mostly in ripples.[67]

Archbold, who claimed to be "the representative of small proprietors," strove at the constitutional convention to defend the inviolability of corporate charters. To make charters alterable, he argued, would prohibit all but the very wealthy from investing their money in internal-improvement companies and other corporations. He pointed out that the

small capitalist is insufficient without the principle of association. What will a single sum of five hundred or one thousand dollars do towards a work of internal improvements? It is plain that small men must have the benefit of the principle of association, if they would effectuate anything. They need the same principle, in order to enable them to compete with the larger capitalist; in order to take away the unjust . . . advantages which the gentlemen from Hamilton county would give to the millionaire.[68]

Six years earlier, Archbold had crossed swords with the hards over the Wooster Bank Bill, at which time it was reported that he personally was handed the draft of the "noxious" bill by a Wooster Bank official to introduce to the legislature.[69] Regardless of how closely Archbold was tied to the Wooster Bank, he was primarily interested in the further development of his rather primitive constituency. Unlike the newer emerging areas of the state, Monroe County was in an older section and surrounded by prosperous counties that had enjoyed the benefits of improvement systems. For Monroe to catch up with its neighbors, in Archbold's opinion, would necessitate bank credit and few if any restrictions on the entrepreneur.

Stark and Wayne counties had been at the center of the conservative Democratic revolt during the controversy over the Wooster Bank

[67] Howe, *Historical Collections of Ohio* (1896 edition), II, 264–68.
[68] *Report of the Debates,* II, 206.
[69] M. A. Goodfellow to William Allen, January 20, 1845, William Allen Papers.

Bill. The major factor in driving representatives of these counties into the soft faction was the considerable influence that the Wooster Bank exercised over politics in that region. A bank faction of soft-money Democrats, including both bank directors and interested politicians, played a major role in disrupting and badly weakening the unity of the party.

Although the influence of the bank was the main impetus behind the soft-money movement, the importance of the Ohio Canal cannot be ignored. It was an effective agent in heightening expectations and preparing the groundwork for the later soft revolt. The completion of the waterway in the early 1830s brought considerable prosperity to the counties it ran through or near. A resident of Stark County during the era recalled the poor times before the Ohio Canal had been built. The people then, he said,

> were wretchedly poor for the want of a market. Within my memory, the farming folks used to start to church Sundays barefoot, carrying their shoes and stockings in a handkerchief until they got to the foot of south hill . . . when they would stop and put them on. At that time wheat brought but twenty-five cents a bushel and had no outlet except by wagon to Cleveland and Pittsburg.[70]

Once completed, the canal opened up the entire area to the market economy. Massillon in Stark County on the canal became the wheat market for Stark, Carroll, Wayne, Holmes, and Richland counties. In 1846 the town was described as "one of the greatest wheat markets in Ohio" and a place characterized as having a "bustling air of business," so that at times the main street was "almost completely blocked by immense wagons of wheat."[71] Wooster, in Wayne County, although not on the canal, also was "a place of much business."[72]

Stark and Wayne counties, however, gave solid hard-money support

[70] Howe, *Historical Collections of Ohio* (1896 edition), II, 613–15.

[71] McClelland and Huntington, *History of the Ohio Canals,* Chapter 11; Howe, *Historical Collections of Ohio* (1896 edition), II, 613–15.

[72] On the stage road between Cleveland and Columbus, Wooster in 1846 had eight churches, "4 grocery, 10 dry goods, 2 hardware, 2 book and 3 drug stores, 1 bank" and "a female seminary in good repute." In 1840 Wooster had a population of 1,913, but this had increased to 2,700 by 1846. Besides the other business enterprise in the town, it was said that "Carriage-making" was "extensively carried on." See Howe, *Historical Collections of Ohio* (1896 edition), II, 832.

in the constitutional convention. Part of this can be explained by the sharp reaction in the counties by hards and moderates against the action of the softs on the Wooster Bank Bill. Since these counties were solidly Democratic, the hards and moderates were eventually able to put down the soft-money insurrection without fearing too much the rather weak Whig party. Furthermore, and perhaps most important, the Wooster Bank failed in 1848,[73] and this event no doubt went a long way to discredit the soft-money men.

4

In retrospect, history seems to have been on the side of the Whigs. The development of canals and railroads to complement the growing agricultural and industrial Ohio economy harmonized with Whig optimism about the material advancement of society and the necessity of banks and credit to underwrite this growth. As a result, most Ohioans who were sympathetic to this view of social development were attracted to the Whig party, and it is not surprising to find highly commercialized or incipient industrial constituencies solidly endorsing the Whigs.

But the Democrats also felt history was on their side. The introduction of paper-money banking had been, they felt, a terrible mistake, a corrupting miscalculation that clouded the vision of many Americans. Banking and speculation, each feeding the other, only fostered speculative and unnatural growth. Natural and healthy economic development would take place if paper money, which enabled the banker to control prices, were eliminated. Counties outside or only peripherally in the market economy, areas hard hit by the earlier Panic of 1819, and sections heavily populated by German-Americans all tended to support the Democratic party.

In 1837 Sam Medary published a list of bank officers and their party affiliations. Of the 405 bank officials, the outspoken editor claimed that 341 were Whigs and 64 Democrats.[74] There is no doubt as to Medary's bias, nor as to the fact that he would have recognized the political capital to be gained by labeling the Whig party the bank party. Yet,

---

[73] Coover, "Ohio Banking Institutions," 319.
[74] Huntington, *Banking and Currency in Ohio,* 162.

allowing for some exaggeration, it is true that the Democratic party, at least after 1840, was not a congenial home for bankers. Democrat Micajah T. Williams, influential organizer and director of an Ohio bank, the Ohio Life Insurance and Trust Company, found in 1840 that he was no longer in sympathy with his party. The radicals had taken over, he concluded, predicting that their "ultra" doctrines would discourage, if not prevent, banking in Ohio.[75] Indeed, Williams' conclusion was an accurate one. From the late 1830s to 1851 the Ohio Democracy was in the control of the hard-money men, who worked mightily to drive banks and paper currency from the state. What is remarkable is that they almost succeeded.

[75] Harry N. Scheiber, "Entrepreneurship and Western Development: The Case of Micajah T. Williams," *The Business History Review,* XXXVII (winter, 1963), 358–64.

CHAPTER VIII

The Northwest

I

THE POLITICAL RESPONSE to the banking issue after 1837 followed a similar pattern in all the northwestern states. As in Ohio, the hard-money men dominated the various Democratic parties and sought either to impose strict reforms upon the banking systems or to abolish note-issuing banks entirely. But, also reflecting the Ohio experience, the Jacksonian leaders were often frustrated in their efforts by a few ever-present soft-money Democrats who defected from the party on crucial banking votes and, in combination with a virtually solid front of Whig opposition, were able to override, limit, or at least modify Democratic objectives. As in Ohio, the Democrats in other northwestern states failed to take positive or effective action to meet the crisis until after the second nationwide bank suspension in 1839. Vigorous Democratic attacks on the banking system from 1839 to the mid-1840s precipitated sharp entrepreneurial counterattacks, and these led to the passage of several free-banking laws. Finally, in response to the tremendous popular desire for more banking facilities, Democrats turned to constitutional solutions.

While the general contours of the political conflicts in the northwestern states were the same, there were some significant variations. These were the result of dissimilar economic and political levels of maturity in the states, contrasting relative strengths of Democratic and Whig parties and differing degrees and types of state involvement in the banking systems. The scope, timing, and intensity of political battles, as well as the degree of militancy reached by the hard-money Democrats, depended in large part on these factors.

2

In the 1830s and 1840s Ohio had the most highly sophisticated economy in the Northwest. This pre-eminence is shown by contrasting the state with Illinois, which was at the time much closer to the frontier in spirit and development.

In the decade of the 1840s Ohio farming operations were highly commercialized or market oriented,[1] and industry was also taking its place as an important economic force. Illinois agriculture, on the other hand, lagged behind at the subsistence or self-sufficient level. Farmers were still largely independent and isolated. It was common for each to raise

his own provisions; tea and coffee were scarcely used, except on some grand occasions. The farmer's sheep furnished wool for his winter clothing; he raised cotton and flax for his summer clothing. His wife and daughters spun, wove, and made it into garments. A little copperas and indigo, with the bark of trees, furnished dye stuffs for coloring. The fur of the raccoon, made him a hat or a cap. The skins of deer or of his cattle, tanned at a neighboring tan-yard, or dressed by himself, made him shoes or moccasins. Boots were rarely seen, even in the towns. And a log cabin, made entirely of wood, without glass, nails, hinges, or locks, furnished the residence of many a contented and happy family. The people were quick and ingenious to supply by invention, and with their own hands, the lack of mechanics and artificers. Each farmer, as a general thing, built his own house, made his own ploughs and harness, bedsteads, chairs, stools, cupboards, and tables.[2]

Whereas in Ohio the canals had opened up the interior of the state to commercial agriculture, it was not until the 1850s that the railroads brought Illinois farmers of the interior counties into the market economy.[3]

[1] Percy W. Bidwell and John I. Falconer, *History of Agriculture in the Northern United States, 1620–1860* (Washington, D.C., 1925), 166. See p. 347, where the authors argue: "It seems safe to say that by 1830 frontier conditions were no longer typical of Ohio." Tennessee and Kentucky, two of the older states of the section, also had developed a commercial agricultural economy by 1837. In 1840 Tennessee and Kentucky were the two leading corn-producing states in the country.

[2] Thomas Ford, *History of Illinois, 1818–1847*, 41, as quoted in *ibid.*, 165.

[3] My argument that Illinois lagged a decade or two behind Ohio in entering

In both 1840 and 1850 Ohio was the third-ranking state in population, the numbers of its inhabitants having risen from just under a million in 1830 to slightly less than 2 million in 1850. Illinois' population jumped more than five times in the same two decades, from just about 150,000 in 1830 to approximately 850,000 at mid century. In 1860 Cincinnati was the sixth-largest city in the country, with 18.3 per cent of its residents engaged in manufacturing, as compared to 4.9 per cent in Chicago.[4]

In 1840 Ohio raised 19.5 per cent of the wheat and 8.9 per cent of the corn grown in the United States, while Illinois grew 3.9 and 6 per cent, respectively. Twenty years later, Illinois farmers were growing 13.8 per cent of the wheat and 13.7 per cent of the corn, while Ohio's production had slipped to 8.7 and 8.8 per cent, respectively.[5]

Thus, the two decades following the Panic were characterized in Ohio by a steady enlargement and sophistication of the economic system. Illinois, on the other hand, was undergoing dramatic change. This rapid transformation of the latter into a market-oriented state is indicated by the rather spectacular development of Chicago as a market center during the 1850s. Early in that decade Chicago exported 2 million bushels of grain, but by 1861 over 50 million bushels were exported.[6]

The turbulent economic stage that Illinois, and Michigan too, were in at the time of the Panic made the effects of the crisis unusually severe there. The situation was further aggravated by the fact that both states had undertaken risky financial schemes immediately prior to the Panic. Legislators, yielding to moments of entrepreneurial zeal, could not have chosen a more inopportune time to act. It was the desire to construct a canal system that prompted the Illinois legislature in the spring of 1837 to expand the capitals of both the state bank and the Bank of Illinois. It was reasoned that since the banks were paying 9 per cent to their investors, the state should increase its investment so

---

the market economy is based on considering each state in its entirety. There were, of course, areas of Ohio, particularly in the northwest, that were not in the market until later, as there were areas of Illinois that are exceptions.

[4] A total of 5.8 per cent of the St. Louis population was engaged in manufacturing in 1860. See Taylor, *Transportation Revolution*, 389.

[5] See charts in Bidwell and Falconer, *History of Agriculture*, 323, 341.

[6] North, *Economic Growth*, 146–53.

as to share in the riches. The profits the state would realize were allocated to pay the interest on the improvement loan. The plan was implemented by increasing the state bank's capital from 2.5 million dollars to 4.5 million dollars, with the state buying the entire amount of new capital. The Bank of Illinois' capital stock was expanded from 300,000 dollars to 1.7 million dollars, with the state subscribing to 1 million dollars of the increase.[7] The same spring the Michigan legislature fell under the spell of the same optimistic spirit and passed the nation's first free-banking act. Within the following year, 11 million dollars of bank capital was authorized for a state with a population of only about 100,000.[8]

Both in Illinois and Michigan the shock of the Panic left the banking systems in ruins. In 1840 the insolvent Michigan banks could claim only 7 cents specie in their vaults for every dollar of obligations in notes and deposits. In 1845 the equally devastated Illinois banks reported 6 cents of specie for every dollar of obligations.[9] No notable pressure for the creation of more banking capital was mounted in either state until the end of the 1840s.

3

At the time of the Panic, political parties in the northwestern states were in different stages of development. In two of the older states, Ohio and Kentucky, comparatively stable political systems had been established early in the Jackson period, and, by the time of the Panic, a good number of voters identified themselves with one party or the other. At the same time, in the newer states of Illinois, Indiana, and Missouri, stable party structure did not evolve until the 1840s.

Early state party systems in the Northwest were not necessarily com-

---

[7] Dowrie, *Banking in Illinois,* 79, and Golembe, "State Banks," 43–44.

[8] The law required bank commissioners to visit each bank every three months, forbade any notes under one dollar, and prohibited a bank's debt to exceed three times the amount of capital stock paid in. The directors and the stockholders were made liable for a bank's obligations, and before any bank could go into operation 30 per cent of each share had to be paid in specie. House *Executive Document No. 172,* 1109–10. See also Utley, "Wild Cat Banking System of Michigan," 209–22.

[9] See Appendix B, Table II.

posed of opposing parties of approximately equal strength. Only in Ohio did a close balance exist [10] between the parties, and this was a major cause of the bitterness with which the banking controversy raged there.

The Whigs had an edge on their Democratic opponents in Tennessee, while in Kentucky they were almost completely dominant. Illinois and Missouri were strongholds for the Democracy. The Illinois Whigs, in fact, never were successful in organizing an efficient and effective party, and the Democracy in neighboring Missouri was second only to New Hampshire in registering large majorities for the party.[11]

When a political organization achieves the sort of powerful pre-eminence that the Whigs had in Kentucky and the Democrats attained in Missouri and Illinois, self-defeating cross currents can arise. Often the more successful a party becomes, the more heterogeneous becomes its following. As more disparate elements are banded together, the party runs an increasingly greater risk of alienating and perhaps splintering off various groups of its adherents and finds it inceasingly difficult to take a position in a controversy and still maintain a united front. One Democratic leader in Missouri complained, "Our majority is *too large;* we shall be much stronger when the number is reduced. . . ." [12]

The defeat of the Ohio Democrats in the state elections in the mid 1840s and the strong initiative taken by the Whigs to introduce more banking capital into the state consolidated the Democrats around the hard-money position. Many blamed the political defeat on attempts to temporize with the banking question. This failure to win voter approval by obscuring the issue, or at least by playing down the differences be-

[10] The Whigs won the presidential canvasses in 1836, 1840, and 1844, while the Democrats gained the ascendancy in 1848 and 1852. The governorship was captured by Democratic candidates in 1838, 1842, 1850, 1851, and 1853.

[11] In Tennessee the Whigs captured every presidential election between the years of 1836 and 1852. They lost three gubernatorial contests: 1839, 1845, and 1849. In Kentucky the Democrats elected a governor in 1832, but the Whigs elected the next four and controlled both houses of the state legislature from 1832 to 1852. See McCormick, *Second American Party System,* 209–35, 258–86, 304–305, 309–10; *Historical Statistics,* 689; and Samuel M. Wilson, *History of Kentucky* (Chicago, 1928), II, 186.

[12] As quoted in Sellers, "The Equilibrium Cycle in Two-Party Politics," 30. Also see V. O. Key, Jr., *Politics, Parties, and Pressure Groups* (New York, 1953), 214.

tween Democrats and Whigs, drove the Ohio Democracy to the reaffirmation of principle and to a militant advocacy of hard-money orthodoxy.[13] Thus, the stability and balance in Ohio politics brought about a closer relationship between party ideology, image, and program. In Ohio the party viewed itself as basically antibank or hard money, and this became the test of party regularity.

In the newer states of the Northwest, as with those in the Southwest, the Democratic brokers were less subject to party discipline because of the absence of a highly organized party structure. Broker politicians on the northwestern frontier, in much the same fashion as Gwin and Claiborne in Mississippi, were therefore able to manage their parties in a far more freewheeling way than their counterparts in Ohio, whose alternative courses of action were severely limited.

4

Ohio was atypical in one respect: it was the only Northwest state that never had a state bank. The Whig bank act of 1845 chartered a class of banks called "state banks," but the state neither had investments in these banks nor exercised any more control over them than over any other banks. Bank controversies in Kentucky, Indiana, Illinois, and Missouri, as well as in Tennessee, were complicated by the fact that these states were directly entangled with the banking systems through state banks that were either partially or entirely government owned. The extent and nature of these ties and the role Democrats played in their origin were important influences on the stances the Democrats took on bank reform. It was only in Ohio that Democrats consistently opposed the argument put forth by neighboring Democrats that state-owned banks were preferable to private banks. Ohio Democrats regarded both as equally dangerous. In 1839 one Ohio radical condemned a plan for creating a state bank on the grounds that it was unconstitutional because the federal Constitution prohibited states from issuing bills of credit. Furthermore, he charged, local banks already had considerable power to do mischief; to consolidate them into a state bank and give them political influence would be disastrous. A state

---

[13] See McCormick, *Second American Party System,* 258–70.

bank "would make its own regulations, either in the State house at Columbus or in the 'Bank parlor'. . . ." [14]

There are several questions that have bearing on the consideration of state banks. Why were they founded? What role did they play? How much control could and should states exercise over them?

It was a great desire for internal improvements that made state banks attractive to legislators in Illinois, Indiana, and Tennessee. The Bank of the State of Tennessee was chartered in 1838 "to raise a fund for the internal improvements and to aid in the establishment of a system of education." The vote on the bank-charter bill was more along sectional than partisan lines, with support coming from eastern and western sections and opposition from the middle of the state. The Whigs split about evenly over the proposal, as did the Democrats, who voted 14 to 12 in favor in the house and 4 to 3 in favor in the senate. [15] The state bank in Indiana was chartered in 1834 and two years later was authorized to make a 10-million-dollar loan for a state internal-improvement system. [16] In these two states and in Illinois heavy state involvement with state banks acted as a restraining force upon Democratic politicians who were concerned that attacks on the banks would result in the curtailment of the improvements and thus in the probable loss to the states of their large investments.

State banks were regarded in a quite different light by Democrats in Missouri and Michigan who were induced to favor the chartering of state banks by their desire to keep a tight control over banking. State banks represented a compromise position between hard-money and entrepreneurial Democrats. The hard-money men accepted state-controlled institutions in lieu of no banks, and the soft-money forces accepted them after failing to win acceptance of a more liberalized banking policy.

The chartering of the state bank in Missouri divided the Democratic party into three groups. The first was composed of intransigent hard-money Democrats who wanted to keep Missouri bankless or to permit

[14] Cincinnati *Advertiser and Journal*, August 7 and 9, 1839.

[15] Stanley John Folmsbee, *Sectionalism and Internal Improvements in Tennessee, 1796–1845* (Philadelphia, 1939), 170–71; Campbell, *Banking in Tennessee*, 94, 104–105.

[16] Harding, "State Bank of Indiana," 3–13; Knox, *History of Banking*, 691–94.

only a bank that lacked note-issuing rights.[17] Another group wanted exclusive state ownership of the bank. The editor of the *Missouri Argus* argued that since the bank profits would be taken from the people they should be returned to the people through their government's ownership of the bank.[18] The third position—and the one that eventually prevailed—was that the state should own one half of the bank's stock and the state legislature should appoint the majority of directors. Most of the Missouri Whigs favored equal division of the stock between state and private investors but wanted the private investors to elect the majority of directors. When in the end a compromise was reached, there were only a few opponents to the establishment of the bank: the radical hard-money Democrats and some Whigs who wanted a national bank and were unwilling to settle for a state bank.[19]

The Bank of the State of Missouri was one of the soundest in the country, the specie ratio after 1837 never falling below 29 cents of specie for every dollar of circulation plus deposits. This did not, however, protect the institution from criticism. For although it was one of the few banks that withstood the specie suspension in 1839, it was under attack from the more commercial areas of the state for its tight money policy, especially for its refusal to accept notes from suspended banks. In response to this pressure, the directors reversed the policy in 1841.[20]

Democratic Governor Thomas Reynolds voiced his disapproval of the action in an address to the legislature in 1842, pointing out that "while our own bank is prohibited from issuing any note of a less denomination than ten dollars, the banks of other States are permitted to circulate within our limits, with impunity, notes of the lowest denomination." [21] In 1843 dissatisfaction came to a head. Democrats

[17] Cable, *Bank of Missouri*, 117–22.

[18] St. Louis *Missouri Argus*, December 23, 1836, as quoted in Primm, *Economic Policy in Missouri*, 25.

[19] Primm, *Economic Policy in Missouri*, 23–24.

[20] *Niles' Register*, April 3, 1841. See Appendix B.

[21] House *Executive Document No. 226*, 989–91. A year earlier Democrats had attempted to cope with this problem. They had sponsored a bill, which passed the house but failed in the senate, that would have made it an "indictable offense to pass or receive a $5 or $10 note." Furthermore, any contracts made or fulfilled with the prohibited notes would have been void. See *Niles' Register*, April 3, 1841.

proposed and passed in the state legislature a resolution stating that "the Bank of the State of Missouri ought not to receive or pay out the paper of any bank that fails or refuses to redeem its notes in gold and silver." It declared the action of the directors in 1841 "unwise, and contrary to the almost unanimously expressed will of the popular branch of the last general assembly." [22]

This resolution led to a party split. Soft-money Democrats who were centered mainly around St. Louis, alarmed at the direction the party's bank policy seemed to be taking, broke from the party in 1843 and 1844. They nominated their own state ticket, which received Whig support, and declared John Tyler their choice for President. [23] David Rice Atchison, later Democratic United States Senator, denounced the action of the soft-money men. He specifically attacked Shadrach Penn, editor of the *Missouri Reporter,* as

doing more to corrupt the Church with his herisies [*sic*] than all the open enemies we have. He had sold himself to all the abominations of the Hawkers and Pedlers [*sic*] of St. Louis. I do hope and trust, that St. Louis will never again elect a Democrat to the legislature; when she does confusion always follows. [24]

By the fall of 1844 the banking controversy had largely ended. Democratic Governor M. M. Marmaduke was able to tell the legislature that "it is believed that at no previous time has our currency been in a sounder or better condition than at present." This was due, he said, to the disappearance of the "worthless and depreciated paper of other States . . . and in its place may now be seen in circulation a fair proportion of silver and gold—the only true representation of value." [25]

After their disastrous experience with free banking, Michigan Democrats turned to the idea of a state bank. Democratic Governor Stevens T. Mason early in 1838 proposed that the legislature charter a state

[22] House *Executive Document No. 226,* 995–96.
[23] Eugene Morrow Violette, *A History of Missouri* (Cape Girdardeau, Mo., 1956), 262–65.
[24] William E. Parrish, *David Rice Atchison of Missouri, Border Politician* (Columbia, Mo., 1961), 32–33.
[25] House *Executive Document No. 226,* 1009. For the Missouri Whigs, see an excellent study by John Vollmer Mering, *The Whig Party in Missouri* (Columbia, Missouri, 1967).

bank, but he did not go into detail as to how it should be organized.[26] In 1839 a report of the bank commissioners recommended the chartering of a state bank, contending that as long as

the control of the cash and credit of the community is in the hands of individuals, rendered irresponsible to moral influence by their corporate capacity, with the temptation and power to acquire wealth at the expense of the community, by a contraction and expansion of paper issues: so long fluctuations in the value of this substitute for money will exist, and the consequent variation in the prices of property and labor, so disastrous to the many, and so beneficial to the few, will inevitably occur.

The commissioners proposed that the free-banking law be repealed and that a "State institution, under the control of the State itself, to be subject at all times to the most rigid scrutiny," be chartered. That same year a state bank was authorized by the Democratic legislature, but it never began operations because of a failure to raise the necessary capital.[27]

The political advantages of a state-controlled bank were not lost on the Tennessee Democrats. It quickly became apparent to them that the state bank could supply the needed credit and still be operated in the public interest.[28] Democratic Governor James K. Polk, before retiring from office in the early 1840s, recommended that insolvent private

[26] Redlich, *Molding of American Banking,* Vol. II, Part 2, 25.

[27] House *Executive Document No. 172,* 1128–29, and Redlich, *Molding of American Banking,* Vol. II, Part 2, 25.

[28] The Tennessee Democrats were swift to grasp the political utility of a state bank. Some of the original Democratic support for the bank came from a desire to discredit Whig agitation for a new national bank and to prevent the Whigs from using the Panic to political advantage. In 1838 James H. Talbot, a west Tennessee Democrat, wrote to James K. Polk, then Democratic congressman from Tennessee, that the late legislature had embarked on "an extensive system of Banking and internal improvement, and if we can only succede [*sic*] in making the election turn upon the question of a National Bank we have them—This System of Bank and internal improvement is all the go, although passed by a very small majority it has become very popular with the people and the members who voted against it are already beginning to apologize—We will say it would be a suicidal act to consent to have a National Bank to destroy our State Bank and with it our whole System of internal improvement Stockholders and all. . . ." See James H. Talbot to James K. Polk, February 16, 1838, as quoted in Folmsbee, *Sectionalism,* 172.

banks be liquidated and "their places supplied by an enlargement of
the capital stock of the Bank of Tennessee, owned exclusively by the
people of the state, and under the control of their immediate
representatives." [29]

The Illinois and Indiana Democrats were not so sanguine about the
operation of the state banks in their states. The major difference was
that in Missouri and Tennessee the public controlled the banks, while
in Illinois and Indiana private investors held the upper hand. In Kentucky the Democrats, as the minority party, were powerless to influence bank policy.

After the Panic Illinois Democrats had been initially reluctant to
take strong action against the state's banks. But in 1839, after the second suspension, they became convinced that the banking system was
beyond saving, and many Democratic county conventions that year
passed resolutions condemning all banks. Of most immediate concern
to them was the lack of control the state had over the State Bank of Illinois. In 1839 a joint committee of the Democratic legislature investigated the bank and concluded that private investors had a dispropor-
tionate amount of power, the state owning 2.1 million dollars of the
approximately 3.64 million dollars capital and yet being allowed to
choose only five of the fourteen directors.[30]

The Indiana Democracy had the same complaint. In 1839, when the
Democrats won a majority in the lower house of the legislature after
several years of political impotence, one Democrat joyfully claimed:

[29] *Niles' Register*, November 6, 1841; Campbell, *Banking in Tennessee*, 99–
100. When Polk took office in 1839, he suggested to the legislature that the banks
be required to resume specie payment, forbidden to declare dividends until six
months after resumption, and prohibited from issuing small notes (eventually
outlawing notes under 20 dollars). See Charles Grier Sellers, Jr., *James K. Polk,
Jacksonian, 1795–1843* (Princeton, N.J., 1957), Chapter XII; Campbell, *Banking
in Tennessee*, 109–10. In response to Polk's appeal the house passed a resolution
38 to 33 compelling the banks to resume specie payment. All but five of those
who voted for the measure were Democrats, and all except eight of those
voting against were Whigs. The senate, however, refused to pass the measure.
See *Niles' Register*, January 11, 1840.

[30] Theodore Calvin Pease, *The Frontier State, 1818–1848* (Chicago, 1919),
307–309; House *Executive Document No. 172*, 876–82; Helderman, *National and
State Banks*, 55–62.

we have the advantage completely: the vicious character of the Banking System is evident: and I hope the opportunity will be seized upon for an entire reform: let the stockholders be made always responsible, in the full value of their private property: let the States, which create these institutions, always guarantee them: and as security, [let the State] retain a complete supervisory power, and control, at all times.[31]

During that legislative session, a committee appointed to investigate the state's banking system charged that illegal acts of the state bank would "vindicate forfeiture" of its charter. It alleged that notes under 5 dollars had been issued in violation of the charter, that merchants had monopolized the bank's loans at the expense of the farmers, and that the favors of the bank had been confined to 5 per cent of the people. Furthermore, the bank was a "government over industry, credit, commerce, and property of the people," and the state was powerless to oversee its management.

Despite the inequities the committee members found in the bank, they called for its reform rather than its destruction. If Indiana did not have its own paper currency, they argued, the state would only be flooded with worthless paper from other states. The committee warned, however, that when "a great controlling money power is organized in a State, it exercises sway over a larger amount of hope, of toil, and of thought, than any other; and never can be sustained, unless . . . it is administered for the general good." [32]

Because of the closely divided legislature in Indiana, little was done to increase the public's power in managing the bank. One hard-money Democrat bitterly complained that the bank had "shot its roots so deep, and in so many branches, that it is not only difficult to eradicate it," but even difficult to curb its excesses. The major stumbling block to more radical action was the fact that the state was deeply indebted to

[31] Nathaniel West to Levi Woodbury, October 18, 1839, Levi Woodbury Papers, Series II. In an earlier letter, the same correspondent suggested that to curb small notes the federal government should impose an excise tax on all notes under 5 dollars. This, of course, was the plan adopted almost thirty years later. Nathaniel West to Levi Woodbury, September 18, 1839, Levi Woodbury Papers, Series II.

[32] House *Executive Document No. 172*, 893–908.

the bank, and the more conservative Democrats refused to support the hard-money portion of the party.[33]

The course of the Kentucky Democrats with regard to the state bank is difficult to trace because the Democrats had so little power there. The Bank of Kentucky had been chartered during the legislative session of 1833–1834, after it had become apparent that there would no longer be a national bank. The charter provided that the state should own two fifths of the 5 million dollars capital. After the Panic of 1837 the Whigs managed to convey to the voters that the Democrats had caused the depression by following a disastrous policy on the national level. This further weakened an already anemic Democracy, and "It now became a more or less settled fact that the state elections should result in Whig victories, and at times they ceased to attract much attention." Thus the Whig majority was free to deal with the banks in as lenient a way as they wished and did periodically legalize the suspension of specie payments until 1842, when the banks resumed permanently. The Democrats did attempt to use the banking issue to their own advantage, and one Democratic candidate in 1840 asserted:

May we not hope that Kentucky will stop short in her hazardous march under the credit system and return to her original principles of republican simplicity? . . . joint stock companies surrounded with privileges denied to the people at large, and splendid and gigantic undertakings to benefit favored districts, are better suited to monarchies than republics.[34]

Despite the differences among Democrats in the Northwest in their attitudes toward state banks, the basic theme remained the same. Whether they saw merit in state participation in the banking system or not, the great majority of the Democrats were hostile and suspicious of banks and at the minimum wanted to make the banks more responsible to the public.

[33] Ethan Brown to Benjamin Tappan, November (date unknown), 1841, and January 31, 1842, Benjamin Tappan Papers, Library of Congress.

[34] William Elsey Connelley and E. M. Coulter, *History of Kentucky* (Chicago, 1922), II, 716–17. Also see *ibid.*, 710, 720; Knox, *History of Banking,* 634–36; Sumner, *History of Banking,* 398–400; Richard H. Collins, *History of Kentucky,* (Covington, Ky., 1882), I, 325; and William C. Mallalieu and Sabri M. Akural, "Kentucky Banks in the Crisis Decade: 1834–1844," *Register of the Kentucky Historical Society,* LXV (October, 1967), 302–303.

5

It was in the years between the second bank suspension in 1839 and the mid 1840s, after which the economy began to revive, that hard-money Democrats achieved their greatest triumphs. The hards demanded, in large part successfully, a broader specie basis for circulations through specie-note ratios, the elimination of weak banks, and the banning of small notes.

During this period in Tennessee, Ohio, and Michigan, there was a drastic reduction in the number of banks. In Michigan the number decreased from twenty-eight in 1839 to one in 1849, in Ohio from thirty-seven in 1840 to eight in 1845, and in Tennessee from twenty-two in 1839 to fourteen in 1846.[35]

Even more important, however, was the increase in the proportion of specie held by northwestern banks in relation to their notes and deposits. In 1837 the banks of that section held on the average a little more than 17 cents for every dollar of circulation plus deposits. By 1844 this ratio had improved to the extent that specie holdings were equal to almost 40 cents on the dollar. Although this was due in part to the attrition of weaker banks, more significantly it was the result of reforms sponsored by the hard-money Democrats. Even in states where there was not a drastic reduction in the number of banks—Indiana, Illinois, and Missouri—the specie to circulation and deposit ratio showed a remarkable improvement. Indiana's ratio increased from 26 cents of specie for every dollar of circulation and deposits in 1837 to 40 cents in 1843, while Illinois showed a gain from 17 cents in 1840 to 33 cents in 1843. Missouri moved from a low of 10 cents in 1837 to 44 cents in 1843 and to a very conservative 75 cents in 1844.[36]

By the middle of the decade of the 1840s in Illinois, the Democratic Governor had concluded that while banks might be useful in commercial communities, "we must be satisfied that we, in the State of Illinois, are better without them. . . ."[37] At the same time, the State of Michigan was virtually bankless. Little currency of any kind was available so

[35] *Comptroller's Report, 1876*, 114–22.   [36] See Appendix B.

[37] As quoted in Sumner, *History of Banking*, 406–11. Also, House *Executive Document No. 226*, 1082–84.

that extensive bartering became necessary for the exchange of goods and merchandise.[38]

The return of good times in the middle 1840s coupled with this shortage of bank capital began to generate tremendous pressure for the creation of new banks. In Ohio, where the lack of adequate bank capital was particularly acute, it was reported that by the late 1840s the state had ten times the population of Rhode Island but only two thirds the banking capital.[39] As a result, Ohio Whigs in 1845 passed an act creating an extensive bank system, and, a few years later, they also passed a free-banking law.

One of the most important outgrowths of this pressure for more banks was the enactment of free-banking laws by Illinois in late 1851 and by Indiana in the spring of 1852. The Indiana measure required that all issues of currency be secured by an equal amount of United States or state stocks and that each bank keep on hand in specie one fourth of its note circulation. The act was less than successful, for within three years of its passage fifty-one of the ninety-four banks organized under it had failed. Party lines were not strictly drawn in voting on the bill. In general the Whigs were opposed, mainly out of loyalty to the state bank, and the Democrats approved. Governor Joseph Wright, a Democrat, signed the bill but did so without enthusiasm.[40] Wright was urged to veto the bill by a Democrat who said he considered the "Free Bank Bill . . . a measure fraught with the downfall of Democracy in this State—a means of monopolizing the legal or metallic currency and then of course the Land—small farms, produce etc. . . ."[41]

As prosperity returned in Illinois, the state experienced an acute shortage of banking facilities and scarcity of money, and sentiment began mounting for the creation of new banks.[42] This reopened the

[38] Thomas M. Cooley, "State Banks Issues in Michigan, A Retrospect of Legislation," Michigan Political Science Association *Publications,* I (May, 1893), 4–22; Knox, *History of Banking,* 736.

[39] Huntington, *Banking and Currency in Ohio,* 208.

[40] Esarey, *State Banking in Indiana,* 279–81; Knox, *History of Banking,* 698–99. Knox says that Wright vetoed it, but there is no other evidence that such was the case. Hammond, *Banks and Politics,* 620–21.

[41] James Elliot to Joseph Wright, May 27, 1852, Joseph Wright Papers, Indiana State Library.

[42] Arthur Charles Cole, *The Era of the Civil War, 1848–1870* (Springfield, Ill., 1919), 92–93.

bank issue as a source of friction within the Democratic party. Augustus C. French, hard-money Democratic Governor, received contradictory reports from local party leaders. One Democrat congratulated French for the "bold ground" he was "taking against that greatest of all political curses, the Banking system." At one time, the correspondent continued, he had thought a free-banking scheme might solve the banking issue and restore party harmony. But the failure of a number of New York free banks had convinced him that the banking system was "possessed of some innate, incurable defect, against which no legislation can guard, or human integrity sustain itself."[43] A Democratic leader from rapidly growing Chicago warned that the people there were in favor of a well-restricted free-banking system. The new constitution had given the party a way out of the banking controversy by requiring the people to vote in a general election on any proposed banking system. French should use this as an escape, his Chicago correspondent wrote him, for to take a strong stand against free banking would cost the Democrats many votes around Chicago.[44]

The agitation for banks built up to a climax in 1851, when a free-banking law, similar to that of New York, was passed. French vetoed it, but it was passed over his veto and was submitted to the people in November of 1851. Between the veto and the general election that fall, French canvassed the state soliciting Democratic opinions. A broker Democratic legislator reported that although he was an antibank man, he had voted in favor of the free-banking law. The banking scheme, he felt, would receive a large majority of the vote in the northern counties of the state. Mildly critical of French's veto, the broker argued that the Governor should have rejected the bill on constitutional grounds alone, which, politically, would have been safer. "The Bank is a dangerous subject to deal with," the writer explained, "and I have a virtuous community to *deal with,*" therefore, "discretion" prevented him from "saying much on this question."[45] Other Democrats sent French

---

[43] A. G. Galloway to Augustus C. French, October 30, 1848, Augustus C. French Papers, Illinois State Historical Library.

[44] F. C. Sherman (last name unclear) to Augustus C. French, December 6, 1848, Augustus C. French Papers.

[45] E. B. Ames to Augustus C. French, April 12 and 13, 1851, Augustus C. French Papers. Other letters discussing the free-banking issue and its reception in the state were: E. Wilcox to Augustus C. French, January 27, 1851; J. B. Wells to Augustus C. French, April 4 and March 4, 1851; Elam Rust to Augustus

more encouraging news. One wrote that the bank bill was becoming more unpopular daily and would be defeated at the polls. He applauded French's veto, which he said would "prove as efficacious to the Democrats of Illinois as . . . the veto of the immortal Jackson of the U.S. Bank Bill proved to the democracy of the whole union." The Governor's strong stand against the banks, he concluded, would save the party.[46]

Sentiment for banks in the state was too great, and the people approved the free-banking scheme in the fall of 1851 by a vote of 54 per cent. The voting indicated a definite sectional split. Northern Illinois went heavily for the bill—some counties around Chicago giving 85 to 95 per cent support—while the southern half of the state was overwhelmingly opposed to its passage.[47] Although the issue was settled, bitterness remained between the hard- and soft-money Democrats. In an intraparty battle to nominate a candidate for governor, Democrats from southern counties wanted to make hard money the test for potential candidates. Northern Democrats violently objected to this, claiming that the "force of circumstances, has made many men at the North go for Banks who otherwise would be against them. . . ." The issue was dead as far as the northern Democrats were concerned.[48]

The entrepreneurial counterattack in the last half of the decade of the 1840s and into the 1850s dramatically multiplied banking capital in the Northwest. Ohio, which had 2.1 million dollars of banking capital in 1845, had increased this amount to a little over 8 million dollars by 1854. From 1851 to 1855 Indiana's bank capital rose from 2 million dol-

---

C. French, April 10 and 14, 1851; and I. N. Haynie to Augustus C. French, October 17, 1851, Augustus C. French Papers. One correspondent (Dan Eaton to unknown, presumably French, January date unknown, 1851, Augustus C. French Papers) reported that many petitions were being circulated in Illinois for the federal government to issue a paper money to protect the people against the "frauds of bankers." Thus it would appear that the historical gap between the hard-money Jacksonians and Greenbackers was quite narrow. Frustrated over the futility of trying to control the currency and the banks at the state level, some hard-money men were attempting to attain a more satisfactory solution through the agency of the federal government.

[46] Elam Rust to Augustus C. French, August 18, 1851, Augustus C. French Papers.

[47] Cole, *The Era of the Civil War,* 95–97.

[48] E. B. Ames to Augustus C. French, December 22, 1851, Augustus C. French Papers.

lars to 7.2 million dollars, while that in Illinois expanded from 1.7 million dollars in 1853 to 5.8 million dollars in 1857. Michigan was practically bankless at the end of the 1840s, with only 139,450 dollars of bank capital in the state. Six years later this had shot up to over 1 million dollars.[49]

6

As a last effort in their war against the banks, northwestern Democrats grasped a new tactic, that of constitutional revision. In the midst of popular cries for banks and credit, the hards sought to revise constitutions, so that banking would be prohibited, and called for popular referendums on new proposals that would enlarge or extend banking systems.

The Ohio hards, after being blocked in their attempts to prohibit banking in the state, had to settle for a constitutional provision calling for voter approval of all subsequent banking measures. Earlier, both Illinois and Michigan had adopted identical constitutional stipulations. In 1847 an Illinois convention dominated 91 to 71 by Democrats failed by one vote to outlaw banking in the state. The convention did incorporate into the new constitution a provision that barred the legislature from reviving or extending bank charters, forbade the state to own stock in any future bank, and prohibited the granting of banking powers without approval by voters at a general election.[50] Three years later Michigan adopted a constitutional provision giving the people the right through referendum to decide on the extent and scope of banking. And it specifically prohibited the creation of banks by special charter.[51]

When a constitutional convention met in Indiana in 1851, the position of the Democrats was more complicated. While enjoying a 95 to 55 edge over the Whigs in the convention, they were not unified. There were those who wanted to prohibit banking altogether and others, critical of the state bank for its rather restrictive loan policy, who called

[49] *Comptroller's Report, 1876,* 114–23.

[50] Helderman, *National and State Banks,* 115–19; Sumner, *History of Banking,* 447–48; Cole, *Era of the Civil War,* 93; Hammond, *Banking and Politics,* 617–18.

[51] Cooley, "State Banks Issues in Michigan," 4–22; Knox, *History of Banking,* 736.

for "separation of bank and state." Edward R. May, a representative of the former group, introduced a resolution outlawing banking, which was defeated 89 to 43. Able Pepper, a Jacksonian officeholder who went along with the latter group of Democrats, argued at the convention that the state and bank must be separated. While he was normally opposed to all banks of issue, he said, the people in his district were not ready to give up notes. The Whigs, in general, supported the state bank.[52] Since the Democrats were badly split, all they could agree upon was a constitutional provision prohibiting the rechartering of the state bank. The document also forbade the establishment of any bank except under general law, forbade the sanctioning by the legislature of any suspension of specie payment, and forbade the state from ever again becoming a stockholder in a bank. Although the new constitution did allow the chartering of a bank with branches, it outlawed state participation in it.[53]

7

The Democratic party was not the party of enterprise in Ohio nor in other northwestern states, and neither the rhetoric nor the economic measures the Democrats supported would lead one to conclude that it was. There was a minority faction of entrepreneurial-minded men within the party, but these Democrats, too, were forced to pay homage, if only ritualistically, to the neo-Jeffersonian hard-money credo.

Exerting tremendous pressure on the party, however, was the increasing sentiment throughout the decade of the 1840s for more banks. The Panic and depression had taken a heavy toll of banking institutions, and most states were left with a shortage of currency and credit. Compounding this situation, more people were being brought into the market economy through the improvement of transportation facilities. And this created a spiraling need for credit and exchange.

Despite this, the hard-money men believed that history was on their side, and although they were not as successful as their counterparts in the Southwest in adopting constitutional prohibitions against banking,

---

[52] Esarey, *State Banking in Indiana,* 265–77; Helderman, *National and State Banks,* 46–55.

[53] Sumner, *History of Banking,* 443–44; Knox, *History of Banking,* 697–98.

this triumph of "correct principle" failed only by a single vote in Illinois and a slight margin in Ohio.

Many brokers agreed with the hards as to the ultimate desirability of the eradication of bank notes, but they realized the increasing political futility and unattractiveness of the position. And although they used the rhetoric of hard money, the brokers did not see the hard-money position in terms of principle. To these men, hard money usually meant bank reform and assurance of adequate state control over banks rather than an ideological commitment. In the years after 1837 the brokers, by offering measures they hoped would provide the basis for a Democratic consensus, labored mightily to keep the party from ripping itself apart over the currency issue.

Free banking as a solution was acceptable to some of the more moderate hards, and it also gained the support of the soft-money Democrats. Indiana, which had not suffered to as great an extent as other western states the consequences of the overbanking mania of the 1830s, provides an example of this. The absence of this experience and the fear of the state bank's monopoly power, which could not be adequately controlled by the state government, prompted many Indiana Democrats to favor the free-banking scheme. Some Democrats in Illinois also lent their support to free banking, but to a lesser degree.

Free banking was only one of the manifestations of this antimonopoly, anticharter sentiment. Charters were viewed by many Democrats as infringements upon the power of the people in that they limited or prohibited public action in certain spheres and secured for corporations privileges that private citizens could not have. While some Democrats who desired the elimination of monopolies were satisfied by the free-banking system, others worried about the entrepreneurial or soft-money aspects and turned to the idea of empowering only the people as a whole to ratify bank charters. Through this plan a majority of the entire community had to consent before restrictions would be made on the people's sovereignty. This plan, too, had the added attraction that it forced a popular referendum on a controversial issue, thus enabling the party to escape taking a direct stand and thereby avoid any intraparty battling.

Ohio, Illinois, and Michigan included new provisions in their constitutions in the late 1840s and early 1850s that required constituent approval of all bank laws. But in Illinois, much to the dismay of the hard-money Democrats, the people used this power to ratify a free-banking law.

Democrats in Missouri and Tennessee were, for the most part, happy with the state-bank arrangement whereby the state owned either part or all of the stock and was able to retain control over the bank. Michigan Democrats evidently saw merit in the state-bank plan but were not able to get it off the ground. The plan did not appeal to Democrats in Illinois and Indiana, where, it was felt, state banks had been established without adequate provisions for public control. This fault, which according to them outweighed any advantages of the system, was reinforced in the minds of Illinois Democrats by the memory of the disastrous experience they had had with a state bank during the Panic and depression. In Indiana the state bank was identified with the Whig party, which added to the distaste the Democrats had for it.

THE EAST

THE EASTERN REGION was economically, socially, and politically the most mature area in the country, and despite the tremendous difference between the South and North, the eastern states did share some common experiences. Many political and economic institutions in the Northeast and Southeast dated from the eighteenth century, and this gave the two sections a certain balance and stability that was, for the most part, lacking in the West.

The Northeast, including New Jersey, Pennsylvania, New York, and the New England states, was the industrial and commercial center of the country and also a prosperous agricultural section. The Erie Canal had opened up not only the interior of New York to the market but much of the West as well, and it was destined to make New York City the major port on the eastern seaboard. Although the growth rate of the Northeast was not nearly so spectacular as that of the younger states of the West, it was a dynamic and vigorous section in its economic prime.

In contrast, the Southeast, including Delaware, Maryland, Virginia, North Carolina, South Carolina, and Georgia, was a section past its prime. The growth rate was sluggish, and the economy was languishing, especially in the section's northernmost states. In the twelve years from 1817 to 1829, it was reported that land values in Virginia had been reduced from 206 million dollars to 90 million dollars.[1] English traveler Harriet Martineau described conditions in South Carolina in

---

[1] Avery Odelle Craven, *Soil Exhaustion as a Factor in the Agricultural History of Virginia and Maryland, 1606–1860* (Gloucester, Mass., 1965), 124.

1835: "Roads nearly impassible in many parts," she wrote, "bridges carried away and not restored, lands exhausted, and dwellings forsaken, are spectacles too common. . . . There is an air of rudeness about the villages, and languor about the towns."[2] Senator Robert Y. Hayne also painted a gloomy picture of conditions there in 1832.

> Look at the state of things now! Our merchants bankrupt or driven away—their capital sunk or transferred to other pursuits—our shipyards broken up—our ships sold! . . . our mechanics in despair; the very grass growing in our streets, and houses falling into ruins; real estate reduced to one-third part of its value, and rents almost to nothing. . . . If we fly from the city to the country, what do we there behold? Fields abandoned; the hospitable mansions of our fathers deserted; agriculture drooping; our slaves, like their masters, working harder, and faring worse. . . .

In earlier, more prosperous years, the senator explained, Charleston had been a city where

> a thriving foreign commerce was . . . carried on direct to Europe. We had native merchants, with large capitals, engaged in foreign trade. We had thirty or forty ships, many of them built, and all owned, in Charleston, and giving employment to a numerous and valuable body of mechanics and tradesmen.[3]

The states of the Southeast gained little in population in the 1830s, and what gain there was seems especially meager when compared with that of the Southwest and Northwest. The population of Maryland, North Carolina, and South Carolina were augmented by only 4.5 per cent, 3 per cent, and 2 per cent, respectively, while Virginia actually lost population. Georgia fared somewhat better, the population there increasing by nearly 30 per cent in the decade.[4]

The banking system in most eastern states had been long established by 1837 and banks were, in general, considerably more responsible than most in the West. By the time of the Panic eastern banks were well integrated into the economic lives of the communities they served and played active and vital roles.

---

[2] As quoted in Charles S. Sydnor, *The Development of Southern Sectionalism, 1819–1848* (Baton Rouge, La., 1948), 249.

[3] Speech to United States Senate as quoted in Frederick Jackson Turner, *The United States, 1830–1850* (Gloucester, Mass., 1958), 150–51.

[4] All figures are approximate, taken from *Historical Statistics*, 13.

Politics in the East were shaped to a considerable extent by this stability. Whereas in the western sections the hard-money position was defined by favoring an exclusive metallic currency, or by at least taking steps to ultimately achieve this goal, hard-money men in the East—at least those in positions of political power—normally stopped short of advocating such action. Eastern radicals were more cognizant of the indispensable services the banks discharged, and, therefore, generally were satisfied with reforms that restricted and regulated bank activities.

Neither of the two eastern sections had been swept up in the economic boom of the 1830s to the degree the two western sections had been. And partially as a result of this, neither the Southeast nor the Northeast suffered from the Panic and depression to the same extent as did the two western sections.

CHAPTER IX

Virginia

I

VIRGINIA, Ohio, and Mississippi represented three different stages of political and economic development in 1837. While Mississippi had the impulsiveness and inexperience of youth and Ohio had the vigor and confidence of approaching maturity, Virginia had passed the period of its economic and political prime. Mississippi and Virginia were both slave states. But in Mississippi the plantation system was expanding and profitable, whereas in Virginia many plantation owners were surrounded with worn-out lands and a surplus labor force. Ohio was opening up the interior of the state to the market economy by an extensive internal-improvement system that would in turn stimulate the development of commerce and local industry. Internal-improvement schemes in Virginia proceeded slowly and seemingly without conviction, and the state never developed a commercial or industrial center like Cincinnati.

Virginia in 1837 remained among the most important and influential states in national politics. To many residents of the Old Dominion, their state had been the flagship in the Democratic flotilla that had scuttled Federalism in 1800 and neo-Federalism in 1828. However, there was a strong sense, too, that Virginia's power, prestige, and political grandeur were on the wane. While Virginians had held the Presidency for thirty-two of the fifty-two years between the inauguration of George Washington and the end of Van Buren's term, no resident of the state had occupied the office since James Monroe.

Perhaps because of the leading role that Virginia had taken and desired to take in the federal government, national political issues assumed a far greater importance there than in either Ohio or Mississippi. For example, the Independent Treasury was a major question in Virginia and split the party like no other issue, while in Ohio and Mississippi it was of relatively little importance in comparison with the question of reforming the state banking systems. It was, in fact, precisely the issue of the Independent Treasury proposal that became so explosive in Virginia as to split off from the Democracy a dedicated group of conservatives, who hoped by their insurgency to change the course of national politics.

The groundwork for the Virginia conservative movement was laid at the Democratic national convention of 1835. Virginia Democrats had gone to the Baltimore conclave fully confident that the Old Dominion's popular native son, William C. Rives, would be given the vice presidential nomination and, thus, become Van Buren's heir apparent. Delegates, however, bypassed the suave, likeable politician—a former United States minister to France who had served in both houses of the United States Congress—in favor of a Kentuckian, Richard M. Johnson.[1] This was a bitter pill for the egotistical Virginian to swallow, particularly so because New York, Virginia's partner in the historic New York-Virginia political axis, threw its support to Johnson. From that moment on, one Virginian politician later wrote, Rives was "lost" to the Van Buren Administration.[2]

Frustrated in his bid for national political leadership, Rives soon became sharply at odds with the administrations of Jackson and later Van Buren over the Specie Circular. The Virginian's restless ambition and conservative views on banking and fiscal measures combined to make him an ideal candidate to lead a revolt against the national leadership. Thus, after the Panic of 1837, when the Van Buren Administration proposed the Independent Treasury, Rives was in the front ranks of the conservative insurgents. He undoubtedly thought this path would lead to the fulfillment of his highest aspirations.

Rives' presidential hopes were not unrealistic. He possessed that intangible quality that gives so many politicians power. His personality, intellect, strength of character, and charm commanded great respect

---

[1] Ambler, *Thomas Ritchie,* 169–73.

[2] John Brockenbrough to Andrew Stevenson, January 1, 1839, Andrew Stevenson Papers.

among Virginia Democrats. Many loyal party members steadfastly refused to condemn Rives even in later years after he had completely broken with the party and was actively courting Whig support.

The forcefulness of Rives' leadership and the devotion he instilled in many of his followers were evident in his relationship with David Campbell, Virginia's conservative Democratic governor. A correspondence between the two men started as a means for "exchanging views" about Virginia politics. However, there was little equality intellectually or otherwise between the two men, and Campbell soon became a willing servant and mouthpiece for Rives.[3]

However proud the Virginians were politically, the economy of the state at the time of the Panic was stagnant. With unproductive lands, a declining population, and no important commercial centers, the state's future looked dreary. But to Rives the banks offered a solution. As important agents of innovation, the banks could lead the way in recapturing the prosperity of Virginia's golden age. If credit were available, planters and farmers could make needed capital improvements to revitalize the land, and merchants would be able to attract produce from the West to Virginia cities, thereby regaining the lucrative direct trade with Europe.[4] An integral part of this dream for the future was the building of a vast internal-improvement system. This, too, would require extensive bank facilities.

Rives' first challenge to the national party was over the Jackson Administration's Specie Circular, which provided that only specie would be acceptable in payment for public lands. Immediately before the nationwide financial panic in 1837, Rives blamed the mounting economic pressure on the Specie Circular. The party, he wrote, should "abstain from . . . experiments and impracticable theories" and not "preach or crusade against the mercantile and business classes of the community, as if every other class, the farmer, the mechanic, the laborer, were not deeply interested in the prosperity of those, who afford a market for the productions of their industry. . . ."[5]

---

[3] See the Rives-Campbell correspondence in the David Campbell Papers, Duke University.

[4] Gray, *History of Agriculture,* II, 924–33. Also, Thomas J. Wertenbaker, *Norfolk: Historic Southern Port* (Durham, N.C., 1931), Chapter 7.

[5] William C. Rives to Thomas Ritchie, May 4, 1837, William C. Rives Papers.

Rives' initial doubts as to the financial wisdom of the Specie Circular were confirmed by the bank stoppage. Thus, he was aghast at the prospect of what he considered to be another such utopian scheme, namely the Independent Treasury proposal to separate the federal government from the banks. The Virginia Democrat was convinced that the party had fallen into destructive hands. A warm friend of the banks, Rives saw these institutions as bulwarks against the re-establishment of a national bank. The Deposit Bank System, he protested to Van Buren, has "worked admirably for the first three years" and has been only "temporarily *thrown out of gear*. . . ." Rives asked the President whether the proposed Independent Treasury System was to "lead . . . to an *exclusive* metallic currency for the country?" If this were the objective, Rives felt it was "visionary" and would lead to one currency for the government and another for the people.[6]

Powerful backing for Rives in the early years came from Thomas Ritchie, long-time editor of the Richmond *Enquirer,* who generally agreed with Rives on the necessity for protecting the banks but differed slightly over the political implications of the Independent Treasury issue. The editor's foremost allegiances, however, were to his party and state. For Ritchie, Rives' attraction was his availability as a presidential candidate who could reassert Virginia's claim as a leader within the Democracy. When it became obvious that Rives had definitely broken with the national administration over the currency question and was threatening to ruin the party, Ritchie repudiated him. For Ritchie was a true political broker to whom personal friendships were secondary to political victory, and his survival in the political jungles of Virginia for almost half a century provides ample testimony to his skill.

It is almost impossible to overemphasize the power and influence the venerable editor wielded within the party. He and his group of like-minded Democrats, mostly from the eastern part of the state and many of them related to each other, were often referred to as the "Richmond Junto."

The most important factor behind the control of Ritchie and his colleagues was the overweening importance that Virginians placed on national political issues as opposed to, and at the expense of, state and

[6] William C. Rives to Martin Van Buren, June 3, 1837, Martin Van Buren Papers.

local ones. This stemmed, no doubt, from the fact that national controversies had been the catalysts behind the formation of the first party system in the state and that Virginia had dominated the Presidency for so long.

Underscoring this preoccupation with national politics was the oligarchic nature of Virginia's political structure. Limited suffrage, eastern domination of state politics, and a highly undemocratic local government arrangement that perpetuated rule by the squirearchy all contributed to the downplaying of local issues and emphasis on national ones. Politics was conducted on a personal, loosely organized basis. House of delegates members were the only officials elected at the county level, and only at presidential elections was there statewide balloting. Governors were elected by the legislature. This discouraged the building of elaborate party machinery on both state and local levels.[7] Without it, it was difficult to channel grassroots discontent in directions in which it might have had some impact on the party. In an attempt to de-emphasize divisive state issues, Ritchie, in his highly political paper, did not indicate party breakdowns on legislative votes on banking, internal-improvement schemes, or other important state questions. Democratic addresses to the people rarely more than mentioned state issues. Gentlemen could differ openly on national issues, but there seems to have been a tacit agreement among the leaders of both parties not to exploit for political advantage those important questions that would have immediate local political, social, or economic implications.

Not all Junto men were as reluctant as Ritchie to support the Independent Treasury or to tackle the question of state bank reform. Peter V. Daniel, a confidant of Van Buren, and Judge Richard E. Parker, brother-in-law of Ritchie, were among those Virginians who vigorously supported the Independent Treasury proposal. Both Daniel, who was appointed Associate Justice of the United States Supreme Court in 1841, and Parker also agreed with those who advocated radical reform of the state's banking system. But, not having a broad base of constituent support nor the public stature of Rives, Daniel and Parker were not in positions to provide leadership for the hard-money sentiment.

Daniel, Parker, and other hard-money men in Virginia generally

[7] See McCormick's, *Second American Party System,* 178–99, for a discussion of Virginia's political structure.

viewed the banks with great suspicion, and it was hoped they could reform and curtail bank activities. Despite the opposition of the influential conservatives, the hard-money men in the legislature consistently
received the majority of the party's support in their efforts to impose
restrictions upon the banks. But in the years separating the Panic and
the final resumption in 1842, the Democrats controlled the legislature
for only one session. Therefore, any action against the suspended banks
was thwarted by the Whigs along with the conservative Democrats.

James McDowell, kinsman of hard-money Senator Thomas Hart
Benton of Missouri, has often been regarded as a hard-money leader
from western Virginia.[8] Yet, in actuality, McDowell was quite moderate in his views toward the Virginia banks and was little suited to provide leadership for the hard-money Democracy. McDowell, who served
as Democratic governor of Virginia from 1843 to 1846, had inherited
enough land and wealth to make him independent of the daily worries
that surrounded the management of his several plantations. During the
1830s, while for several terms he represented the Moderate Strong
Whig Rockbridge County in the house of delegates, the Whigs of
Rockbridge could find few who agreed with them more on the value
and benefit of an internal-improvement system. As early as 1832
McDowell had demanded improvements that would unite "the navigable waters of the Ohio with the tide of the James." [9]

Although he was a strong supporter of Van Buren's Independent
Treasury plan, McDowell had little quarrel with the Virginia banks,
holding a sizable amount of bank stock. In 1838 he joined with the
Whigs and a handful of other Democrats to vote down a bill sponsored
by the hard-money men that would have given the legislature the
power to repeal, alter, or amend bank charters. His action does not
seem to have stemmed from any abstract belief in the sanctity of private property. In the early 1830s he had caused a considerable stir by
arguing that the state had the right to seize newborn slaves for gradual
emancipation if the owners would not surrender them or the state
could not afford to purchase them.[10]

[8] Ambler, *Thomas Ritchie,* 211.
[9] James Glen Collier, "The Political Career of James McDowell, 1830–1851,"
unpublished Ph.D. thesis, 1963, University of North Carolina, 4–12, 61–62, 87.
Also, Edgar P. Nicholson, "James McDowell," *The John P. Branch Historical
Papers of Randolph-Macon College,* IV (June, 1914), 12.
[10] *Ibid.*

Still, it would be a mistake to think of McDowell in entrepreneurial terms. A late convert to Presbyterianism, he was a pious man and as governor even refused to allow dancing or the drinking of wine in the governor's mansion.[11] His travels on business affairs to the West instilled in him a healthy suspicion of the banks and the speculating mania and inflation that could result from unchecked credit. "I have been much bothered in getting here and have had almost to line my way with dollars," he wrote his wife from Mississippi. "Such a country for extortion as no man should come into who can keep away: at all events no man should make his money elsewhere to spend it here," for "you can hardly ask a man for the time of day but he charges you for it."[12]

McDowell's position is illustrative of the dilemma some of the more moderate Democrats within the hard-money Democracy found themselves in. Although they supported the Independent Treasury plan, they were extremely uneasy about taking strong and radical action against the banks. There were several reasons for this. The Virginia banking system had been conservative and responsible. The state was one of the few in which small notes did not circulate.[13] The banks were closely linked with the Virginia government through state investment in the banks and state appointments to bank directorships. And the Virginia Democrats, having for a long time held the reins of power in the state, were in large part responsible for and closely tied to the banks. Two bank presidents were Democrats: John Brockenbrough of the Bank of Virginia, and James Rawlings of the Farmers' Bank.[14]

2

The suspension of specie payments by the Virginia banks in the middle of May, 1837, drew attention, at least temporarily, away from the

[11] Collier, "Political Career of James McDowell," 7, 11; W. H. T. Squires, *Through Centuries Three: A Short History of the People of Virginia* (Portsmouth, Va., 1929), 445; Oren F. Morton, *A History of Rockbridge County Virginia* (Staunton, Va., 1920), 266.

[12] James McDowell to Mrs. Susanna S. McDowell, April 26, 1837, James McDowell, Jr., Papers, University of North Carolina. See also letters of April 4, 1837; April 12, 1837; and March 29, 1839.

[13] At least this was true in the early 1830s. See Gouge, *Paper Money and Banking*, 56–57.

[14] Ambler, *Thomas Ritchie*, 27–28.

national and to the state level. In Virginia, as in most states, specie suspension made bank charters liable for forfeiture, and this led to a general outcry in the Old Dominion for a special session of the legislature,
with the object of suspending penalties against the banks. Among the
proponents of this course of action was Thomas Ritchie, who asked the
legislature to relieve the banks but to couple this favor with rigid restrictions limiting bank circulations.[15]

The appeal for a special session was made to the new governor,
David Campbell. Egotistical, politically ambitious, and easily seduced
by flattery, Campbell had quickly fallen under Rives' influence following his election as governor the preceding winter. A resident of Abington in the extreme southwestern part of Virginia, Campbell had a natural dislike and suspicion of the Tidewater wing of the Virginia
Democracy. His view of the Virginia aristocracy revealed his deep
sense of inferiority over being a westerner. There never was, he
claimed,

in any country a more arrogant aristocracy than the educated class of old
Virginians. They think the world does not produce their equals—and they
are in truth as light and airy and as unsubstantial as their bloodhorses.
Many of them now are repudiating their old republican principles, being
the only thing that ever gave them character.[16]

Campbell's initial reaction was not to call the legislature,[17] but the
combination of public pressure, the urging of Rives, and the realization
that he might advance his own political stock decided him in favor of
a special session. "To save the Banks," he wrote to his wife, "and I
may say the country from great losses I am taking great responsibility
upon myself" and "have decided today to call the legislature
together."[18]

The bank suspension and the impending special session stimulated a

[15] Richmond, Va., *Enquirer*, May 16, 1837.
[16] David Campbell to William B. Campbell, February 21, 1837, David Campbell Papers.
[17] David Campbell to Maria Hamilton Campbell, May 14, 1837, David Campbell Papers.
[18] David Campbell to Maria Hamilton Campbell, May 15, 1837; John F. May
to David Campbell, May 13, 1837; Frederick County Citizens to David Campbell, May 13, 1837; James Rawlins to David Campbell, May 15, 1837; Maurice H.
Garland to David Campbell, May 16, 1837; David Campbell Papers.

lively debate in the Richmond *Enquirer*. Ritchie attempted to stall any action against the banks but invited discussion of all points of view in his paper's columns. He warned, however, that he would not support those who favored "crushing the Banks" because "it would let in by far more evils than it would cure." At the same time, he wrote,

the experience of the last few weeks has essentially shaken our confidence in the banking system. . . . It is eminently defective; and demands radical reform. But at *this moment,* it is impossible to reform it thoroughly, without producing more injuries than we can hope to remove.[19]

It would appear that the large majority of Ritchie's correspondents were hostile to the banking system, but the antagonists did not, in general, run to the extreme of calling for an immediate winding up of the banks. Some recommended prohibition of notes under 100 dollars, while others wanted to gradually eliminate banks until there would be only one in each state.[20] Such halfway measures did not appeal to one correspondent, "A Democrat in Earnest," who opposed the special session because he felt that it would simply legalize the banks' violation of the law. "It is passing strange," he said,

that a system so fraudulent, so anti-Republican, so dangerous, should ever have been saddled upon us. Shall we so far forget our duty to ourselves, and the obligations we owe to our children, as to attempt to patch up and perpetuate such a system . . . ? No! Let us blot out every corporation that violates its charter.[21]

The most economically sophisticated essay to appear in the *Enquirer* was by "Civis," who asserted that one of the greatest weaknesses in the banking system was its failure to maintain the convertibility of paper. The banks, he felt, had underwritten too many long-term projects, such as buying lands and slaves and building roads and canals. Conceding that Virginia banks were among the soundest in the country, he pointed out that in 1836 even they had scarcely one seventh of their "circulation in specie, and the greater part of the balance is 'accommodation paper,' on short dates apparently, but really on indefinite time. . . ." For safe banking operations, "Civis" argued, a bank should

[19] Richmond *Enquirer,* June 2 and June 9, 1837.
[20] *Ibid.,* May 23, 1837, and June 9, 1837.
[21] *Ibid.,* May 26, 1837. Other essays by "A Democrat in Earnest" were in the issues of May 23 and June 2, 1837.

have one third of its circulation in specie and the remainder in short-term paper. "Civis" concluded that at best the paper system was an evil and a poor substitute for gold and silver. Not only was an exclusive metallic currency desirable, but it was possible to attain.[22]

Conservative opinions were also expressed in the *Enquirer*. One correspondent, "Jefferson," warned his Democratic friends that the Whig party was capitalizing upon the unrest to renew its campaign for a new national bank. The Whig strategy, he said, was to dupe the Democratic party into destroying the local banks, thereby removing the greatest obstacles in their path.[23]

Within the Democratic party leadership, even among the hard-money men, there was no immediate demand for eliminating all banks. Peter V. Daniel believed that although "the utter extinction of all Banks throughout the world" would be "the greatest possible good which could be done to mankind," the banks had to be allowed to suspend specie payment or else there would be ruinous consequences for the state and the people.[24] Reform was what Richard E. Parker called for; and he tried to convince his brother-in-law, Mr. Ritchie, of "the absolute necessity at this time of taking a decided part against the Banking System." Parker hoped that the legislature would take advantage of the suspension of specie payments and impose new restrictions on the banks.[25]

Rives agreed that the banks should resume specie payment at the earliest possible time and should be prohibited from extending their note issues while suspended. But since the local banks were the only practical substitute for a national bank, Rives said, they must be sustained. In a letter to Campbell, he warned the Governor to be wary of those Democrats who were "for putting down all Banks, both State and Federal, and enforcing an exclusive metallic currency." The hard-money men's notions were "visionary and impracticable" and they could "have no other effect than to . . . derange all the business interests and operations of the community. . . ."[26]

Campbell agreed with Rives. But the Governor felt that there were

[22] *Ibid.,* June 6, 1837.					[23] *Ibid.,* June 2, 1837.

[24] Peter V. Daniel to David Campbell, May 15, 1837, David Campbell Papers.

[25] Richard E. Parker explains the position he took with Ritchie in a letter to Benjamin F. Butler, May 29, 1837, Martin Van Buren Papers.

[26] William C. Rives to David Campbell, May 22, 1837, David Campbell Papers.

only a few men who were of the hard-money belief and that he would be able to keep them in line.[27] Campbell thought highly of his powers of persuasion. He wrote to his wife that Ritchie came to see him every two or three days "red hot for hard money" but that after reasoning with him, the Governor got Ritchie "back on the proper track. . . ."[28]

In his message to the special session of the legislature, Campbell advised against making any radical changes in Virginia's banking system, which had "been long since introduced" and in which the state had considerable investments. *"There are those* who would have no banks," the Governor warned, "either State or Federal, and are for enforcing an exclusive metallic circulation." This, Campbell believed, was "wholly impracticable, and the agitation of it at this period could have no other effect than still further to derange . . . and oppress every interest in the community." The Governor called on the legislature to "relieve the banks from the penalties and disabilities incurred by them, and to authorize for a limited period the suspension of specie payments." He did not call for even the most modest reform but simply mentioned that "care should be taken to guard against abuses."[29]

Rives congratulated Campbell on his message, for it was a clarion call for all Democrats to rally and to resist the hard-money notions within the party. The only way to save the Van Buren Administration, Rives told Campbell, was to rescue the President from such reckless advisors as Frank P. Blair, who had boasted that the Virginia legislature would not legalize suspension and would declare war against the entire banking system.[30] This flattery was not lost on Campbell, who wrote to his wife that his "bold and independent . . . stand" had caused such a favorable reaction that he was "now the strongest man in the State" and could have any office in Virginia for the asking.[31]

The special legislative session proved any fears of the conservatives

[27] David Campbell to Maria H. Campbell, June 1, 1837, David Campbell Papers.
[28] David Campbell to Maria H. Campbell, June 3, 1837, David Campbell Papers.
[29] Richmond *Enquirer,* June 13, 1837; *Niles' Register,* June 17, 1837.
[30] William C. Rives to David Campbell, June 12, 1837, and June 18, 1837, David Campbell Papers.
[31] David Campbell to Maria H. Campbell, June 19, 1837, David Campbell Papers.

to be groundless. The hard-money Democrats failed to mount enough opposition to block legislative relief for the banks. The bill passed the house of delegates by a wide majority of 88 to 18, with all the negative votes being cast by Democrats. On a resolution to allow the banks to issue small notes, the hard-money Democrats marshalled a respectable opposition, but the resolution passed 64 to 52, with nineteen Democrats and forty-five Whigs voting for and fifty Democrats and two Whigs voting against.[32]

Hugh Garland, hard-money Democrat from Mecklenburg County, perhaps represented the majority sentiment among the Democratic delegates. Regarding "the whole banking system as it exists in this country as an evil," he said that

[when] the fit occasion has arrived, I am prepared to divorce them entirely from all connection with the Government, State and Federal—to tear asunder that unnatural connection which has been injurious and corrupting to both parties—to take from them the high prerogatives of making the money, the circulating medium of this Commonwealth, just what they please—the sovereign power of elevating or depressing the property of our citizens, just as it may suit their view of profit or speculation—I am prepared to make them what they ought to be—commercial institutions, confined to mercantile operations placed under the closest restrictions, and based on the full and entire responsibility of those who manage and enjoy the benefits of them.

But, Garland urged, this reform should not be undertaken by the special session. The next legislature, already elected, would have time and information to formulate plans of reform. The special session would merely bolster up the sagging banks, leaving their ultimate fate to subsequent legislatures.[33] Garland's attitude might explain why so few Democrats voted against the bank-relief bill as compared to the number who voted against allowing banks the privilege of issuing small notes.

Ritchie praised the legislature's work. At the beginning of the session he had feared that the hard-money Democrats "would strive to cripple the banks," but he was pleased to note that they "came forward at the first sitting of the House, and displayed the most liberal desire" to help Virginia's banking institutions.[34]

[32] Richmond *Enquirer*, June 20, 1837, and June 23, 1837.
[33] *Ibid.*, June 20, 1837.   [34] *Ibid.*, June 27, 1837.

Not all Democrats were pleased with the lenient course of the legislature. A hard-money man wrote to Blair, editor of the Washington *Globe,* that the legislature's gentle treatment of the banks had "excited the indignation of most of our friends here." Blair was told that "the voice of Richmond, the course of the press, or of the Legislature" should not be taken "as a fair indication of the sentiments of our people." The newspapers and the cities where they were published were, he said, under the influence of the banks and speculators. Blair's correspondent continued:

I shall not fail to deal plainly and frankly with friend Ritchie, as I have hitherto done. I long for leisure to scold him, for wronging his best friends, and endangering the best of causes by his *timidity,* his slang about "ultra-ism" . . . when in truth, we have hesitated, faltered, and flinched, in carrying out—no, not carrying out, but proposing even the most cautious reforms. . . . But I fear Mr. Ritchie is so situated that *he dare not* come out against the banks, do what they may.[35]

A like-minded correspondent, writing in the *Enquirer,* charged that "our State government has tamely knuckled to the bank power, shamefully sacrificed the rights and interests of the *many* to the selfish and unjust demands of the *few."* Warning Ritchie and the Democratic readers of the *Enquirer* that although the advocates of an exclusive metallic currency were "in a small minority . . . there is a strong and strengthening majority of the people who go for a radical reform, or total extermination of our present paper system." Ritchie, in an editorial that accompanied the letter, denied that the state government was under the control of the banks and pledged his support to reorganizing and reforming the banking system. But Ritchie cautioned against "any rash transactions, any violent measures," or "the immediate crushing of those State institutions that have suspended specie payments. . . ."[36]

[35] Thomas H. Averett to Frank P. Blair, June 28, 1837, Martin Van Buren Papers. Almost five years later Ritchie admitted publicly that he was indebted to the banks but denied vigorously that this had influenced him. Richmond *Enquirer,* March 1, 1842.

[36] Richmond *Enquirer,* July 11, 1837.

3

After the special session, the Virginia conservatives were supremely optimistic about their chances to control the state party. The failure of the hard-money Democrats to block the bank-relief legislation lulled the softs into a false sense of security. Rives and his followers were to be rudely jolted from their euphoria during the legislative session of 1838, when it became clear that the majority of the party would not support a confrontation and split with the national administration.

But by the summer of 1837 no national policy had been formulated, and there were many rumors as to the course of action the Van Buren Administration would take to meet the crisis. Many conservatives felt that the hard-money wing of the party, led by Senator Thomas Hart Benton of Missouri and editor Blair of the *Globe,* had been discredited by the financial disarrangement. This, it was hoped, would force the President to turn to Rives and other critics of the hard-money position. Rives believed that the party and the Van Buren Administration were at a major turning point. Van Buren did not have the popularity Jackson had, he reasoned, and for the wily New Yorker to maintain the same unpopular hard-money position Jackson had pursued would be ruinous.[37]

The Virginia conservatives also were confident of their basis of support within the state. During the special session, in their estimation, there had been no more than twenty to thirty hard-money Democrats, and Governor Campbell and other conservatives were certain they could by persuasion and opposition reduce this number. They knew they would have to be cautious and not provoke the hard-money men into forming a third party. Nor should they occupy the same ground with the advocates of a national bank.[38] Thus the conservatives felt

---

[37] The *Madisonian* was established that summer as a conservative Democratic organ in Washington, D.C. Some Virginia conservatives believed Van Buren might repudiate the *Globe* in favor of the *Madisonian.* W. B. Hodgson to William C. Rives, July 13, 1837, William C. Rives Papers, and William C. Rives to David Campbell, August 26, 1837, David Campbell Papers.

[38] Edmund Fontaine to William C. Rives, June 26, 1837, William C. Rives Papers. See also William C. Rives to David Campbell, July 8, 1837, David Campbell Papers; J. T. Anderson to William C. Rives, July 8, 1837, and W. B.

they must clearly establish their position and the position of the Democratic party in the middle ground between the hard-money "bank destructionists" and the Whigs who supported the re-establishment of a national bank.

Van Buren's message to the special session of Congress in the fall of 1837 and his formal recommendation of the Independent Treasury dispelled any notions the conservatives might have had of winning the President over to their position. David Campbell thought that Van Buren must be under some delusion, and he predicted that the proposal, which was "directly to do the most serious injury to the State Banks," would destroy the party.[39] Campbell also recognized that Van Buren's course of action was awakening the people's prejudices against the banks and wrote to Rives that the Independent Treasury scheme was more popular than the conservatives had originally supposed.[40]

To strengthen the conservative position, Rives suggested to Governor Campbell that in his annual address he warn the legislature to guard against any scheme that would crush the banks. It should be pointed out, Rives instructed the Governor, that the state had a deep interest in maintaining the credit of the banks. Not only did they supply the currency, but the state had large sums invested in them for public education and internal improvements. An exclusive metallic currency, Rives declared, in a growing country like the United States, where the credit system has stimulated so many improvements, was completely out of touch with the times.[41] Campbell faithfully followed this advice.[42]

Ritchie, although he opposed the Independent Treasury, was mainly interested in keeping the party together. In preference to a national

---

Hodgson to William C. Rives, July 13, 1837, William C. Rives Papers. J. T. Anderson informed Rives that seven eighths or nine tenths of the last legislature opposed the hard-money schemes. See letter of July 25, 1837, in William C. Rives Papers.

[39] David Campbell to William C. Rives, November 4, 1838, and David Campbell to Unknown, November 25, 1837, David Campbell Papers.

[40] David Campbell to William C. Rives, October 18, 1837, William C. Rives Papers. See also Charles Hurston to William C. Rives, July 26, 1837, William C. Rives Papers, and William C. Rives to David Campbell, October 16, 1837, David Campbell Papers.

[41] William C. Rives to David Campbell, October 31, 1837, and November 28, 1837, David Campbell Papers.

[42] See Campbell's message in the Richmond *Enquirer,* January 2, 1838.

bank, he supported the administration's plan. But his first choice was for adoption of a compromise special deposit system that would keep federal funds in the state banks but prohibit the banks from using the federal money.[43]

Through the *Enquirer,* Ritchie hoped that all Democratic viewpoints would be expressed. "The Democrats are taking the field under various names, and with different banners—and so long as they contend with the weapons of argument, not the fiery arrows of denunciation, the discussion may profit our country without injuring our party." And, he continued, "with this spirit, we may bid defiance to the common enemy, the Bank of the U. States." [44]

Behind the scenes, Ritchie was working to bring the two feuding sides together. He wrote to Rives, advising him to be very cautious, as a wise and prudent man would not brave executive power.[45] Ritchie tried to convince Van Buren that the Deposit Bank System had not had a fair trial. The proposed Independent Treasury, he said, "would increase the already too large power of the Executive. . . ." Furthermore, the plan was alien to old Republican principles, which held that state officers should be used as much as possible "to save the expense and patronage of creating a new batch of Federal agents." Although he was not certain, Ritchie thought that "the majority of the Democratic Party *in Virginia,* . . . [would] be opposed to the Sub-Treasury System, as compaired [*sic*] with the State Banks." [46]

It must have been extremely disappointing to the conservatives to find John Brockenbrough, close friend and relative of Ritchie and president of the Bank of Virginia, a strong supporter of the Independent Treasury. In fact, the respected banker had been instrumental in first suggesting the plan to Van Buren. Brockenbrough felt that because there was "too little . . . cohesion" between the state banks "to afford any prospect of regulating the currency through that channel," federal funds should never be kept by a bank of discount but instead by some

[43] Ambler, *Thomas Ritchie,* 200.

[44] See Richmond *Enquirer,* August 15 and 18, September 1 and 8, 1837.

[45] Thomas Ritchie to William C. Rives, August 10, 1838, William C. Rives Papers.

[46] Thomas Ritchie to Martin Van Buren, August 20, 1837, Martin Van Buren Papers.

independent agency.[47] A responsible banker who was greatly concerned with the stability and reputation of his bank, Brockenbrough undoubtedly felt that the Deposit System's tendency was to cause the weaker banks to undercut the stronger ones. If the plan were not replaced by the Independent Treasury, a new national bank would surely result.[48]

Although Brockenbrough supported the establishment of the Independent Treasury, he was far from being a hard-money man. "The chimerical idea of establishing in this country a mere metallic currency is too silly for any man of sense to dwell on," he argued. The credit system was necessary and preferable even when "carried to the excess it has been" in a "rising and enterprising country like ours. . . ."[49]

Supporters of the Independent Treasury tried to avoid an open split with the conservatives. "Our party seems to be battling on the very brink of a dangerous precipice," Brockenbrough wrote to Rives, "and unless we continue united we must fall over."[50] Judge Parker warned

[47] John Brockenbrough to William C. Rives, May 20, 1837, William C. Rives Papers, and John Brockenbrough to Martin Van Buren, May 22, 1837, Martin Van Buren Papers.

[48] Brockenbrough's misgivings about the workings of the Deposit Bank System had been reinforced in the fall of 1837 when large amounts of federal funds in paper of banks in the South and West had flooded into the Bank of Virginia. The Virginia banker told Secretary of Treasury Levi Woodbury, "we received it for the convenience of the Treasury Department not for our own." Brockenbrough had assumed that the money was intended for expenditure in Virginia, where it would "gradually be disbursed . . . in the paper of the Banks of Virginia and occasional small sums of specie." This had not been the case. For drafts for public funds on the Bank of Virginia had been given to agents in northern towns whose demands for immediate payment in specie from the Bank of Virginia had been backed up with threats to sue. Brockenbrough then had appealed to Van Buren, pointing out that the ordinary federal expenditures in Virginia would draw every federal dollar from his bank. Furthermore, this pressure on the Bank of Virginia would give "strength to the assertion of the conservatives that it is the design of the Government to cripple and crush the Deposite Banks. . . ." See letters from John Brockenbrough to Levi Woodbury, October 25, 1837, Levi Woodbury Papers, Series II, and John Brockenbrough to Martin Van Buren, May 22, 1837, Martin Van Buren Papers.

[49] John Brockenbrough to William C. Rives, May 20, 1837, William C. Rives Papers, and John Brockenbrough to Martin Van Buren, May 22, 1837, Martin Van Buren Papers.

[50] John Brockenbrough to William C. Rives, August 5, 1837, Martin Van Buren Papers.

Rives that it would be "unwise and unpatriotic . . . for the friends of the State Banks to unite with the Whigs." He recognized Rives' plight, however, and hoped that Rives could maintain his principles "and yet not violently . . . offend that large and *increasing* party, who are opposed to Banks. . . ." [51]

The heavily Democratic legislature [52] that opened in January, 1838, became a battleground between those who favored the Independent Treasury and those who were opposed to it. This represented the climax of the conservatives' attempt to dominate the Virginia Democratic party.

David Campbell wrote Rives that leaders of the Independent Treasury party were going to attempt to get the legislature to approve by resolution Van Buren's bank-divorce plan. But Campbell believed that "if we do not permit incautious friends to be inveigled from their principles and misled by this balmy proposition of compromise which haunts the brain of Mr. Ritchie so much, we have and can maintain a decided majority of our own party." [53]

At the same time, Van Buren was informed by Richard E. Parker that of the members elected the past year to the legislature "as friends of the administration; a clear and decided majority are in favor of *all* the recommendations of your first message, and the small number who dissent, admit the liberal and conciliatory spirit of your last message, and avow themselves firm supporters of your administration." Resolutions supporting the Independent Treasury were going to be offered by John R. Edmunds of Halifax County, he reported. Concluding, Parker hopefully predicted "that no third party of any consequence can be raised to distract or divide." [54]

[51] Richard E. Parker to William C. Rives, September 14, 1837, and November 15, 1837, William C. Rives Papers. Amos Kendall wrote to Claiborne W. Gooch that if he could get Rives to retrace his steps, Gooch would render a great service to Rives and the country. Amos Kendall to Claiborne W. Gooch, September 10, 1837, Gooch Family Papers, University of Virginia. See also Walter Coles to Andrew Stevenson, September 15, 1837, Andrew Stevenson Papers.

[52] There were eighty-seven Democrats and forty-seven Whigs according to Henry H. Simms' classification in his *The Rise of Whigs in Virginia, 1824–1840* (Richmond, Va., 1929), 178–81.

[53] David Campbell to William C. Rives, January 16, 1838, William C. Rives Papers.

[54] Richard E. Parker to Martin Van Buren, January 18, 1838, Martin Van Buren Papers.

Actually, Edmunds' resolutions were quite mild and moderate, but their introduction began a long and bitter fight over the questions of whether Virginia's United States senators should be instructed on the Independent Treasury bill and if so, what the instructions should be. Edmunds resolved "that no connexion between the Federal Government and Banking Corporations is established by the Federal Constitution, and that, in the opinion of this Assembly, no such connexion, for the purpose of collecting the Federal revenue is necessary." This first resolution clearly endorsed the Sub-Treasury, but a second one clouded the issue. It provided that "the revenue of the Federal Government, when collected, should be so kept and disbursed as never to be mingled with the funds of the Banks, or used in any manner as a means of banking operations." This echoed Ritchie's compromise scheme. Other resolutions offered by Edmunds condemned a national bank, praised the President, and pledged support to the "essential and prominent measures of the present Federal Administration. . . ." [55]

Ritchie enthusiastically received the resolutions, especially the second one. With some modification, he was hopeful that they would be "acceptable to a large majority of the friends of the Administration." [56] But he was to be disappointed. "It is now too late to talk of compromise," Rives wrote to Campbell. The Edmunds resolutions were unacceptable to Rives for he considered them as an endorsement of the Sub-Treasury.[57]

Peter V. Daniel reported to Van Buren the state of the hard-money Democracy in Virginia. "How far it will be practicable *here* to cooperate with the republicans in Congress, in asserting our independence of the Banks; has been and now is, a question" anxiously being discussed. There was need "for speaking out, and speaking out strongly. . . ." If the hard-money men did not clarify their position, Daniel felt, the views of the conservative Democratic Governor, who had been the "disappointment and mortification of almost every one concerned in elevating him to office," and of the *Enquirer* would be accepted as the doctrines of the Virginia Democracy. "As for Ritchie . . . he must now be given up as incorrigible." The editor had demanded such compro-

[55] Richmond *Enquirer,* January 20, 1838.　　[56] *Ibid.*
[57] William C. Rives to David Campbell, January 20, 1838, David Campbell Papers.

mises in the Edmunds resolutions, Daniel concluded, that "no identity of feeling, or useful cooperation can ever be reasonably expected" from Ritchie, for "he is inseparably wedded to Rives and the Banks. . . ."[58]

Numerous other resolutions, hard, soft, and moderate in persuasion, were presented to the Virginia legislature. But the broker Democrats, led by Ritchie, were finally able to get all resolutions indefinitely tabled. "May we not," Ritchie said, "dare to advise our friends, on both sides of the House, to move not at all, if they cannot move together."[59]

4

The spring election of 1838 marked a major turning point in the Virginia conservatives' strategy. Prior to the election, Rives and his followers had attempted to control the Virginia Democracy. But they had badly misread the political signs. Most Democrats were not willing to break with the national administration over the Independent Treasury issue, and the more strident and vocal the conservatives became in their opposition to the proposal, the more isolated they became. Many Democrats who ordinarily might have sympathized with the conservatives withheld their support when it appeared the party was going to be ripped apart over the issue. Thus, the conservatives concluded that to remain as Democrats would result in their political extinction. Their only viable alternative, therefore, was to establish themselves as a separate political entity outside both parties.[60] The conservatives hoped

[58] Peter V. Daniel to Martin Van Buren, January 23, 1838, Martin Van Buren Papers.

[59] By a majority of ten, some "of the Whigs, most of the Sub-Treasury gentlemen, and those Republicans who are the friends of conciliation and compromise" united to table the currency resolutions. The Whigs and Democratic conservatives were, in general, for taking them up. One factor in shutting off debate on the currency resolutions was the fear that there would be no time for consideration of internal-improvement projects. See the Richmond *Enquirer,* January 25; February 20, 22, and 24; March 1, 13, and 22, 1838.

[60] Third-party plans were not new in the spring of 1838. The *Madisonian* had carried articles regarding the formation of a third party in the last month of 1837. But in Virginia the bulk of Rives' followers entertained hopes of controlling the state party as late as the spring of 1838. For information regarding the new tack of the conservatives see William C. Rives to David Campbell, May 3, 1838, David Campbell Papers, and William Shands to William C. Rives, May 23, 1838, William C. Rives Papers.

that Van Buren had made himself so odious by his Independent Treasury proposal and that Whig leader Henry Clay was so disliked that men of conservative principles from both parties would rally to their banner.

The immediate objective for the conservatives that spring was to win enough strength in the next legislature to assure the re-election of their leader, William C. Rives, to the Senate. The plan was to oppose Independent Treasury Democratic candidates wherever possible and to appeal to the people on a platform endorsing Rives and the Deposit Bank System. This led to a fervid battle. John Letcher reported that he and James McDowell, both of whom were Independent Treasury Democrats, had been defeated unexpectedly. Blaming Ritchie and Rives, Letcher charged that the latter had

scattered Hundreds of his late Currency speech throughout Western Virginia, for the purpose of operating upon the people and insuring a return of *his* own friends to the next Legislature. But instead of elevating his conservative friends to power, it has only had the effect of returning "Whigs" who will in the election of an U. S. Senator, at the next session of the Legislature . . . select from their own ranks.[61]

The election by two votes of a conservative over an Independent Treasury Democrat in Madison County was declared by one observer to be "the severest contest . . . ever known in the county." [62]

The conservatives' campaign strategy was a major factor in the election of a Whig plurality to the Virginia legislature that spring. Therefore, one of the most delicate maneuvers with which the conservatives were faced was that of persuading the Virginia Whigs that it might be in their interest to support Rives in his quest for re-election to the Senate. Rives was congratulated by one Whig on the outcome of the Virginia spring election, which was "*precisely* and *exactly* the result most conspicuous to yourself *personally*—and what is infinitely more important *to your party*—(I mean the Conservatives)." Another Whig advised Rives not to take the attacks upon him by the Richmond *Whig* seriously because "they are not approved of by the Whigs proper." [63]

[61] John Letcher to Ely Moore, April 28, 1838, and John Letcher to Martin Van Buren, May 12, 1838, Martin Van Buren Papers.

[62] Richmond *Enquirer,* May 4, 1838. See also issue of May 1, 1838.

[63] Jno. Pendleton to William C. Rives, May 16, 1838; Thomas S. Haywood to William C. Rives, June 14, 1838, William C. Rives Papers.

Yet at the same time there was the great danger that through this close cooperation the conservatives might be swallowed by the Whig party.[64] This worried Thomas Allen, editor of the conservatives' national newspaper, the *Madisonian*. In New York, Ohio, and Missouri, he pointed out in the fall of 1838, conservatives already were either thoroughly identified with the Whigs or were pledged to the election of William Henry Harrison in 1840. In Maine, some voted with the Whigs, some voted an independent ticket, and others stayed away from the polls, while in Pennsylvania the soft-money support was thrown on the side of the Sub-Treasury Democrats. Only in Virginia, Allen said, did the conservatives follow the true course of independence and commitment to the Deposit Bank System. They did not, as in other states, simply leave the Democratic party and immediately seek the most profitable alliance with new friends.[65]

Despite Allen's pessimism over the lack of nationwide unity within the conservative movement, Nathaniel P. Tallmadge predicted to his Virginia colleague that political success would be theirs. Many conservatives would like to see Rives nominated for the Presidency, he felt, but realized that it would be premature. All, however, "look forward to the time when the old fashioned Republicans will be united on old principles, and will maintain themselves against the *Ultraists* of both parties," and then, Tallmadge assured Rives, his "services will be required." [66]

Although by the spring of 1838 it was apparent that there would be no conciliation between the conservatives and the Independent Treasury Democrats, Ritchie stubbornly refused to accept the obvious truth. Instead he worked tirelessly for acceptance of his special deposit system as a compromise measure [67] and attempted to focus the attention of

[64] J. C. Clark to William C. Rives, November 4, 1838, William C. Rives Papers. James Garland wrote Rives that he did not intend to go into the Whig party. James Garland to William C. Rives, November 14, 1838, William C. Rives Papers.

[65] Thomas Allen to William C. Rives, September 30, 1838, William C. Rives Papers.

[66] N. P. Tallmadge to William C. Rives, August 26, 1838, William C. Rives Papers.

[67] Thomas Ritchie to Unknown, May (date unknown), 1838, Martin Van Buren Papers. In a letter to Rives, Ritchie urged acceptance of the special deposit system as a compromise. Thomas Ritchie to William C. Rives, July 4,

the party on a common enemy. "The Philistines are upon you," he warned, and the "Bank of the U. States threatens your liberties." [68] In his role as mediator, Ritchie barely averted personal political disaster. Early in 1838, James McDowell and other Independent Treasury Democratic leaders, tired of Ritchie's hedging, planned to establish a rival Democratic press in Richmond. The scheme did not materialize, but the threat of the withdrawal of the main body of the Democratic party's support put considerable pressure on the Richmond editor.[69]

By the fall of 1838, Ritchie was losing his enthusiasm for defending Rives [70] and was coming to realize the futility of any talk of compromise. Peter V. Daniel reported to Van Buren that the *Enquirer* had "become cooled in its love" for Rives and was "deserting openly, if it has not already deserted, for it is shouting loudly for victories achieved under the banner of the Independent Treasury, and proclaims its determination *'to sink or swim with Mr. Van Buren.'*" Rives, Daniel said, should have known that Ritchie's political horizon was "limited to the State of Virginia." In the past, Daniel claimed, Ritchie had felt that the unfortunate connection between Virginia and her banks obligated the state

to sustain these Banks to any and every extent, and therefore he sided with them: he now believes that the State will not countenance an outbreak with [the] administration . . . therefore to keep with the majority . . . he will abandon Mr. Rives if necessary, and save himself from falling from the earth. I suspect too that Ritchie's own involvements with the Banks have had their influence.[71]

A few months later, in January, 1839, Ritchie called upon the conservatives to decide whether they were going to support the Van Buren Administration or not. "Any man who prefers a Whig candidate to Mr.

1838, William C. Rives Papers. Throughout that spring and summer, through the columns of the *Enquirer,* Ritchie had urged conciliation. See the Richmond *Enquirer,* May 11, June 15, and August 7, 1838.

[68] Richmond *Enquirer,* March 13, April 7, and April 24, 1838.

[69] See two undated letters from Thomas Ritchie to James McDowell in January, 1838, in James McDowell Papers, University of North Carolina.

[70] Ritchie, in turn, had been given up by the conservatives. See David Campbell to William C. Rives, September 9, 1838, William C. Rives Papers, and William C. Rives to Campbell, September 23, 1838, David Campbell Papers.

[71] Peter V. Daniel to Martin Van Buren, October 20, 1838, Martin Van Buren Papers.

Van Buren," Ritchie contended, "or who is not disposed to lend a liberal support to the present Administration, had better join the Whig ranks at once. . . ."[72]

The solicitation of Whig votes to re-elect Rives to the Senate in the legislative session of 1839 proved unsuccessful. The conservatives did, however, prevent the election of any other candidate. The Whigs were not able to detach enough conservative votes to elect a Whig, and enough Whigs disliked Rives so intensely that they were able to prevent his election.[73] Thus the impasse in the legislature prevented the filling of Virginia's second Senate seat.

Although there were great expectations by conservative leaders for maintaining their identity as a separate party, there was scant possibility from the beginning that any such plan could succeed. The issue that they chose to stake their political future on—the Deposit Bank System in preference to the Independent Treasury or a national bank— was not one likely to attract a large popular following. Many men who were drawn to the movement in the beginning withdrew their support and returned to Democratic orthodoxy when they realized that the Independent Treasury was not an ultra radical scheme designed to destroy the banks. The second suspension of specie payment in 1839 further discredited the banks. This, coupled with Rives' course, which brought the conservatives into close cooperation with the Whigs, alienated many original conservative supporters. By 1840 the Rives conservatives existed in name only and were in reality merely an appendage of the Whig party. Rives was rewarded for his support of the Whig presidential nominee and re-elected to the Senate, but the conservatives quickly discovered they would have little influence with the victorious Whig administration.[74]

[72] Richmond *Enquirer,* January 31, 1839. Ritchie felt that Rives had discredited himself to such an extent by seeking Whig support for re-election that the editor recommended to his former colleague that he retire from public life. See Thomas Ritchie to Andrew Stevenson, May 4, 1839, Andrew Stevenson Papers.

[73] "To the People of Albemarle," a printed broadside by Thomas Gilmer and V. W. Southhall, February 25, 1839, William C. Rives Papers.

[74] The William C. Rives Papers, Library of Congress, and the David Campbell Papers, Duke University, are excellent for following the Virginia conservatives from the Democratic party to their futile efforts to remain independent and to their ultimate destination, the Whig party. See Daniel Webster to Wil-

5

The Independent Treasury issue was not the only dimension of the battle between the conservatives and the hard-money men in the Virginia Democratic party. Concurrent with the clash over the national issue, which led to the exodus of Rives and his followers from the party, the Virginia Democrats were quarreling among themselves over the state banking question. Despite the schisms, the hard-money men held a majority in the party throughout the period, and most Democrats could usually be expected to support measures to enforce stockholder liability, to make bank charters repealable, and to inaugurate stricter specie-note ratios, usually three or two to one. The bulk of the party also opposed granting banks the privilege of issuing small notes, increasing the banking capital, and continuing to defer the penalties against the suspended banks. But the Democrats were normally unsuccessful in their attempts to impose tighter controls on the banks. From the initial suspension in 1837 to the final resumption in 1842, they controlled the legislature for only the first two years. And although the second and third suspensions in 1839 and 1841 strengthened the hard-money position within the party, the Whigs, combined with a small number of conservative Democrats, effectually overrode the protestations of the hard-money men.[75]

Just weeks before the financial panic in the spring of 1837 forced banks throughout the country to suspend specie payment, the Virginia legislature had enacted a general banking law for the purpose of standardizing banking regulations and providing a sound basis for the expansion of banking facilities in the state. Among other things the act stipulated that banks could not go into operation until three fifths of the capital had been paid in, could issue only paper redeemable in specie, could not issue notes for amounts less than 10 dollars (and after 1840 less than 20 dollars), would have to maintain a specie-note ratio of

---

liam C. Rives, December 7, 1840, William C. Rives Papers, for a highly insulting letter to Rives and one that gave the conservative leader a good indication of the kind of treatment he might expect from the Whigs.

[75] Party affiliations for the legislatures from 1834–1840 were taken from the Appendix in Simms, *Rise of Whigs in Virginia*.

at least one to five, would be liable for 15 per cent damages and forfeiture of their charters in case specie payments were suspended, and could make no loans for longer than six months. The state, through gubernatorial appointment of bank directors, was given considerable power over the banks, but not control of them.[76]

Although the General Banking Law won overwhelming acceptance in the Virginia house of delegates and passed by a vote of 84 to 31, more than one third of the total Democratic membership voted against it.[77] Arthur Smith, a hard-money Democratic delegate from the Isle of Wight, urged the house to adopt a specie-note ratio of two to one. George Booker from Buckingham County supported Smith and warned that the Virginia banks were operating precariously with eight or nine dollars of notes in circulation to every dollar of specie in their vaults. Thus the delegate from Buckingham called for a conservative specie-note ratio "that could not be overturned." [78]

As has been shown, the special session of the legislature in the spring of 1837 gave the banks temporary relief from penalties incurred by suspension of specie payment immediately after the Panic. Thus the following year the heavily Democratic legislature was faced with the problem of deciding whether simply to extend the relief or to attempt to reform the banks.

Governor David Campbell warned in his message to the legislature that it would be ruinous to "abandon suddenly the banking system . . . or to restrict it in such manner, as to deny to the community the facilities to which it has been accustomed." The suspension, the Governor argued, arose from factors outside the control of the banks. He admitted that the credit system presented "temptations to speculation," but this was not of a magnitude to necessitate any "attempt to annihilate all

[76] At the same session the legislature chartered a new bank with branches and increased the capital of other Virginia banks. This represented the largest capital increase ever authorized during a single legislative session to that date and added 5 million dollars to Virginia's bank capital. If the banks accepted the terms of the law increasing the bank capital, their charters were extended to 1857. See Starnes, *Branch Banking in Virginia*, 80–86.

[77] Of the eighty-four voting in favor of the measure, forty-four were Democrats and forty were Whigs, and of those opposing the bill, twenty-six were Democrats and five were Whigs. Vote in Richmond *Enquirer*, March 18, 1837.

[78] Richmond *Enquirer*, March 18, 1837.

credit." [79] The legislature's mood was no more radical than that of the Governor, much to the dismay of the hard-money Democrats. The conservatives prevented the adoption of a resolution supporting the Independent Treasury and united with the Whigs to prevent any substantial bank reform. Penalties against the banks were suspended again.[80]

The Governor's message was denounced by hard-money men, one of whom feared the influence "of corporate monopolies," which had "spread . . . like a pestilence, by the rearing of a Bank in almost every village. . . ." [81] A correspondent in the *Enquirer* asked of the legislature: "Are we to be guiled and duped longer by a set of Banks rotten to the core?" As for the legislators supporting the banks, he warned that the people would hold them accountable at the polls. "We begin to think," he went on,

that the very atmosphere of Richmond is not congenial to fair legislation. Too much Bank influence, too many parties, too much good eating and champaigne [*sic*]; else why so much flinching? Thousands that six or nine months since were in favor of Banks, cry now, Down with the swindling institutions, and let the worst come to the worst. . . . Rely on it, the days of our present system of banking are numbered.[82]

A hard-money Democrat, John Woolfolk of Orange County, attempted to amend the relief bill by including a section that would have given the legislature "the power to repeal, alter or amend, the charters of all the Banks who avail themselves of this act, at . . . will and pleasure." This amendment was at first accepted by the house but later reconsidered and rejected when some who had voted for it realized its implications. The Whigs and soft-money Democrats were horrified by the "monstrous proposition," which would have struck at the very heart of the rights of property. One Whig claimed that he had taken

[79] *Ibid.,* January 2, 1838.   [80] *Ibid.,* March 31, 1838.

[81] Peter V. Daniel to Martin Van Buren, January 23, 1838, Martin Van Buren Papers.

[82] Richmond *Enquirer,* March 15, 1837. Richard E. Parker wrote to Van Buren that he was greatly distressed at the unity of the "money power" and feared that "our public virtue is too weak to oppose it, in this period of general distress." Parker believed, however, that a division could be created by "opposing the resuming, against the non-resuming banks—the money power of New York against that of Philadelphia." Richard E. Parker to Martin Van Buren, April 10, 1838, Martin Van Buren Papers.

its defeat for granted and that there were not "ten men in all Virginia, who would have voted for such a proposition." The final vote on Woolfolk's amendment was fifty-four Democrats and three Whigs in favor, and thirty-eight Whigs and twenty-four Democrats against.[83]

By the time the next legislature met in January, 1839, the banks had temporarily resumed specie payment. The Whigs, as the majority party, decided to take advantage of this occasion to increase Virginia's banking capital. Their bill provided that should a bank accept an increase in capital, it must also agree to abide by the provisions of the general bank law of 1837. A house resolution testing support for increasing the bank capital passed 80 to 44. A total of fifty-eight Whigs and twenty-two Democrats voted for it, while thirty-three Democrats and ten Whigs opposed the resolution.[84]

The second suspension in the fall of 1839 further discredited the banks and those conservatives who had risked their political fortunes in defending them. Still, the Whig-dominated legislature of 1839–1840 was in no mood for reform. By an 83 to 40 vote, the house of delegates passed a temporary relief measure, once more excusing the banks from penalties for suspending specie payments. Of those voting yea, nineteen were Democrats and sixty-four Whigs. A total of thirty-seven Democrats and three Whigs voted against the bill.[85]

The legislature's temporizing with the banks prompted a violent reaction from some hard-money men. "THE SPECIE STANDARD—*a radical reform, or total extermination of our present paper system,* must become the motto—the rallying cry of every freeman," demanded an *Enquirer* correspondent. The hard-money men were particularly angered because state laws were constantly being violated by the banks. By law, bank

[83] Richmond *Enquirer,* March 10, 1838.

[84] Sumner, *History of Banking,* 314; Richmond *Enquirer,* March 9, and April 9, 1839; *Niles' Register,* May 4, 1839. The party affiliation of one member of the house of delegates is not known. According to a classification of one of Rives' lieutenants, thirteen of the twenty-two Democrats who voted for the measure were committed to voting for Rives for Senator. Of those voting against the bill, only two Democrats were going to support Rives. See J. Sherrard to William C. Rives, February 1, 1839, William C. Rives Papers.

[85] Richmond *Enquirer,* December 7, 1839. Rives asked Campbell if the forty who voted against the relief bill were for putting down the banks altogether. William C. Rives to David Campbell, December 8, 1839, David Campbell Papers.

suspension resulted in loss of charter, but in practice the legislature constantly waived the law to protect the banks, thus making the regulation worthless. This led to the repeated charge that the banks were above the law. The banks must be taught, one Democrat insisted, that "the laws shall not be broken with impunity—that they shall be *obedient* to the laws, not *masters* of the law-making power. . . ."[86]

The banks resumed only to suspend for a third time in 1841. Each suspension magnified the hard-money Democrats' antagonism toward the banks, and each converted a number of the more moderate Democratic brethren to take a more decided stand against the banks. Even Ritchie called the bank system "eminently defective, and rotten in its operations."[87] Although never very specific, Ritchie did at one point suggest that bank issues should be curtailed to the amount needed for the commercial and business wants of the country.[88]

The 1841–1842 legislature, in which the Whigs had a slight edge,[89] was advised to grant the banks additional relief from penalties by the Democratic governor, John Rutherfoord, the son of a well-to-do merchant family and a relative of Jacksonian diplomat Andrew Stevenson.[90] Although agreeing more with the softs than the hards on the bank issue, Rutherfoord, as a broker Democrat, worked to prevent the question from destroying the party.

A close friend of Rives, Rutherfoord had been solicited by the conservative leader immediately after the Panic to write articles for the press exposing the "dangerous extravagance" of some of the "ultra notions."[91] Rutherfoord answered Rives that he regretted that the press of business affairs kept him from taking up his pen to expose the visionary schemes of some Democrats. He warned Rives, however, that opposition to the administration's policy must be conducted with great tact, because the Whigs were striving to create dissension within the Democratic party that would ultimately lead to the election of a Whig

---

[86] Richmond *Enquirer*, December 21, 1839.   [87] *Ibid.*, October 26, 1841.

[88] See *ibid.*, November 19 and December 11, 1841.

[89] There were sixty-eight Whigs and sixty-six Democrats in the House of Delegates according to the *Niles' Register*, May 29, 1841.

[90] There is a biographical sketch of John Rutherfoord in the John Rutherfoord Papers, Duke University.

[91] William C. Rives to John Rutherfoord, June 10, 1873, John Rutherfoord Papers.

President and a new national bank.[92] When it became evident that Rives was jeopardizing the very existence of the party, Rutherfoord broke with the conservatives. Becoming governor upon the resignation of his Whig predecessor, Rutherfoord boasted that he could be elected for a second term but could not afford to serve because he would have to give up his insurance company agency, as the governorship made it extremely difficult to collect rents and stock dividends.[93]

Rutherfoord, obviously, was not the kind of man to give leadership to bank-reform sentiment. In his message to the legislature, he recognized that the recklessness of many banks had created a strong prejudice against all of them. Although admitting the need for bank reform, he cautioned the legislature not to resort to a "harsh or violent remedy" and recommended that the banks be extended "reasonable indulgence." He felt it necessary for the state to have some control over the issue of bank notes but believed this would never be effective as long as the state remained a stockholder in the banks. The state could not adequately safeguard the public interest as long as it was anxious for bank profits.[94]

This legislative session turned out to be similar to earlier ones in which the Whigs and conservative Democrats allied to protect the banks. The house of delegates passed a resolution instructing the committee on banks to report a bill to relieve the banks, with fifty-seven Whigs and nine Democrats favoring the measure and fifty-four Democrats and four Whigs in opposition.[95] The same day in December the house granted the banks the privilege of issuing notes under 5 dollars until the following April 1. This was passed by fifty-nine Whigs and six Democrats over the opposition of fifty-four Democrats and one Whig.[96] An often-tried Democratic reform, "to make the stockholders liable to the amount of the par value of their stock, for

[92] John Rutherfoord to William C. Rives, August 2, 1837, William C. Rives Papers.

[93] John Rutherfoord to John C. Rutherfoord, February 11, 1842, John Rutherfoord Papers.

[94] Richmond *Enquirer*, December 7, 1841.

[95] The party affiliations used in this and the following votes in the house of delegates are from the *Niles' Register*, May 29, 1841. The votes will be only close approximations because a few of the legislators' party affiliations are not known.

[96] Richmond *Enquirer*, December 18, 1841.

the payment of all liabilities of such Banks," was rejected by the house, 65 to 42. Voting in favor of the measure were thirty-nine Democrats and three Whigs, while fifty-two Whigs and thirteen Democrats recorded noes.[97]

Despite the fact that the banks were not paying specie, an attempt was made to charter a new bank in Albemarle County, the home of William C. Rives, at Scottsville on the James River. A motion to postpone the project failed in the house, with thirty-one Democrats and eleven Whigs voting to postpone and forty-seven Whigs and twenty-one Democrats desiring the immediate chartering of the bank. In the senate, however, eleven Democrats and six Whigs allied against two Democrats and eight Whigs to postpone the bill indefinitely. Ritchie argued that it was not the proper time for establishing a new bank. "Pause, pause," he begged the legislature, while "we are festering under the banking system—goaded almost to madness, crushed almost beneath the wheels of the Juggernaut. . . ." No more banks should be chartered until "they are better guarded" and "until we put upon them all the restrictions, which our dear-bought experience urges upon us."[98]

One of the most heated battles of the legislature was over what date should be set for the banks to resume. The hard-money Democrats wanted an almost immediate resumption, whereas the Whigs and Democratic softs desired to allow the banks considerable time to get back on their feet. Hard-money Democrat Joel Holleman favored forcing the banks to resume in less than two months, by May 1, arguing that the banks had been relieved of penalties for four successive years, sufficient time to allow them to put their affairs in order. Instead of preparing for resumption, the banks had irresponsibly "increased their liabilities," he charged. Furthermore, "the *bone and sinew* of the country were rising in masses, and with an indignant voice calling upon these institutions to do their duty, and comply with the obligations they had contracted with the community." Holleman claimed that the reason the banks were against an early resumption was that stockholders feared they would not receive their dividends, and the directors of the banks, who owed almost 600,000 dollars to their institutions, believed it would weigh against their own personal interests. Finally, the

[97] *Ibid.*, March 19, 1842.   [98] *Ibid.*, February 22 and March 17, 1842.

fact that fifty members of the legislature owed the banks a combined total of 111,000 dollars, Holleman believed, militated against an early resumption.[99] The first of May as the resumption date was rejected 64 to 54, with forty-nine Democrats and five Whigs favoring it and fifty-four Whigs and ten Democrats voting in the negative. The legislature ultimately agreed on November 1, 1842.[100]

The directors of the state's banks met in Richmond the following summer and decided to resume specie payment September 15, a month and a half before the legislature's deadline.[101] This ended the bank question as an important political issue in Virginia. By the mid-1840s the Virginia banks reported a specie to circulation ratio of 1 to 2.8 and a ratio of specie to circulation and deposits of 1 to 4. This reflected the soundness of the Virginia banks and their very conservative and, for the most part, responsible management. After the Panic of 1837, while many banks failed in other states, all the Virginia banks survived.[102]

This steady record, coupled with the state's partial ownership and control of the banks, constituted a major influence inhibiting the development of a successful antibank movement. Other factors as well, such as the lack of hard-money leadership, the relative unimportance of state issues as compared with national ones, and the enormous power of Ritchie and the other broker Democrats, all combined to render the numerically superior hard-money Democrats politically ineffectual. Despite all of this, it is remarkable how much strength the hards mustered within the Democratic party. On virtually all of the legislative bank votes, the overwhelming majority of Democrats supported the more radical position, whether it be opposing relief to the banks or supporting the legislature's right to amend, alter, or repeal bank charters, while only a relatively small number of Democrats sided with the Whigs.

[99] *Ibid.*, March 24, 1842.   [100] *Ibid.*, March 17 and 26, 1842.
[101] *Ibid.*, July 15, 1842.   [102] Starnes, *Branch Banking in Virginia*, 100–102.

CHAPTER X

Virginia Constituencies

I

VIRGINIA had once been the largest, wealthiest, and most powerful state in the Union. But by the 1830s the formerly rich Tidewater agricultural region had been languishing for a number of years, and the few commercial centers in the state were unable to compete for western business because of a lack of both capital and an efficient internal-improvement system. Psychologically and economically this had a profound political impact upon citizens of the Old Dominion, who in the 1830s and 1840s were making a concerted effort to regain their lost political power and prestige as well as their economic solvency.

The Tidewater region, extending from the coast to the first falls on the rivers, was worst hit by an agricultural depression that dated from the eighteenth century. Faced with a declining white population, depleted soils that would no longer profitably grow tobacco, and a growing slave population that many felt could no longer be efficiently used, these planters of the 1830s were desperately trying to find some way out of their genteel poverty. Recalling days when the Tidewater had been a wealthy tobacco-producing area, one Virginian plaintively questioned,

Where . . . are our arts, our literature, our manufacture, our commerce? . . . What has become of our political rank and eminence in the Union? . . . Whither has the Genius of Virginia fled? . . . Virginia has now declined and is declining—she has sunk to be the third, and will soon sink lower on the scale.[1]

[1] As quoted in Robert P. Sutton, "Nostalgia, Pessimism, and Malaise: The Doomed Aristocrat in Late-Jeffersonian Virginia," *Virginia Magazine of History and Biography*, LXXVI (January, 1968), 46–47.

Some Tidewater planters, however, were turning to new agricultural techniques and new crops as a means of recouping their fortunes. New methods of ploughing, crop rotation, and the use of manures were among the measures urged by agricultural reformers. To some extent they were successful. Edmund Ruffin was, perhaps, the most influential reformer, and he is credited with persuading enough Tidewater farmers and planters to use marl so that the value of land in the Tidewater increased by more than 17 million dollars from 1838 to 1850. Corn, oats, grasses, peas, and some wheat were the major crops of the area, and truck gardening, begun in the late 1830s, increased in importance up until the Civil War.[2]

The Piedmont was the adjoining section to the west, commencing at the fall line and running westward to the Blue Ridge Mountains. It and the Tidewater were the oldest sections, and, like the Tidewater, the Piedmont suffered from a declining white population. In fact, in nearly half of the Piedmont and Tidewater counties east of the Blue Ridge the white population was reduced from 1810 to 1840. The center of the tobacco-producing area was in the southern Piedmont, while the northern and upland counties raised wheat.[3]

Further west still was the great Valley of Virginia, lying between the Blue Ridge Mountains on the east and the Alleghenies on the west. This was a fertile area originally settled by Scotch-Irish and Germans, who established prosperous, self-sufficient communities. Transportation for

[2] See Map 5. Information about the Tidewater comes from Henry Howe, *Historical Collections of Virginia* (Charleston, S.C., 1849), 129; Joseph Martin, *A Comprehensive Description of Virginia, and the District of Columbia* (Richmond, Va., date unknown, probably 1835), 99; and Craven, *Soil Exhaustion,* 142. For a discussion of Virginia agriculture in the decade following the bank controversy, see Emmett B. Fields, "The Agricultural Population of Virginia, 1850–1860" (unpublished Ph.D. thesis, Vanderbilt University, 1953), 122–23. Fields selects fifteen sample counties and argues that the "plain folk" of the Old South have been ignored by historians, who have misrepresented ante-bellum society as being made up only of planters, poor whites, and slaves. Fields modifies this traditional view but still concludes that 18 per cent of Virginia's agricultural population owned 59 per cent of the land, while 45 per cent owned 41 per cent and 37 per cent were landless.

[3] Richard Edwards, *Statistical Gazetteer of the State of Virginia* (Richmond, 1855), 77; Howe, *Historical Collections of Virginia,* 129; Craven, *Soil Exhaustion,* 123. See also Sutton, "Nostalgia, Pessimism, and Malaise," 41.

marketing crops was a problem for some Valley counties, and, as late as 1820, it was reported that the farmers there could sell only products that they could walk to market. The principal Valley crop was wheat, but corn and oats also were grown, as well as some tobacco in the southern portion of the area.[4]

From the Alleghenies to the Ohio River lay the Trans-Allegheny section, a large mountainous and sparsely populated region. Residents there were mainly engaged in subsistence agriculture, especially the raising of livestock, but by the 1830s and 1840s attempts also were being made to exploit the area's vast mineral resources. Perhaps because of the remoteness of this region and its inaccessibility to markets, the state of Virginia had only a tenuous hold on the loyalty of these far western Virginians. Separated from the rest of the state by a mountain barrier, most of these Virginians looked west rather than east, as their lifeline to the world and routes of commerce were the Ohio and Mississippi river systems. Furthermore, these westerners became increasingly alienated over what they felt was a system of unfair representation in the Virginia legislature, a feud that was resolved only by the secession of certain western counties from the state during the Civil War.[5]

The geography of Virginia played an important role in shaping the political, social, and economic development of the state. The rivers and the mountains were perhaps the most important geographical features. During the Colonial Period, the numerous and excellent waterways permitted ocean-going vessels to travel far inland and load the planters' staples at the plantations. This eliminated the need for commercial centers to act as middlemen in collecting and dispersing the goods of the countryside. Thus Virginia remained predominantly rural. Virginia's rivers also prevented the sharp political and economic dichotomy between Tidewater and Piedmont areas. Because the streams were navigable for quite some distance into the state's interior, many Piedmont

---

[4] Charles Henry Ambler, *Sectionalism in Virginia from 1776 to 1861* (Chicago, 1910), 2, 13–14; Edwards, *Statistical Gazetteer of Virginia, 77;* and Martin, *A Comprehensive Description of Virginia,* 99.

[5] Martin, *A Comprehensive Description of Virgina,* 99–100; Howe, *Historical Collections of Virginia,* 129; Edwards, *Statistical Gazetteer,* 77; Ambler, *Sectionalism in Virginia,* 1–6, 137, 170.

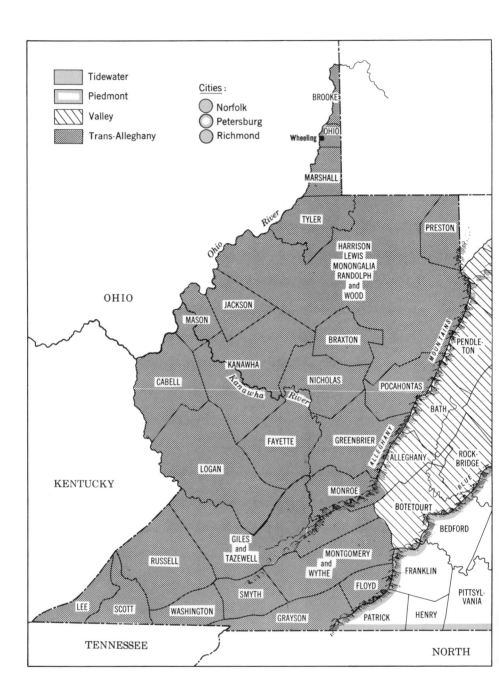

Tidewater
Piedmont
Valley
Trans-Alleghany

Cities:
Norfolk
Petersburg
Richmond

OHIO

KENTUCKY

TENNESSEE

BROOKE
OHIO
Wheeling
MARSHALL
TYLER
PRESTON
HARRISON
LEWIS
MONONGALIA
RANDOLPH
and
WOOD
PENDLE-TON
JACKSON
MASON
BRAXTON
KANAWHA
CABELL
NICHOLAS
POCAHONTAS
BATH
FAYETTE
GREENBRIER
ALLEGHANY
ROCK-BRIDGE
LOGAN
MONROE
BOTETOURT
BEDFORD
GILES
and
TAZEWELL
MONTGOMERY
and
WYTHE
FRANKLIN
RUSSELL
FLOYD
PITTSYL-VANIA
SMYTH
HENRY
LEE
SCOTT
WASHINGTON
GRAYSON
PATRICK
NORTH

Ohio
River
Kanawha
River
MOUNTAINS
ALLEGHANY
BLUE

MAP 5. VIRGINIA GEOGRAPHIC SECTIONS

counties developed a large plantation agricultural system.[6] The James, Potomac, Shenandoah, Rappahannock, Pamunkey, York, and Roanoke all opened up extensive inland areas to commercial agriculture. In the Trans-Allegheny, the Ohio and the Kanawha had the same effect.

As the western area of the state developed, however, there was an increasing need for internal-improvement projects to supplement the excellent rivers and bring the interior into the market economy. But as late as 1851 little had been done, and a commercial convention of that year complained that other states had been more responsive to western needs than Virginia.

The stagnation of our commerce is to be attributed to physical obstacles which separate the productive interior from our seaboard, whilst the enterprise of other States and cities has actually constructed improvements for the . . . factorage of our produce. . . .

It is thus that towns in Western Virginia have sprung up, manufactures have been established, minerals have been made available, agricultural produce has been created, all of which seeks a market in the cities of Cincinnati, New Orleans, Philadelphia and Baltimore; whilst even Savannah, in Georgia, has participated in those productions of Virginia, which could not have paid the cost of exportation eastward to the Chesapeake cities of Virginia. The cities enumerated have supplied the Valley and Western Virginia with merchandise in exchange for its productions. The commerce of Virginia, like some fountains choked up and neglected, cheers with its shattered streamlet every region except that to which its free and fertilizing current would naturally and gladly have directed itself.[7]

As a result of this funneling off of western produce through other market cities in adjoining states, Virginia never developed a large commercial city to compete with Baltimore, Philadelphia, or New York. But this did not stop men of enterprise from dreaming that internal-improvement projects would make Virginia "one of the most successful commercial States of the Union, and its ports, so long forsaken," would become "the marts of a trade not surpassed by that of the present great emporia of the country."[8] The most ambitious project was the James River and Kanawha Canal, which was supposed to link Tidewater

---

[6] See Jackson Turner Main for a discussion of how geography influenced Virginia politics in the 1780s. *The Antifederalists, Critics of the Constitution, 1781–1788* (Chapel Hill, N.C., 1961), 28–31.

[7] Edwards, *Statistical Gazetteer*, 139. [8] *Ibid.*, 97.

Virginia with the Ohio River and become "second only in extent and importance to the Erie Canal. . . ." But by the early 1850s the canal had not yet been completed beyond the Alleghenies.[9]

Despite the weakness of the transportation system in Virginia, however, a fairly substantial manufacturing and mining industry did develop. In 1840 Virginia had more than 11.3 million dollars invested in manufacturing, while ten years later this figure had grown to 18.1 million dollars. Five industries—flour milling, tobacco processing, construction, cotton manufacturing, and iron manufacturing—each had over 1 million dollars capital investment in 1840.[10] Richmond, the center of the flour-milling industry, developed a lucrative business with South America, that at times surpassed Baltimore's trade. Brazil was the major recipient of Virginia flour, importing over 80,500 barrels in 1845.[11] Tobacco still was a major agricultural and industrial product of the state, as Virginia produced "almost 45 per cent of all tobacco manufactured in the United States. . . ." The four most important centers of tobacco manufacturing, in order of importance, were Richmond, Petersburg, Lynchburg, and Danville.[12]

Despite the fact that the state had rich mineral resources, they were not fully exploited in the period before the Civil War. In 1851 a manufacturers' convention concluded that it was both mortifying and astonishing

that Virginia, with an area of coal measures covering not less than 21,000 square miles . . . capable of yielding all the varieties of British coal, and of equal quality, should be reduced to the . . . production of less than 200,000 tons of the value of $650,000, while Great Britain, with little more than half the extent of coal measures, produces annually, 37,000,000 tons, of about the value of . . . $180,000,000. . . .[13]

[9] *Ibid.*, 97, 133.

[10] In 1840 the capital investment in flour mills was 5,184,669 dollars; in tobacco processing, 1,526,080 dollars; construction, 1,367,393 dollars; cotton manufacturing, 1,299,020 dollars; and iron manufacturing, 1,246,650 dollars. See Howe, *Historical Collections of Virginia*, 130, and Edwards, *Statistical Gazetteer*, 87.

[11] Craven, *Soil Exhaustion*, 132.

[12] Joseph Clarke Robert, *The Tobacco Kingdom; Plantation, Market, and Factory in Virginia and North Carolina, 1800–1860* (Durham, N.C., 1938), 165, 178–81.

[13] Edwards, *Statistical Gazetteer*, 75.

It was the lack of adequate transportation resources that prevented the early development of Virginia's coal fields. With the exception of some mining in the Tidewater, the great bulk of the coal reserves was in and around the Kanawha Valley in western Virginia. Despite attempts to improve the Kanawha River so that miners could ship their coal to the Ohio River, the Kanawha remained navigable only about six months a year. As a result, the coal mined there was practically all used locally in the making of salt.[14]

2

Throughout the ante-bellum period, Virginia politics remained aristocratic and dominated by the landed gentry. The constitution of 1831 did bring some electoral reform, but still one third of the adult white males were disenfranchised. Each county government was totally under the control of the local oligarchy, a group of men not elected by the public but instead appointed for indefinite terms by the governor. Because of the relatively few elective offices and the aristocratic nature of Virginia politics and society, political parties were not highly organized and Virginia politicians tended to be more individualistic and independent of the party than their counterparts in other states.[15]

Prior to 1833–1834 there had been little anti-Democratic strength in the state. Adams carried only about 20 per cent of the city and county constituencies in 1828, while Clay won less than 10 per cent in 1832.[16] Jackson's strong stand against South Carolina in the Nullification crisis and his withdrawal of the federal deposits from the Bank of the United States alienated a number of his early supporters, however, and in the presidential elections from 1836 to 1844 a vigorous opposition to the Democrats developed. In fact, during those years the Whig and Democratic parties were of more nearly equal strength in Virginia

[14] James T. Laing, "The Early Development of the Coal Industry in the Western Counties of Virginia, 1800–1865," *West Virginia History*, XXVII (January, 1966), 145–49, and Otis K. Rice, "Coal Mining in the Kanawha Valley to 1861: A View of Industrialization in the Old South," *Journal of Southern History*, XXXI (November, 1965), 394–96.

[15] McCormick, *Second American Party System*, 178–85.

[16] See Map 6. For 1828 and 1832 elections see Simms, *Rise of Whigs in Virginia*, 33, 62.

than they were in either Ohio, where the Whigs had a decided edge, or Mississippi, where the Democrats had a comfortable majority. Political opinion in Virginia was considerably more polarized than in Ohio but slightly less so than in Mississippi.[17]

In Virginia, as in Mississippi and in Ohio, there was a correlation between wealth and Whiggery and between lack of wealth and Democratic voting. The Virginia correlation was smaller than those in Ohio and Mississippi but nevertheless significant. In the Virginia Tidewater and Piedmont there was not too much difference in wealth between Whig and Democratic constituencies but in the Valley and Trans-Allegheny sections the more traditional correlation between Whiggery and wealth existed.[18]

While wealth appears to be a fairly reliable index of Whig and Democratic strength in the western half of Virginia, other factors played a more prominent role in the eastern half. The Tidewater and Piedmont shared a longer political history, and there the Whig and Democratic parties represented, at least in part, a re-emergence of past feuds and antagonisms stemming from party factionalism in the Revolutionary era. One historian, for example, has shown there to have been a rather persistent split during the 1780s between two areas of

[17] Although the strongest Democratic and Whig constituencies (according to voting in presidential contests from 1836–1844) in Virginia were separated by a greater number of percentage points (79) than in Mississippi (64) and Ohio (46), this is to be expected due to the fact that the constituencies in Virginia are far more numerous. Statistically the variation in Virginia opinion can be shown by employing the formula to compute the Semi-Interquartile Range. This shows that 50 per cent of Virginia constituencies were within 9.50 percentage points of the median constituency. The median constituency in Virginia gave an average of 52.92 per cent of its votes to the Democrats, less than the 56.13 per cent the median constituency gave in Mississippi but more than the 46.67 per cent the median constituency gave in Ohio. See Footnote 22, Chapter VII, and Appendix A, Table III. For the 1836–1844 time period, Virginia voting constituencies considered in this book include the counties, cities, and county groups enumerated in Appendix A, Table III.

[18] In the Tidewater, for example, the mean rank in wealth for Whig constituencies was 70, while the mean Democratic rank was 66. In the Piedmont, Whig and Democratic mean ranks in wealth were 79 and 81.5, respectively. Constituencies were ranked from poorest to richest. On the other hand, in the Valley, the Democratic mean rank for wealth was 41, far below the Whig rank of 57. The same was true of the Trans-Allegheny, where the Democratic mean rank was 11 and the Whig rank 29. See Appendix A, Table III.

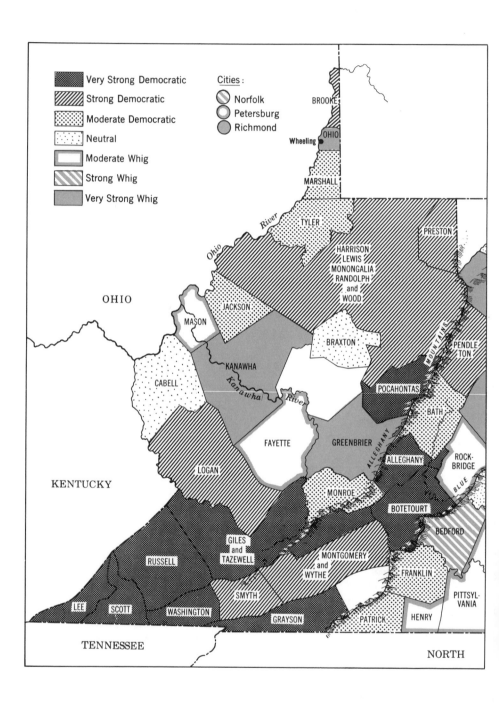

Very Strong Democratic
Strong Democratic
Moderate Democratic
Neutral
Moderate Whig
Strong Whig
Very Strong Whig

Cities:
Norfolk
Petersburg
Richmond

OHIO

KENTUCKY

TENNESSEE

NORTH

BROOKE
OHIO
Wheeling
MARSHALL
TYLER
PRESTON
HARRISON
LEWIS
MONONGALIA
RANDOLPH
and
WOOD
PENDLE-
TON
JACKSON
MASON
BRAXTON
CABELL
KANAWHA
POCAHONTAS
BATH
River
Kanawha
FAYETTE
GREENBRIER
ALLEGHANY
ROCK-
BRIDGE
LOGAN
MONROE
BOTETOURT
BEDFORD
GILES
and
TAZEWELL
MONTGOMERY
and
WYTHE
FRANKLIN
RUSSELL
PITTSYL-
VANIA
SMYTH
LEE
SCOTT
WASHINGTON
GRAYSON
PATRICK
HENRY

Ohio River

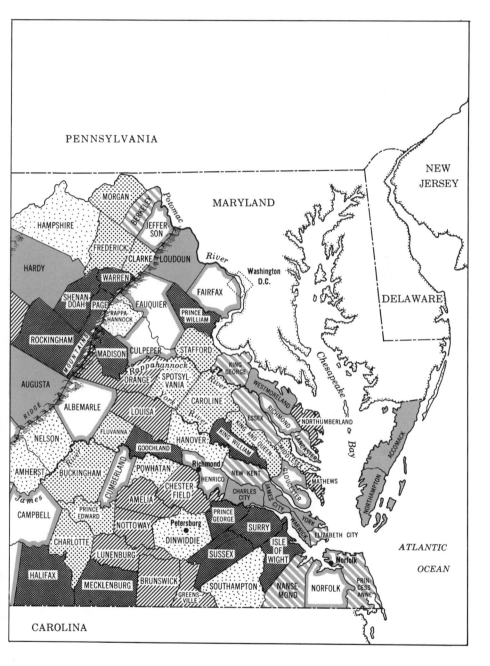

MAP 6. DEMOCRATIC AND WHIG STRENGTH IN VIRGINIA, 1836–1844

(*Data not available for unlabeled counties—Nicholas and Floyd*)

Virginia: the Southside (or the counties in the Tidewater and Piedmont situated south of the James River) and the Northern Neck (the
region bounded by the Potomac and Rappahannock rivers and extending as far west as to include the two uppermost Valley counties). And,
while allowing for the considerable change that had taken place in the
intervening years, this Northern Neck-Southside division of the 1780s
was still distinguishable in the Jacksonian era. During the Confederation period, it is claimed that

Virginia east of the Blue Ridge was separated into Federal and Antifederal
territory by a line which was irregular but clearly defined. The major sections which had opposed each other during the Confederation period were
the Southside and Northern Neck, and the same alignment existed over
the Constitution. The Northern Neck . . . was Federal by a great majority.
. . . The Southside was even more solidly Antifederal. The James-York
River counties had supported the Northern Neck in the past and continued
to do so, with some exception; indeed along the James, Federalist delegates
were to be found even beyond the fall line. The remaining "Tidewater"
counties had never shown a really consistent pattern of behavior, but those
nearest to the coast were now Federal, those inland (with the above-
mentioned exceptions along the rivers) were Antifederal. It is perhaps this
alignment which has given rise to the belief that the division in Virginia
was between east and west, whereas the division was really between the
Northern Neck plus the York-James counties versus the Southside, or
southern Piedmont.[19]

During the 1780s the Northern Neck counties tended to favor
strengthening the Confederation government and initiating tax measures to pay the debt. The Southside counties, on the other hand, were
generally suspicious of increasing the power of the central government
and anxious to postpone the payment of the debt. Although issues had
changed considerably by the Jacksonian period, there is evidence that
the historic Federal-Antifederal division had re-emerged as a Whig-
Democratic one, if only in outline and not in detail. Of the twenty-

[19] Main, *Antifederalists*, 231. For a more detailed discussion of the sectional
nature of Virginia politics, see Jackson T. Main, "Sections and Politics in Virginia, 1781–1787," *William and Mary Quarterly*, 3rd Series, XII (January, 1955),
97–111. By the time of the Jackson period the two Valley counties that Main
includes with the Northern Neck, Berkeley and Frederick, had split to make two
new counties: Clark and Jefferson.

seven Tidewater and Piedmont counties that can be classified Whig by their voting in presidential elections from 1836–1844, eighteen had supported ratification of the Constitution, seven had opposed, and two had been divided. Of the thirty-one counties in the two sections that can be classified Democratic by the voting in the 1836–1844 presidential elections, nineteen had opposed ratification of the Constitution, eight had been Federalist, and four divided.[20]

Thus, in the Jacksonian period as in the Confederation era, the political division in the eastern half of Virginia was not the Piedmont versus the Tidewater but rather a much more complex division involving history, geography, and economics.

The overwhelming majority of Whig support in Virginia came from the Tidewater and Piedmont and, with the exception of the coastal counties of Nansemond, Norfolk, and Princess Anne, and a few others to the west, was concentrated north of the James River. The Whigs consistently carried forty county and city constituencies in the presidential elections from 1836 to 1844 and thirty of these were in the Piedmont and Tidewater regions. The Whigs drew their support from a number of quite different types of areas. They were strong in a certain number of the languishing Tidewater counties, although there is some evidence that this was only a temporary phenomenon. The Whigs also appeared to have considerable backing in regions of general farming where slave forces had been reduced and land improved by the use of fertilizer. And finally, in the Valley and the Trans-Allegheny the Whig constituencies were clearly the wealthiest. Throughout the entire state the more urbanized and commercialized areas were strong in their support of the Whig party. Of the twenty-three constituencies that either had banks or were authorized to have banks in 1839, thirteen were Whig and seven were soft-money Democratic.[21]

[20] See Map 6, pp. 256–57. The county-by-county vote in Virginia on the adoption of the Constitution is shown in a map illustrating Norman J. Risjord's "The Virginia Federalists," *Journal of Southern History,* XXXIII (November, 1967), 494. Culpeper County was excluded from the list of Whig counties, because in the interim it had split into two counties and was in 1836–1844 no longer the same entity as in 1788.

[21] Richmond *Enquirer,* April 9, 1839. The question of whether a constituency was soft or hard money in its attitude was determined by analyzing the vote on twelve bank bills or resolutions spanning the years 1837–1842. (1) Vote on General Bank Bill, Richmond *Enquirer,* March 18, 1837. (2) Resolution to allow

In the 1832 presidential election the Democrats carried all but two of the Tidewater constituencies. Four years later the Whigs had the majority vote in nineteen of the thirty-six constituencies in the section. The most obvious reason for this dramatic development was opposition to Andrew Jackson's strong and positive denunciation of South Carolina's attempt to nullify the federal tariff. Other Tidewater gentlemen withdrew their allegiance when the Old General removed the federal deposits from the Bank of the United States. To these members of the Tidewater gentry, Jackson's vigorous use of executive power violated the principles of strict construction and state rights. Even those who remained within the Democratic party were made extremely uneasy by Jackson's actions, and Ritchie's paper ran long and intricately-argued essays discussing Nullification and its doctrinal relationship to the hallowed principles of '98. When a resolution was introduced into the Virginia legislature supporting Jackson and denying the right of secession, it was voted down overwhelmingly, 107 to 24.[22]

The Tidewater Whig gentlemen were unique. In Ohio, Mississippi, and other areas of Virginia the party represented the more commercially minded men who were optimistic and confident of the future. The typical Virginia Tidewater Whig, however, has been described as a "southern mugwump," who, suspicious of democracy and estranged by Virginia's lost pre-eminence in national politics, came to feel that history in some sense had passed him by and thus adopted "strident means of expressing his feelings of bitterness and alienation." [23]

The difference between Tidewater Whigs and Democrats, however, must be one of emphasis rather than degree. Men such as Abel Upshur

---

banks to issue small notes, *ibid.*, June 23, 1837. (3) Resolution to allow the legislature to repeal, alter, or amend bank charters, *ibid.*, March 19, 1838. (4) Resolution to force banks to report debtors, *ibid.*, March 9, 1839. (5) Resolution on increasing banking capital, *ibid.*, March 9, 1839. (6) Bill to give temporary relief to the banks, *ibid.*, December 7, 1839. (7) Bill to allow banks to issue small notes, *ibid.*, February 4, 1841. (8) Bill to relieve the banks from penalties, *ibid.*, March 4, 1841. (9) Bill to allow banks to issue notes under 5 dollars, *ibid.*, December 18, 1841. (10) Resolution to postpone indefinitely the creation of a new bank, *ibid.*, February 22, 1842. (11) Resolution in favor of immediate specie resumption, *ibid.*, March 17, 1842. (12) Bill to make stockholders liable, *ibid.*, March 19, 1842.

[22] Simms, *Rise of Whigs in Virginia*, 67, 73.

[23] William R. Taylor, *Cavalier and Yankee: The Old South and American National Character* (Garden City, N.Y., 1963), 35-36, 39.

and Edmund Ruffin, who became Whigs, would surely have found the political philosophy of Democrat Peter V. Daniel congenial with their own. Unlike the situation in most other states, there was no unanimity among Tidewater Whigs on the banking question. Most, it is true, supported the party's policy of protecting the Virginia banks against the reform attempts of the Democrats, but five Tidewater Whig constituencies did give occasional support to the hard-money Democracy. Upshur, for instance, had the more traditional Whig view of banking and urged that the state banking system in Virginia be expanded to the point that each community would be assured an adequate currency.[24] But Ruffin, the planter, agricultural reformer, and polemicist, was opposed to banks. Founder of the Association for Promoting Currency and Banking Reform, he charged that

The paper banking system is essentially and necessarily fraudulent. . . . The object, as well as the effect, of the paper-money system is to enable those who have earned or accumulated nothing by labor, to exchange this *nothing* for the *something,* and often the *everything* earned by the labor of others.[25]

The same argument might have been used by any one of dozens of hard-money Democrats. Most members of the Tidewater gentry appear to have been suffering from the same malady. Nostalgic about Virginia's past, some even left politics. To those who remained active, a primary objective seems to have been recapturing Virginia's former illustrious role in national politics. Those who stayed in the Democratic party undoubtedly felt that this objective could best be achieved there, while those who entered the Whig ranks felt that Andrew Jackson had ruined the Democratic party to the point that it was beyond redemption and that Virginia's political future lay outside the Democratic party. There is evidence that Whig strength in the Tidewater began to decline after 1840. Upshur, for example, after much wavering, did vote for Harrison in 1840, but only out of loyalty to Tyler. An uneasy Whig, Ruffin threw his support to Tyler once he became President.[26]

[24] Claude H. Hall, *Abel Parker Upshur: Conservative Virginian, 1790–1844* (Madison, Wisc., 1963), 110–11.

[25] As quoted in Avery Craven, *Edmund Ruffin, Southerner; A Study in Secession* (New York, 1932), 69–70.

[26] *Ibid.,* 47–48; Hall, *Abel Parker Upshur,* 110–11; and Ambler, *Thomas Ritchie,* 225–26.

An analysis of the nineteen Tidewater constituencies that voted Whig in the presidential election of 1836 reveals a dramatic tapering off by 1844. In fourteen of these, the Democrats gained appreciably, averaging over a 19-per-cent increase.[27] Thus it would appear that many Tidewater residents found only temporary solace in the commercially minded Whig party. To be sure, the positions on the annexation of Texas taken by Clay and Polk were such that many Tidewater Whigs were attracted to Polk's banner. Nevertheless, beyond the Texas issue, given the *Weltanschauung* of both Democratic and Whig Tidewater gentlemen, the Democratic party with its emphasis upon strict construction and state rights was bound, in the long run, to be more attractive. The marriage between some of the heirs of Jefferson, John Randolph, and John Taylor of Caroline with Clay and Webster was a rocky one that could not last.

Although both Democrats and Whigs drew support from the declining areas in eastern Virginia, the Whigs seem to have been more popular than the Democrats in the better agricultural areas north of the James. The northern portions of the Tidewater and especially the Piedmont appear to have developed in the ante-bellum period into areas of well-balanced general agriculture, where a regular system of crop rotation was used and in general a more scientific approach to farming was practiced. George Washington, upon being asked for advice about choice locations for settlement in the United States, replied that the "eastern side of the Blue Ridge, between the Potomac and the James," combined the "most advantages" and was "the most desirable." [28]

One historian of southern agriculture has referred to an area including Culpeper, Fauquier, Loudoun, and Prince William counties, as "one of the most important general farming regions in the South." [29] Of these four counties, Culpeper and Fauquier were Moderate Whig, Loudoun was Very Strong Whig, and Prince William was Very Strong Democratic. Farmers in Loudoun County were pioneers in agricultural improvement; the use of gypsum was introduced as a fertilizer as early as 1784. Loudoun reformers were successful in convincing

[27] See election statistics in Walter Burnham's *Presidential Ballots* (Baltimore, 1955), 818–42, 852–64, 948–51.

[28] Martin, *Comprehensive Description of Virginia*, 19, 99.

[29] Lewis Cecil Gray, *History of Agriculture in the Southern United States to 1860* (Gloucester, Mass., 1958), II, 919–20.

their neighbors to adopt better farming techniques, such as deep ploughing and crop rotation.[30] Westmoreland and James City, two other Very Strong Whig constituencies, are also mentioned as counties where there was some evidence of agricultural improvement.[31] Obviously, most of the eastern half of Virginia remained unimproved. Ruffin estimated that near the end of the ante-bellum period only about 5 per cent of the Tidewater land had been revived.

No systematic, county-by-county analysis of Virginia agriculture for the Jacksonian period is available. However, there are impressionistic indications that in the Tidewater alone the improved agricultural areas, or at least those with better land, tended to be Whig, while the ones with poorer, unimproved land tended to be Democratic. The average market value of farm land and buildings in the Tidewater for the Whig counties in 1850 was 11.44 dollars, while the Democratic average value was 7.35 dollars. Thus the average value in the Democratic counties was only about two thirds that in the Whig counties. If only the Democratic counties south of the James—where the Democrats had a virtual monopoly—are considered, the average value of land for the Democratic counties falls to 5 dollars an acre.[32] Furthermore, a comparison of slaveholding in 1840 in the Tidewater region indicates that mean slaveholding in the Whig constituencies was .81 slaves per member of the free population, while the Democratic mean was 1.01 slaves per free capita. This is a rough indicator that perhaps the once-large and wealthy plantations with their numerous slaves in the Northern Neck were being slowly transformed into more diversified farms by the selling of slaves and the improvement of land. In the Democratic constituencies there was perhaps a tendency to remain "slave poor," the

[30] Craven, *Soil Exhaustion,* 90, 94, 95, 98.

[31] *Ibid.,* 93–94, 143, and Martin, *Comprehensive Description of Virginia,* 288–92.

[32] Thomas J. Pressly and William H. Scofield, *Farm Real Estate Values in the United States by Counties, 1850–1959* (Seattle, Wash., 1965), 42–44. Fields, in his "Agricultural Population of Virginia," points out that the Tidewater soils north of the James River were different from those south of it. North of the river the soil was Sassafras, which before the Civil War was producing corn and wheat. "South of the James on moderately well drained lands is Norfolk soil," states Fields, who further explains that although it "is considered very unproductive naturally" it "responds well to fertilization. Counties of this area were usually low in production before 1860." See pages 48–49.

planters keeping more slaves than were economically necessary to work their land.

In the western half of the state the Whigs were greatly outnumbered by the Democrats. In the Valley eleven constituencies were Democratic, five Whig, and one Neutral, and in the Trans-Allegheny seventeen were Democratic, five Whig, and two Neutral. As has been mentioned, there is a very clear correlation between wealth and Whiggery in the western areas. Those constituencies with strong commercial and industrial interests were attracted to the Whigs by their more positive attitude toward banking and the building of internal-improvement systems.

Augusta and Rockbridge represent the extremes within the Whig camp in the Valley section. Augusta was a Very Strong Whig constituency and the third wealthiest county in the Valley. Its city of Staunton, for example, was a flourishing town with "many mercantile and mechanical establishments," a bank, and "a large business with the surrounding country."[33] Rockbridge, in the Moderate Whig category, although only average in wealth among Valley counties, had an incipient iron industry and hopes for further development. In 1835, one iron works made 30 tons of pig iron a week and employed sixty-five persons. Slaves were hired from east of the Blue Ridge by the ironmongers to work in the industry. A major handicap to the development of the industry, however, was the lack of transportation. And despite considerable sentiment within the county for improved communications with the east, a canal did not reach Lexington until 1852.[34]

The Whigs also had small footholds in the extreme west of the state, especially in Kanawha and Ohio counties, which were in the Very Strong Whig category. Kanawha was bisected by the Kanawha River, which was navigable to the Ohio River for six months of the year. Charleston, Kanawha's prosperous county seat, was located on the river and could boast of a branch of the Bank of Virginia and of being the center of a salt industry that employed nearly three thousand persons. A traveler described the valley around 1840:

It is nearly 20 miles below the falls before the Kanawha valley widens into something like a plain, and opens its beautiful vista to the eye. The moun-

---

[33] Howe, *Historical Collections of Virginia*, 177–84, and Martin, *Comprehensive Description of Virginia*, 103–104.

[34] Morton, *Rockbridge County Virginia*, Chapters 20 and 21.

tains which enclose it on either side become gradually depressed into hills; and, for the first time, the dense, dark volumes of smoke which ascend from the salt-furnaces, announce the busy and bustling scene which enlivens the highway to the village of Charleston. What a scene of animation, indeed, contrasted with the deep solitudes from which the traveler has but just emerged. Here he is feasted with a continuous succession of green meadows and cultivated fields, teeming with flocks and herds, and adorned by commodious and even elegant mansions. The chimneys of the salt manufactories pour forth, at short intervals of space, their curling masses of black vapor, while swarms of laborers, and others connected with these establishments, are continually passing to and fro, presenting a pleasing *coup d'oeil* of incessant activity and industry. Nature, indeed, seems to have been prodigal in her bounties to this interesting region. The contiguous forests having been almost stripped to supply fuel to the salt-furnaces. . . .[35]

The city of Wheeling in Ohio County mushroomed in the years 1820 to 1840. Its spectacular population growth during these two decades, from 1,567 to 7,885, made it the largest town in western Virginia in 1840 and the fourth largest city in the state. Located on the banks of the Ohio River and blessed with rich coal deposits, the county annually mined over a million bushels of coal, which could be easily transported to market.[36]

The Tidewater cities of Richmond and Norfolk, the two largest commercial areas of the state, were heavily Whig. And Petersburg, the largest city of the Piedmont, with a population of 11,136 in 1840, was Moderate Whig. The location of Richmond, near the mouth of the James River, enabled the city's merchants to tap the market of interior Virginia. With a population of 20,153, Richmond in 1840 had "17 Foreign commercial and 29 commission-houses," with a capital of

$3,062,000; 256 retail stores, cap. $1,646,450; 3 lumber yards, cap. $24,000; 4 furnaces, and 8 forges . . . , cap. $317,900; machinery produced . . . $128,000; 1 cotton factory . . . , cap. $175,000; tobacco manufactories, cap. $492,250; 1 paper factory, cap. $75,000; 3 flouring-mills, 2 grist-mills, 3 saw-mills, total cap. $61,000. . . .[37]

Norfolk, with the best harbor in the state, was undergoing an economic transition. While the city's merchants were losing the European commerce that had once been so important, coastal trade was growing

[35] Howe, *Historical Collections of Virginia*, 343–47.   [36] *Ibid.*, 407–17.
[37] *Ibid.*, 309.

rapidly. Southern Virginia and northern North Carolina shipments were funneled into Norfolk through the Dismal Swamp Canal, connecting the Chesapeake Bay with Albemarle Sound. With 10,920 inhabitants, the city ranked third in population among Virginia cities in 1840, behind Richmond and Petersburg.

In 1840 Petersburg was second only to Richmond in the production of tobacco products and was the trade center for the Virginia-North Carolina tobacco belt. The city had that year eight tobacco factories representing a capital investment of $310,000, and six of these employed fifty or more persons. By the middle 1840s the city could claim "6 commercial and 8 commission houses engaged in foreign trade . . . 121 retail stores . . . 2 lumber yards, 1 furnace, 6 forges, 1 woollen factory . . . 2 flouring mills, 1 grist-mill, 2 saw-mills, 2 printing offices. . . ."[38]

3

Democratic strength came from four different areas of Virginia: the declining agricultural region in the Tidewater (especially south of the James River), the wealthy tobacco region in the southern Piedmont, the farmlands in the Valley—populated heavily by persons of German descent—and sparsely settled areas in the mountains of the Trans-Allegheny section.

Although the Tidewater Democrats shared the same gloomy ethos as their Whig brethren, the Democrats seemed even more pessimistic about the future and more alienated from the commercial society represented by the banks. These Democratic heirs of John Taylor of Caroline and his cult of agrarianism presented a solid phalanx in opposition to the Virginia banks. The burden of the past hung heavily around the necks of these Tidewater Virginia planters. Overcultivation of tobacco forced either the abandonment of the land or conversion to the raising of grain crops. However, since wheat and corn required less cultivation, the planters' large slave gangs could be used only at reduced efficiency. This forced the conscientious planter into a real dilemma.

---

[38] Robert, *Tobacco Kingdom*, 185–86; and Howe, *Historical Collections of Virginia*, 242. A railroad was built from Norfolk County to Weldon, North Carolina, on the Roanoke but proved to be disappointing. See Thomas J. Wertenbaker, *Norfolk: Historic Southern Port* (Durham, N.C., 1931), 392–404.

Social custom and a sense of morality prohibited some planters from selling surplus slaves to the lower South.[39] If the past was a burden to these Tidewater planters, it also represented their glory. Indeed, these Virginia Democrats responded like other "groups which have lost their social positions" and "seek more violently than ever to impose on all groups the older values of a society which they once represented." [40] The promise the banks offered to other groups held no such attraction for Tidewater Democrats.

Two Very Strong Democratic Tidewater counties, Sussex and Isle of Wight, are good examples of the declining agricultural area south of the James River. Sussex lost 25 per cent of its white population from the tax rolls in a single two-year period.[41] Isle of Wight, one of the eight original shires, also showed a rather dramatic decline of white population, decreasing from 8,339 in 1830 to 6,186 in 1840. The slave population, however, increased from 2,178 to 3,786.[42] This latter increase was of economic advantage to the Isle of Wight planter only if he chose to sell his excess slaves to the slave-hungry regions in the Southwest. And in the decade of the 1830s, with the large increase in slaves, it is unlikely that Isle of Wight planters did this.

Arthur Smith, the Democratic representative from Isle of Wight in the house of delegates immediately after the Panic, was against giving the banks any quarter. Smith was a descendant of a leading family of Isle of Wight, his forebear being the original owner of the land on which the county's largest village, Smithfield, was laid out in 1752. Smith was described by a contemporary as "one of the most eminent men this county has ever produced. He was a man of charming simplicity of character and sacrificed his social career to his conscience." [43] Smith's position on banking was like that of other Democratic representatives from the Virginia Tidewater. The banks and the commercial change they wrought, they believed, had corrupted the morals of many of their countrymen, tempting them into selling their principles for a

[39] Gray, *History of Southern Agriculture*, II, 908–11.

[40] This is Daniel Bell's definition of status politics in his *End of Ideology*, 111.

[41] Sutton, "Nostalgia, Pessimism, and Malaise," 41.

[42] Martin, *Comprehensive Description of Virginia*, 196; Howe, *Historical Collections of Virginia*, 315.

[43] John Bennett Boddie, *Seventeenth Century Isle of Wight County Virginia* (Chicago, 1938), 253.

bank loan. These hard-money Jacksonians were concerned about the crass materialism around them, but part of their indignation surely stemmed from the jealousy they must have felt when they observed the wealth and increasing influence of the newer sections of the state. To allay this sense of decadence, they became the trustees of an older, simpler, and purer order.

The southern part of the Piedmont, with its heavy tobacco-growing areas, also was strongly Democratic. This was part of the region south of the James River that had been solidly opposed to the ratification of the Federal Constitution and had been a bastion of Republican strength in the 1790s. The top twenty tobacco-growing counties in 1839 were in this area, and twelve were Democratic, four Whig, and four Neutral.[44] The solid support for the Democrats in the tobacco country accounts for the fact that the Piedmont was the only section in which the Democratic mean rank in wealth was slightly higher than that of the Whigs. Furthermore, there was a significant difference in slaveholding, the Democratic constituencies having a mean holding in 1840 between 1.353 and 1.403 slaves per free capita and the Whigs having only .914.[45]

Other consistent Democratic sentiment in Virginia came from the newer, more isolated, and thinly populated counties. In the Valley, Bath and Alleghany were mountainous and had little land under cultivation. It was estimated that only one eighth of Bath County was arable.[46] In the Trans-Allegheny region, the first, second, fourth, and fifth poorest constituencies in the state, Grayson, Scott, Lee, and Russell counties, were in the Very Strong Democratic category. Interestingly enough the Moderate Whig Fayette County, the ninth poorest constituency in the state, gave occasional support to the hard-money Democrats.

As in Ohio, the German-Americans who settled in Virginia gave strong support to the Democratic party. The bulk of the German population settled in the Valley, where the counties of Shenandoah, Rockingham, and Page were populated from two thirds to three fourths by German-Americans. Significantly these three counties were three of the

[44] For an analysis of the nationalist and antinationalist regions in Virginia in the 1790s, see Risjord, "Virginia Federalists," 486–517. For the tobacco production rankings, see Robert, *Tobacco Kingdom*, 47.

[45] See Appendix A, Table III.

[46] Martin, *Comprehensive Description of Virginia*, 103, 308–309, 319–31.

top four Democratic constituencies in Virginia, with each giving *at least* 86.23 per cent of its vote to the Jacksonians.[47] One early settler in Page County recalled that around the turn of the nineteenth century: "Nothing was spoken in this part of the country but the German language. . . ."[48] German was taught in the schools of Shenandoah County well into the nineteenth century.[49]

The Valley was a wealthy, self-sufficient, agricultural area, but also one of few slaves. Most farmers evidently were in the market economy but not completely dependent on it. The period was described as a "time of general prosperity and relative independence, our people producing on their farms, in their homes, and in their numerous small shops and factories nearly everything that was necessary to their welfare and comfort." The wagons that were used by the local teamsters were produced locally, as was the wool and linen clothes many wore.[50] In the early 1850s the Virginia legislature authorized Shenandoah County to vote on the question of whether to subscribe to a railroad. The record is not clear, but either the sentiment was so strong against the taking of stock that a vote was never taken or a vote was taken and the plan was overwhelmingly defeated.[51]

The large population of German-Americans in the Valley no doubt played a major role in keeping this area on the side of the hard-money Democracy. As in Ohio, generally the kind of society the Germans built in Virginia was not conducive to the development of an entrepreneurial spirit. Settling in the eighteenth century in compact communities, the Virginia Germans continued a thrifty and frugal existence well into the nineteenth century.

Both their peasant training and their remoteness from markets inclined them toward a diversified system of farming involving a large measure of self-sufficiency. They were accustomed to the production of Irish potatoes and small grain, from which they made their bread, fattened their hogs, brewed their beer, and distilled their whiskey, the provision of abundant

[47] See Appendix A, Table III.

[48] Harry M. Strickler, *A History of Page County Virginia* (Richmond, Va., 1952), 105–106.

[49] Martin, *Comprehensive Description of Virginia*, 445–52.

[50] John W. Wayland, *A History of Shenandoah County Virginia,* (Strasburg, Va., 1927), 288–89.

[51] *Ibid.*, 293.

orchards, and the raising of flax and hemp from which to spin and weave their clothing.[52]

As in Mississippi and Ohio, a clear majority of Virginia Democrats, at least as represented in the legislature, could be classified as hard-money men. From 1837 to 1842, sixty-four house of delegates voting districts were represented always or nearly always by Democrats. On twelve separate banking issues that spanned the period, Democratic legislators from forty-four of these constituencies gave practically solid support to the hard-money position. Six additional constituencies that were evenly divided between Whigs and Democrats gave support to the hard-money cause when a Democrat was in the legislature.

The soft-money Democratic strongholds were scattered around the state, although few were found in the Tidewater. They were, for example, normally prosperous agricultural counties, each with one or more flourishing towns or villages to give economic unity. Furthermore, there generally were good lines of communications with outside markets. All four of the most solid soft-money Democratic counties, Brooke, Washington, Prince Edward, and Frederick, had banks or were authorized to have them by the Bank Expansion Act of 1839.

Brooke and Washington were the most westerly counties of solid soft-money support. Brooke, the northernmost county in the state, was on the Ohio River. Wellsburg, the county seat of two thousand inhabitants, was described around 1840 as a "thriving, business place" containing

9 mercantile stores, 2 academies . . . 1 white flint-glass works, 1 glass-cutting establishment, 1 paper-mill, 1 large cotton factory, 2 extensive potteries, 1 steam saw-mill, 5 large warehouses, 1 newspaper printing office, 6 extensive flouring mills in it and the vicinity, 1 woolen factory, [and] a branch of the N. W. Va. Bank. . . .[53]

Washington County was the home of conservative Democratic Governor David Campbell. Abingdon was the county seat and was "by far the most considerable and flourishing town in sw. Virginia. . . ." It was "surrounded by a fertile, flourishing, and thickly-settled agricul-

---

[52] Gray, *History of Southern Agriculture,* I, 122–23. Gray in this specific passage is describing an earlier period, but these same characteristics were also evident in the 1830s.

[53] Howe, *Historical Collections of Virginia,* 193–202.

tural country" and contained "several large mercantile stores, 2 newspaper printing offices . . . a variety of mechanical and manufacturing establishments and a population of over 1000." [54]

Botetourt was another predominantly soft-money Democratic county west of the Blue Ridge. From it, two rivers, the James and Roanoke, were navigable to the Tidewater. Fincastle was the county seat, although Buchanan and Pattonsburg across from one another on the James River had the county's only bank and two tobacco factories. John T. Anderson of Fincastle, who represented Botetourt County in the Virginia senate from 1834 to 1842, was an early follower of Rives.[55]

Another Valley county, Frederick, was Democratic but soft in persuasion. Like many other conservative areas, it had an important commercial center, Winchester, which was, outside of Wheeling, the largest town in Virginia west of the Blue Ridge and was blessed with two banks.[56]

In the tobacco-rich and Democratically strong southern Piedmont there was some soft-money sentiment in the counties that were closely divided politically. Two Moderate Democratic counties, Prince Edward and Franklin, were represented by soft-money Democrats or Whigs in the legislature almost exclusively in the period from 1837 to 1842. In fact, Franklin County, while preferring by a small margin Democratic presidential nominees, sent mainly Whigs to the lower house of the legislature. Of the Neutral counties, Dinwiddie, Nelson, and Amherst sent Whigs or softs to the legislature most of the time.

The difference between Prince Edward and another Piedmont county, hard-money Louisa, perhaps gives some indication of the general contrast between hard- and soft-money constituencies. A contemporary in the mid-1830s described the Strong Democratic Louisa as having soil "originally of at least middling fertility; but by every species of mismanagement (amid which overcropping, frequent grazing, bad ploughing, scanty manuring, and the culture of tobacco, stand con-

---

[54] *Ibid.,* 497–99.

[55] *Ibid.,* 202–203; Martin, *Comprehensive Description of Virginia,* 327–30; and John T. Anderson to William C. Rives, July 8 and 25, 1837, William C. Rives Papers. Also see Robert Douthat Stoner, *The Seed-Bed of the Republic, A Study of the Pioneers in the Upper (Southern) Valley of Virginia* (Kingsport, Tenn., 1962), 292, 402.

[56] Howe, *Historical Collection of Virginia,* 272–73.

spicuous), it has become pitiably barren." Of the fourteen hundred dwellings in the county, none "can pretend to elegance or grandeur; for the greater number is of one story . . . wooden, either framed or made with logs." No more than twenty were made of brick and "even painting is rare." [57]

Residents in Prince Edward, however, had little about which to complain. It was a wealthy area, and Farmville was the "fourth tobacco market in Virginia; and the quality of its tobacco . . . [was] nowhere surpassed." Located on the Appomattox River, Farmville in the mid-1840s had "2 tobacco warehouses, 10 tobacco factories, 7 or 8 mercantile stores, a branch of the Farmers' Bank . . . and a population of about 1400." [58] One of Rives' supporters in the Virginia legislature, Nathaniel E. Venable, was a leading merchant there and was among the residents who petitioned the legislature for the incorporation of a bank in Farmville. In the middle 1840s he led a revolt of the bank's stockholders and was consequently elected head of the board of directors.[59]

4

The politics of banking in Virginia was similar in broad outline to that in Mississippi and Ohio. In all three of the states there was a significant correlation between the wealthier constituencies and the Whigs, and the poorer ones and the Democrats. The statewide correlation, however, can be deceiving, because wealth seems to have been a more important factor in dividing the Whig and Democratic constituences in the two western sections of Virginia than in the two eastern ones.

There were major differences between Virginia and the two western states. Both Ohio and Mississippi had growing populations and expanding economies. Thus most residents of the two states believed in the promise of the future, and the development of their states seemed to confirm this hope. To many Virginians in the 1830s, however, the

---

[57] Martin, *Comprehensive Description of Virginia*, 217–19.

[58] Howe, *Historical Collections of Virginia*, 432; also, Robert, *Tobacco Kingdom*, 166.

[59] Herbert Clarence Bradshaw, *History of Prince Edward County, Virginia: From Its Earliest Settlements Through Its Establishment in 1754 to Its Bicentennial Year* (Richmond, Va., 1955), 321–22, 326–27.

future was not to be anticipated but to be stoically endured. The Whigs and soft-money Democrats on the better farmlands, or in areas of rising expectations, did not in general completely share this gloomy outlook. Virginia's future could be bright if the most were made of the commercial, industrial, and agricultural resources of the state. Banks and banking capital were vitally needed for the task.

A further complicating factor in Virginia politics was the Virginian's sense of the past. There was a strong emotional attachment to the Old Republican principles of 1798 and 1799. This, however, proved to be an ambiguous legacy. State rights Whigs, Rives' conservatives, and hard-money Democrats all claimed to be its heirs.

CHAPTER XI

The Southeast

I

LIKE VIRGINIA, the other southeastern states [1] did not participate in the boom of the 1830s, and so they too escaped many of the disastrous consequences of the financial crisis. In 1840 the Governor of South Carolina observed that "amid the general pressure of the times we have suffered but little. . . ." [2] The circulation of notes in the Southeast as a whole declined from a high of 28 million dollars in 1837 to a low of 12 million dollars in 1843, a contraction not nearly as severe as that in the Southwest, where the circulation fell from almost 31 million dollars to 3 million dollars between 1840 and 1843. [3] From 1824 to 1836 the discount rate of the notes of the southeastern banks at Philadelphia never fell below 5 per cent, with the exception of North Carolina in 1838 and Georgia in 1834. [4] Furthermore, the specie ratio after 1835 never dropped below 16 cents of specie for every dollar of circulation plus deposits. The figures also show that, in general, the southeastern banks began a slow conservative contraction of their liabilities after the Panic. [5]

There was less hard-money reaction to the Panic on the part of Democrats in the Southeast than in either the Northwest or Southwest.

---

[1] Included in southeastern section along with Virginia are Delaware, Georgia, Maryland, North Carolina, and South Carolina.

[2] Quoted in Sydnor, *Southern Sectionalism,* 264.

[3] All figures are approximate, taken from Berry, *Western Prices,* 588–89. See Alfred Glaze Smith, Jr., *Economic Readjustment of an Old Cotton State: South Carolina, 1820–1860* (Columbia, S.C., 1958), 202.

[4] Van Fenstermaker, *American Commercial Banking,* 85.

[5] See Appendix B, Table III.

In most states of the Southeast the overwhelming attitude within the party was one of indulgence and reform. There were several reasons for this. The Panic and depression had not hit the Southeast as hard as the western sections. On the whole, banks in the Southeast had acted with more restraint. And, in some states of the Southeast the banks were closely tied with state internal-improvement and education funds, thus making the Democratic party loath to take strong action against them.

2

Because the southeastern states were economically, socially, and politically more mature than their sister states in the Southwest, the politics of the Southeast was more stable and better balanced. Only in Virginia did the electorate give Democratic presidential candidates their support for the entire period from 1828 to 1856. South Carolina was second only to Virginia as a consistent Democratic state. After giving its support to Jackson in 1828, South Carolina followed John C. Calhoun out of the party. When Calhoun and his followers rejoined the Democrats in 1837, the state returned its backing to Democratic presidential aspirants unwaveringly from 1840 to 1856. Out of the eight presidential elections from 1828 to 1856, North Carolina and Georgia gave Whig candidates their favor three times, while Maryland gave the Democrats its support only in 1828, 1832, and 1852. The strongest Whig state in the Southeast was Delaware, where the Democracy was virtually shut out of all statewide elections until 1850.[6]

However, it can be misleading to focus attention only on national politics as a means of determining party strength within a state. Despite Maryland's proclivities for Whig presidential candidates, the Democrats managed to dominate the gubernatorial contests after 1838.[7] In the crucial years after the Panic, Virginia and North Carolina legislatures were mainly under Whig control. In Virginia this was due in

---

[6] North Carolina voted Whig from 1840 to 1848, while Georgia was Whig in 1836, 1840, and 1848. *Historical Statistics,* 689; John A. Monroe, "Party Battles, 1789–1850," in *Delaware: A History of the First State,* Henry Clay Reed, editor, (New York, 1947), I, 159; McCormick, *Second American Party System,* 153–54.

[7] McCormick, *Second American Party System,* 154–66.

large part to the fact that the influential Rives had split off from the party. North Carolina Democrats were frozen out of power because they had poor leadership to contend with an efficient Whig organization. Indeed, it was not until 1839 that the state's Democrats discarded their informal and less efficient means of political management and streamlined their party structure.[8]

The political situation in Georgia was perhaps the most unusual in the section. Until the middle 1830s, Georgia politics was characterized by vigorous contests between local parties that had no attachment to the developing national parties or issues. The anti-Jackson or State Rights men did not call themselves Whigs until 1843.[9]

Delaware was a politically conservative state and "was distinguished above all other states for the stability of its politics."[10] The Whigs were remarkably successful in Delaware, and this has been attributed to the fact that "they advocated causes which Delawareans wanted—a strong Union, a solid banking structure, a protective tariff, and peace with the world so that Delaware's farms and factories might flourish."[11] The Democrats swept the elections in 1850, but prior to that time they had won only three statewide campaigns, electing governors in 1832 and 1846 and a congressman in 1838. Despite this rather meager record of achievement, the Democrats did manage to poll an average of 48 per cent of the vote in statewide contests.[12]

Politics in Virginia and South Carolina were quite similar, both oligarchic in nature and oriented strongly to national issues. The conditions were ideal for men with national ambitions, such as Rives and Calhoun. The highly undemocratic political structure in South Carolina allowed the Calhoun clique to use the state as a political base, for the most part ignoring local issues in order to concentrate all efforts on elevating their native son to the Presidency. Calhoun had left the Democratic party during the Nullification crisis of the early 1830s, returning in 1837 to add his support to Van Buren's Independent Treasury pro-

---

[8] *Ibid.*, 199–209; J. G. DeRoulhac Hamilton, *Party Politics in North Carolina, 1835–1860* (Chapel Hill, N.C., 1916), 76–78.

[9] McCormick, *Second American Party System*, 236–46.

[10] *Ibid.*, 147.   [11] Monroe, "Party Battles," 153.

[12] *Ibid.*, 159, and McCormick, *Second American Party System*, 153–54.

posal. The Calhoun men, although surprised by this switch,[13] mustered their forces and pushed resolutions endorsing the scheme through the South Carolina legislature in the 1837–1838 session. This maneuver was denounced by some, who claimed that not ten people in the state had supported the Independent Treasury System until Calhoun had thrown his support to the administration. The action was further criticized on the grounds that South Carolina should remain united and not be divided by questions of finance.[14]

3

Softening or at least shifting the focus and emphasis of the southeastern Democratic attack on the banks was the heavy state involvement in the banking systems, especially in Virginia, South Carolina, and Georgia. Closely related to this was a widespread belief, held by Democrats as well as Whigs, that some kind of credit was necessary. Democrats, therefore, supported state-owned and/or controlled institutions in preference to privately operated ones. In the Northwest, Democrats in Tennessee and Missouri also had come to this decision.

The Bank of the State of South Carolina was one of the few banks outside the Northeast that was able to sustain specie payments after the general suspension in the fall of 1839. In fact, all the banks in South Carolina were so conservatively operated that from 1783 to 1861 not one bank failed.[15] Managed in the 1840s by Franklin H. Elmore, a political lieutenant of Calhoun, the state-owned bank was an important economic and political force in the state. This was recognized by one South Carolinian who wrote that the "Bank controlled the State and Colonel Elmore controlled the bank." [16]

Although Calhoun had persuaded the Democrats to support the Independent Treasury, this move was not translated into any action

---

[13] Laura A. White, *Robert Barnwell Rhett: Father of Secession* (New York, 1931), 33–34.

[14] *Ibid.*, 41–42.

[15] Knox, *History of Banking,* 567. Van Fenstermaker maintains that one bank failed in 1826, in *American Commercial Banking,* 178. Sumner, *History of Banking,* 355–57.

[16] As quoted in White, *Robert Barnwell Rhett,* 59–60.

against the banks in the state. The same legislature that endorsed the plan showed none of the traditional Democratic distaste for small notes. On the contrary, it authorized the Bank of the State of South Carolina to issue notes for 25 and 50 cents.[17] Governor Patrick Noble, a Calhoun Democrat, was mildly critical of the banks in an address to the legislature in 1838. Although charging that inherent evils in the banking system had brought about the economic dislocation, he called for no specific reforms other than to recommend that future charters be granted under a general law that would reserve the right of the legislature to make reforms as required to protect the public's interest.[18]

In the 1840s sentiment against the state bank swelled within the Democratic party. In 1843 a resolution was introduced, but not adopted, calling for the bank's abolition.[19] A few years later, in a series of articles, Democrat C. G. Memminger attacked the bank and its management, alleging that its loans had been "most unequally distributed," the funds being "monopolized by a few individuals, and chiefly by the officers and Directors." Furthermore, he pointed out, "a large debt, due by the Nesbit Manufacturing Company, has stood for many years, without one cent of principle or interest paid. . . ."[20] Although it is not clear how valid Memminger's accusations were, it is true that Elmore was closely associated with the Nesbit Company. Memminger, who was later to become secretary of the Confederate treasury, was a Charleston banker. Undoubtedly his criticism was motivated, at least in part, by the jealousy and antagonism that existed between supporters of the state bank and the privately owned banks. In 1843, for example, the Bank of Charleston was chartered over the opposition of the advocates of the state-owned bank, who would have preferred that the legislature simply increase the capital of the Bank of the State of South

[17] Sumner, *History of Banking*, 240. It is interesting to note that the highly particularistic state had the second highest number of Bank of the United States stockholders. South Carolina ranked second only to Pennsylvania. House *Executive Document No. 172*, 348.

[18] Charleston *Courier*, November 28, 1838.

[19] House *Executive Document No. 226*, 633.

[20] Undated clipping entitled "To the People of St. Philip's and St. Michael's Parishes, No. five," in a scrapbook of clippings in the Franklin H. Elmore Papers, Library of Congress.

Carolina.[21] Resolutions were adopted by the state senate in 1848 calling for an inquiry into the Nesbit Company's debt to the bank, which amounted to over 91,000 dollars.[22]

Attacks on the bank mounted, and in 1849 Democratic Governor W. B. Seabrook charged that the state bank was "a dangerous institution, anti-Republican in its character and tendency, and the evils inevitably arising from the connection of a monied corporation and the State increase and ramify the longer the rights and privileges of the former are extended." It was ridiculous, he thought, for a state so committed to the Independent Treasury scheme to so conspicuously violate the principle of separation of bank and state. Furthermore,

to grant to the members of a community almost exclusively devoted to rural pursuits unusual facilities for commanding money, is to inflict on them and their posterity an unmitigated evil; that the more numerous and difficult the obstacles in the way of receiving bank accommodation by that class the greater their contentment and the more certain their success in their vocation.[23]

But despite the increasing criticism, the bank remained in business until 1870.[24]

The banking issue in Georgia revolved around the Central Bank, chartered in 1828 for the purpose of supplementing the work of commercial banks by furnishing credit to persons not able to get accommodations from them. It was an entirely state-owned bank, its capital consisting of money in the state treasury, shares owned by the state in other banks, and all debts owed to the state.[25]

The economic depression following the Panic did not bring a strong hard-money reaction in the Georgia Democracy. The main body of the party championed the cause of the Central Bank against the hard-money men in the party and against the Whigs, who represented the interests of the commercial banks. In 1839 the Democratically con-

---

[21] Knox, *History of Banking*, 566–67.

[22] Resolutions offered in the senate, December 13, 1848. Undated clipping from a scrapbook of clippings in the Franklin H. Elmore Papers.

[23] Sumner, *History of Banking*, 432; Knox, *History of Banking*, 565.

[24] Knox, *History of Banking*, 565, maintains the bank lasted until 1870, while Van Fenstermaker, *American Commercial Banking*, 178, says 1856.

[25] Thomas Payne Govan, "Banking and the Credit System in Georgia, 1810–1860," *The Journal of Southern History*, IV (May, 1938), 172.

trolled legislature passed a bill allowing the Central Bank "to issue double the amount of its capital" and repealing "the clause in the old charter, . . . [which restricts] the circulation to the amount of specie on hand . . . as well as that which limits the indebtedness to the amount of capital. . . ." It was reported that of the forty-eight senators voting for the bill, forty-four were "friends of the federal administration." [26] That same year Democratic Governor Charles McDonald praised the Central Bank and blamed the private banks for the disorders in the currency, maintaining that the latter had disregarded the law and should be made to resume specie payment or to liquidate.[27]

As the depression deepened, the Democratic hard-money men joined the main body of the party in rallying to the support of the Central Bank. In the small farming regions, hard-money strongholds, some Democrats began to argue that commercial banks should be restricted to the wholesale trade. Farmers and artisans should not be burdened, they insisted, with the depreciated commercial notes and should use specie or Central Bank currency exclusively for exchange.[28] Democratic friends of the Central Bank demanded too much of it, requiring it to issue too many notes. In the summer of 1843 the bank failed, despite efforts to save it. The election of a Whig governor, George W. Crawford, in the fall of that year sealed its fate. At the next legislative session the bank was ordered to wind up its affairs and do no further business.[29]

Maryland, unlike Georgia, South Carolina, and Virginia, had no system of banks under direct or partial control of the state government, although in the early 1830s Democrats had tried without success to establish a state bank to provide banking capital in areas of the state where it was lacking.[30] Without the complicating factor of a state

---

[26] *Niles' Register,* January 18, 1840. During the same legislative session an attempt was made to repeal the free-banking law passed a year earlier, but this effort failed.

[27] Milton Sydman Heath, *Constructive Liberalism: Role of the State in Economic Development in Georgia to 1860* (Cambridge, Mass., 1954), 207–208, 214–15.

[28] *Ibid.,* 208.

[29] Sumner, *History of Banking,* 367–70; Paul Murray, *The Whig Party in Georgia, 1825–1853* (Chapel Hill, N.C., 1948), 199; Govan, "Banking in Georgia" (article), 174.

[30] Bryan, *State Banking in Maryland,* 81–84.

bank, Maryland politics was cast in a more traditional mold, with the radicals condemning all banks and the softs and the Whigs rushing to their defense. Immediately following the bank suspension in the spring of 1837, a public meeting was held in Baltimore at which radical hard-money and conservative Democrats were widely split over the banking controversy. The radicals, in resolutions presented at the gathering, contended that the banking system was "a well matured system of fraud and deception;—impoverishing the great mass of the people, whilst it enables the few to amass princely fortunes at their expense . . . by inducing the incautious to engage in unprofitable speculations . . . and by over issues. . . ." Significantly, the resolutions, despite the inflammatory rhetoric, called merely for the resumption of specie payments "if not immediately, as soon as possible." This sentiment was not acceptable to the conservative Democrats, who put forth their own resolutions at the gathering. They maintained that they would "stand by the present administration, encourage and sustain them in the effort to correct existing evils, and to restore our currency to its wonted healthfulness. . . ." But the idea of an exclusive metallic currency they debunked as "impracticable and visionary in the extreme. . . . Rather, these conservatives took the unusual view that a healthy circulating medium could be attained only by a national bank "with proper checks and balances" and "with branches established (by consent of the states), in every state of the union. . . ." [31]

Despite the feuding, the Democrats elected William Grason governor the next year. In his message to the legislature in 1839, Grason called for the fixing of "the loans and discounts of every bank . . . at a certain limit, beyond which they could never be carried without causing a forfeiture of . . . charter. . . ." The Governor also wanted to see each bank forbidden to "issue, pay or receive any note for a less sum than five dollars . . . or to refuse to redeem its obligations, till its specie was entirely exhausted." Grason concluded, however, that no regulations would succeed unless the legislators were willing to repeal the charters of banks unwilling to conform to law.[32]

The next year Governor Grason wrote to Van Buren explaining his plight:

[31] See account of meeting in *Niles' Register,* June 3, 1837.
[32] *Niles' Register,* January 4, 1840.

The great body of people are tired of banks, yet their representatives, many of them of our party, instead of reducing their number, content themselves with imposing . . . restrictions upon their future operations. In this state we now have the power to get rid of a portion of them by the direct action of the Legislature. Yet I do not find a man in favour of this course. Indeed last winter the Legislature was . . . [for] establishing a real estate bank, and some of our friends were in favour of it. The whig Senate will of course reject my . . . bill for the regulation of the banks. But if the House of Delegates would adopt some decisive measure, free from . . . obscurities, the whigs would incur a heavy responsibility by rejecting it.

The penalties against the banks, he continued, would be sufficient if *"they were enforced."* [33]

In December, 1840, Grason again condemned small notes and warned the legislature against expecting the general government under the newly elected Whig administration to cure the currency ills. Worried over the prospect of the establishment of a Whig-inspired national bank, the Governor maintained that if too much paper were in circulation and too many banks in operation, it would be the fault of the individual states, and a new national bank would be no solution. "The States," he said, "have ample power over their corporations and their own paper money. . . ." [34]

In 1841 a Democratic legislature passed a law that gave the Governor the power to close up those banks that refused to pay specie or that issued small notes in violation of the law.[35] But Maryland banks still did not resume specie payment. The next year, however, the legislature, by a wide margin, passed resolutions forcing the banks to resume by May 1, 1842.[36]

In both North Carolina and Delaware the Democratic party was not powerful enough to have much influence on shaping banking policy. This weakness, however, did not keep the North Carolina Democrats from adopting a militant antibank position. The views of former United States Senator Bedford Brown were, perhaps, representative of

[33] William Grason to Martin Van Buren, January 8, 1840, Martin Van Buren Papers.

[34] House *Executive Document No. 111*, 158–59.

[35] Knox, *History of Banking*, 506–507; Bryan, *State Banking in Maryland*, 105.

[36] Bryan, *State Banking in Maryland*, 107; *Niles' Register*, March 12, 1842; Knox, *History of Banking*, 504–505.

the majority opinion in the Democratic ranks. In 1842 he introduced a bill in the state legislature calling for forfeiture of charter if a bank suspended specie payment for a total of thirty days a year. At the same session he sharply criticized the proposal of one Democratic leader to issue a million dollars in treasury notes for financial relief. The Democratic party, Brown stated firmly, was the party of hard money.[37]

Another Democrat, Thomas Loring, was read out of the party in 1843 for an editorial he published on the subject in the *North Carolina Standard*. His newspaper contended that

the business habits of the age cannot be divested of the facilities afforded by banking institutions. . . . We believe that specie-paying banks ought to be sustained in all their lawful operations, by the approving voice of the people and the government; especially those in whose business the *government may be a partner*. We have insisted that the banks should redeem their notes in specie, when demanded—as we are opposed to an irredeemable currency in any and every shape.[38]

Loring, although simply expressing the sentiment of many Democrats in other states, evidently was out of step with the party in his state, which was closely aligned with a more orthodox hard-money position.

The Delaware banks apparently were operated in a conservative manner, and all indications are that the banking issue was of slight importance. The legislature did have to suspend penalties against the banks for stopping specie payment on their notes.[39] But evidently all the banks survived the business collapse. One historian of banking writing in the late nineteenth century concluded that in Delaware bank "failures have been almost unknown." [40] In 1842, after Delaware banks had resumed specie payment, a Wilmington newspaper editor commented that the

ability and credit of our moneyed institutions have not been impaired or destroyed by the intermeddling of headlong and ignorant legislatures. . . . For a state, in these times of depression and embarrassment, to be not only out of debt, but to have a half a million of dollars surplus, is something

[37] Clarence Clifford Norton, *The Democratic Party in Ante-Bellum North Carolina: 1835–1861* (Chapel Hill, N.C., 1930), 56.
[38] *North Carolina Standard*, January 11, 1843, as quoted in *ibid.*, 57–58.
[39] Sumner, *History of Banking*, 347.
[40] Knox, *History of Banking*, 468.

to boast of; and we do feel a pride when we consider the safe and un-
burdened condition of *Delaware*.[41]

4

The Democratic party in Virginia and the other states of the southeastern section, in contrast to the Southwest and Northwest, did not
develop as strong nor as militant a hard-money movement. In Virginia, South Carolina, and Georgia, Democrats supported institutions
that were either entirely or largely state owned. This appears to have
been a characteristic of the Democracy throughout the country. When
hard-money men were unable to win backing for a strong antibank
position, a compromise was often worked out: the party would oppose
privately owned banks in favor of a state-owned and controlled institution.

The Panic, of course, did not wreak the terrible havoc in the Southeast that it did in the two western sections. But perhaps a major factor
in stunting the growth of strong, militant, hard-money Democratic factions there was the concentration upon national politics to the
exclusion of state issues. This was particularly true of Virginia and
South Carolina. Both were old states whose politicians were long used
to playing important national political roles. In both, parties had been
organized initially from the national level on national questions, and
political leaders were able to sustain the national focus because of undemocratic state political systems. Democratic leaders in Virginia and
South Carolina recognized the importance of playing down local divisive issues and keeping Democrats in the states harmonious. For without this, their national positions would have been considerably weakened.

[41] Wilmington, Delaware, *Gazette* as quoted in *Niles' Register,* April 9, 1842.

CHAPTER XII

Pennsylvania and New York

I

AT THE TIME of the Panic, the Middle Atlantic and New England states of the Northeast had the most sophisticated and diversified economies in the country. This highly commercialized area also had the highest proportion of urbanized population. In 1840 about 18 or 19 per cent of the northeasterners were city dwellers, as compared with the Southeast, which ranked second, where 8 per cent were city dwellers.[1]

New York and Pennsylvania deserve special attention. They were the most important states in the section, with Philadelphia and New York City serving as the financial and commercial capitals of the nation. Furthermore, these two states, along with Virginia, had provided the key support for the Jeffersonian coalition as well as for the development of the Jacksonian alliance. New York and, to a lesser degree, Pennsylvania have been treated in great detail by historians, and indeed the complexity and intricacy of their economic and political institutions deserve thorough and careful analysis. For the purpose of this work, however, a summary treatment is given here to place the two states in proper perspective with the other states of the northeastern section, as well as with the other states of the Union.

2

Pennsylvania had a unique position in the country throughout the war that raged between the Jacksonians and the banks, primarily because Philadelphia, as the home of the Second Bank of the United

[1] North, *Economic Growth*, 258.

States and its predecessor, had long been the financial and banking capital of the nation. Jackson's veto of the national bank had thus been both a national and a state issue for the Pennsylvania Democrats, many of whom had always viewed the "Monster" with suspicion. There were others, though, who saw the bank as intricately meshed in the national and state economies and predicted that its removal from the scene would bring ruin to the state.

Ironically, the months before the Panic had been a time of harmony within the Democratic party in Pennsylvania despite the fact that the Bank had long been a source of party friction. A year earlier internal feuding between the various factions had ceased when the Whigs, along with a handful of entrepreneurial Democrats, had given the old Bank of the United States a state charter. The resurrection of the hated bank as an issue overshadowed, at least for a time, any of the petty personal jealousies that had plagued the Jacksonians.[2]

At the time of the Panic the relationship between Pennsylvania and the banks was further complicated by the close ties that existed between many of the banks and state-sponsored internal-improvement projects that were underway in the various sections of the state. Many of these projects, of course, were designed to ease transportation difficulties in the backwoods areas, usually bastions of hard-money strength. Funds for the improvements were raised both by bank loans to the state and through bonuses paid by banks to the state for their charters. So it was only natural that the Panic would almost instantly disrupt the temporary party harmony, which had been achieved largely on the rather simplistic issue of Democratic antagonism to one bank, the Second Bank of the United States, without regard to the other banks.

Although there were some cries for radical reform, most Democratic politicians were split between the conservatives and the moderate wing of the hard-money Democracy. The smaller group, the soft-money men, feared any tampering with the banking system and generally voted with the Whigs against reforms. Paper currency and bank credit were needed, these men argued, to finance internal improvements and to encourage corporate enterprises. Too vigorous action against the banks would destroy or seriously weaken a business climate conducive to expansion.

[2] Snyder *Jacksonian Heritage*, Chapters 4 and 5.

The more moderate hards who called for a thorough reform of the banking system and the few radical Democrats favoring the abolition of all bank notes worked together as another group, representing the bulk of the party. They attempted to bring the banks under greater public control and were mainly interested in the maintenance of a sound currency immediately redeemable in specie.

After the Panic struck and the banks suspended, there was in Pennsylvania a strong sense of guilt and the need for financial and political retribution. "Now is the time to stand firm," a Democrat wrote Van Buren, "and redeem the country from the flood of Bank rags with which it is inundated." There would be some "Temporary embarrassment and inconvenience," but

the storm will soon pass over, and like those in the natural world will purify the atmosphere, and impart an elasticity, refreshing and invigorating. I shall be perhaps myself a sufferer, having just before the storm . . . entered into wholesale mercantile pursuits with a friend, and having many thousands of dollars now out on notes received for goods sold, and money advanced, but I am willing to risk all rather than succumb to mercantile gamblers and corrupt stock jobbers.[3]

On May 15, 1837, the largest Pennsylvania public meeting that had ever been assembled was called to order in the Statehouse yard at Philadelphia to protest the banks' actions. Resolutions were passed by the reported throng of more than twenty thousand condemning the Whigs for having contrived the banking crisis in order to force the Democratic administration to repeal the Specie Circular "and to compel the people to submit to the establishment of a national bank." Participants further resolved that they

[are opposed] to monopolies of every description—more especially moneyed monopolies; that we consider the banking system a system of fraud and oppression; that we believe hard money to be the only just and legal currency, and that we will therefore hereafter give our suffrages to no man, who is not hostile to all banks, and in favor of no other circulating medium than that of gold and silver.[4]

A major factor behind this sentiment for hard-money currency in Philadelphia and other eastern cities was that many, including small manu-

[3] George Lehman to Martin Van Buren, May 11, 1837, Martin Van Buren Papers.
[4] *Niles' Register*, May 27, 1837.

facturers and artisans, believed that an inflationary paper currency made it easier for foreign goods to sell in the United States. On the other hand, an all specie or deflationary currency would protect domestic manufacturers by making it more difficult for foreign goods to be sold. The Philadelphia meeting called for "full and ample protection for the "domestic manufactures of our country" and argued "that such protection, can only be afforded by establishing a currency of gold and silver. . . ." [5]

A week later another mass meeting was held, but the resolutions were not as militant as those the week before. The banks were reminded of their responsibilities under Pennsylvania laws, which required that banks forfeit their charters if specie payment were not resumed within ninety days and prohibited the payment of dividends while notes were not being paid in specie. Furthermore, delegates at the constitutional convention devoted to revising the state's fundamental law were asked to "introduce into our new constitution the most positive . . . provisions against the mad spirit of creating banks, corporations and monopolies, which has heretofore existed in our state." [6]

Henry D. Gilpin, a former government director of the Bank of the

---

[5] *Ibid*. See also, Henry D. Gilpin to Martin Van Buren, May 15, 1837, Martin Van Buren Papers. Gilpin told Van Buren that the meeting was organized *"entirely* by the working classes; without consultation or cooperation with any of those who usually take the lead in such matters."

It would appear that some radical Jacksonians, like radicals in the Revolutionary era, many of them being urban artisans, could be counted on to support radical politics if it would result in the protection of their small manufacturing or handicraft activities. In the earlier instance, they gave strong support to the nonimportation agreements, which, of course, acted as an effective protective tariff against the cheaper British manufactured goods.

The Jacksonians' logic was fallacious. An *inflationary* monetary policy would make a protective tariff more effective and stimulate exports, for "if the foreign exchange value of the local currency depreciated faster than its domestic purchasing power, exporting will be rendered more profitable." As quoted in Sharkey, *Money, Class and Party,* 150. Both Sharkey (Chapter IV) and Irwin Unger in his *The Greenback Era, A Social and Political History of American Finance, 1865–1879* (Princeton, N.J., 1964), 59, point out that after the Civil War some industrialists opposed contraction because they felt it would have the effect of lowering the protective tariff. Unger, however, does not see the tariff issue as being quite as important a factor in stimulating opposition to contraction as Sharkey does.

[6] *Niles' Register,* June 3, 1837.

United States, leading Philadelphia Democrat, and Van Buren's Attorney General during the last two years of his administration, was responsible for helping to direct the antibank sentiment in a more politically responsible direction. The Democratic broker wrote to Van Buren that the meeting's resolutions had been "put into shape" by him. The views expressed were those of the mass of the people but had been "somewhat softened down." There was, Van Buren was told, an "intense indignation against the banking and speculation mania," and although the meeting claimed no political ties, they were "with us to a man." [7]

First evidence of a split within the party over banking was at the constitutional convention of 1837. Although the Democrats had a slim margin of one among the convention delegates, the recommendation of the majority of the committee on banks was for no change in banking provisions in the new constitution. This conservative recommendation was upheld by convention delegates.

Reforms were called for, however, in a minority report filed by Democrat Charles J. Ingersoll condemning the state's banking system. But the renegade politician failed to get his report considered by the convention; the delegates voted against printing it, 67 to 57. [8]

Growing up in the midst of Federalist Philadelphia as a member of a wealthy and fashionable family, Ingersoll earlier had shocked his friends and relatives by becoming somewhat of a "radical" nonconformist. As a Jeffersonian Republican, Ingersoll served in Congress and later was appointed United States District Attorney. Ingersoll's biographer said that his subject's "career is mainly interesting because of his courage and vigor in championing causes and groups which were unpopular in his own social environment." [9]

Ingersoll contended in his report that delegates at the previous constitutional convention nearly a half century earlier had not envisioned that the banks would become, as they had, among "our most important institutions," with power to place value on property, determine prices,

[7] Henry D. Gilpin to Martin Van Buren, May 22, 1837, Martin Van Buren Papers.

[8] *Niles' Register,* June 3, 1837; Hartz, *Economic Policy and Democratic Thought,* 252.

[9] E. Digby Baltzell, *An American Business Aristocracy* (New York, 1962), 155–56.

and fix the wages of industry. Now, he maintained, "the condition of the currency regulates every thing else," and "currency is the life's blood of the body politic." This situation, according to Ingersoll, necessitated the reevaluation of the relationship between the state and the banking system.[10]

Ingersoll suggested limiting the amount of capital in each bank, gradually suppressing small notes under 20 dollars, and making stockholders' private property liable for debts and liabilities of the banking corporation. There was no plan to maintain a fixed specie-currency ratio, as Democrats in other states often proposed. One aspect of the report, however, was more radical. This was a proposal to reserve the right of the state to alter or repeal any bank charter. Its effect was to reopen the question of the sanctity of a corporate charter, settled earlier in the Dartmouth College case. In support of this idea, Thomas Earle, a radical Democrat, claimed that each

generation should act for itself. If one generation was free to say we will have banks and other corporations, the following generations might say we will have no banks, and no corporations. . . . Let each generation, as it comes upon the stage, manage its own affairs, in its own way.[11]

The majority of Democrats in the campaign of 1837 refused to take a strong affirmative bank-reform position, preferring, instead, to remain noncommittal.[12] This was not true of Ingersoll, who ran unsuccessfully for Congress that year on a radical hard-money platform. "Let the people have hard money," he argued.

Let them insist upon it. Let them try it. Let them compromise with nothing short of it. Let hard money be the will of the people. . . . Suppress paper money, and give American industry fair play, with its superior ingenuity, enterprise, versatility and perseverance. . . .[13]

During the campaign of 1837 the Whigs had a decided tactical advantage over Ingersoll. On the one hand, they played up his aristocratic background. Ingersoll was a man, they maintained, "who looks upon common people through gold specs and ornaments his fingers with costly diamonds." [14] But on the other, they could exploit his radi-

[10] *Niles' Register*, June 3, 1837.
[11] *Ibid.*; Hartz, *Economic Policy and Democratic Thought*, 252.
[12] Snyder, *Jacksonian Heritage*, 114–15.   [13] *Niles' Register*, June 24, 1837.
[14] As quoted in Snyder, *Jacksonian Heritage*, 90.

calism for their own purposes. In an attempt to frighten conservative Democrats from voting for the Democratic candidate, the Whigs all but ignored their own candidate and emphasized the dangers of Ingersoll's economic radicalism. The plan worked, and Ingersoll was defeated in a constituency that was normally Democratic.[15]

At least one Democratic newspaper agreed with Ingersoll on the importance of the banking issue in the election. The paper claimed that the election would decide "whether the Banks shall rule the Government, or the Government rule the Banks." If the Whigs won, the banks would take their victory as a mandate in favor of suspension of specie payment, but "if the Democrats are successful the banks will be compelled to redeem their notes or else wind up their affairs." [16]

In the election that fall, the Democrats gained control of the house, but were in a minority in the senate. James Buchanan, United States Senator from Pennsylvania, wrote to Jackson that owing to "the infamous system of gerrymandering resorted to by the Legislature which rechartered the Bank [United States Bank of Pennsylvania]; there will still be a majority against us of five in the Senate." Therefore, the Democrats would "be able to do nothing efficient against the dangerous Institution until after our Governor's election, which will take place next year." [17]

Buchanan was right in his prediction of Democratic ineffectiveness in the state legislature. An attempt was made by a virtually united Democratic party to pass a bank-reform bill, but it was frustrated by the Whig-dominated senate. The bill would have prohibited notes under 10 dollars, eliminated the system of banks paying the state bonuses for charter privileges, and required that the banks sell their stock at auction, issue annual reports, yield excess profits to the state, and redeem their notes in specie. The bill passed the house by a party vote, all but a few Democrats voting for it and the Whigs and Antimasons voting against it.[18]

During the same legislative session a split between Democrats devel-

---

[15] *Ibid.*, 114.   [16] *Ibid.*, 114–15.

[17] James Buchanan to Andrew Jackson, October 26, 1837, in *The Works of James Buchanan, Comprising His Speeches, State Papers, and Private Correspondence* (Philadelphia, 1908–1911), III, 325, edited by John Bassett Moore.

[18] Snyder, *Jacksonian Heritage*, 120–21.

oped over the Independent Treasury. Despite the Democratic majority in the house, the Whigs passed a resolution in both houses instructing the United States Senators and requesting the Congressmen to postpone action on the Independent Treasury Bill until the following session. As an inducement for conservative Democratic support, the resolution stated "that we have full confidence in Martin Van Buren, and in the wisdom and intelligence of our democratic senators and representatives in congress." The legislators were further called upon "to vote for such a mode of receiving, keeping, and disbursing, the public moneys as will separate, as far as practicable, the banks from the government." [19]

Seven Democrats in the lower house deserted the party to vote for the resolution. "Here then we have before us," one disgusted Democrat told Van Buren, "a practical illustration of the immense and alarming power of the banks, whose agents have been and now are as thick as bees prowling about the halls of both houses of our legislature." [20]

In the spring of 1838 the Democrats nominated David R. Porter for governor. He once had been an ironmaker, but his business failed in the Panic of 1819 and he was by 1838 a successful farmer. While in the state senate he had supported the Independent Treasury but was nevertheless still considered a friend of the banks. [21] One Pennsylvania Jacksonian advised Van Buren that he did not consider Porter *"as safe"* as some Democrats who might have been nominated, but that Porter would probably be elected, "provided he removes some suspicion" which has "gotten afloat, namely, that he is pledged . . . to assist the Conservatives in their Bank and anti-Sub-Treasury schemes." [22]

Porter's campaign proved successful, but the suspicion of the new governor was warranted. If Porter never openly became a conservative, it was only because he felt that his political aspirations would be frustrated by such a move. He could best be described as a political broker with conservative sympathies. William C. Rives was assured that Porter was with the conservatives. "Indeed, *Porter* himself said to me," a Pennsylvania conservative wrote the Virginian, "that *M'Kean* was very

[19] *Niles' Register*, February 24, 1838.

[20] S. Salisbury to Martin Van Buren, February 17, 1838, Martin Van Buren Papers.

[21] Snyder, *Jacksonian Heritage*, 123.

[22] Henry Augustus Muhlenberg to Martin Van Buren, March 12, 1838, Martin Van Buren Papers.

instrumental in producing his election."[23] The McKean referred to was Samuel McKean, who had split from the party earlier in the decade. While in the United States Senate he had alienated the party by voting in favor of Henry Clay's resolution to restore the deposits to the Bank of the United States.[24]

In 1839 a Democratic newspaper summed up the difference on the bank issue between the two factions within the party. One group, the paper maintained, temporized with the banks, while the other "will go for making stockholders individually liable for their notes, the appointment of bank commissioners to watch the banks, and prevent them from cheating the people, and the annulling of all who are not in condition to resume immediate specie payment."[25]

Porter, in his message the next year, attempted to adopt a position midway between conservatives and the hards. He warned the legislators that "the banking system has, for good or for evil, stamped its influence on every commercial, manufacturing and agricultural interest among our citizens" and insisted that a "judicious credit system is . . . indispensable to an enlightened business community." Therefore he recommended that the state be indulgent and give reasonable time for specie payment resumption. The Governor, however, did approve of certain reform measures. He supported the prohibition of small notes and wanted to see this extended to small notes from banks of other states. He called for the appointment of bank commissioners to examine the condition of banks, for the prohibition of post notes, and for the limitation of stockholder dividends to a maximum of 7 per cent. Making bank directors personally liable for the bank circulation exceeding the ratio of 3 dollars for every one of specie was another reform the Governor felt would improve the stability of the banking system.[26]

A newspaper dubbed by the Democratic Albany *Argus* as the New York organ of the bank claimed that Governor Porter "came out openly a conservative" in this address to the legislature. The *Argus* put off judgment until Porter's entire speech could be scrutinized, although

[23] John W. Ashmead to William C. Rives, December 1, 1838, William C. Rives Papers.
[24] Snyder, *Jacksonian Heritage*, 43.
[25] Harrisburg, Pennsylvania, *Iron Gray* as quoted in *Niles' Register*, November 30, 1839.
[26] *Niles' Register*, January 25, 1840.

the paper did indicate that the Governor should have called for an early specie resumption. Two days later the *Argus,* in a long article, defended Porter, contending that this address did not place the Governor in the conservative camp.[27] There were those who differed from the *Argus,* however. Thomas Allen, conservative editor of the *Madisonian,* said that Porter's message was "Conservative to the backbone." [28]

Many Pennsylvania Democrats denounced Porter for being too indulgent with the banks. The house, under the leadership of the Democrats, passed a resolution demanding immediate specie resumption. The senate passed a similar but not identical measure, but the two houses failed to compromise their differences. The senate finally passed another bill that gave the banks almost a year before specie resumption was demanded, and twenty Democrats in the house deserted their original stand for immediate resumption and voted with the Whigs to accept the senate bill.[29]

The Democratic party condemned the bill as "passed by the Whigs and anti-masons, together with a few apostate democrats" and as deserving "the eternal and everlasting execration of every genuine democrat in the commonwealth." [30] Governor Porter also was blamed for the lenient position the legislature took on the question of specie resumption. In a special message the Governor had strongly indicated that an immediate resumption bill would meet with his extreme disfavor and perhaps even a veto. If the Whigs triumph in Pennsylvania "it will be because of the course the Governor is taking," an irate Democrat wrote the President. The "faction headed by Simon Cameron, [and] Lloyd Wharton . . . are doing the party great mischief," and they along "with Porter must be put down, they are a venal and corrupt pack." [31]

[27] Albany, New York, *Argus,* January 13 and 15, 1840.

[28] Thomas Allen to William C. Rives, January 10, 1840, William C. Rives Papers. James Garland of Virginia called the message "decidedly *conservative.*" James Garland to William C. Rives, January 11, 1840, William C. Rives Papers.

[29] *Niles' Register,* February 8, March 7, and April 4, 1840; Snyder, *Jacksonian Heritage,* 139–41.

[30] *Niles' Register,* May 16, 1840.

[31] J. Thompson to Martin Van Buren, February 7, 1840, Martin Van Buren Papers.

A more moderate and practical Democrat believed that Porter would "be pretty well sustained throughout the State." Furthermore, he did not think that public opinion is very strong at this time in favor of an early resumption of specie payments, but it is evidently averse to a remote one. The graineries of the farmers never were so full, and had they their produce sold, and their money for it, hasty resumption could not affect us with that reliable and respectable portion of our friends. Whereas if a speedy resumption should be forced, the banks go down, prices fall, and [there is] nothing but depreciated money to buy the produce of the farmer with, it is hard to tell the extent of complaints, and how far they would be ascribed to hasty Legislation. Under all the circumstances, policy dictates great prudence and forbearance.[32]

James Buchanan, always the broker, agreed and tried to split the difference. Mildly critical of the Governor, Buchanan told Porter that his warning against harsh measures toward the banks had been greeted with "exultation" by the Whigs. But the Pennsylvania Senator hastily added that he now believed "that the storm has passed away."[33]

The banks did resume specie payment in January, 1841, but failed to sustain it, suspending again almost immediately. In response the Whigs drew up the Relief Bill, which waived indefinitely the penalties against suspended banks. The bill called upon the banks to lend to the state 3 million dollars for internal-improvement projects and, in return, to receive permission to issue one-, two-, and five-dollar notes. Porter vetoed the bill, but the Whigs, undaunted, resubmitted it, this time excluding from its privileges the United States Bank of Pennsylvania. A few Democrats who saw the bill as the only way to continue public-works projects deserted the party and voted with the Whigs to override the Governor's veto.[34]

Although leaders urged that these Democrats not be driven from the party, rank-and-file party members and some newspapers were not so tolerant. One newspaper, which labeled the deserters traitors "who could forget everything in their thirst for gold!," urged the people to

---

[32] Levi Reynolds, Jr., to Martin Van Buren, February 6, 1840, Martin Van Buren Papers.

[33] James Buchanan to David R. Porter, February 24, 1840, David R. Porter Papers, Historical Society of Pennsylvania.

[34] *Niles' Register,* April 3, 1841; Snyder, *Jacksonian Heritage,* 155–56.

"brand them with the mark of blackest infamy, and teach your children to mention their names as you would mention with execration the traitor Arnold, the traitor Burr, or the traitor Hull." [35]

The intraparty battle came to a climax after the election of 1841, when the Democrats re-elected Governor Porter and retained control of the legislature. The conservative Democrats nominated one of their men, Hendrick B. Wright,[36] for speaker of the house. The Governor, unwilling to alienate the hards, endorsed Wright but did not do so publicly. The hards supported J. Ross Snowden, an advocate of bank reform who had led the Democratic minority against the Relief Bill, for speaker. The party caucused, and both factions agreed to back Snowden. In exchange the conservatives received several key committee assignments, Wright being appointed chairman of the internal-improvement committee.[37]

That winter, as the legislature met, the financial and economic condition of Pennsylvania was as serious as it had been at any time since 1837. The revenue raised by the Relief Bill had been inadequate, and there were indications of growing sentiment that internal improvements had been a bad investment. The banks were still not making specie payment and were urging further extension of suspension of penalties against them. Some Democrats favored selling off the improvements and repudiating the remaining debt; however most hard-money and soft-money Democrats agreed that the debt should be paid and the banks made to resume specie payment immediately. Consequently the Democrat-controlled legislature, after considering the idea of calling for only gradual resumption over five years, passed a resolution demanding immediate resumption. The return of good times the following year virtually ended the controversy over banking in Pennsylvania.[38]

[35] As quoted in Snyder, *Jacksonian Heritage*, 157–58.

[36] Later, Wright was elected the presiding officer at the Democratic National Convention in 1844 and was instrumental in denying the nomination to Van Buren. See James C. N. Paul, *Rift in the Democracy* (New York, 1961).

[37] Snyder, *Jacksonian Heritage*, 158–60.

[38] *Ibid.*, 158–63; *Niles' Register*, March 12, 1842.

3

Few would deny that the pre-Panic Democracy in New York—especially those in the clique of party leaders called the Albany Regency—had close ties with the state banking system.[39] The Mechanics' and Farmers' Bank of Albany is the most conspicuous example of the entrepreneurial affiliations of some of the New York Jacksonians. Benjamin Knower, president of the bank, was Governor William Marcy's father-in-law; Thomas W. Olcott, also a member of the Albany Regency, was the bank's cashier. Edwin Crosswell, a Regency leader and editor of the influential state newspaper, the Albany *Argus,* was another Jacksonian businessman who at the time of the Panic "was up to his neck in the Canal Bank of Albany and other speculations." [40] The involvement of some members of the Albany Regency with the banks made the New York Democracy vulnerable to internal divisions after the Panic of 1837. In fact, the Van Buren Administration's steps to meet the crisis split the party into several factions.

The conservatives led by Rives' colleague, United States Senator Nathaniel P. Tallmadge, recoiled in horror at the Van Buren Administration's decision to separate federal finances from the state banks and to

[39] Frank Otto Gatell makes a careful distinction between the bank operations of Albany and New York City. He argues that although the Albany Regency did have close connections with the Albany banks this did not mean they had equally close involvements with the New York City banks, nor did it mean that the Regency could be counted upon to champion the city banks' interests. Instead, Gatell maintains, the economic interests of the New York country banks were quite different from the city ones. Concluding, he raises damaging questions, if not completely destructive ones, about the validity of the thesis that the attack on the Second Bank of the United States was motivated to a large degree by the Van Buren-led New York Democrats who were seeking to replace Chestnut Street with Wall Street as the economic and financial center of the country. See Gatell's "Sober Second Thoughts on Van Buren, the Albany Regency, and the Wall Street Conspiracy," *The Journal of American History,* LIII (June, 1966), 19–40.

[40] As quoted in Benson, *Concept of Jacksonian Democracy,* 68. For information on careers of other Regency leaders, see *ibid.,* 65–70, as well as Ivor Debenham Spencer, *The Victor and the Spoils: A Life of William L. Marcy* (Providence, R.I., 1959), Chapter III, and Jabez D. Hammond, *The History of Political Parties in the State of New York from the Ratification of the Federal Constitution to December, 1840* (Albany, N.Y., 1842), II, 298–99.

create an Independent Treasury. To these softs who eventually left the party, the national administration's call for such an institution meant that the radical wing of the party led by Frank P. Blair and Thomas H. Benton had gained the ascendancy. On the state level, it meant that the dreaded radicals of New York City, who for several years had been critical of the party and its connection with the banks, were to be appealed to and accepted as allies against the banks. In a letter to the *Argus,* Tallmadge argued that he was "in favor of a well regulated credit system, and opposed to the chimerical scheme of *exclusive metallic* currency." He maintained that the "credit system is the distinguishing feature between despotism and liberty; it is the offspring of free institutions: it is found to exist, and its influence is felt, in proportion to the freedom enjoyed by any people." Continuing, Tallmadge pointed out that the banks were responsible for the prosperity of the nation,

and he who should at this day recommend an entire abandonment of our credit system for a *sole and exclusive metallic* currency, would be deemed no less visionary than he who should attempt to substitute a Pennsylvania wagon, for a locomotive or a canal packet, or should endeavor to stem the resistless current of the Mississippi in a flat boat, instead of those splendid palaces which now move majestically on its waters. . . . Shall we attempt to overthrow, subvert and destroy a system which has produced all these blessings? [41]

In many ways sympathetic to Tallmadge's argument were broker politicians, such as Governor Marcy, editor Crosswell, and former Governor Enos Thompson Throop. But, although deeply critical of the Independent Treasury and unhappy over any alliance with the New York City radicals, these men were nevertheless unwilling to follow their opposition through to its logical end—the breaking up of the party.

The hard-money men or radicals constituted a rather diversified group, ranging from New York City radicals to long-time party members, such as Azariah C. Flagg, who after the Panic saw an opportunity to reorganize the party along more radical lines dedicated to reforming the banking system.

As in many other states, the bank suspension raised an immediate political problem. New York law called for penalties, including forfei-

[41] *Niles' Register,* June 24, 1837.

ture of charters, to be levied against the banks for suspending specie payments. Thus the Democratic-controlled legislature in the spring of 1837 was faced with the dilemma of deciding whether it should legalize the suspension, incurring the odium of the radicals, or refuse to aid the banks, risking the economic and political consequences. Throop reported to Van Buren that a committee had been dispatched to Albany to urge upon the legislature the immediate passage of a law suspending parts of the Safety Fund Law that called for forfeiture of charter upon nonpayment of specie. Throop told the President that the only obstacle the committee members "expect to encounter to their application is Flagg. . . ." But, Van Buren was warned, "if the Banks are prostrated," the nation would "groan for years." [42] Churchill C. Cambreleng, a close associate of both Flagg and Van Buren, was of a different mind. He advised legislators against suspending bank penalties, and if they did, they would "deserve the reprobation of the country." [43]

Van Buren was sent a long analysis of the state of the party by United States Senator Silas Wright. Crosswell, the President was told,

is as he usually is, a most fine, honest, true hearted man and labours to keep peace on all sides, but is so deeply immersed in . . . speculations as to be too far in the power of the moneyed institutions. The same division runs through the Legislature and in the senate we have a few very bad men who labour industriously to blow the spark to the flames. . . . I cannot apprehend any seism [*sic*] that will do harm, but I do not doubt we are to lose certain individuals as we have always done when we get too strong and our friends . . . connect public duty with their private pockets. Sometimes we have been compelled to sink below the surface to permit this rotten matter to float off, and were it two years earlier I should fear a defeat might be necessary at this time; but as the presidential election of 1836 is past I have, as yet, no fear . . . for I shall not consider a reduction of our strength in the Legislature an injury even if that should be a consequence which I doubt.[44]

[42] Enos Thompson Throop to Martin Van Buren, May 10, 1837, Martin Van Buren Papers.

[43] Churchill C. Cambreleng to Martin Van Buren, May 10, 1837, Martin Van Buren Papers; Churchill C. Cambreleng to Azariah C. Flagg, May 10, 1837, Azariah C. Flagg Papers, New York Public Library.

[44] Silas Wright to Martin Van Buren, May 13, 1837, Martin Van Buren Papers.

Despite the opposition of some of the leading Democrats, the New York legislature in May, 1837, legalized the specie suspension by the wide margin of 95 to 19. The Democrats did refuse, however, to suspend the law prohibiting notes under 5 dollars.[45]

The radicals reacted vehemently, labeling this indulgent action, passed with the approval of the majority of Democrats in the legislature, as traitorous. At a public meeting in New York City a resolution was adopted asserting that the "present is an opportune season for entirely eradicating the curse of paper money." As in Philadelphia these radicals were concerned about the effect of an inflationary currency on imports. They condemned the banks for turning the "balance of trade against . . . [them]." Furthermore, they argued that if an exclusive metallic currency were to be adopted, it would "render this a selling instead of [a] buying nation." [46]

Governor Marcy found himself condemned as a supporter of the suspension of penalties law. Marcy recognized that suspended banks were an evil but asked his radical critics "if the immediate annihilation of one hundred banks which had ten millions of the public money on deposit and to which the people of the state owed seventy five millions would not have been an evil?" [47] The Governor justified his action in a letter to Van Buren. Marcy acknowledged that he was heavily in debt but protested that this had not been a factor in his actions. He told Van Buren that if the banks had been made to forfeit their charters, the vast debt owed to the banks would have been subject to immediate payment. This would have caused vast economic dislocation and business failure, throwing large numbers of laborers out of work. Continuing, Marcy defended the use of a mixed currency of paper and specie, arguing that "an attempt to introduce specie as the *sole* circulating medium would be unsuccessful" as would "a paper system without a specie basis. . . ." [48]

Cambreleng was thoroughly disgusted by the legislature's actions. Condemning the speculators within the Democratic ranks, he asserted

---

[45] *Niles' Register*, May 20, 1837.   [46] *Niles' Register*, May 27, 1837.

[47] William L. Marcy to P. M. Wetmore, June 16, 1837, William L. Marcy Papers, Library of Congress.

[48] William L. Marcy to Martin Van Buren, May 25, 1837, Martin Van Buren Papers.

that it "would be better for some people at Albany if they had less to do with banks and speculation or if they would do us the favor to throw aside their democracy or rather their professed democracy," for you "cannot make a democrat out of a bank director. . . ." Cambreleng's anger at the relief bank bill was due partially, at least, to the influence the country banks had exerted on the legislature for the adoption of provisions favorable to their interests and unfavorable to the city banks. The result had been a law providing that in order for a bank to be protected from penalties, it had to accept for payment of debts any notes of any other bank covered by the New York law. Cambreleng claimed that this would cripple the city banks, for "the whole weight of our country bank circulation amounting to millions is thrown upon them." [49]

That summer, in 1837, another Democratic public meeting was held in New York City. As before, the law legalizing suspension of specie payments was denounced, but unlike before no call for an exclusive metallic currency was issued. At the summer meeting Democrats who wanted to "preserve and regulate, but not destroy" said that they favored a "well regulated credit system." The main complaints leveled at the banking system were directed against "*all* special legislation whereby privileges are granted to the few and withheld from the many." Such legislation was attacked as a restraint of "natural freedom, and totally averse to the plain doctrines of democracy." The resolutions recommended a free banking law "*open to all,* with salutary regulations" rendering "each corporation and its stockholders amenable to the common law of debtor and creditor. . . ." [50]

The motives and exact position of the radical New York Democrats is difficult to assess. One of the major impulses behind the anticharter doctrine was an intense egalitarianism. As corporations had been used to limit the power of a king in the past, many felt that charters were being used in the nineteenth century to limit the sovereignty of the people. While in some states this sentiment led to an assertion of legis-

---

[49] Churchill C. Cambreleng to Abraham Van Buren, May 30, 1837, Martin Van Buren Papers. Marcy had opposed this provision of the bill but signed it, with misgivings. See William L. Marcy to P. M. Wetmore, May 14 and 16, 1837, William L. Marcy Papers.

[50] *Niles' Register,* August 12, 1837.

lative authority to amend or alter bank charters, in New York it would appear that it was manifested in a desire for free banking. The radical *Evening Post,* for example, was among the newspapers that supported the Whig-sponsored free-banking proposal in New York the following year.[51]

Governor Marcy reacted negatively to the Van Buren Administration's formal announcement in the fall of 1837 of its intention to separate government finances from the banks through the Independent Treasury, which he regarded as a confirmation and acceptance of New York radicals by the President. Long a target of radical abuse, the disheartened Marcy now felt that his attackers wore the mantle of the respectability of Democratic orthodoxy. "Who then," he asked his old friend P. M. Wetmore, "shall shield us, I ask, from the wrath of the loco-focos." [52]

The insolence of the radicals, Marcy wrote,

who pretend they have (and . . . [it] appears they certainly have) a full endorsement of all their doctrines by the president, is almost insufferable and operates powerfully to create and confirm our threatened divisions. This faction will, and as to the issue proposed to be joined it is their right to take the lead in our political affairs. They regard themselves as the fathers of the Church and even Mr. V. B. is only one of their recent converts. Is it reasonable to expect that the democrats of the state will range themselves under the banners of Ming, Leggett . . . and others of better repute of Washington. . . .[53]

The New York election in the fall of 1837 was a disaster for the Democrats and marked the end of the long dominance of the Regency over New York politics. While the 1836 election had given the Democrats 121 seats out of a total of 160 seats in the house and senate, the election of 1837 gave the Whigs 111 seats, a 101 to 27 majority in the house but a 10 to 22 minority in the senate.[54]

The financial crisis had split the New York party badly. The hardmoney men were convinced that the defeat had been caused by the

[51] McFaul, "Politics of Jacksonian Finance," 224–25.

[52] William L. Marcy to P. M. Wetmore, September 9, 1837, William L. Marcy Papers.

[53] William L. Marcy to Albert Gallup, September 23, 1837, William L. Marcy Papers.

[54] *Niles' Register,* November 18 and 25, 1837.

party's straying from true principle. "We must," Cambreleng wrote to Van Buren, "once in ten years be whipped into our principles."[55] Another hard-money man wrote to Flagg, enraged over the conduct of the party:

I now write to tell you the tone of the Argus is altogether too tame for the tone of my stomach. Full grown democrats require stronger food than the notes of conciliation and compromise and resumption of specie payments at an early day and causes that may or may not retard the resumption and the prattle about the dissensions and distractions and unhappy differences. . . . What in hell is the difference between democratic principles this year and last year? With an honest democrat they are the same yesterday, today and forever—The Banks are precisely what Gen. Jackson called them in his letters to Blair and "never was baser treachery & perfidy exhibited" than has been exhibited by them and those connected with them at the recent County elections. . . . What has the democracy to do with the compromise with conciliation?—as well might the lamb think of compromise or conciliation with the wolf.[56]

The brokers did not agree with the radicals' analysis of the election. Throop argued that for the Democrats to regain the ascendancy in the state, the "State banks must be brought to our aid or at least not driven into the opposition." The defeat could be ascribed mainly, Throop argued, "to the belief that the administration was determined to break down the state banking system. . . ."[57]

The bank issue reached a climax in the spring of 1838, when the Whig-dominated legislature passed the free-banking act. The Democrats objected to the free-banking bill during the legislative sessions on the grounds that there was not sufficient protection for the note holders. They proposed unlimited liability on stockholders and a one-to-five specie-note ratio. The Whigs, however, would accept only a ratio of one-to-eight.[58]

Despite the inadequacy of the free-banking law, some Democrats

[55] Churchill C. Cambreleng to Martin Van Buren, November 9, 1837, Martin Van Buren Papers.

[56] Preston King to Azariah C. Flagg, November 22, 1837, Azariah C. Flagg Papers, New York Public Library.

[57] Enos Thompson Throop to Martin Van Buren, November 23, 1837, Martin Van Buren Papers.

[58] McFaul, "Politics of Jacksonian Finance," 221–30; Redlich, *Molding of American Banking*, II, Part 2, 9; and Hammond, *Banks and Politics*, 596.

saw a certain political advantage in its passage. For a number of years the Whigs and New York City radicals had argued that the Albany Regency had opposed the creation of new banking capital to protect its own bank monopoly. "We had therefore," one Democrat wrote Van Buren, "to encounter the opposition, as well of a large portion of those who were in favor of Free banking . . . [and] those who were interested in Banks." The free banking law would still this criticism.[59]

Later Flagg, as state comptroller, reported on the effect of the new free-banking act. The main trouble with it, as he saw it, was the failure of the banks to protect the holders of bank notes from loss by the depreciation of the currency. The prompt redemption of notes in specie was the only way to sustain the value of paper currency. He argued that the "assurance that securities are pledged for the ultimate redemption of the bills will not keep them at par, unless the redemption of them in specie is kept good." The specie basis of the currency must be increased, he felt, either by forbidding small notes or increasing the amount of specie in banks. Flagg recommended that the banks be required to keep at least 20 per cent of their circulation in specie and that they be prohibited from issuing more notes when their supply of specie fell short of this.[60]

The Whig-dominated legislature, however, did not follow Flagg's advice and in 1840 it repealed the small specie-reserve requirement that had provided some restraint.[61]

4

Within the hard-money wing of the New York and Pennsylvania Democracy, a strong theme of egalitarianism was present. In Pennsylvania this led some Democrats to attempt to incorporate into the 1838 state constitution a clause that would have allowed the legislature to alter, amend, or repeal bank charters. The radicals argued that inviolable bank charters were an abridgement of the basic rights of the people, and, as one said, each generation should be allowed to "manage its

[59] Jabez D. Hammond to Martin Van Buren, May 16, 1838, Martin Van Buren Papers.

[60] House *Executive Document No. 227*, 201–209.

[61] Redlich, *Molding of American Banking*, II, Part 2, 9.

own affairs, in its own way." In New York this radical egalitarianism prompted some hard-money Democrats to support free banking, which might appear, at least on the surface, to be somewhat incompatible with a hard-money position. This seeming contradiction raises an important question: to what extent, if any, was the desire on the part of Democratic radicals for free banking a reflection of this egalitarianism and hatred of monopolies and to what extent, if any, was it a part of an entrepreneurial movement to open up and democratize business? The type of radical hard-money sentiment that was strong within the movement for free banking in New York seems to belie the emphasis that some historians have placed upon the entrepreneurial impulse as motivating the radical Democrats. One historian, who has noted the seeming inconsistency of the radicals' position—antimonopoly freeing of enterprise joined to a strong attachment to hard money—concludes that these men had little concern for the needs of an expanding economy and that their primary dedication was to a deflationary monetary policy.[62] Substantiating this conclusion is the evidence that a number of New York hard-money men supported a deflationary monetary policy in the belief that it would protect them from the inflow of foreign goods and make the protective tariff more effective.

While the radicals were often the most vocal members of the party, the brokers and the more moderate hard-money men dominated the Democracy in Pennsylvania and New York. And, although the conservative Democrats, who were stronger in these two states than in the West, and the Whigs accused the hard-money men of advocating the dissolution of the banking and credit system, there is little evidence that a significant number of Democratic politicians were willing to go beyond reforms to broaden the specie base of the currency and to make banks more responsible to the public.

[62] Carl N. Degler, "The Locofocos: Urban 'Agrarians,'" *The Journal of Economic History* (September, 1956), XVI, 322–33. Degler emphasizes the Democratic devotion to a deflationary monetary policy in contrast to Hofstadter and Redlich, who stress the entrepreneurial side of the radicals.

CHAPTER XIII

The Northeast

I

LOOKING BACK over his long career, Horace Greeley, reformer, Whig politician, and editor of the New York *Tribune,* recalled the distress caused by the Panic of 1837.

Manufactories were stopped, and their "hands" thrown out of work. Trade was almost stagnant. Bankruptcies among men of business were rather the rule than the exception. Property was sacrificed at auction—often at sheriff's or assignee's sale—for a fraction of its value; and thousands, who had fondly dreamed themselves millionnaires, or on the point of becoming such, awoke to the fact that they were bankrupt.[1]

There are indications, however, that the economic collapse did not hit Pennsylvania, New York, and the other states of the Northeast as hard as the states in the other three sections. The price indices of Charleston, Cincinnati, New Orleans, and Philadelphia demonstrate that prices in Philadelphia declined only about half as much as in the other three cities. While the Philadelphia price index dipped from about 98 in 1836 to 75 in 1843, the Charleston index dropped from 121 to 66, the Cincinnati index from 145 to 72, and the New Orleans index from 132 to 70.[2] Although specie ratios would indicate that northeastern banks were as overextended as those elsewhere, generally they were sound institutions and better able to weather the storm than those elsewhere. In great part this was because the public had confidence in them and because their loans were more liquid. Banks in and north of New York managed to keep paying specie in 1839 when the second

[1] Horace Greeley, *Recollections of a Busy Life* (New York, 1869), 123.
[2] *Historical Statistics,* 119–22.

suspension was started by the failure of the United States Bank of Pennsylvania.[3]

Contributing to the relative stability of Northeastern banks were the Suffolk Bank System, through which country banks deposited funds in Boston banks where their notes were redeemed at par, thus establishing a currency of standard value throughout New England, and New York's Safety Fund plan, which required each bank to contribute a certain percentage of its notes to a common fund from which notes of a failed bank would be redeemed at face value.

In the years immediately before the Panic the state of New York was in an enviable position. Completion of the Erie Canal in the mid-1820s had confirmed and assured the future dominance of the port of New York over eastern rivals. By this early date New York already was "the great commercial emporium of America," and by the time the other ports had awakened "to all that New York had been quietly accomplishing . . . it was too late for them to catch up."[4] In the period from 1821 to 1860, New York easily outdistanced rivals in capturing the major portion of the export and import market. In imports, New York was first (handling 60.3 per cent of the market) followed by Boston (15.7 per cent), Philadelphia (7.5 per cent), New Orleans (6.6 per cent), and Baltimore (3.2 per cent). New York had a narrower lead in exports with 32.9 per cent of the market and was trailed by New Orleans (24.5 per cent), Boston (8.4 per cent), Charleston (6.7 per cent), Mobile (6.3 per cent), Savannah (4.0 per cent), Baltimore (3.7 per cent), and Philadelphia (3.6 per cent).[5]

Pennsylvanians quickly recognized that the Erie Canal would siphon off western goods to New York and put Philadelphia increasingly at a trade disadvantage. Although handicapped by almost insurmountable natural obstacles, the state planned the elaborate and expensive Pennsylvania Canal, which was

a railroad from Philadelphia to Columbia on the Susquehanna, a canal from that point northward along the Susquehanna and westward along

---

[3] See Appendix B, Table IV. Knox, *History of Banking,* 329, 390; Sumner, *History of Banking,* Chapter 14.

[4] Robert Greenhalgh Albion, *The Rise of New York Port (1815–1860)* New York, 1939), 15.

[5] *Ibid.,* 389.

the Juniata to Hollidaysburg, a railroad to provide a portage across the Alleghenies, and a canal along the Kiskiminetas and Allegheny rivers to Pittsburg.[6]

By 1836 Pennsylvania had expended over 22 million dollars on internal improvements. But in general the system suffered from poor planning and construction and "was moulded by the prevalence of local interests, in violation of the plain dictates of sound policy."[7] As a result, Philadelphia was in lowly eighth place among American cities as far as exports during the ante-bellum period.

Commerce was just one aspect of the Northeast's diverse economy. The section's industry employed 75 per cent of all American workers engaged in manufacturing in 1850 and 71 per cent in 1860. By the start of the Civil War the textile industry was the largest in terms of men employed, and 75 per cent of the cloth manufactured in the nation came from New England, while 23 per cent came from the Middle Atlantic states.[8]

Massachusetts was making the transition from a commercial to an industrial state in the 1820s when the state's favorite son, Daniel Webster, agonized over the tariff issue. By the late 1840s Lowell, Massachusetts, produced one sixth of all textiles manufactured in the United States and had grown from a population of 3,532 in 1828 to 28,841 in 1846. It was estimated that the city's textile mills were so profitable and dividends so high that an investor could double his capital in five years.[9]

Northeastern farmers also found themselves living in a time of transition and were forced to make adjustments. Improvement of transportation facilities that brought western products east faster and more cheaply made it unprofitable by 1860 for the northeastern farmer to grow wheat and corn or to raise hogs, beef, cattle, or sheep. It has been reported that "Dairying based upon hay and pasture dominated the ag-

[6] Snyder, *Jacksonian Heritage,* 11.
[7] Mathew Carey, *Brief View of the System of Internal Improvement of the State of Pennsylvania* (Philadelphia, 1831), 18, as quoted in *ibid.*
[8] North, *Economic Growth,* 159–61.
[9] J. D. B. De Bow, *The Industrial Resources, Etc., of the Southern and Western States* (New Orleans, 1852), II, 75–76.

riculture of the East in 1860, with whole milk, butter, and cheese as the sources of income." [10]

2

The northeastern states, for the most part, had been involved in the first party system and had vigorously participated in the political battles between the Republicans and Federalists. Thus by the 1820s, when the second American party system was beginning to take shape, the states in the section already had reached a level of political maturity unmatched by the newer states to the west, and most of them did fairly early in the Jackson period re-establish balanced and stable two-party systems. Pennsylvania and Vermont present possible exceptions, with Vermont maintaining three instead of two parties down to the Civil War and Pennsylvania failing to establish a stable two-party system until as late as 1840.[11]

There was great difference among the states as to party strength. New Hampshire was the strongest Democratic state in the nation, the Democrats winning the presidential elections there from 1832 to 1852 and not losing a gubernatorial election until 1846. Maine was another banner Democratic state, giving the Whig presidential candidate its support only in 1840 and between the years 1830 and 1854 electing Whig governors only in 1837 and 1840. Among the Middle Atlantic states Pennsylvania more consistently supported the Democracy than did its neighbors, New York and New Jersey. From 1828 to 1856 the Democrats won the support of Pennsylvanians in all the presidential contests except 1840 and 1848. In New York, the Democracy lost the same two elections as well as the 1856 canvass. The opposition met with more success in New Jersey, giving up the state's electoral vote to the Democrats only in 1832, 1852, and 1856.[12]

Vermont and Massachusetts were the two strongest Whig states. In neither state from 1828 to 1856 did a Democratic presidential nominee

[10] Bidwell and Falconer, *History of Agriculture in the Northern United States,* 450.
[11] McCormick, *Second American Party System,* chapters III and IV.
[12] *Ibid.,* 50–62; *Historical Statistics,* 684–89.

win.[13] In state elections the Democrats had little more success. It was not until 1839 that the Massachusetts Democrats captured the governorship and enjoyed a short-lived victory. The Vermont Democracy was consistently in the minority, but did poll about 45 per cent of the vote.[14] In Rhode Island, the Democrats were a little more successful, winning the state's electoral votes in 1836 and 1852.[15]

3

The Antimasonic party was a political phenomenon that complicated politics in the Northeast. It was strongest in Vermont and Pennsylvania, but the Antimasons also played an influential role in the politics of New York and Massachusetts. One historian relies heavily upon the opposition of the New York Antimasonic party to the Albany Regency to discredit the traditional notion of the Jacksonians as reformers. "Except for the illusions that the Jacksonian Democracy concept has fostered," he argues, "it seems unlikely that historians would have come to associate the Jackson party with the democratic, egalitarian, and social reform movements of 1825 to 1850." It was Antimasonry rather than the Van Buren Democracy, he says, that projected the image of a radical, egalitarian, populistic democracy and "represented an impassioned, leveling attack by members of the 'lower classes' against the village and urban 'aristocracy.'" Calling for the "Abolition of All Licensed Monopolies," the Antimasons directed their attack at the Albany Regency who, they felt, denied equal rights and privileges by using "control of the legislature to strengthen its political machine by rewarding supporters with highly-prized charters and punishing opponents by denying them charters." [16]

The New York experience was atypical. In none of the other three states that developed substantial Antimason parties did the Democratic party emerge from such a strong, well-organized faction as the Albany

[13] *Historical Statistics,* 684–89.
[14] McCormick, *Second American Party System,* 36–49, 69–76.
[15] *Historical Statistics,* 684–89.
[16] Lee Benson, *The Concept of Jacksonian Democracy: New York as a Test Case* (Princeton, N.J., 1961), 24, 37, 38. Quotations from this work reprinted courtesy of Princeton University Press, copyright © 1961 Princeton University Press.

Regency. The Regency, holding considerable power in the 1820s, was indeed responsible for the creation of a number of the state's banks and had a number of bankers in or close to the party leadership. Thus by the late 1820s and early 1830s the New York Democratic party, because of its Albany Regency antecedents and its dedication to the protection of the political and economic establishment of the state, projected a rather conservative image. And this conservatism of the Regency largely determined the nature of the Antimason program and attack. In other words, the Regency was the "negative reference group" for the Antimasons.[17]

In Pennsylvania also the Antimasons opposed the Democrats, but the radical credentials of the third party are open to question. The leader of the group was Thaddeus Stevens, one of the country's ablest political opportunists and the man who personally guided the bill to grant a state charter to the Second Bank of the United States through the Pennsylvania legislature.[18] In the state's constitutional convention he was one of the leaders of the Whig-Antimason coalition that was formed to oppose any radical changes in the frame of government.[19] After the Panic, when the Democrats suggested banking reforms, the Whigs and Antimasons claimed that the Democrats were

breathing nothing but destruction to the banking and credit systems of the Commonwealth. . . . Men of no practical experience in the affairs of life— beardless enthusiasts, full of crude and chimerical notions of reform, and with no better idea of a banking institution than such might be picked up in the various but unmeaning vocabulary of a village newspaper. . . .[20]

If the conservatism of the Pennsylvania Antimasons is at variance with the radicalism of the third party in New York, the indications of

[17] See *ibid.,* 27, for the definition of a negative reference group. Benson quotes from Robert K. Merton, *Social Theory and Social Structure,* rev. ed. (Glencoe, Ill., 1957), who writes that the concept of a negative reference group "is a general concept designed to earmark that pattern of hostile relations between groups or collectivities in which the actions, attitudes and values of one are *dependent* upon the actions, attitudes and values of the other to which it stands in opposition" (see pp. 300–301).
[18] Ralph Korngold, *Thaddeus Stevens: A Being Darkly Wise and Rudely Great* (New York, 1955), 40–42.
[19] Snyder, *Jacksonian Heritage,* Chapter VI.
[20] Henry R. Mueller, *The Whig Party in Pennsylvania* (New York, 1922), 61–62.

cooperation between Antimasons and Democrats in Rhode Island and
Vermont also point to the conclusion that the New York experience
was atypical. In Rhode Island Democrats and Antimasons often united
against the National Republicans and later against the Whigs.[21] In
Vermont the Antimasons constituted the largest party in the state in
the early 1830s, but by the middle of the decade they were forced to
choose sides among the major parties.

When the Whigs and Antimasons merged in 1836, many of the latter,
accepting the designation of "Jack Masons," aligned with the Democrats.
Early in 1837 a conference of Democratic and Jacksonian-Antimasonic
politicians agreed to unite in issuing a call for the next state convention,
signifying the merger of one Antimasonic faction with the Democrats.[22]

An analysis of the Massachusetts Democracy's relationship with the
Antimasons is instructive. In contrast to New York, the Adams men,
National Republicans or Whigs, there represented the establishment
and controlled the state until the end of the decade of the 1830s. Initially led by rather conservative men, the Democrats did not offer an
attractive political alternative until after the Panic of 1837, at which
time more radical leaders assumed power.

When the suspension of specie payments thrust the banking question
into the forefront, Massachusetts Democrats were under the direction
of David Henshaw, a wholesale druggist and bank promoter from Boston. Snubbed by the old merchant families as a parvenu, Henshaw,
nevertheless, was extremely successful and influential, both as businessman and party leader.[23] However, his political power was challenged
in the spring of 1837 after the banks had been discredited by their suspension of specie payments. The executive committee of the Democratic representatives in the Massachusetts legislature wrote to Van

[21] Charles McCarthy, *The Antimasonic Party: A Study of Political Antimasonry in the United States, 1827–1840* (Washington, D.C., 1903), 551–52.

[22] McCormick, *Second American Party System,* 75. Also see McCarthy, *Antimasonic Party,* 514. McCarthy claims that William Henry Harrison's letter
against the Masons "made it easy for the Antimasons of Vermont to become
Whigs." He adds, however, that "Many of their prominent leaders, nevertheless,
became followers of Van Buren."

[23] See, Arthur B. Darling, *Political Changes in Massachusetts, 1824–1848: A
Study of Liberal Movements in Politics* (New Haven, Conn., 1925), 6, 15, for a
discussion of Henshaw's business interests.

Buren that "banks have been the known enemies of our republican government from their beginnings; and should never have been tolerated by Republicans." The President was warned that there were so many debtors to the banks in the cities that they could control the entire community, "and so far as Democrats are involved in this dilemma of interest, on one side, and principle on the other; it is impossible to expect a cordial opposition to the Whigs." [24]

Benjamin F. Hallett, an Antimason turned Democrat, in his newspaper the *Advocate,* attacked all banks as being as dangerous as the old Bank of the United States. He denounced monopolies and corporations with special rights and demanded a hard-money currency supplemented by paper money not controlled by the banks.[25] He and other Massachusetts radicals, however, did not advocate an exclusive metallic currency, favoring specie combined with some kind of treasury notes.

The Massachusetts party was faced with glaring inconsistencies that weakened its antibank position. One Democrat complained to Van Buren that every time the party advocated the separation of the government from banks and influence, it was pointed out "that the offices of Government are generally bestowed upon Bank Men and those having the greatest interest in sustaining the whig System of Bank corruption." David Henshaw, J. K. Simpson, and their relatives and friends all were closely involved with the banks, and many enjoyed lucrative federal jobs by virtue of the patronage system. These "office holders and conservatives by the most unjustifiable course" Van Buren was told, "have managed to secure a majority of both *State and County Committees* to recommend and advocate their pretensions, [and] this has been done by obtaining the control of Banks and granting discounts to irresponsible persons by which means their aid is secured in promoting their selfish designs. . . ." [26]

Henshaw defended the banks from all attacks. Within a year after the Panic, however, the more radical forces within the party had wrested control away from him. First sign of the change came in 1837, when a Democratic convention was taken over from the conservatives

[24] Executive Committee to Martin Van Buren, May (date unknown), 1837, Martin Van Buren Papers.

[25] Darling, *Political Changes in Massachusetts,* 206–207.

[26] Ralph Huntington to Martin Van Buren, January 27, 1838, Martin Van Buren Papers.

and excessive paper money was condemned. The next year George Bancroft was appointed collector of the port of Boston, a powerful post for controlling the party. He and Marcus Morton, the perennial Democratic gubernatorial candidate, rebuilt the party, eliminating the conservative Henshaw.[27]

The ascendancy of Bancroft to the leadership of the Massachusetts Democracy cleared the way for the Democrats to absorb the Antimason as well as the Workingmen groups. Bancroft, in the preceding years, had spent considerable time cultivating the Antimasons and Workingmen and had acted as a liaison man between the two radical groups and the Democratic party.[28] Henshaw's deposition did not, however, put the party entirely into the hands of the radical Democracy, for Bancroft's hard-money credentials were not without serious flaw. Involved with the Bank of Michigan, Bancroft urged Secretary of the Treasury Woodbury in 1840 not to press the bank for debts owed the federal government.

The treasurer has recently been drawing on the Bank of Michigan . . . much beyond their means to pay. . . . This exhausted their immediate resources. . . . May I beg of you not to draw any sums beyond what Mr. Jones left word the Bank could meet.[29]

A month later, Bancroft again wrote the secretary, this time offering a compromise plan by which the government would get its money, but gradually so as not to bankrupt the bank. The debt, between 70,000 dollars and 80,000 dollars, was to be paid monthly in installments of 15,000 dollars, on the condition that the federal government would not bring legal action against the bank.[30]

Bancroft's dominance in the party as the collector of the port did not go unchallenged. One Democrat warned Woodbury that Bancroft was "surrounding himself . . . with persons having no political preferences except where they can make money, and [they] depend wholly upon . . . [Bancroft]." Furthermore it was "*exceedingly* unsafe," he warned,

[27] Darling, *Political Changes in Massachusetts*, 204–19.

[28] Russel B. Nye, *George Bancroft, Brahmin Rebel* (New York, 1944), Chapter IV.

[29] George Bancroft to Levi Woodbury, July 7, 1840, Levi Woodbury Papers, Series II.

[30] *Ibid.*, August 14, 1840, Levi Woodbury Papers, Series I.

to allow Bancroft to fill all the places in the Customs with persons having no other recommendation than that they are *wholly* his creatures. He is a man quite as likely to run east tomorrow because he is running west today. Having not the slightest notion of consistency or honorable obligation, and capable of manufacturing principles to suit any occasion, you can never be sure that you may not find him before long bitterly against you.[31]

In 1839 the Democrats finally, but barely, succeeded in elevating Morton to the governor's chair. This election in 1839 and Morton's re-election in 1842 proved to be hollow victories. In both instances Democrats in the legislature could not muster enough strength to overcome Whig opposition and as a result were unable to enact any sort of a legislative program.[32]

The Panic of 1837 forced the hands of many Democratic brokers, discrediting those who had been conspicuous in their defense of the banking system. Some party leaders, like Bancroft were able to take advantage of this and move the party in a more radical direction, making it more attractive to some Antimasons as well as to other radicals who had been disenchanted by earlier conservative Democratic leadership.[33]

It is clear that after 1837 the Democracy in New York became more appealing to New York City radicals. The exact course of the rank-and-file Antimasons is not clear. With respect to all of the states that spawned a sizeable Antimasonic movement, there is need for a close analysis of what happened to the Antimason vote once the party disintegrated. Too many generalizations, which are at best misleading, are based only on the political course of the Antimason leadership.

---

[31] Robert Rantoul to unknown (probably Levi Woodbury), March 7, 1839, Levi Woodbury Papers, Series II. The Van Buren men were to learn the wisdom of this warning much to their sorrow, almost five years later, when Bancroft deserted Van Buren at the Democratic convention in favor of Polk.

[32] *Niles' Register,* February 8, 1840; Darling, *Political Changes in Massachusetts,* 251–300.

[33] McCarthy, in his *Antimasonic Party,* 525, concludes somewhat ambiguously that: "The Antimasons of Massachusetts, with the exception of a few radicals, were completely united with the Whig party in the election of 1836." It is not clear whether this 1836 alliance was maintained, nor was there any analysis of voting returns to bolster his impressionistic evidence. McCarthy does seem to stress, however, that the aristocratic image projected by the Whigs made that party unattractive to many Antimasons.

4

In the Northeast anticharter egalitarianism manifested itself in two ways. In New York, as opposed to the rest of the East, it led radicals to support a free-banking law. This was due in large part to the dilemma the New Yorkers faced. Many New York banks prior to the passage of the free-banking act owed their charters to the support of the Albany Regency. Not to support a free-banking act, many radical Democrats concluded, would add credence to the Whig argument that the state Democratic party was dedicated to protecting the monopoly of the banks with special charters. Furthermore, they believed, a free-banking act would eliminate the corrupting influence the banks had on the state's political structure.

In Pennsylvania this egalitarian sentiment motivated Democrats to propose that the legislature be given the right to alter, amend, or rescind any bank charter, whether granted in the past or to be granted in the future. This proposition represented the main thrust of the radicals' proposals at the constitutional convention. The radical Democrats in New Jersey sponsored a similar constitutional change. Later, Democrats there urged the state constitutional convention that met in 1844 to adopt an amendment calling for a three-fifths vote in the legislature to charter a bank and establish a limit of twenty years for a bank charter. Furthermore they recommended the inclusion of a clause permitting the legislature to alter or repeal any charter by a three-fifths vote. The Democrats failed, however; their proposals were defeated by a close party vote.[34] New Hampshire Democrats were able to get their state legislature to go on record denying the irrevocability of bank charters. This also was attempted by Vermont Democrats but unsuccessfully.

New Hampshire had the strongest Democratic party in New England, and under the leadership of Isaac Hill (United States Senator from 1831–1836 and state governor from 1836–1839) it kept tight control over state politics. However, by the decade of the 1840s a severe split had developed. A conservative faction led by Hill feared that the zeal of the radicals in the party would impair the economic develop-

[34] John Cadman, *The Corporation in New Jersey: Business and Politics, 1791–1875* (Cambridge, Mass., 1949), 97.

ment of the state, and the radicals, for their part, were concerned about the increasing power of corporations and the lack of public control.[35] This factionalism, however, had not prevented the 1839 legislature from passing a joint resolution reaffirming the right of the people, through their elected representatives, "to alter, amend or abrogate any act of incorporation heretofore granted, or which may hereafter be granted . . . when in the opinion of the legislature the public good may require such alteration, amendment or abrogation. . . ."[36]

Anticharter sentiment in New Hampshire was similar to that in Pennsylvania. In both states Democrats feared the gradual whittling away of the people's power by charter grants and the frightening prospect of private corporations becoming so powerful that they could control the government. This fear of special legislation in chartering corporations was expressed by a later Democratic governor of the state, John Page, who maintained that corporations were chartered

with a sole view to avoid personal responsibility, to enable individuals to transact business under their corporate name, with an exemption from all responsibility. . . . The number and power of corporations in this country have been extended to an alarming degree, and it may require the utmost vigilence and efforts of our people, as well as their legislatures, to retain the government of the country in opposition to so many and so powerful combinations.[37]

Hill and his followers evidently did not share Page's apprehension. In 1842 Hill's newspaper condemned "the Democratic young lawyers . . . who joined the democracy to destroy it by advocating ridiculous doctrines. . . ."[38] Among these "ridiculous doctrines," in Hill's view, was unlimited stockholder liability, a dangerous concept that would threaten the economic progress and prosperity of the state.[39] Whether the conservatives were so protective toward banking corporations, it is not clear. But it does appear that most New Hampshire Democrats feared the power of the banks and disliked paper currency. They gen-

---

[35] Richard H. Sewell, *John P. Hale and the Politics of Abolition* (Cambridge, Mass., 1965), 21–24.

[36] *Niles' Register,* July 27, 1839.

[37] As quoted in Everett S. Stackpole, *History of New Hampshire* (New York, 1916), III, 116.

[38] As quoted in Sewell, *John P. Hale,* 23.   [39] *Ibid.*

erally concluded, however, that there was little they could do about either, except to regulate the banks more closely.

If New Hampshire was solidly Democratic, Vermont was just as solidly Whig. The Democrats, until the middle 1840s at least, never controlled either the legislature or the governorship. In 1839 there was an apparent split in the Democratic party. The Whigs that year designated their convention the "Democratic-Whig" convention, and among those in attendance was Ezra Meech, a former Democratic candidate for governor who never rejoined his original party. Despite the division, the Democrats ran well and almost captured the legislature. Their platform promised bank reform.[40] The Whig Governor, obviously responding to Democratic campaign charges, told the Vermont legislature that despite the charges of monopoly raised against the banks, he considered the banks indispensable to the state.[41] The Democrats attempted to pass a resolution similar to the one in New Hampshire, asserting the legislature's absolute power over past, present, and future bank charters. But they were not successful.[42]

5

The banking issue in the Northeast did not remain a divisive political issue as long as it did in the other sections. In comparison with the rest of the country, banks in the Northeast acted with more restraint and responsibility, and Democrats could have made little political capital by advocating an exclusive metallic currency. Thus Democrats were forced to walk a tightrope—answering Whig and conservative charges that they were intent upon destroying the entire banking system and, at the same time, satisfying followers who were deeply suspicious of banks and paper currency and who fervently disliked the special privileges in bank charters.

Banks were such an integral part of each state's economy that Democrats felt that any attempt to remove this malignancy might well kill the patient. Generally, the party urged the adoption of such reforms as

---

[40] Walter Hill Crockett, *Vermont, The Green Mountain State* (New York, 1921), 304–305.
[41] *Ibid.*   [42] *Niles' Register,* November 30, 1839.

prohibition of small notes, requirement of adequate specie reserve for notes, and stockholder liability.

Another reason the bank controversy ended sooner in the Northeast than elsewhere was that there, by the middle of the century, the relative importance of banks was waning. Other financial institutions and "great corporations . . . formed for other purposes . . . grew so great as to overshadow the banks." And in "the older parts of the country . . . the accumulation of capital had now become so great that the old banking system of paper-money-mongering was out of date." [43]

At the time of the Panic the Democratic party in the Northeast was firmly in the hands of the brokers. This, of course, meant different things in different states. In New York, and to a lesser extent in Massachusetts, the broker-leaders of the party were closely identified with the state banking system. When the economic collapse came, and there was a reaction against the banks, this was an important factor in discrediting the broker leadership, which in turn led to the strengthening of the more radical element within the party. In Pennsylvania, however, this did not happen, and therefore the brokers faced no major threats to their management of party affairs.

[43] Sumner, *History of Banking,* 414–15. Sumner makes this comment about banks throughout the country; however, I find it more accurately applied only to banks in the Northeast.

CONCLUSION

I

BY THE DECADE of the 1850s banking was no longer a major divisive issue in the states. The Panic of 1837 was but a distant memory to most Americans, and the threatening clouds of civil war already were on the horizon. For almost a decade and a half after 1837, however, banking had been a bitterly contested question, separating not only Democrat from Whig but also Democrat from Democrat.

The Democratic party did not engage in the battle over banks and currency as the party of the entrepreneur in an age of enterprise. In contrast, the party's appeal was in the nature of a plaintive warning against the increasing commercialization and vulgarization of American life. If the laissez faire logic of the Jacksonian antibank and anticorporate argument eventually led to the enthronement of the business ethic in the last half of the nineteenth century, it is one of history's cruelest paradoxes.

After the Panic of 1837, although the rhetoric of the two parties sometimes obscured their real positions, it is clear that the Whigs were the champions of the banks against the "radicalism" of the Jacksonians. Despite internal feuding, the main body of the Democratic party supported radical reform of the banks and, in some cases, their destruction. The party reflected, in both ethos and program, the hard-money position.

The commercialization of the country and the extension of the market economy were major innovative factors that stimulated profound and unsettling economic and social changes in ante-bellum America. The Panic of 1837 threw these changes into sharp relief and underscored some of their less attractive manifestations. The Democratic party became the instrument through which protest against this change was funneled and offered a stingingly critical analysis of the agents of this transformation—the banks.

Hard money has been an elusive concept for historians to define, perhaps in part because it had widely varying meanings to the Jacksonians themselves. The level of a state's economic development and the extent to which a state was entangled with its banking system were major factors in defining the nature of hard-money radicalism within its boundaries. In the newer western sections, where banks often were unstable and erratic in their behavior and where there was not a consensus that banking services were vital to the well-being of the economy, there was strong sentiment for doing away with the banks in the name of hard money and establishing a specie currency, responsible only to the natural laws, to replace a paper money, subject to the caprice and avarice of the banker. Paper-money banking, many Jacksonians felt, violated the natural laws of economics. Gold and silver were the only natural money; paper currency was unnatural, evil, and disruptive.

Initially, Democratic efforts to bring legislative action against the banks in the two western sections were complicated by the close financial ties many of the states had with the banks at the time of the Panic. In the Southwest the states had involved themselves extensively with the banks by underwriting the necessary loans to raise capital for the plantation banks, while in Illinois, Indiana, and Tennessee state banks had been used to raise funds for the building of internal-improvement systems. The Panic so weakened the banks of Mississippi, Alabama, and Arkansas in the Southwest and Illinois and Michigan in the Northwest that after an initial effort to bring order and reform to a chaotic and over-extended banking system, the Democrats moved to put the broken banks out of business. While banks were important to the economic lives of all the states in the two sections, this was particularly true of Louisiana and Ohio, the two most economically mature states in the West. Yet hard-money Democrats were successful in Louisiana in constitutionally prohibiting the creation of new banks, and in Ohio they passed two general bank laws that were so strict that bankers refused to accept their terms.

Thus in the two western sections some of the states were virtually bankless by 1845, and in all there had been a dramatic reduction in the amount of bank capital. The Democrats, who were then faced with a strong drive for more bank capital supported by the Whigs and softs, sought some way to solve permanently the banking question. Attempting to follow the lead of the Louisiana Democrats, some hoped to constitutionally prohibit banking in their states. Their efforts, for the most part, were to no avail, and the forces of enterprise were able to expand the banking capital in the western states.

In the two eastern sections, hard money normally meant reform of the banks, and eastern hard-money men called for specie–note ratios, stockholder liability clauses, elimination of small notes, and an end to inviolable bank charters. The increased use of specie was seen as a laissez faire reform device that would add a kind of automatic balance to the banking system, making it more responsible to the public interest. The milder response of the eastern hard-money Democrats in comparison to the western radicals was due to several factors. The eastern banking system, for the most part, dated from the eighteenth century. Thus, banks had been accepted by many easterners as vital economic institutions, and were, in comparison with the West, operated in a stable and conservative fashion. Banks were particularly essential to the economic life of the complex commercial and industrial economy of the Northeast, the banking and trading center of the country. No matter how hated the banks were, most northeastern radicals recognized the futility and political peril of destroying them. Furthermore, the Panic and depression did not strike the eastern half of the country, particularly the Southeast, as hard as it did the West. The Southeast had not participated in the boom of the 1830s to the extent of the other sections. Consequently, when the crash came, the section escaped much of the severe contraction. This circumstance, along with the close involvement of some of the southeastern states with the banking system, tempered and hindered Democratic reform efforts. In Virginia, South Carolina, and Georgia, state investment in banks played a large role in inhibiting reform.

In addition to the level of a state's economic maturity, the stage of its political development also was an important factor in shaping Democratic response. In Ohio, for example, politics were more democratic and more ideologically oriented. There seems to have been an intense antibank, hard-money commitment on the part of Democratic grass-roots supporters, and this, coupled with the democratic nature of Ohio politics, forced party leaders to be more responsive and more radical. In Mississippi, there appears to have been the same strong antibank sentiment within the ranks of the Democratic party. However, since the political structure was newer, more fluid, and less democratic, politics remained in the hands of political brokers like William M. Gwin. Less responsive to constituent pressures and more manipulative in their operations, the Mississippi brokers used the overwhelming antibank sentiment to control the party, trying to channel this energy in politically advantageous, but not politically destructive, directions. Virginia, perhaps, was less democratic and more nationally oriented than either Ohio or Mississippi. As a consequence the party managers of the Virginia Democracy were able to control the party without too much fear of a grassroots insurgency.

A good indication of the differences between eastern and western Democrats on the banking issue was a mocking editorial in the Jackson *Mississippian* in 1846, written in response to the call of a Pennsylvania Democratic governor for bank reform. The governor's message, according to the *Mississippian,* eloquently embodied "the most orthordox [*sic*] views of the democratic party upon the banking system," pointing out the "evil tendency of the system and its disastrous consequences. . . ." Thus, after the governor had expressed "his conviction of the utter insufficiency of any legislative enactment, ever yet tried, to protect the public against bank swindling and fraud," the Mississippi editor reasoned, the only possible conclusion the governor could arrive at was to demand "*a total extinguishment* of the banks." But much to the journalist's astonishment, the governor instead came "to the most lame and impotent conclusion of continuing them in existence, and renewing expired charters with the additional check of '*individual liability*'—'*monthly returns,*' and the '*periodical publications of the same*'. . . ." The Mississippi editor concluded that

if it were customary for the older States to derive lessons of wisdom from the experience of the younger, Pennsylvania might well learn from Mississippi more to convince her of the utter impotency of checks and guards upon bank swindling, than a thousand years of theorizing and experimenting will teach her.[1]

2

In all three states there was a significant correlation between the wealthier constituencies and the Whigs, and the poorer ones and the Democrats. Yet in Virginia and Ohio, the statewide correlation can be deceiving. In the southwestern counties and those of the Western Reserve in Ohio as well as the Tidewater and Piedmont areas in Virginia, wealth or the lack of it does not seem to have been an important factor in the division between Democratic and Whig constituencies. The correlation between wealth and political affiliation was considerably more striking in the less developed and underpopulated areas of Ohio and Virginia as well as in the entire state of Mississippi.

Typical Whig constituencies were those that were fully participating in the market economy. They ranged from areas heavily involved in commercial agriculture to urban centers of industry and commerce. Perhaps, as one historian has noted, the most outstanding characteristic of the Whigs was their enthusiasm regarding the future of the country.[2] This enthusiasm, more often than not, manifested itself in economic terms. Henry Clay's vision of the good society was of a commercial and industrial America, interlaced with roads and canals to facilitate the transfer of goods from one section to another. Clay and his Whig followers also envisioned a country with ample banking institutions to provide currency, credit, and exchange. The soft-money Democrats, in many cases, were Whigs who just happened to be Democrats. In all three of the states, Mississippi, Ohio, and Virginia, the Democratic constituencies that supported the softs were very similar to Whig areas in wealth and in participation in the market.

Hard-money Democratic strength came from several different sources: areas outside the market economy and ones of declining wealth, power, and prestige; northeastern cities (which had long con-

[1] Jackson *Mississippian,* April 22, 1846.
[2] Glyndon G. Van Deusen, "Some Aspects of Whig Thought and Theory in the Jacksonian Period," *American Historical Review,* LXIII (January, 1958), 305–22.

tained pockets of radicalism); and from constituencies heavily populated by persons of German descent. Citizens in all had in common
feelings of envy, fear, and disapproval toward banks, which symbolized
privilege and uncontrolled power.

Before 1837 Americans living outside the market viewed the banks
ambivalently. But the Panic and resulting economic and monetary
chaos reinforced their fears. In the following years, as many of these
isolated areas were brought into the market economy, there still remained a lingering suspicion of banks.

The Virginia Tidewater and urban centers of the Northeast were
dissimilar, yet there were strongholds of antibank, hard-money attitudes in both. The urban radicals blended their hard-money orthodoxy
with a kind of laissez faire egalitarianism, while the nostalgia-ridden
Tidewater planters hated the banks, which to them represented the
commercialism that was undermining and destroying the old order.

The spirit of enterprise was not particularly attractive to most German-Americans. Clannish, industrious, and frugal, these stolid folk
were extremely suspicious of anything that smacked of speculation.
Strongly Democratic in sympathy, it was reported that some Germans
were still "voting for Jackson long after his death, even after the Civil
War!"[3] There are some indications that this skepticism of risk-taking
and entrepreneurialism was not a characteristic only acquired by the
Germans in the American environment. One Prussian official complained in 1839 that the

capitalists here are not inclined to pay industrial enterprises their proper
due. Even the soundest of incorporation projects fail to attract interest.
Rather than making funds available to industry, capitalists prefer to invest
their fortunes in government securities or mortgages, and to enjoy the
fruits of their investment with the greatest possible amount of peace and
calm.[4]

Communities that were established by the Germans in America, as
well as the ones that had developed in the declining Virginia Tidewater, were "heavily weighted in economic fields toward tradition and

[3] Robert Remini, *The Election of Andrew Jackson* (Philadelphia, 1963), 104.

[4] As quoted in Rondo Cameron, *Banking in the Early Stages of Industrialism:
A Study in Comparative Economic History* (New York, 1967), footnote on pages
154–55.

continuity." One scholar has pointed out that these are characteristics typical of societies not highly motivated toward entrepreneurial innovation. He further describes these societies as ones

slow to adapt to economic change, slow to receive many of the products of mass production (as against hand craftsmanship) and slower still to accept the new methods and relationships involved. Psychological and cultural resistances to mechanization, and the cheapness of labor and services have alike made for continuation of established means and forms. The motivation to remain with the circular flow has been notably stronger, the incentives to innovate correspondingly weaker.[5]

3

The election of 1844 was the first time in American history that a political party had been able to regain the Presidency once it had lost it. Thus, it is not surprising to find soft-money Democratic leaders, such as Rives and Tallmadge, in the late 1830s confident of their political futures. The hard-money wing of the party, these softs concluded, was hopelessly deluded by a commitment to an outworn agrarian radicalism that was completely out of touch with the political and economic reality of the nineteenth century. The hards were destined to destroy themselves and the Democratic party, and the softs hoped to be able to reconstruct a new party upon the ruins of the old. Yet the soft-money Democrats were overconfident of their own strength and misjudged the strength of the hards as well as the popular appeal of the hard-money ideology.

Bray Hammond argues that the Jacksonian attack upon the banks had negative and destructive results.

[5] Although John E. Sawyer is considering a much broader topic, his insights into social traits that accelerate or inhibit the development of entrepreneurial drives are useful for understanding the German communities in Virginia and Ohio. Lewis Cecil Gray's conclusions in his *History of Agriculture in the Southern United States to 1860* regarding the farming operations in the Virginia Tidewater would indicate that Sawyer's analysis could be applied to that section as well. Sawyer, "The Entrepreneur and the Social Order, France and the United States," in *Men in Business, Essays on the Historical Role of the Entrepreneur,* edited by William Miller (New York, 1962), 16–17.

So in the extraordinarily dynamic period of business enterprise extending from the election of Andrew Jackson in 1828 to the election of Abraham Lincoln in 1860, blunders in banking were profuse. So was dishonesty, though neither blundering nor dishonesty prevailed. Banking was both good and bad. From the point of governmental responsibility and what the monetary system should have been, the imperfections were awful, mainly because of the anarchic destructiveness of the Jacksonians, who had ended control of a function inherently requiring control.[6]

By focusing upon the Jacksonians' destruction of the Bank of the United States, Hammond misinterprets the actions of the Democrats. It is true that after the demise of the Deposit Bank System, the Democrats abandoned the idea of federal control over the banking system. But the battle against the banks was not abandoned. It simply shifted to the states.

Although hard-money Jacksonianism was based upon an anachronistic view of society and played upon the fears and antagonisms raised by a swiftly changing environment, its legacy was a vital and enduring one. The Democratic critique of the banking system after 1837, while not always translated into legislation, was still an important factor in making the banks more sensitive and responsible to public needs. The hards' advocacy of reforms, such as specie-note ratios, unlimited liability of stockholders and directors, and small-note laws, and their desire for the abolition of banks were aimed at one objective—the restriction or elimination of the virtually unlimited power that ante-bellum bankers had over prices, the money supply, and the economic cycle. By insisting upon a currency with a larger specie base and urging that the amount of a bank's legal liabilities be tied directly to a set percentage of the specie the bank actually held in its vaults, the Democrats hoped to establish specie as a kind of internal regulating device in the American banking system. The relatively stable and more responsible conduct of the country's banks from the early 1840s to the Civil War was due in large part to Democratic sponsored bank reforms and the vigorous hard-money critique.

Sectionalism, the inexorable expansion of the market economy, the return of good times, and the more responsible operation of the banking system ended the banking question as a divisive issue in ante-bel-

[6] Hammond, *Banks and Politics*, 676.

lum politics. By mid-century, in most states, an uneasy consensus had been worked out between the hards, softs, and Whigs on banking. The entrepreneurial-minded softs and the Whigs acknowledged the need for and were willing to accept more regulation of the banking system. The more radical hards, especially in the West, remained unreconciled to the banks and hoped for their eventual destruction. This position, however, became more and more utopian, and the more moderate hards recognized the dwindling appeal of their position and, therefore, reluctantly accepted accommodation.

After the Civil War, currency and banking reforms were inflationary, not deflationary as were the Jacksonian ones, and did not come from within the Democratic party. The agrarian radicalism that had pervaded the Jacksonian movement did not find a congenial home in either of the major parties of the post-bellum era. Nevertheless, there is a strong theme of continuity linking hard-money Jacksonian with Greenbacker and Populist. In all three movements, the means may have differed, but the end was the same: democratic control over banking and currency.

APPENDICES

Appendix A

COMPUTATION OF CORRELATION COEFFICIENTS
BETWEEN DEMOCRATIC STRENGTH AND
VARIOUS MEASURES OF ECONOMIC STANDING
IN MISSISSIPPI, OHIO, AND VIRGINIA,
AND BETWEEN DEMOCRATIC STRENGTH AND
SLAVEHOLDING IN MISSISSIPPI AND VIRGINIA [1]

AFTER ANALYZING the Democratic party and its relation to the banking issue in Mississippi, Ohio, and Virginia, the next logical research questions arose: from where did the support for the party come within each state, and, what kind of generalizations can be made about the nature of political support in both parties? To provide a statistical basis for the analysis, rank-difference correlation coefficients were computed in order to test the hypothesis that a relationship existed between economic wealth, in terms of taxable real and personal property, and political strength and also between slaveholding and political strength. More specifically, the hypothesis tested was that poorer constituencies were more likely to have voted Democratic, while wealthier constituencies were more likely to have voted Whig.

Rank-difference correlation coefficients were computed according to the method described by Henry E. Garrett in his *Statistics in Psychology and Education* (New York, 1949), 343–47. The formula for coefficients, p, is given by

$$p = 1 - \frac{6 \Sigma D^2}{N (N^2 - 1)}$$

where D is the difference between ranks and N is the number of counties in the array.

Constituencies in the three states were ranked according to Democratic political strength and wealth, and in Virginia and Mississippi they were ranked according to slaveholding as well. Then the coefficient of rank correlation, a statistical measure of the association between two rankings, was computed. Basically, this measure indicates how nearly, on the average, individual constituencies obtained the same ranks in terms both of wealth and of political standing or in terms both of slaveholding and political standing. The wider the difference between two factors, the lower the correlation coefficient will be. It must in all cases, however, be a number between 0.000 (which represents no correlation) and $\pm$ 1.000 (which represents a perfect correlation, positive or negative as the case may be). In this analysis no negative correlations were expected or obtained, so that all the coefficients were numbers between 0.000 and $+$ 1.000. The statistical significance of p is generally accepted or rejected in relation to one of two probability criteria or levels: the .05 level which indicates that the odds against such a correlation occurring by chance are at least 20 to 1, or at the .01 level, which indicates that the odds against such a correlation occurring by chance are at least 100 to 1.

TABLE I

DATA FOR CALCULATION OF RANK ORDER CORRELATION
COEFFICIENT BETWEEN DEMOCRATIC STRENGTH AND
TAXABLE WEALTH IN MISSISSIPPI, 1836–1844, AND
BETWEEN DEMOCRATIC STRENGTH AND SLAVEHOLDING
IN MISSISSIPPI, 1836–1844

RESULTS:

p(Democratic Strength–Lack of Wealth) $=$ .771 (significant at .01 level)

p(Democratic Strength–Lower Slaveholding) $=$ .768 (significant at .01 level)

Mississippi Constituency 1836–1844 [2]	*Per Cent of Votes Cast for Democratic Nominees* [3]	*Demo-cratic Rank*	*Tax Per Capita Paid in 1845 (in dollars)* [4]	*Eco-nomic Rank*	*Average Slave-holding in 1840* [5]	*Rank in Slave-holding*
Very Strong Democratic [6]						
Jackson	92.97	1	0.450	5	0.28	7
Lawrence	84.67	2	0.778	19	0.62	23
Clarke	77.13	3	0.598	13	0.44	17
Itawamba	76.07	4	0.427	4	0.15	4
Lauderdale	75.43	5	0.541	10	0.34	9
Covington	74.90	6.5	0.531	9	0.46	19
Smith	74.90	6.5	0.494	7	0.27	5
Newton	70.83	8	0.800	21	0.28	6
Scott	70.40	9	0.952	24	0.39	15
Marion	69.43	10	0.984	25	0.81	31
Jones	69.10	11	0.187	1	0.15	3
Tishomingo	67.50	12	0.407	3	0.14	2
Neshoba	66.73	13	0.643	15	0.44	16
Pike	66.43	14	0.799	20	0.63	24
Jasper	65.43	15	0.590	12	0.46	18

Mississippi Constituency 1836–1844 [2]	Per Cent of Votes Cast for Democratic Nominees [3]	Democratic Rank	Tax Per Capita Paid in 1845 (in dollars) [4]	Economic Rank	Average Slaveholding in 1840 [5]	Rank in Slaveholding
Strong Democratic						
Winston	64.63	16	1.018	26	0.52	21
Chickasaw	64.33	17	1.251	30	0.38	14
Monroe	62.57	18	1.450	33	0.79	30
Franklin	61.10	19	1.644	35	1.30	38
Simpson	59.83	20	0.498	8	0.37	13
Moderate Democratic						
Wayne	57.37	21	0.903	22	0.86	33
Hancock [7]	57.33	22	0.692	17	0.46	20
Copiah	57.13	23	1.145	29	0.73	27
Oktibbeha	57.00	24	1.806	37	1.06	36
Kemper	56.60	25	0.766	18	0.66	25
Pontotoc	56.30	26	0.947	23	0.55	22
Tippah	56.13	27	0.674	16	0.29	8
Lowndes	54.57	28	2.643	42	1.53	41
Leake	54.40	29	0.377	2	0.10	1
Greene	54.03	30	0.456	6	0.36	12
Attala	53.83	31	0.553	11	0.34	10
Neutral						
Choctaw	52.20	32	0.617	14	0.35	11
Panola	52.03	33	2.605	41	1.08	37
De Soto	51.00	34	1.808	38	0.76	28
Yalobusha	50.17	35	1.092	27	0.84	32
Noxubee	49.43	36	2.814	43	1.61	42
Marshall	47.60	37	1.355	31	0.89	34
Moderate Whig						
Lafayette	46.93	38	1.139	28	0.77	29
Bolivar [8]	46.47	39	10.547	52	2.52	47
Carroll	45.87	40	1.623	34	1.04	35
Rankin	45.23	41	1.428	32	0.67	26
Claiborne	44.70	42	4.980	50	2.93	50
Amite	43.07	43	1.739	36	1.52	40
Holmes	42.60	44	2.031	39	1.43	39

TABLE I (*Continued*)

Mississippi Constituency 1836–1844[2]	Per Cent of Votes Cast for Democratic Nominees[3]	Democratic Rank	Tax Per Capita Paid in 1845 (in dollars)[4]	Economic Rank	Average Slave-holding in 1840[5]	Rank in Slave-holding
Strong Whig						
Talahatchie	42.27	45	2.193	40	1.84	44
Jefferson	41.33	46	4.172	46	3.71	52
Hinds	39.20	47	2.878	44	1.80	43
Yazoo	37.60	48	4.824	47	2.34	46
Adams	36.40	49	8.373	51	2.74	48
Very Strong Whig						
Madison	34.57	50	4.869	49	2.89	49
Washington[9]	33.33	51	23.911	53	10.04	53
Warren	32.87	52	4.825	48	1.97	45
Wilkinson	29.37	53	3.913	45	3.30	51

TABLE II

DATA FOR CALCULATION OF RANK ORDER CORRELATION
COEFFICIENT BETWEEN DEMOCRATIC STRENGTH AND
AGGREGATE REAL ESTATE WEALTH IN OHIO, 1836–1844

RESULT:

$p_{\text{(Democratic Strength–Lack of Wealth)}} = .428$ (significant at .01 level)

Ohio Constituency 1836–1844[10]	Per Cent of Votes Cast for Democratic Nominees[11]	Democratic Rank	Per Capita Wealth, 1840 (in dollars)[12]	Economic Rank
Very Strong Democratic				
Paulding	67.63	1	30.436	9
Monroe	67.33	2	15.999	1
Holmes	65.27	3	33.251	13
Strong Democratic				
Mercer	64.20	4	26.975	7
Butler	62.87	5	96.103	63
Hocking	62.03	6	23.270	4
Hancock	59.50	7	44.328	22
Richland	59.37	8	43.437	20
Fairfield	59.20	9	74.110	52

Ohio Constituency 1836–1844 [10]	Per Cent of Votes Cast for Democratic Nominees [11]	Democratic Rank	Per Capita Wealth, 1840 (in dollars) [12]	Economic Rank
Perry	59.00	10	37.919	16
Putnam	58.90	11	32.527	11
Wayne	57.87	12	52.465	32
Moderate Democratic				
Adams	55.40	13	54.450	34
Crawford	55.03	14	41.965	18
Coshocton	54.83	15	47.100	25
Brown	54.73	16	61.264	41
Clermont	54.67	17	70.382	49
Seneca	54.37	18	51.487	29
Knox	53.77	19	58.580	39
Hamilton	52.97	20	114.398	69
Allen	52.93	21	31.973	10
Neutral				
Sandusky [13]	52.43	22	66.558	45
Licking	52.40	23.5	79.275	56
Williams	52.40	23.5	33.557	14
Pike	51.37	25	56.497	37
Columbiana	51.34	26.5	49.723	27
Jackson	51.34	26.5	20.197	3
Jefferson	51.30	28	65.491	44
Morgan	51.13	29	34.011	15
Henry	49.50	30	51.877	31
Shelby	48.60	31	48.792	26
Highland	48.47	32	54.642	35
Darke	48.40	33	43.567	21
Carroll	47.67	34	26.463	6
Moderate Whig				
Harrison	46.97	35.5	39.593	17
Montgomery	46.97	35.5	99.108	65
Marion	46.47	37	69.440	48
Medina, Portage, and Stark [14]	46.33	38	58.303	38
Tuscarawas	46.00	39	42.687	19

TABLE II (*Continued*)

Ohio Constituency 1836–1844 [10]	Per Cent of Votes Cast for Democratic Nominees [11]	Democratic Rank	Per Capita Wealth, 1840 (in dollars) [12]	Economic Rank
Belmont	45.87	40	49.856	28
Hardin	45.77	41	84.508	60
Guernsey	45.60	42	25.664	5
Wood	44.83	43	81.952	59
Trumbull	44.70	44	65.412	43
Pickaway	44.57	45	107.341	67
Lorain	43.97	46	55.737	36
Huron [15]	43.13	47	53.595	33
Fayette	42.93	48	63.903	42
Washington	42.87	49	45.965	24
Delaware	42.70	50	66.886	46
Strong Whig				
Ross	41.43	51	114.333	68
Athens	41.27	52	45.388	23
Franklin	40.63	53	152.641	71
Union	40.50	54	81.108	57
Muskingum	39.37	55	76.548	54
Lucas	39.00	56	148.831	70
Champaign	37.53	57	73.182	51
Lawrence	37.30	58	18.515	2
Preble	37.23	59	69.226	47
Scioto	36.90	60	72.519	50
Meigs	36.83	61	32.602	12
Miami	36.77	62	81.494	58
Warren	36.67	63	97.301	64
Clinton	36.10	64	78.276	55
Gallia	35.87	65	28.753	8
Very Strong Whig				
Logan	34.53	66	61.092	40
Madison	34.27	67	102.471	66
Cuyahoga and Geauga [16]	34.07	68	74.925	53
Greene	33.57	69	89.697	61
Clark	28.60	70	95.759	62
Ashtabula	21.17	71	51.811	30

TABLE III

*DATA FOR CALCULATION OF RANK ORDER CORRELATION
COEFFICIENT BETWEEN DEMOCRATIC STRENGTH AND
TAXABLE WEALTH IN VIRGINIA, 1836–1844, AND
BETWEEN DEMOCRATIC STRENGTH AND SLAVEHOLDING
IN VIRGINIA, 1836–1844*

RESULTS:

p(Democratic Strength–Lack of Wealth) $= .206$ (significant at .05 level)

p(Democratic Strength–Lower Slaveholding) $= .074$ (insignificant)

Virginia Constituency 1836–1844 [17]	Per Cent of Votes Cast for Democratic Nominees [18]	Demo- cratic Rank	Tax Per Capita Paid in 1840 (in dollars) [19]	Eco- nomic Rank	Average Slave- holding in 1840 [20]	Rank in Slave- holding
Very Strong Democratic						
Page	92.63	1	0.345	31	0.144	25
Shenandoah	91.57	2	0.287	20	0.098	18.5
Madison	90.07	3	0.645	75	1.129	81
Rockingham	86.23	4	0.426	47	0.123	22
Isle of Wight	84.07	5	0.365	35	0.612	51
Sussex	76.90	6	0.730	93	1.555	100
Halifax	74.93	7	0.687	83	1.213	88
Scott	74.50	8.5	0.143	2	0.049	12
King William	74.50	8.5	0.842	98	1.663	104
Goochland	73.43	10	0.844	99	1.291	92
Warren	73.13	11	0.407	41	0.342	39
Lee	73.03	12	0.155	4	0.074	15
Washington	73.00	13	0.320	25	0.188	29
Pocahontas	71.73	14	0.296	21	0.081	17
Prince William	71.70	15	0.425	46	0.543	47
Grayson [21]	71.17	16	0.096	1	0.057	13
Alleghany	70.63	17	0.330	27	0.248	33
Giles and Tazewell [22]	67.67	18.5	0.208	13	0.118	21
Botetourt [23]	67.67	18.5	0.412	44	0.353	41
Russell	66.80	20	0.160	5	0.098	18.5
Mecklenburg	66.67	21	0.705	91	1.353	95
Surry	65.90	22	0.410	43	0.787	61
Prince George [24]	65.33	23	0.703	89	1.270	90
Strong Democratic						
Louisa	64.93	24	0.665	80	1.403	97
Northumberland	64.20	25	0.331	28	0.693	55
Orange [25]	63.77	26	0.657	78	1.136	83
Amelia	63.60	27	1.049	106	2.130	108

TABLE III (*Continued*)

Virginia Constituency 1836–1844 [17]	Per Cent of Votes Cast for Democratic Nominees [18]	Demo- cratic Rank	Tax Per Capita Paid in 1840 (in dollars) [19]	Eco- nomic Rank	Average Slave- holding in 1840 [20]	Rank in Slave- holding
Logan	63.53	28	0.246	15	0.036	11
Chesterfield [26]	63.33	29	0.695	86	1.030	76
Smyth	62.20	30	0.285	19	0.147	26
Brunswick	62.13	31	0.622	71	1.589	103
Brooke	61.70	32	0.313	24	0.012	2.5
Greensville	61.67	33	1.187	108	2.084	107
Montgomery and Wythe [27]	61.17	34	0.306	23	0.257	34
Lunenburg	60.13	35	0.654	76.5	1.578	102
Nottoway	59.87	36	1.047	105	2.670	109
Harrison, Lewis, Monon- galia, Randolph, and Wood [28]	59.54	37	0.164	6	0.035	9.5
Mathews	59.53	38	0.354	33	0.801	63
Preston	58.90	39	0.185	10	0.013	4
Pendleton	58.60	40	0.227	14	0.071	14
Moderate Democratic						
Bath	57.43	41	0.408	42	0.322	37
Prince Edward	57.33	42.5	0.940	101	1.561	101
Tyler	57.33	42.5	0.176	8	0.012	2.5
Morgan	55.80	44	0.267	18	0.033	8
Stafford	55.70	45	0.421	45	0.740	58
Frederick	55.60	46	0.475	55	0.193	30
King and Queen	55.57	47	0.585	69	1.205	87
Buckingham	55.23	48	0.751	94	1.417	98
Monroe	54.77	49	0.198	11.5	0.115	20
Middlesex	54.37	50	0.540	66	1.012	75
Caroline	54.10	51.5	0.627	73.5	1.375	96
Clarke	54.10	51.5	1.394	109	1.098	80
Fluvanna	53.37	53	0.535	63	0.889	70
Franklin	53.33	54	0.259	17	0.483	44
Charlotte	52.97	55	0.961	103	1.736	105
Spotsylvania	52.87	56	0.670	82	1.003	74
Marshall	52.70	57	0.250	16	0.007	1
Patrick	52.67	58	0.167	7	0.300	36
Jackson	52.53	59	0.198	11.5	0.018	6

Virginia Constituency 1836–1844 [17]	Per Cent of Votes Cast for Democratic Nominees [18]	Democratic Rank	Tax Per Capita Paid in 1840 (in dollars) [19]	Economic Rank	Average Slaveholding in 1840 [20]	Rank in Slaveholding
Neutral						
Powhatan	52.00	60.5	1.018	104	1.835	106
Hanover	52.00	60.5	0.698	87	1.277	91
Southampton	51.67	62	0.439	50	0.822	66
Braxton	51.53	63	0.149	3	0.025	7
Cabell [29]	50.63	64	0.882	100	0.075	16
Rappahannock	49.53	65	0.467	54	0.655	53
Amherst	49.43	66	0.441	51	0.850	67
Dinwiddie [30]	49.10	67	0.567	68	1.234	89
Hampshire	48.93	68	0.305	22	0.129	23
Nelson	48.13	69	0.522	61	0.944	72
Moderate Whig						
Albemarle	47.27	70	0.690	84	1.062	78
Petersburg, City of	46.50	71	0.817	97	0.485	45
Fairfax	46.30	72	0.460	53	0.584	49
Fayette	46.27	73	0.184	9	0.035	9.5
Richmond	45.90	74.5	0.381	38	0.656	54
Culpeper	45.90	74.5	0.654	76.5	1.140	84
Rockbridge	45.80	76	0.348	32	0.326	38
Cumberland	45.60	77	1.178	107	2.826	110
Mason	45.03	78	0.333	29	0.135	24
Norfolk [31]	44.90	79	0.479	56	0.567	48
Henrico [32]	44.87	80	0.700	88	0.796	62
Campbell	44.83	81	0.695	85	0.914	71
Fauquier	44.67	82	0.704	90	0.957	73
Jefferson [33]	44.50	83	0.533	62	0.419	43
Gloucester	44.07	84	0.539	65	1.133	82
Henry	43.63	85	0.340	30	0.636	52
Pittsylvania	43.20	86	0.405	40	0.779	59
Strong Whig						
Bedford	42.23	87	0.394	39	0.782	60
New Kent	41.93	88	0.553	67	1.190	86
Berkeley	41.23	89	0.486	57	0.212	31
Lancaster	40.17	90	0.595	70	1.153	85
Essex	39.60	91	0.668	81	1.484	99
Elizabeth City	39.37	92	0.538	64	0.855	68
King George	36.97	93	0.722	92	1.329	93

TABLE III (*Continued*)

Virginia Constituency 1836–1844[17]	Per Cent of Votes Cast for Democratic Nominees [18]	Demo-cratic Rank	Tax Per Capita Paid in 1840 (in dollars) [19]	Eco-nomic Rank	Average Slave-holding in 1840 [20]	Rank in Slave-holding
Nansemond	36.57	94	0.434	49	0.723	56
Norfolk, City of	36.40	95	0.958	102	0.514	46
Princess Anne	35.37	96	0.494	59	0.735	57
Very Strong Whig						
Greenbrier	34.90	97	0.492	58	0.162	27
Hardy	32.63	98	0.443	52	0.174	28
Kanawha	30.17	99	0.321	26	0.233	32
Augusta	28.83	100	0.508	60	0.267	35
Ohio	28.47	101	0.368	36	0.016	5
Accomack	24.83	102	0.355	34	0.371	42
Richmond, City of	24.50	103	3.962	110	0.594	50
Loudoun	22.80	104	0.660	79	0.348	40
Westmoreland	21.93	105	0.427	48	0.811	65
York [34]	20.00	106	0.380	37	0.810	64
Charles City	18.50	107	0.627	73.5	1.039	77
James City [35]	16.70	108	0.811	96	1.063	79
Northampton	13.80	109	0.625	72	0.884	69
Warwick	13.50	110	0.785	95	1.330	94

NOTES TO TABLES

1. The use of statistical techniques has allowed me, I hope, to be clearer, more logical, and persuasive in presenting my argument about the nature of political support in Mississippi, Ohio, and Virginia. However, it should be made clear that any attempt to "quantify" a historical problem raises a number of difficulties. By using rank-difference correlations to indicate the closeness of the association between wealth and politics or slaveholding and politics, I do not wish to imply that I believe that the economic factor is the sole motivating force in shaping political response. Indeed, I have used the correlations and political and economic rankings only as the underlying foundation for my analysis and hopefully have enriched the discussion by an impressionistic consideration of factors that do not lend themselves to quantification, such as geographic, social, and ethnocultural characteristics.

In one way the use of statistical data makes answers neater and more precise, but it also suggests many questions. For example, I have used counties (and, in a few instances, cities) as the basic electoral units for analysis, recognizing that there are certain drawbacks to this approach. I am not as skeptical of this data as is Professor Thomas B. Alexander, but he and his associates do have a point when they argue, in "The Basis of Alabama's Ante-Bellum Two-Party System" (pp. 247, 255), that a county can be too large an entity to study "economic factors in relation to voter preferences" because "the parties were often fairly closely balanced in a county, and the various neighborhoods may have differed greatly in soil characteristics and other aspects of economic significance." Certainly, under ideal conditions it would be preferable to examine local constituencies even smaller than counties. However, when one wishes to examine a state as a whole, or several states, the question is not whether to use county data or local data, but whether to use county data or no data. Reliable social and economic data earlier than that in the 1850 Census are difficult to uncover, even for counties. But data including election returns for smaller geographic units are virtually non-existent and never available on a consistent, parallel, and systematic basis throughout a single state, much less three states.

Above and beyond Professor Alexander's contention, there are inherent problems in using ecological correlations, and readers should be warned against drawing the wrong kind of conclusions from them. Social, economic, and political characteristics of a constituency cannot be transferred to individuals within the constituency. In other words, if a strong Jacksonian county has few slaves per capita and little taxable wealth, this does not necessarily mean that all Jacksonians within that county will have few slaves and small amounts of taxable real and personal property. (See Lynn L. Marshall, "The Genesis of Grassroots Democracy in Kentucky," *Mid-America: An Historical Review,* XLVII, October, 1965, footnote on page 279; and W. A. Robinson, "Ecological Correlations and the Behavior of Individuals," *American Sociological Review,* XV, 1950, 16–38). Therefore, readers should infer only that certain characteristics seem to be typical of Whig constituencies and other characteristics seem to be typical of Democratic constituencies.

With all apologies made, it remains to be said that it is my belief that an honest and objective appraisal of admittedly imperfect data is better than no appraisal.

2. Included are all Mississippi counties formed by 1836, except Coahoma, Perry, and Tunica, which have been excluded because no returns were submitted by these counties for the presidential election of 1836.

3. Counties are ranked—from the strongest to the weakest in Democratic standing—on the basis of percentage of votes cast for Democratic nominees in the presidential elections of 1836, 1840, and 1844. Each election is weighted equally. Election data were obtained from Walter Burnham's *Presidential Ballots* (Baltimore, 1955), 554–71, 924–26. Presidential elections were used to determine constituency political affiliation in order to provide uniformity of data for the three states. For example, gubernatorial elections might have been used to determine affiliations in Ohio, but they would have been of limited value in organizing data for Mississippi, where more than two candidates contended for the office in several of the elections. In Virginia the governor was elected by the legislature, and presidential elections provided the only statewide political canvass.

4. Counties are ranked—from the poorest to the wealthiest per capita (free

population only)—on the basis of aggregate (real estate and personal) taxes paid in 1845 (as reported in the Jackson *Mississippian,* October 29, 1845). County populations for 1845 were estimated by computing the geographic mean between the 1840 and 1850 free populations. Population data were obtained from: Department of State, *Compendium of the Sixth Census* (Washington, D.C., 1841), 56–59; and J. D. B. De Bow, *Statistical View of the United States; . . . Being a Compendium of the Seventh Census* (Washington, D.C., 1854), 260.

5. Counties are ranked—from lowest to highest—on the basis of the number of slaves per capita (free population only) in 1840. Slave and free population data were obtained from: Department of State, *Compendium of the Sixth Census,* 56–59.

6. For information about categories, see Footnote 10, Chapter IV.

7. Data on Harrison County (formed in 1841 from Hancock County) are included here with Hancock County.

8. Data on Sunflower County (formed in 1844 from Bolivar County) are included here with Bolivar County.

9. Data on Issaquena County (formed in 1844 from Washington County) are included here with Washington County.

10. Included are all Ohio counties formed by 1836 except Van Wert, which has been excluded because no returns were submitted by this county for the presidential elections of 1836 and 1840. County boundary changes between 1836 and 1844 necessitated county groupings in a few instances.

11. Constituencies are ranked—from strongest to weakest in Democratic standing—on the basis of the percentage of votes cast for Democratic nominees in the presidential elections of 1836, 1840 and 1844. Each election is weighted equally. Election data were obtained from Burnham's *Presidential Ballots,* 678–96, 937–38.

12. Constituencies are ranked—from poorest to wealthiest per capita (free population only)—on the basis of "Grand Aggregate of Real Estate and Improvements as Equalized" in 1840, as computed by John Brough, Auditor of Ohio, in a special report submitted to the Ohio General Assembly on Feb. 24, 1841. Included in the total were the values of lands, improvements, and town lots, including buildings. See Ohio General Assembly, "Special Report of the Auditor of the State," *Executive Document No. 69* (Columbus, 1841). County populations for 1840 were obtained from: Department of State, *Compendium of the Sixth Census,* 76–79.

13. Data on Ottawa County (formed in 1840 from Sandusky County) are included here with Sandusky County.

14. The formation of Summit County in 1840 from Medina, Portage, and Stark counties necessitated grouping these counties together. Data on Summit also are included, after 1840.

15. Data on Erie County (formed in 1838 from Huron County) are included here with Huron County.

16. The formation of Lake County in 1840 from Cuyahoga and Geauga counties necessitated grouping these counties together. Data on Lake also are included, after 1840.

17. Included are all Virginia counties formed by 1836 except Floyd, whose 1836 presidential election returns were not accepted as valid by the state, and

Nicholas, about which there is no information regarding the returns for the 1844 presidential election. County boundary changes between 1836 and 1844 necessitated county groupings in a few instances. Also listed are three cities that voted separately: Norfolk, Petersburg, and Richmond.

18. Constituencies are ranked—from strongest to weakest in Democratic standing—on the basis of the percentage of votes cast for Democratic nominees in the presidential elections are 1836, 1840, and 1844. Each election is weighted equally. Election data was obtained from Burnham's *Presidential Ballots,* 818–42, 852–64, 948–51.

19. Constituencies are ranked—from poorest to wealthiest per capita (free population only)—on the basis of land and personal property taxes paid in 1840. Tax data was obtained from: Manuscript Land and Personal Property Tax Lists, Virginia State Library, Richmond. Also Manuscript Land Tax Lists, State Auditor's Office, Charleston, West Virginia. County populations for 1840 were obtained from: Department of State, *Compendium of the Sixth Census,* 32–39.

20. Constituencies are ranked—from lowest to highest—on the basis of the number of slaves per capita (free population only) in 1840. Slave and free population data were obtained from: Department of State, *Compendium of the Sixth Census,* 32–39.

21. Data on Carroll County (formed in 1842 from Grayson County) are included here with Grayson County.

22. The formation of Mercer County in 1837 from Giles and Tazewell counties necessitated grouping these counties together. Data on Mercer also are included, after 1837.

23. Data on Roanoke County (formed in 1838 from Botetourt County) are included here with Botetourt County.

24. Not including City of Petersburg.

25. Data on Greene County (formed in 1838 from Orange County) are included here with Orange County.

26. Not including cities of Petersburg or Richmond.

27. The formation of Pulaski County in 1839 from Montgomery and Wythe counties necessitated grouping these counties together. Data on Pulaski County also are included, after 1839.

28. The formation of Marion County in 1842 (from Harrison and Monongalia), Barbour County in 1843 (from Harrison, Lewis, and Randolph counties), Ritchie County in 1843 (from Harrison, Lewis, and Wood counties), and Taylor County in 1844 (from Barbour, Harrison, and Marion counties) necessitated grouping all these counties together. Also included are data on Marion, Barbour, Ritchie, and Taylor counties, after each was formed.

29. Data on Wayne County (formed in 1842 from Cabell County) are included here with Cabell County.

30. Not including City of Petersburg.

31. Including City of Portsmouth but excluding City of Norfolk.

32. Not including City of Richmond.

33. Data on the 1840 land tax for Jefferson County are not available. Therefore, the 1840 land tax has been estimated here by computing the geographic mean between the 1839 and 1841 taxes.

34. Not including City of Williamsburg.

35. Including City of Williamsburg. Data for the 1839 and 1840 personal property taxes for the City of Williamsburg are not available. Therefore the 1840 personal property tax for the city has been estimated here by computing the geographic mean between the 1838 and 1841 taxes.

Appendix B

COMPUTATION OF THE AVERAGE SPECIE HOLDINGS OF BANKS IN RELATION TO THEIR NOTE CIRCULATIONS AND DEPOSITS IN THE VARIOUS SECTIONS AND STATES FROM 1834 TO 1850
Figures show the average amount of specie held by banks for each dollar of their obligations in notes and deposits. Statistics are compiled from Comptroller's Report, 1876, 96–121. The designation, "N.A." indicates that data are not available.

TABLE I
SOUTHWESTERN STATES

Year	Alabama	Louisiana	Mississippi	Arkansas	Average in Southwest
1834	0.151	N.A.	0.055	N.A.	0.103
1835	0.194	0.231	0.083	N.A.	0.169
1836	0.168	0.138	0.060	N.A.	0.122
1837	0.155	0.160	0.131	N.A.	0.149
1838	0.056	0.182	0.063	1.012	0.328
1839	0.144	0.286	N.A.	0.530	0.320
1840	N.A.	0.292	0.036	0.151	0.160
1841	0.158	0.332	N.A.	0.179	0.223
1842	0.253	N.A.	0.004	N.A.	0.013
1843	0.043	0.693	N.A.	N.A.	0.368
1844	0.900	0.963	N.A.	N.A.	0.932
1845	0.832	0.788	N.A.	0.065	0.842
1846	0.488	0.486	N.A.	N.A.	0.487
1847	N.A.	0.449	N.A.	N.A.	0.449
1848	0.398	0.613	N.A.	N.A.	0.505
1849	0.218	0.647	N.A.	N.A.	0.432
1850	0.346	0.526	N.A.	N.A.	0.436

TABLE II
NORTHWESTERN STATES

Year	Ohio	Tennessee	Kentucky	Indiana	Illinois
1834	N.A.	0.052	N.A.	N.A.	N.A.
1835	0.234	0.075	0.024	1.288	0.802
1836	0.185	0.037	0.208	0.238	0.309
1837	0.198	0.058	0.193	0.256	0.247
1838	0.260	0.145	0.298	0.375	0.246
1839	0.241	0.339	0.222	0.391	0.186
1840	0.264	N.A.	0.253	0.304	0.167
1841	0.191	0.203	0.234	0.323	0.206
1842	N.A.	0.245	0.322	0.354	N.A.
1843	0.293	0.362	0.433	0.398	0.334
1844	0.288	0.314	0.380	0.382	N.A.
1845	0.266	0.348	0.381	0.327	0.064
1846	0.166	0.289	0.325	0.275	N.A.
1847	0.200	0.216	0.361	0.265	N.A.
1848	0.202	0.249	0.345	0.255	N.A.
1849	0.224	0.257	0.321	0.299	N.A.
1850	0.215	0.219	0.302	0.324	N.A.

Year	Michigan	Wisconsin	Missouri	Average in Northwest
1834	N.A.	N.A.	N.A.	0.052
1835	0.085	N.A.	0.295	0.400
1836	0.052	N.A.	0.269	0.185
1837	0.151	N.A.	0.099	0.172
1838	0.143	0.452	0.745	0.333
1839	0.128	0.190	0.390	0.261
1840	0.071	0.349	0.355	0.252
1841	0.165	N.A.	0.759	0.297
1842	N.A.	N.A.	0.295	0.304
1843	0.357	N.A.	0.440	0.374
1844	0.260	N.A.	0.755	0.396
1845	0.302	N.A.	0.416	0.301
1846	0.213	0.280	0.406	0.279
1847	0.238	N.A.	0.511	0.298
1848	0.216	N.A.	0.614	0.313
1849	0.195	N.A.	0.564	0.310
1850	0.120	N.A.	0.479	0.276

TABLE III
SOUTHEASTERN STATES

Year	Delaware	Virginia	North Carolina	South Carolina	Georgia	Maryland	Average in Southeast
1834	N.A.	0.111	0.057	0.201	N.A.	0.131	0.125
1835	N.A.	0.133	N.A.	0.217	0.378	N.A.	0.182
1836	0.157	0.132	0.116	0.136	0.231	0.187	0.160
1837	0.133	0.113	0.188	0.167	0.260	0.140	0.167
1838	0.108	0.134	0.233	0.274	0.260	0.197	0.201
1839	0.128	0.208	0.268	0.275	0.318	0.209	0.234
1840	N.A.	0.198	0.212	0.341	0.173	0.211	0.227
1841	0.133	0.241	0.311	0.290	0.253	0.275	0.251
1842	0.165	0.230	0.341	0.218	0.146	0.326	0.238
1843	0.169	0.301	0.441	0.286	0.398	0.538	0.354
1844	0.177	0.282	0.368	0.307	N.A.	0.610	0.349
1845	0.138	0.252	0.366	0.275	N.A.	0.336	0.273
1846	0.125	0.213	0.351	0.143	0.291	N.A.	0.225
1847	0.164	0.247	0.357	0.134	0.329	0.319	0.258
1848	0.171	0.223	0.377	0.163	0.333	0.307	0.262
1849	0.123	0.207	0.384	0.142	0.266	0.317	0.240
1850	0.157	0.205	0.341	0.159	N.A.	0.298	0.232

TABLE IV
NORTHEASTERN STATES

Year	Maine	New Hampshire	Massachusetts	Vermont	Rhode Island
1834	0.060	0.256	0.055	0.033	0.133
1835	0.055	N.A.	0.051	N.A.	0.169
1836	0.108	0.229	0.074	0.032	N.A.
1837	0.098	0.281	0.062	0.056	0.061
1838	0.136	0.094	0.126	0.066	0.134
1839	0.085	0.092	0.126	0.057	0.134
1840	0.103	0.128	0.169	0.090	0.212
1841	0.103	0.117	0.187	0.052	0.108
1842	0.077	0.127	0.189	0.084	0.126
1843	0.106	0.128	0.376	0.050	0.139
1844	0.088	0.097	0.189	0.046	0.086
1845	0.062	0.075	0.129	0.078	0.069

TABLE IV (*Continued*)

Year	Maine	New Hampshire	Massachusetts	Vermont	Rhode Island
1846	0.076	0.066	0.127	0.047	0.073
1847	0.113	0.071	0.144	0.039	0.077
1848	0.152	0.083	0.121	0.060	0.081
1849	0.100	0.080	0.104	0.046	0.066
1850	0.123	0.068	0.106	0.037	0.074

Year	Connecticut	New York	New Jersey	Pennsylvania	Average in Northeast
1834	0.033	0.072	N.A.	0.144	0.098
1835	0.033	0.196	N.A.	0.207	0.117
1836	N.A.	0.123	N.A.	0.160	0.121
1837	0.076	0.119	0.116	0.117	0.110
1838	0.192	0.146	0.193	0.192	0.142
1839	0.095	0.175	0.187	0.168	0.124
1840	0.156	0.216	0.137	0.166	0.153
1841	0.114	0.168	0.169	0.195	0.135
1842	0.130	0.171	0.229	0.138	0.141
1843	0.128	0.270	0.185	0.289	0.186
1844	0.083	0.208	0.149	0.272	0.135
1845	0.075	0.149	0.139	0.200	0.108
1846	0.075	0.154	0.135	0.177	0.100
1847	0.074	0.166	0.186	N.A.	0.109
1848	0.075	0.122	0.152	0.158	0.112
1849	0.091	0.097	0.140	0.176	0.100
1850	0.082	0.109	0.141	0.141	0.098

BIBLIOGRAPHY

I. MANUSCRIPT COLLECTIONS

William Allen Papers. Library of Congress. Washington, D.C.
James Martin Bell Papers. Duke University. Durham, N.C.
Nicholas Biddle Papers. Library of Congress. Washington, D.C.
Sidney Breese Papers. Illinois State Historical Library. Springfield, Ill.
James Buchanan Papers. Library of Congress. Washington, D.C.
————. State Historical Society of Pennsylvania. Philadelphia, Pa.
Simon Cameron Papers. Library of Congress. Washington, D.C.
David Campbell Papers. Duke University. Durham, N.C.
Salmon P. Chase Papers. Library of Congress. Washington, D.C.
John Francis Hamtramck Claiborne Papers. Library of Congress. Washington, D.C.
————. Mississippi Department of Archives and History. Jackson, Miss.
————. Southern Historical Collection. University of North Carolina. Chapel Hill, N.C.
Peter V. Daniel Papers. University of Virginia. Charlottesville, Va.
Jefferson Davis Papers. Library of Congress. Washington, D.C.
Andrew Jackson Donelson Papers. Library of Congress. Washington, D.C.
Stephen A. Douglas Papers. Illinois State Historical Library. Springfield, Ill.
George Coke Dromgoole Papers. Southern Historical Collection. University of North Carolina. Chapel Hill, N.C.
George Coke Dromgoole and Richard B. Robinson Papers. Duke University. Durham, N.C.
Edgehill-Randolph Papers. University of Virginia. Charlottesville, Va.
Franklin H. Elmore Papers. Library of Congress. Washington, D.C.
John Fairfield Papers. Library of Congress. Washington, D.C.
Azariah C. Flagg Papers. New York Public Library. New York, N.Y.
Augustus C. French Papers. Illinois State Historical Library. Springfield, Ill.
Gooch Family Papers. University of Virginia. Charlottesville, Va.
William M. Gwin Papers. Bancroft Library. University of California. Berkeley, Calif.
Charles Hammond Papers. Ohio Historical Society. Columbus, Ohio.
Hunter and Garnett Family Papers. University of Virginia. Charlottesville, Va.

Charles Jared Ingersoll Papers. Historical Society of Pennsylvania. Philadelphia, Pa.

Andrew Jackson Papers. Library of Congress. Washington, D.C.

John A. McClernand Papers. Illinois State Historical Library. Springfield, Ill.

McDowell Family Papers. University of Virginia. Charlottesville, Va.

James McDowell, Jr., Papers. Duke University. Durham, N.C.

———. Southern Historical Collection. University of North Carolina. Chapel Hill, N.C.

Duncan McLaurin Papers. Duke University. Durham, N.C.

William H. McLaurin Papers. Southern Historical Collection. University of North Carolina. Chapel Hill, N.C.

Alexander Gallatin McNutt Papers. Duke University. Durham, N.C.

William L. Marcy Papers. Library of Congress. Washington, D.C.

Samuel Medary Papers. Ohio Historical Society. Columbus, Ohio.

William Medill Papers. Library of Congress. Washington, D.C.

Mississippi Governors' Executive Journal and Official Correspondence. Mississippi Department of Archives and History. Jackson, Miss.

Ohio Governors' Official Papers. Ohio Historical Society. Columbus, Ohio.

David R. Porter Papers. Historical Society of Pennsylvania. Philadelphia, Pa.

John A. Quitman Papers. Southern Historical Collection. University of North Carolina. Chapel Hill, N.C.

———. University of Virginia. Charlottesville, Va.

Charles Reemelin Papers. Cincinnati Historical Society. Cincinnati, Ohio.

Thomas Ritchie Papers. Library of Congress. Washington, D.C.

Thomas Ritchie Miscellaneous Papers. University of Virginia. Charlottesville, Va.

Ritchie-Harrison Papers. College of William and Mary. Williamsburg, Va.

William C. Rives Papers. Library of Congress. Washington, D.C.

John Rutherfoord Papers. Duke University. Durham, N.C.

Simon Ryder Papers. Illinois State Historical Library. Springfield, Ill.

Edwin McMasters Stanton Papers. Library of Congress. Washington, D.C.

Andrew Stevenson Papers. Library of Congress. Washington, D.C.

Alexander H. H. Stuart Papers. University of Virginia. Charlottesville, Va.

Benjamin Tappan Papers. Library of Congress. Washington, D.C.

Benjamin Tappan Papers. Ohio Historical Society. Columbus, Ohio.

Tazewell Family Papers. Virginia State Library. Richmond, Va.

Lyman Trumbull Papers. Illinois State Historical Library. Springfield, Ill.

John Tyler Papers. Library of Congress. Washington, D.C.

Martin Van Buren Papers. Library of Congress. Washington, D.C.

Virginia Executive Letter Books. Virginia State Library. Richmond, Va.

Virginia Manuscript Land and Personal Property Tax Lists, 1840. Virginia State Library. Richmond, Va.

Benjamin Wade Papers. Library of Congress. Washington, D.C.

Robert J. Walker Papers. Library of Congress. Washington, D.C.

Gideon Welles Papers. Library of Congress. Washington, D.C.

West Virginia Manuscript Land Tax Lists, 1840. State Auditor's Office. Charleston, W. Va.

Levi Woodbury Papers. Library of Congress. Washington, D.C.

Joseph Wright Papers. Indiana State Library. Indianapolis, Ind.

Hendrick B. Wright Papers. Wyoming Historical and Geological Society Library. Wilkes-Barre, Pa.

Silas Wright, Jr., Papers. New York Public Library. New York, N.Y.

II. PRINTED CORRESPONDENCE, PERSONAL MEMOIRS, TRAVEL ACCOUNTS, AND GAZETEERS

Anonymous. *Nine Years of Democratic Rule in Mississippi: Being Notes Upon the Political History of the State, From the Beginning of the Year 1838 to the Present Time.* Jackson, Miss., 1847.

Baldwin, Joseph G. *The Flush Times of Alabama and Mississippi: A Series of Sketches.* San Francisco, 1889.

Benton, Thomas Hart. *Thirty Years' View; Or a History of the Working of the American Government for Thirty Years, from 1820–1850.* 2 vols. New York, 1854–1856.

Besancon, Lorenzo Augustus. *Besancon's Annual Register of the State of Mississippi.* Natchez, Miss., 1838.

Biddle, Nicholas. *The Correspondence of Nicholas Biddle Dealing with National Affairs, 1807–1844.* Edited by Reginald C. McGrane. Boston, 1919.

Buchanan, James. *The Works of James Buchanan, Comprising His Speeches, State Papers, and Private Correspondence.* Edited by John Bassett Moore. 12 vols. Philadelphia, 1908–1911.

Cist, Charles. *Cincinnati in 1841: Its Early Annals and Future Prospects.* Cincinnati, 1841.

Claiborne, John Francis Hamtramck. "A Trip Through the Piney Woods," Mississippi Historical Society *Publications,* IX (1906), 487–538.

Davis, Jefferson. *Jefferson Davis, Constitutionalist, His Letters, Papers, Speeches.* Edited by Dunbar Rowland. 10 vols. Jackson, Miss., 1923.

Davis, Reuben. *Recollections of Mississippi and Mississippians.* Boston, 1889.

Dix, Morgan, compiler. *Memoirs of John Adams Dix.* 2 vols. New York, 1883.

Edwards, Richard, editor. *Statistical Gazetteer of the State of Virginia.* Richmond, 1855.

Garrett, William. *Reminiscences of Public Men in Alabama for Thirty Years.* Atlanta, 1872.

Greeley, Horace. *Recollections of a Busy Life: Including Reminiscences of American Politics and Politicians, From the Opening of the Missouri Contest to the Downfall of Slavery.* New York, 1869.

Howells, William Cooper. *Recollections of Life in Ohio, From 1813–1840.* Cincinnati, 1895.

Hunter, Robert M. T. *Correspondence of Robert M. T. Hunter, 1826–1876.* Edited by Charles H. Ambler. American Historical Association *Annual Report,* 1916, II. Washington, D.C., 1918.

Jackson, Andrew. *Correspondence of Andrew Jackson.* Edited by John Spencer Bassett. 7 vols. Washington D.C., 1926–1935.

Jenkins, Warren. *The Ohio Gazetteer and Traveller's Guide.* Revised edition. Columbus, 1841.

Koerner, Gustave. *Memoirs of Gustave Koerner, 1809–1896.* Edited by Thomas J. McCormack. 2 vols. Cedar Rapids, Iowa, 1909.

Martin, Joseph. *A Comprehensive Description of Virginia and the District of Columbia: Containing a Copious Collection of Geographical, Statistical, Political, Commercial, Religious, Moral, and Miscellaneous Information, Chiefly From Original Sources.* Richmond, Va., date unknown, probably 1835.

Martineau, Harriet. *Society in America,* I. London, 1837.

McCulloch, Hugh. *Men and Measures of Half a Century.* New York, 1888.

Orr, J. A. "A Trip from Houston to Jackson, Miss., in 1845," *Publications of the Mississippi Historical Society,* IX (1906), 173–78.

Prentiss, George L., editor. *A Memoir of S. S. Prentiss.* 2 vols. New York, 1861.

Quitman, John A. *Life and Correspondence of John A. Quitman.* Edited by John Francis Hamtramck Claiborne. 2 vols. New York, 1860.

Steele, Mrs. Eliza R. *A Summer Journey in the West.* New York, 1841.

Trollope, Mrs. Frances. *Domestic Manners of the Americans.* New York, 1949.

Whealen, John J. "The Jackson-Dawson Correspondence," Historical and Philosophical Society of Ohio *Bulletin,* XVI (January, 1958).

Wills, William H. "A Southern Traveler's Diary, 1840," *Publications of the Southern History Association,* VII (1903), 349–52 and 427–32; VIII (1904), 23–39 and 129–38.

Wise, Henry A. *Seven Decades of the Union.* Philadelphia, 1881.

III. FEDERAL AND STATE DOCUMENTS

Louisiana. *Proceedings and Debates of the Convention of Louisiana.* 1844.

Louisiana House of Representatives. *Journal.* 1837–1838, 1841–1842.

Mississippi House of Representatives. *Journal.* 1838, 1842, 1843 (special session).

Mississippi Senate. *Journal.* 1838.

Ohio. *Report of the Debates and Proceedings of the Convention for the Revision of the Constitution of the State of Ohio, 1850–1851.*

Ohio General Assembly. "Special Report of the Auditor of the State," *Executive Document No. 69* (Columbus, Ohio, 1841).

Richardson, James D. *A Compilation of the Messages and Papers of the Presidents.* 11 vols. Washington, D.C., 1911.

United States Bureau of the Census. *Historical Statistics of the United States, Colonial Times to 1957.*

United States Comptroller of the Currency. *Annual Report for 1876.*

United States Department of State. *Compendium of the Enumeration of the Inhabitants and Statistics of the United States, as Obtained at the Department of State, From the Returns of the Sixth Census.* Washington, D.C., 1841.

United States House of Representatives. *Executive Document No. 227 (Letter from the Secretary of Treasury Transmitting Statements, and, in Relation to the Condition of the State Banks).* 25th Congress, 3rd Session.

———. *Executive Document No. 172 (Letter from the Secretary of the Treasury Transmitting Statements Showing the Condition of the State Banks).* 26th Congress, 1st Session.

———. *Executive Document No. 111 (Letter from the Secretary of the Treasury, in Obedience to the Resolution of the House of Representatives of July 10, 1832, Statements Showing the Condition of the Several State Banks).* 26th Congress, 2nd Session.

———. *Executive Document No. 226 (Report of the Secretary of the*

Treasury, of the Return of the State Banks from 1841 to 1846). 29th Congress, 1st Session.

United States Senate. *Executive Document No. 471 (Report from the Secretary of Treasury)*. 25th Congress, 2nd Session.

IV. NEWSPAPERS AND PERIODICALS

Albany (N.Y.) *Argus.*
Boston (Mass.) *Columbian Centinel.*
Charleston (S.C.) *Courier.*
Chillicothe (Ohio) *Scioto Gazette.*
Cincinnati (Ohio) *Advertiser and Journal.*
Cincinnati (Ohio) *Enquirer.*
Cleveland (Ohio) *Plain Dealer.*
Columbus (Ohio) *Daily Journal and Register.*
Columbus *Ohio State Journal.*
Columbus (Ohio) *New Constitution.*
Jackson (Miss.) *Mississippian.*
Jackson (Miss.) *Southern Sun.*
Jackson (Miss.) *Southron.*
Jackson (Miss.) *Statesman.*
Jackson (Miss.) *State Telegraph.*
Jackson (Miss.) *Tri-Weekly Mississippian.*
Natchez (Miss.) *Free Trader.*
New Orleans (La.) *Daily Picayune.*
Niles' Register (Baltimore and Washington, D.C.).
Port Gibson (Miss.) *Correspondent.*
Richmond (Va.) *Enquirer.*
Richmond (Va.) *Whig.*
Washington (D.C.) *Globe.*
Whig Almanac (New York, N.Y.)

V. GENERAL WORKS

Abernathy, Thomas P. "Andrew Jackson and the Rise of Southwestern Democracy," *American Historical Review*, XXXII, (October, 1927), 64–77.

Adams, James Truslow. *New England in the Republic, 1776–1850.* Boston, 1926.

Atherton, Lewis E. *The Pioneer Merchant in Mid-America.* Columbia, Mo., 1939.

Baker, Henry F. *Banks and Banking in the United States.* Boston, 1853.

———. "Outline History of Banking in the United States: A Sketch of the Progress of Banking in the Several States of the United States," *Bankers' Magazine and Statistical Register,* IX (July, 1854), 1–16, and XI (August–December, 1856), 81–89, 161–76, 241–56, 321–41, 417–30.

Bell, Daniel. *The End of Ideology: On the Exhaustion of Political Ideas in the Fifties.* New York, 1965.

Benson, Lee. "Research Problems in American Political Historiography," in Mirra Komarovsky, editor, *Common Frontiers of the Social Sciences.* Glencoe, Ill., 1957.

Berry, Thomas Senior. *Western Prices Before 1861: A Study of the Cincinnati Market.* Cambridge, Mass., 1943.

Bidwell, Percy W., and John I. Falconer. *History of Agriculture in the Northern United States, 1620–1860.* Washington, D.C., 1925.

Blau, Joseph L., editor. *Social Theories of Jacksonian Democracy: Representative Writings of the Period 1825–1850.* New York, 1947.

Brown, Richard H. "The Missouri Crisis, Slavery, and the Politics of Jacksonianism," *South Atlantic Quarterly,* LXV (Winter, 1966), 55–72.

Bruchey, Stuart. *The Roots of American Economic Growth, 1607–1861: An Essay in Social Causation.* New York, 1965.

Buley, R. Carlyle. *The Old Northwest, Pioneer Period, 1815–1840.* 2 vols. Indianapolis, Ind., 1950.

Burnham, Walter. *Presidential Ballots.* Baltimore, 1955.

Callender, Guy S. "The Early Transportation and Banking Enterprises of the States in Relation to the Growth of Corporations," *Quarterly Journal of Economics,* XVII (November, 1902), 111–62.

Cameron, Rondo. *Banking in the Early Stages of Industrialization: A Study in Comparative Economic History.* New York, 1967.

Campbell, Angus, Philip E. Converse, Warren E. Miller, and Donald E. Stokes. *The American Voter: An Abridgment.* New York, 1964.

Carroll, E. Malcolm. *Origins of the Whig Party.* Durham, N.C., 1925.

Cochran, Thomas C., and William Miller. *The Age of Enterprise: A Social History of Industrial America.* Revised edition. New York, 1961.

Cole, Arthur C. *The Whig Party in the South.* Washington, D.C., 1913.

Cole, Arthur Harrison. *Wholesale Commodity Prices in the United States, 1700–1861.* Cambridge, Mass., 1938.

Concise Dictionary of American Biography. New York, 1964.

Cone, Leon Winston, Jr. "Martin Van Buren: The Architect of the Democratic Party, 1837–1840." Unpublished Ph.D. thesis, University of Chicago, 1950.

Current, Richard N. *Daniel Webster and the Rise of National Conservatism.* Boston, 1955.

Dangerfield, George. *The Awakening of American Nationalism, 1815–1828.* New York, 1965.

———. *The Era of Good Feelings.* London, 1953.

Davis, Lance E. "The New England Textile Mills and the Capital Markets: A Study of Industrial Borrowing," *Journal of Economic History,* XX (March, 1960), 1–30.

Davis, William T., editor. *The New England States, Their Constitutional, Judicial, Educational, Commercial, Professional and Industrial History.* 4 vols. Boston, 1897.

De Bow, J. D. B. *Encyclopedia of the Trade and Commerce of the United States, More Particularly of the Southern and Western States.* London, 1854.

———. *The Industrial Resources, Etc., of the Southern and Western States.* 3 vols. New Orleans, 1852–1854.

Destler, Chester McArthur. *American Radicalism, 1865–1901.* Chicago, 1966.

Dewey, Davis R. *State Banking Before the Civil War.* Washington, D.C., 1910.

Dorfman, Joseph. *The Economic Mind in American Civilization, 1606–1918.* 3 vols. New York, 1946–1949.

Duverger, Maurice. *Political Parties, Their Organization and Activity in the Modern State.* London, 1962.

Eaton, Clement. *Henry Clay and the Art of American Politics.* Boston, 1957.

Faust, Albert Bernhardt. *The German Element in the United States; With Special Reference to its Political, Moral, Social, and Educational Influence.* 2 vols. Boston, 1909.

Fine, Sidney. *Laissez Faire and the General Welfare State: A Study of Conflict in American Thought, 1865–1901.* Ann Arbor, Mich., 1964.

Formisano, Ronald P., and William G. Shade. "The Concept of Agrarian Radicalism," *Mid-America,* LII (January, 1970), 3–30.

Foulke, Roy A. *The Sinews of American Commerce.* New York, 1941.

Garrett, Henry E. *Statistics in Psychology and Education.* New York, 1949.

Gatell, Frank Otto. "Sober Second Thoughts on Van Buren, The Albany Regency, and the Wall Street Conspiracy," *Journal of American History,* LIII (June, 1966), 19–40.

——. "Spoils of the Bank War: Political Bias in the Selection of Pet Banks," *American Historical Review,* LXX (October, 1964), 35–58.

Gates, Paul W. *The Farmers' Age: Agriculture, 1815–1860.* New York, 1960.

Genovese, Eugene D. *The Political Economy of Slavery: Studies in the Economy and Society of the Slave South.* New York, 1965.

Golembe, Carter H. "State Banks and the Economic Development of the West, 1830–1844." Unpublished Ph.D. thesis, Columbia University, 1952.

Goodman, William. *The Two-Party System in the United States.* 2nd edition. Princeton, N.J., 1960.

Goodrich, Carter. "Local Planning of Internal Improvements," *Political Science Quarterly,* LXVI (September, 1951), 411–45.

——. "National Planning of Internal Improvements," *Political Science Quarterly,* LXIII (March, 1948), 16–44.

——. "The Revulsion Against Internal Improvements," *Journal of Economic History,* X (November, 1950), 145–69.

Gouge, William M. *A Short History of Paper Money and Banking in the United States.* Philadelphia, 1833.

Govan, Thomas Payne. *Nicholas Biddle, Nationalist and Public Banker, 1786–1844.* Chicago, 1959.

Grace Madelein, Sister M. *Monetary and Banking Theories of Jacksonian Democracy.* Philadelphia, 1943.

Gray, Lewis Cecil. *History of Agriculture in the Southern United States to 1860.* 2 vols. Gloucester, Mass., 1958.

Green, Fletcher M. *Constitutional Development in the South Atlantic States, 1776–1860: A Study in the Evolution of Democracy.* Chapel Hill, N.C., 1930.

Greer, Thomas H. "Economic and Social Effects of the Depression of 1819 in the Old Northwest," *Indiana Magazine of History,* XLIV (September, 1948), 227–43.

Hamilton, Holman. *Prologue to Conflict: The Crisis and Compromise of 1850.* New York, 1966.

Hammond, Bray. *Banks and Politics in America: From the Revolution to the Civil War.* Princeton, 1957.

——. "Long and Short Term Credit in Early American Banking," *Quarterly Journal of Economics,* XLIX (November, 1934), 79–103.

———. "The North's Empty Purse," *American Historical Review,* LXVII (October, 1961), 1–18.

Handlin, Oscar, and Mary Flug Handlin. "Origins of the American Business Corporation," *Journal of Economic History,* V (May, 1945), 1–23.

Helderman, Leonard C. *National and State Banks: A Study of Their Origins.* Boston, 1931.

Hicks, John D. *The Populist Revolt: A History of the Farmers' Alliance and the People's Party* (Lincoln, Neb., 1961).

Hofstadter, Richard. *The American Political Tradition and the Men Who Made It.* New York, 1957.

———. *Age of Reform: From Bryan to F.D.R.* New York, 1960.

Holdsworth, J. T. "Lessons of State Banking Before the Civil War," Academy of Political Science *Proceedings,* I (January, 1911), 210–24.

Information Please Almanac Atlas and Yearbook, 1962. New York, 1961.

Key, V. O., Jr. *Politics, Parties, and Pressure Groups.* New York, 1953.

———. *Southern Politics in State and Nation.* New York, 1949.

Klement, Frank L. *The Copperheads in the Middle West.* Chicago, 1960.

Knox, John Jay. *A History of Banking in the United States.* New York, 1900.

Lane, Robert E. *Political Life: Why and How People Get Involved in Politics.* New York, 1965.

Lebowitz, Michael A. "The Significance of Claptrap in American History," *Studies on the Left,* III (Winter, 1963), 79–94.

Leonetti, Vincent Joseph. "The Effects of Certain Early 19th Century State Banking Laws and Institutions." Unpublished M.A. thesis, University of California at Berkeley, 1962.

Lively, Robert A. "The American System: A Review Article," *Business History Review,* XXIX (March, 1955), 81–96.

Lynch, William O. *Fifty Years of Party Warfare (1789–1837).* Indianapolis, 1931.

McCarthy, Charles. *The Antimasonic Party: A Study of Political Antimasonry in the United States, 1827–1840.* Washington, D.C., 1903.

McCormick, Richard P. "New Perspectives on Jacksonian Politics," *American Historical Review,* LXV (January, 1960), 288–301.

———. *The Second American Party System: Party Formation in the Jacksonian Era.* Chapel Hill, N.C., 1966.

Macesich, George. "Sources of Monetary Disturbances in the United States, 1834–45," *Journal of Economic History,* XX (September, 1960), 407–26.

McFaul, John Michael. "The Politics of Jacksonian Finance." Unpublished Ph.D. thesis, University of California at Berkeley, 1963.

McFaul, John Michael, and Frank Otto Gatell. "The Outcast Insider: Reuben M. Whitney and the Bank War," *Pennsylvania Magazine of History and Biography*, XCI (April, 1967), 115–44.

McGrane, Reginald C. *Foreign Bondholders and American State Debts*. New York, 1935.

———. *The Panic of 1837: Some Financial Problems of the Jacksonian Era*. Chicago, 1924.

MacLeod, Henry Dunning. *A History of Banking in Great Britain*. New York, 1896.

Main, Jackson Turner. *The Antifederalists, Critics of the Constitution, 1781–1788*. Chapel Hill, N.C., 1961.

Marshall, Lynn L. "The Authorship of Jackson's Bank Veto Message," *Mississippi Valley Historical Review*, L (December, 1963), 466–67.

———. "The Genesis of Grassroots Democracy in Kentucky," *Mid-America: An Historical Review*, XLVII (October, 1965), 269–87.

Merrill, Horace Samuel. *Bourbon Democracy of the Middle West, 1865–1896*. Baton Rouge, La., 1953.

Meyer, Balthasar H. *History of Transportation in the United States Before 1860*. Washington, D.C., 1917.

Meyers, Marvin. *The Jacksonian Persuasion, Politics and Belief*. New York, 1960.

Miller, Harry Edward. *Banking Theories in the United States Before 1860*. Cambridge, Mass., 1927.

Nettels, Curtis P. *The Emergence of a National Economy, 1775–1815*. New York, 1962.

North, Douglass C. *The Economic Growth of the United States, 1790–1860*. Englewood Cliffs, N.J., 1961.

Ostrogorski, Moisei. *Democracy and the Organization of Political Parties*. Abridged edition, edited by Seymour Martin Lipset. 2 vols. Garden City, N.Y., 1964.

Owsley, Frank Lawrence. *Plain Folk of the Old South*. Baton Rouge, La., 1949.

Parton, James. *Life of Andrew Jackson*. 3 vols. New York, 1860.

Paul, James C. N. *Rift in the Democracy*. New York, 1961.

Pessen, Edward. *Jacksonian America: Society, Personality, and Politics*. Homewood, Ill., 1969.

Pessen, Edward. "The Workingmen's Movement of the Jacksonian Era," *Mississippi Valley Historical Review*, XLIII (December, 1956), 428–43.

Phillips, Ulrich Bonnell. *Life and Labor in the Old South*. New York, 1929.

Pressly, Thomas J., and William H. Scofield. *Farm Real Estate Values in the United States by Counties, 1850–1959.* Seattle, Wash., 1965.

Ranney, Austin, editor. *Essays on the Behavioral Study of Politics.* Urbana, Ill., 1962.

Redlich, Fritz. *The Molding of American Banking: Men and Ideas.* 2 vols. New York, 1951.

Remini, Robert V. *The Election of Andrew Jackson.* Philadelphia, 1963.

Rezneck, Samuel. "Social History of an American Depression, 1837–1843," *American Historical Review,* XL (July, 1935), 662–87.

Robinson, W. A. "Ecological Correlations and the Behavior of Individuals," *American Sociological Review,* XV (1950), 16–38.

Ross, F. A. *The Old World in the New.* New York, 1914.

Rostow, W. W. "The Take-Off Into Self-Sustained Growth," *Economic Journal,* LXVI (March, 1956), 25–48.

Rothan, Reverend Emmet H. *The German Catholic Immigrant in the United States (1830–1860).* Washington, D.C., 1946.

Rothbard, Murray N. *The Panic of 1819: Reactions and Policies.* New York, 1962.

Sawyer, John E. "The Entrepreneur and the Social Order, France and the United States," in William Miller, editor, *Men in Business: Essays on the Historical Role of the Entrepreneur* (New York, 1962).

Scheiber, Harry N. "The Pet Banks in Jacksonian Politics and Finance, 1833–1841," *Journal of Economic History,* XXIII (June, 1963), 196–214.

Schlesinger, Arthur M., Jr. *The Age of Jackson.* Boston, 1945.

———. Review of Walter B. Smith's *Economic Aspects of the Second Bank of the United States,* in *American Historical Review,* LIX (October, 1953), 140–41.

Schmidt, Louis Bernard. "Internal Commerce and the Development of National Economy Before 1860," *Journal of Political Economy,* XLVII (December, 1939), 798–822.

Sellers, Charles Grier, Jr. "Andrew Jackson Versus the Historians," *Mississippi Valley Historical Review,* XLIV (March, 1958), 615–34.

———. "The Equilibrium Cycle in Two-Party Politics," *Public Opinion Quarterly,* XXIX (Spring, 1965), 16–38.

———. *James K. Polk, Jacksonian, 1795–1843.* Princeton, N.J., 1957.

———. "Who Were the Southern Whigs?" *American Historical Review,* LIX (January, 1954), 335–46.

Sharkey, Robert P. *Money, Class, and Party: An Economic Study of Civil War and Reconstruction.* Baltimore, 1959.

Smith, Walter B., and Arthur Harrison Cole. *Fluctuations in American Business, 1790–1860.* Cambridge, Mass., 1935.

Sumner, William Graham. *A History of Banking in the United States.* New York, 1896.

Sydnor, Charles S. *The Development of Southern Sectionalism, 1819–1848.* Baton Rouge, La., 1948.

Taylor, George Rogers. *The Transportation Revolution, 1815–1860.* New York, 1958.

Taylor, William R. *Cavalier and Yankee: The Old South and American National Character.* Garden City, N.Y., 1963.

Taylor of Caroline, John. *Construction Construed and Constitutions Vindicated.* Richmond, Va., 1820.

———. *An Inquiry Into the Principles and Policy of the Government of the United States.* New Haven, Conn., 1950.

Trescott, Paul B. *Financing American Enterprise: The Story of Commercial Banking.* New York, 1963.

Tucker, George. "Banks or No Banks," *Hunt's Merchants' Magazine and Commercial Review,* XXXVIII (February, 1858), 147–57.

———. *The Theory of Money and Banks Investigated.* New York, 1964.

Turner, Frederick Jackson. *The United States, 1830–1850.* Gloucester, Mass., 1958.

Unger, Irwin. *The Greenback Era: A Social and Political History of American Finance, 1865–1879.* Princeton, N.J., 1964.

Van Deusen, Glyndon G. *Horace Greeley, Nineteenth-Century Crusader.* New York, 1964.

———. *The Jacksonian Era, 1828–1848.* New York, 1959.

———. "Some Aspects of Whig Thought and Theory in the Jacksonian Period," *American Historical Review,* LXIII (January, 1958), 305–22.

Van Fenstermaker, Joseph. *The Development of American Commercial Banking, 1782–1837.* Kent, Ohio, 1965.

Wade, Richard C. *Slavery in the Cities: The South 1820–1860.* New York, 1964.

———. *The Urban Frontier: The Rise of Western Cities, 1790–1830.* Cambridge, Mass., 1959.

Webster, Homer J. "History of the Democratic Party Organization in the Northwest, 1824–1840," *Ohio Archaeological and Historical Publications,* XXIV (January, 1915), 1–120.

Wilburn, Jean Alexander. *Biddle's Bank: The Crucial Years.* New York, 1967.

Wilensky, Harold. "The Skidder: Ideological Adjustments of Downward

Mobile Workers," *American Sociological Review*, XXIV (1959), 215–31.
Wiltse, Charles M. *John C. Calhoun*. 3 vols. Indianapolis, 1944–1951.
Wirth, Max. *The History of Banking in Germany and Austria-Hungary*. New York, 1896.

VI. WORKS PERTAINING TO INDIVIDUAL STATES

ALABAMA

Abernathy, Thomas P. *The Formative Period in Alabama, 1815–1828*. Montgomery, Ala., 1922.
Alexander, Thomas B., Kit C. Carter, Jack R. Lister, Jerry C. Oldshue, and Winfred G. Sandlin. "Who Were the Alabama Whigs?" *The Alabama Review*, XVI (January, 1963), 5–19.
Alexander, Thomas B., Peggy Duckworth Elmore, Frank M. Lowrey, and Mary Jane Pickens Skinner. "The Basis of Alabama's Two-Party System," *The Alabama Review*, XIX (October, 1966), 243–76.
Brantley, William N. *Banking in Alabama, 1816–1860*. Birmingham, Ala., 1961.
Jackson, Carlton. "A History of the Whig Party in Alabama, 1828–1860." Unpublished Ph.D. thesis, University of Georgia, 1962.
McWhiney, Grady. "Were the Whigs a Class Party in Alabama?" *Journal of Southern History*, XXIII (November, 1957), 510–22.
Moore, Albert B. *History of Alabama*. University, Ala., 1935.
Scroggs, William O. "Pioneer Banking in Alabama," in *Facts and Factors in Economic History, Articles by Former Students of Edwin Francis Gay*. Cambridge, Mass., 1932.

ARKANSAS

Meek, Melinda. "The Life of Archibald Yell," *Arkansas Historical Quarterly*, XXVI (Spring, 1967), 11–23; (Summer, 1967), 162–84; (Autumn, 1967), 226–43; (Winter, 1967), 353–78.
Worley, Ted R. "Arkansas and the Money Crisis of 1836–37," *Journal of Southern History*, XV (May, 1949), 178–91.
———. "The Arkansas State Bank: Ante-Bellum Period," *Arkansas Historical Quarterly*, XXIII (spring, 1964), 65–73.
———. "The Control of the Real Estate Bank of the State of Arkansas, 1836–1855," *Mississippi Valley Historical Review*, XXXVII (December, 1950), 403–26.
Worthen, W. B. *Early Banking in Arkansas*. Little Rock, Ark., 1906.

CONNECTICUT

Morse, Jarvis Means. *A Neglected Period of Connecticut's History, 1818–1850.* New Haven, Conn., 1933.

Woodward, John Gurley. "Currency and Banking in Connecticut," in William T. Davis, editor, *The New England States, Their Constitutional, Judicial, Educational, Commerical, Professional and Industrial History.* 4 vols. Boston, 1897.

DELAWARE

Conrad, Henry C. *History of the State of Delaware, from the Earliest Settlements to the Year 1907.* 3 vols. Wilmington, Dela., 1908.

Monroe, John A. "Party Battles, 1789–1850" in Henry Clay Reed, editor, *Delaware: A History of the First State.* 3 vols. New York, 1947.

Scharf, John Thomas. *History of Delaware, 1609–1888.* 2 vols. Philadelphia, 1888.

GEORGIA

Govan, Thomas Payne. "Banking and the Credit System in Georgia, 1810–1860," *Journal of Southern History,* IV (May, 1938), 164–84.

———. "Banking and the Credit System in Georgia, 1810–1860." Unpublished Ph.D. thesis, Vanderbilt University, 1938.

Heath, Milton Sydman. *Constructive Liberalism: Role of the State in Economic Development in Georgia to 1860.* Cambridge, Mass., 1954.

Murray, Paul. *The Whig Party in Georgia, 1825–1853.* Chapel Hill, N.C., 1948.

ILLINOIS

Cole, Arthur Charles. *The Era of the Civil War, 1848–1870.* Springfield, Ill., 1919.

Dowrie, George William. *The Development of Banking in Illinois, 1817–1863.* Urbana, Ill., 1913.

Eilert, John W. "Illinois Business Incorporations, 1816–1869," *Business History Review,* XXXVII (Autumn, 1963), 169–81.

Ford, Thomas. *A History of Illinois From Its Commencement as a State in 1818 to 1847.* Chicago, 1854.

Krug, Mark M. *Lyman Trumbull: Conservative Radical.* New York, 1965.

Pease, Theodore Calvin. *The Frontier State, 1818–1848.* Chicago, 1919.

Thompson, Charles Manfred. *The Illinois Whigs Before 1846.* Urbana, Ill., 1915.

———. "A Study of the Administration of Thomas Ford, Governor of Illinois, 1842–46," *Illinois Historical Collections,* VII (1911).

INDIANA

Esarey, Logan. "The Organization of the Jackson Party in Indiana," Mississippi Valley Historical Association *Proceedings,* VII (1913–1914).
———. *State Banking in Indiana, 1814–1873.* Bloomington, Ind., 1912.
Harding, W. F. "The State Bank of Indiana," *Journal of Political Economy,* IV (December, 1895), 1–36.
Leonard, Adam A. "Personal Politics in Indiana, 1816–1840," *Indiana Magazine of History,* XIX (March, 1923), 1–56.

KENTUCKY

Collins, Richard H. *History of Kentucky.* 2 vols. Covington, Ky., 1882.
Connelley, William Elsey, and E. M. Coulter. *History of Kentucky.* 5 vols. Chicago, 1922.
Mallalieu, William C., and Sabri M. Akural. "Kentucky Banks in the Crisis Decade: 1834–1844," *Register of the Kentucky Historical Society,* LXV (October, 1967).
Wilson, Samuel M. *History of Kentucky.* 4 vols. Chicago, 1928.

LOUISIANA

Caldwell, Stephen A. *A Banking History of Louisiana.* Baton Rouge, La., 1935.
Greer, James K. "Louisiana Politics, 1845–1861," *Louisiana Historical Quarterly,* XII (July, 1929), 381–425; (October, 1929), 555–610; XIII (January, 1930), 67–116; (April, 1930), 257–303; (July, 1930), 444–83; (October, 1930), 617–54.
Howard, Perry H. *Political Tendencies in Louisiana, 1812–1952.* Baton Rouge, La., 1957.
Neu, Irene. "Louisiana Politics and the Bank Act of 1842." Unpublished paper read at the December, 1964, meeting of the American Historical Association.
Reed, Merl E. *New Orleans and the Railroads: The Struggle for Commercial Empire, 1830–1860.* Baton Rouge, La., 1966.
Sears, Louis Martin. *John Slidell.* Durham, N.C., 1925.
Shugg, Roger W. *Origins of Class Struggle in Louisiana: A Social History of White Farmers and Laborers During Slavery and After, 1840–1875.* Baton Rouge, La., 1939.

MAINE

Chadbourne, W. W. *A History of Banking in Maine, 1779–1930.* Orono, Maine, 1936.
Hatch, Louis Clinton, editor. *Maine, A History.* 3 vols. New York, 1919.

MARYLAND

Bryan, Alfred Cookman. *History of State Banking in Maryland.* Baltimore, 1899.
Scharf, J. Thomas. *History of Maryland, From the Earliest Period to the Present Day.* 3 vols. Baltimore, 1879.

MASSACHUSETTS

Darling, Arthur B., *Political Changes in Massachusetts, 1824–1848: A Study of Liberal Movements in Politics.* New Haven, Conn., 1925.
Handlin, Oscar, and Mary Flug Handlin. *Commonwealth, A Study of Government in the American Economy: Massachusetts, 1774–1861.* New York, 1947.
Nye, Russel B. *George Bancroft, Brahmin Rebel.* New York, 1944.
Scheiber, Harry N. "George Bancroft and the Bank of Michigan, 1837–1841," *Michigan History,* XLIV (March, 1960).
Whitney, David R. *The Suffolk Bank.* Cambridge, Mass., 1878.

MICHIGAN

Cooley, Thomas M. "State Banks Issues in Michigan, A Retrospect of Legislation," Michigan Political Science Association *Publications,* I (May, 1893), 4–22.
Streeter, Floyd Benjamin. *Political Parties in Michigan, 1837–1860.* Lansing, Mich., 1918.
Utley, H. M. "The Wild Cat Banking System of Michigan," *Report of the Pioneer Society of the State of Michigan Together with Reports of County, Town, and District Pioneer Societies,* V (1884), 209–22.

MISSISSIPPI

Brough, Charles Hillman. "The History of Banking in Mississippi," Mississippi Historical Society *Publications,* III (1900), 317–40.
Carroll, Thomas Battle. *Historical Sketches of Oktibbeha County Mississippi.* Edited and amended by Alfred Benjamin Butts, Alfred Garner and Frederic Davis Mellen. Gulfport, Miss., 1931.
Claiborne, John Francis Hamtramck. *Mississippi, As a Province, Territory*

and State, with Bibliographical Notices of Eminent Citizens. Jackson, Miss., 1880.

Dickey, Dallas C. *Seargent S. Prentiss: Whig Orator of the Old South.* Baton Rouge, La., 1945.

Ingraham, Joseph Holt. *The South-West, By a Yankee.* 2 vols. New York, 1835.

James, D. Clayton. *Antebellum Natchez.* Baton Rouge, 1968.

Kamper, Anna Alice. "A Social and Economic History of Ante-Bellum Bolivar County, Mississippi." Unpublished M.A. thesis, University of Alabama, 1942.

Kirwan, Albert D. *Revolt of the Rednecks: Mississippi Politics: 1876–1925.* Lexington, Ky., 1951.

Lowe, E. N. *A Preliminary Study of Soils of Mississippi.* Nashville, Tenn., 1911.

Lowry, R., and W. H. McCardle. *A History of Mississippi.* Jackson, Miss., 1891.

Lynch, James D. *Bench and Bar of Mississippi.* Publisher and date of publication unknown.

Miles, Edwin Arthur. *Jacksonian Democracy in Mississippi.* Chapel Hill, N.C., 1960.

Ranck, James Byrne. *Albert Gallatin Brown: Radical Southern Nationalist.* New York, 1937.

Rowland, Dunbar. *History of Mississippi, the Heart of the South.* 2 vols. Chicago, 1925.

Rowland, Dunbar, editor. *Mississippi: Comprising Sketches of Counties, Towns, Events, Institutions, and Persons, Arranged in Cyclopedic Form.* 3 vols. Atlanta, Ga., 1907.

Shenton, James B. *Robert John Walker: A Politician From Jackson to Lincoln.* New York, 1961.

Sumners, Mary Floyd. "Politics in Tishomingo County, 1836–1860," *Journal of Mississippi History,* XXVIII (May, 1966), 133–51.

Sydnor, Charles Sackett. *A Gentleman of the Old Natchez Region: Benjamin L. C. Wailes.* Durham, N.C., 1938.

——. *Slavery in Mississippi.* New York, 1933.

Walmsley, James Elliott. "The Presidential Campaign of 1844 in Mississippi," Mississippi Historical Society *Publications,* IX (1906), 179–97.

Weaver, Herbert. *Mississippi Farmers, 1850–1860.* Nashville, Tenn., 1945.

Winston, E. T. *Story of Pontotoc.* Pontotoc, Miss., 1931.

Winston, James E. "The Mississippi Whigs and the Tariff, 1834–1844," *Mississippi Valley Historical Review,* XXII (March, 1936), 505–24.

Works Projects Administration. "Jones County, Mississippi." Manuscript, Mississippi Department of Archives and History, Jackson, 1937.

———. "Oktibbeha County, Mississippi." Manuscript, Mississippi Department of Archives and History, Jackson, 1937.

———. "Wayne County, Mississippi." Manuscript, Mississippi Department of Archives and History, Jackson, 1936.

Young, David Nathaniel. "The Mississippi Whigs, 1834–1860." Unpublished Ph.D. thesis, University of Alabama, 1968.

MISSOURI

Anderson, Hattie M. "The Evolution of a Frontier Society in Missouri, 1815–1828," *Missouri Historical Review*, XXXII (April, 1938).

Cable, J. R. *The Bank of the State of Missouri*. New York, 1923.

Chambers, William Nisbet. *Old Bullion Benton: Senator From the New West, Thomas Hart Benton, 1782–1858*. Boston, 1956.

Dorsey, Dorothy B. "The Panic and Depression of 1837–43 in Missouri," *Missouri Historical Review*, XXX (January, 1936), 132–61.

———. "The Panic of 1819 in Missouri," *Missouri Historical Review*, XXIX (January, 1935), 79–91.

Jones, Breckenridge. "A Hundred Years of Banking in Missouri," *Missouri Historical Review* (January, 1921).

Mering, John Vollmer. *The Whig Party in Missouri*. Columbia, Mo., 1967.

Parrish, William E. *David Rice Atchison of Missouri, Border Politician*. Columbia, Mo., 1961.

Primm, James Neal. *Economic Policy in the Development of a Western State, Missouri, 1820–1860*. Cambridge, Mass., 1954.

Sharp, James Roger. "Governor Daniel Dunklin's Jacksonian Democracy in Missouri, 1832–1836," *Missouri Historical Review*, LVI (April, 1962), 217–29.

Violette, Eugene Morrow. *A History of Missouri*. Cape Girardeau, Mo., 1956.

NEW HAMPSHIRE

Grant, Philip A., Jr. "The Bank Controversy and New Hampshire Politics, 1834–35," *Historical New Hampshire*, XXIII (Autumn, 1968), 19–36.

Sewell, Richard H. *John P. Hale and the Politics of Abolition*. Cambridge, Mass., 1965.

Stackpole, Everett S. *History of New Hampshire*. 4 vols. New York, 1916.

NEW JERSEY

Cadman, John. *The Corporation in New Jersey: Business and Politics, 1791–1875.* Cambridge, Mass., 1949.

NEW YORK

Albion, Robert Greenhalgh. *The Rise of New York Port (1815–1860).* New York, 1939.

Alexander, Dealva Stanwood. *A Political History of the State of New York.* 3 vols. New York, 1906.

Benson, Lee. *The Concept of Jacksonian Democracy: New York as a Test Case.* Princeton, N.J., 1961.

Byrdsall, F. *The History of the Loco-Foco or Equal Rights Party, Its Movements, Conventions and Proceedings with Short Characteristic Sketches of its Prominent Men.* New York, 1842.

Chaddock, Robert E. *The Safety Fund Banking System in New York, 1829–1866.* Washington, D.C., 1910.

Degler, Carl N. "The Locofocos: Urban 'Agrarians,'" *Journal of Economic History,* XVI (September, 1956), 322–33.

Donovan, Herbert D. A. *The Barnburners: A Study of the Internal Movements in the Political History of New York State and the Resulting Changes in Political Affiliation, 1830–1852.* New York, 1925.

Flagg, Azariah C. *Banks and Banking in the State of New York From the Adoption of the Constitution in 1777 to 1864.* New York, 1868.

Fox, Dixon Ryan. *The Decline of Aristocracy in the Politics of New York, 1801–1840.* New York, 1965.

Hammond, Jabez D. *The History of Political Parties in the State of New-York, From the Ratification of the Federal Constitution to December, 1840.* 2 vols. Albany, N.Y., 1842.

———. *Life and Times of Silas Wright, Late Governor of the State of New York.* Syracuse, N.Y., 1848.

Hugins, Walter. *Jacksonian Democracy and the Working Class: A Study of the New York Workingmen's Movement, 1829–1837.* Stanford, Calif., 1960.

Spencer, Ivor Debenham. *The Victor and the Spoils: A Life of William L. Marcy.* Providence, R. I., 1959.

Trimble, William. "Diverging Tendencies in New York Democracy in the Period of the Locofocos," *American Historical Review,* XXIV (April, 1919).

NORTH CAROLINA

Boyd, William K. "Currency and Banking in North Carolina, 1790–1836," *Trinity College Historical Society*, X, 52–86.

Hamilton, J. G. De Roulhac. *Party Politics in North Carolina, 1835–1860*. Chapel Hill, N.C., 1916.

Hoffmann, William S. *Andrew Jackson and North Carolina Politics*. Chapel Hill, N.C., 1958.

Norton, Clarence Clifford. *The Democratic Party in Ante-Bellum North Carolina, 1835–1861*. Chapel Hill, N.C., 1930.

OHIO

Baer, Elizabeth. "William S. Groesbeck," *Bulletin of the Historical and Philosophical Society of Ohio*, XX (April, 1962), 111–22.

Bates, James L. *Alfred Kelley, His Life and Work*. Columbus, Ohio, 1888.

Baughin, William A. "The Development of Nativism in Cincinnati," *Bulletin of the Cincinnati Historical Society*, XII (October, 1964), 240–55.

Bogart, Ernest Ludlow. *Financial History of Ohio*. Urbana, Ill., 1912.

———. *Internal Improvements and State Debt in Ohio: An Essay in Economic History*. London, 1924.

Chaddock, Robert E. *Ohio Before 1850: A Study of the Early Influence of Pennsylvania and Southern Populations in Ohio*. New York, 1908.

Coover, A. B. "Ohio Banking Institutions, 1803–1866," *Ohio Archaeological and Historical Quarterly*, XXI (April–July, 1912), 296–320.

Davis, Harold E. "Economic Basis of Ohio Politics, 1820–1840," *Ohio Archaeological and Historical Quarterly*, XLVII (1938), 288–318.

———. "Social and Economic Basis of the Whig Party in Ohio, 1828–1840." Unpublished Ph.D. thesis, Western Reserve University, 1933.

Dorn, Helen P. "Samuel Medary, Journalist and Politician, 1801–1864," *Ohio Archaeological and Historical Quarterly*, LII (1944), 14–38.

Downes, Randolph Chandler. "Evolution of Ohio County Boundaries," *Ohio Archaeological and Historical Quarterly*, XXXVI (July, 1927), 340–477.

Finn, Chester. "The Ohio Canals: Public Enterprise on the Frontier," *Ohio Archaeological and Historical Quarterly*, LI (January–March, 1942), 1–28.

Ford, Henry A., and Mrs. Kate B. Ford, compilers. *History of Cincinnati, Ohio*. Cleveland, 1881.

Gephart, William F. *Transportation and Industrial Development in the Middle West.* New York, 1909.

Gilkey, Elliot Howard. *The Ohio Hundred Year Book: A Hand Book of the Public Men and Public Institutions of Ohio From the Formation of the North-West Territory (1787) to July 1, 1901.* Columbus, Ohio. 1901.

Greve, Charles Theodore. *Centennial History of Cincinnati and Representative Citizens.* Chicago, 1904.

Harlow, Alvin Fay. *The Serene Cincinnatians.* New York, 1950.

Henlein, Paul C. *The Cattle Kingdom in the Ohio Valley, 1783–1860.* Lexington, Ky., 1959.

Holt, Edgar A. "Party Politics in Ohio, 1840–1850," *Ohio Archaeological and Historical Quarterly,* XXXVII (July, 1928), 439–591, and XXXVIII (January, 1929), 47–182.

Hooper, Osman Castle. "John Brough," *Ohio Archaeological and Historical Quarterly,* XIII (January, 1904), 40–70.

Howe, Henry. *Historical Collections of Ohio, An Encyclopedia of the State.* Cincinnati, 1847.

———. *Historical Collections of Ohio, An Encyclopedia of the State.* 2 vols. Norwalk, Ohio, 1896.

———. *Historical Collections of Ohio, An Encyclopedia of the State.* 2 vols. Cincinnati, 1907.

Hubbart, Henry Clyde. *The Older Middle West, 1840–1880, Its Social, Economic and Political Life and Sectional Tendencies Before, During and After the Civil War.* New York, 1936.

Huntington, Charles Clifford. *A History of Banking and Currency in Ohio Before the Civil War.* Columbus, Ohio, 1915.

Jones, Wilbur D. "Some Cincinnati German Societies a Century Ago," *Bulletin of the Historical and Philosophical Society of Ohio,* XX (January, 1962), 38–43.

Knapp, H. S. *History of the Maumee Valley Commencing With its Occupation by the French in 1680.* Toledo, Ohio, 1877.

Lloyd, W. A., J. I. Falconer, and C. E. Thorne. *The Agriculture of Ohio: Bulletin 326 of the Ohio Agricultural Experiment Station.* Wooster, Ohio, 1918.

Lottick, Kenneth V. "Culture Transplantation in the Connecticut Reserve," *Bulletin of the Historical and Philosophical Society of Ohio,* XVII (July, 1959), 155–66.

McClelland, C. P., and Charles Clifford Huntington. *History of the Ohio Canals, Their Construction, Cost, Use and Partial Abandonment.* Columbus, Ohio, 1905.

McGrane, Reginald Charles. *William Allen: A Study in Western Democracy.* Columbus, Ohio, 1925.

Morris, B. Franklin, editor. *The Life of Thomas Morris: Pioneer and Long a Legislator of Ohio, and U. S. Senator from 1833 to 1839.* Cincinnati, 1856.

Northrop, N. B. *Pioneer History of Medina County.* Medina, Ohio, 1861.

Ohio Historical Society. *The Governors of Ohio.* Columbus, Ohio, 1954.

Price, Erwin H. "The Election of 1848 in Ohio," *Ohio Archaeological and Historical Quarterly,* XXXVI (April, 1927), 188–311.

Randall, Emilius O., and Daniel J. Ryan. *History of Ohio: The Rise and Progress of an American State.* 5 vols. New York, 1912.

Ratcliffe, Donald. "Political Divisions in Ohio in the Years of Jacksonian Democracy." Unpublished Bachelor of Philosophy Thesis, Oxford University, 1966.

Roseboom, Eugene, H. *The Civil War Era, 1850–1873.* Columbus, Ohio, 1944.

———. "Ohio in the Presidential Election of 1824," *Ohio Archaeological and Historical Quarterly,* XXVI (April, 1917), 157–223.

Scheiber, Harry N. "Entrepreneurship and Western Development: The Case of Micajah T. Williams," *The Business History Review,* XXXVII (winter, 1963), 345–68.

Stevens, Harry R. *The Early Jackson Party in Ohio.* Durham, N.C., 1957.

Upton, Harriet Taylor. *History of the Western Reserve.* 3 vols. Chicago, 1910.

Webster, Homer J. "History of the Democratic Party Organization in the Northwest, 1824–1840," *Ohio Archaeological and Historical Publications,* XXIV (January, 1915), 1–120.

Weisenburger, Francis P. *The Passing of the Frontier, 1825–1850.* Columbus, Ohio, 1941.

Wittke, Carl. "The Germans of Cincinnati," *Bulletin of the Historical and Philosophical Society of Ohio,* XX (January, 1962), 3–14.

———. *We Who Built America: The Saga of the Immigrant.* Revised edition. Cleveland, 1967.

PENNSYLVANIA

Baltzell, E. Digby. *An American Business Aristocracy.* New York, 1962.

Bartlett, Marguerite G. *The Chief Phases of Pennsylvania Politics in the Jacksonian Period.* Allentown, Pa., 1919.

Ferguson, Russell J. *Early Western Pennsylvania Politics.* Pittsburgh, Pa., 1938.

Geary, Sister M. Theophane. *A History of Third Parties in Pennsylvania, 1840–1860.* Washington, D.C., 1938.

Hartz, Louis. *Economic Policy and Democratic Thought: Pennsylvania, 1776–1860.* Cambridge, Mass., 1948.

Holdsworth, John T. *Financing an Empire: History of Banking in Pennsylvania.* 4 vols. Chicago, 1928.

Hussey, Miriam. *Wholesale Prices in Philadelphia, 1784–1861.* Philadelphia, 1936.

Kehl, James A. *Ill Feeling in the Era of Good Feeling: Western Pennsylvania Political Battles, 1815–25.* Pittsburgh, Pa., 1956.

Klein, Philip Shriver. *Pennsylvania Politics, 1817–1832: A Game Without Rules.* Philadelphia, 1940.

———. *President James Buchanan, A Biography.* University Park, Pa., 1962.

Korngold, Ralph. *Thaddeus Stevens; A Being Darkly Wise and Rudely Great.* New York, 1955.

Meigs, William M. *The Life of Charles Jared Ingersoll.* Philadelphia, 1900.

Mueller, Henry R. *The Whig Party in Pennsylvania.* New York, 1922.

Snyder, Charles McCool. *The Jacksonian Heritage: Pennsylvania Politics, 1833–1848.* Harrisburg, Pa., 1958.

SOUTH CAROLINA

Smith, Alfred Glaze, Jr. *Economic Readjustment of an Old Cotton State: South Carolina, 1820–1860.* Columbia, S.C., 1958.

White, Laura A. *Robert Barnwell Rhett: Father of Secession.* New York, 1931.

TENNESSEE

Abernathy, Thomas P. "The Early Development of Commerce and Banking in Tennessee," *Mississippi Valley Historical Review,* XIV (December, 1927), 311–25.

———."The Origin of the Whig Party in Tennessee," *Mississippi Valley Historical Review,* XII (March, 1926), 504–22.

Campbell, Claude A. *The Development of Banking in Tennessee.* Nashville, Tenn., 1932.

Folmsbee, Stanley John. *Sectionalism and Internal Improvements in Tennessee, 1796–1845.* Philadelphia, 1939.

Parks, Joseph Howard. *Felix Grundy, Champion of Democracy.* Baton Rouge, La., 1940.

Sellers, Charles Grier, Jr. "Banking and Politics in Jackson's Tennessee,

1817–1827," *Mississippi Valley Historical Review,* XLI (June, 1954), 61–84.

———. "Jackson Men with Feet of Clay," *American Historical Review,* LXII (April, 1957), 537–51.

VERMONT

Crockett, Walter Hill. *Vermont, the Green Mountain State.* 4 vols. New York, 1921.

Grant, Philip A., Jr. "The Antimasons Retain Control of the Green Mountain State," *Vermont History,* XXXIV (July, 1966), 169–87.

VIRGINIA

Abbott, Richard H. "Yankee Farmers in Northern Virginia, 1840–1860," *Virginia Magazine of History and Biography,* LXXVI (January, 1968), 56–63.

Agee, Helene B. *Facets of Goochland (Virginia) County's History.* Richmond, Va., 1962.

Ambler, Charles Henry. *Sectionalism in Virginia from 1776 to 1861.* Chicago, 1910.

———. *Thomas Ritchie, A Study in Virginia Politics.* Richmond, Va., 1913.

———. "Virginia and the Presidential Succession, 1840–1844," in *Essays in American History: Dedicated to Frederick Jackson Turner.* New York, 1910.

Boddie, John Bennett. *Seventeenth Century Isle of Wight County Virginia.* Chicago, 1938.

Bradshaw, Herbert Clarence. *History of Prince Edward County, Virginia: From its Earliest Settlements Through its Establishment in 1754 to its Bicentennial Year.* Richmond, Va., 1955.

Braverman, Howard. "The Economic and Political Background of the Conservative Revolt in Virginia," *Virginia Magazine of History and Biography,* LX (April, 1952), 266–87.

Clement, Maud Carter. *The History of Pittsylvania County Virginia.* Lynchburg, Va., 1929.

Collier, James Glen. "The Political Career of James McDowell, 1830–1851." Unpublished Ph.D. thesis, University of North Carolina, 1963.

Craven, Avery Odell. *Edmund Ruffin, Southerner: A Study in Secession.* New York, 1932.

———. *Soil Exhaustion as a Factor in the Agricultural History of Virginia and Maryland, 1606–1860.* Gloucester, Mass., 1965.

Curry, Richard Orr. *A House Divided: A Study of Statehood Politics and the Copperhead Movement in West Virginia.* Pittsburgh, Pa., 1964.

Dunaway, Wyland Fuller. *History of the James River and Kanawha Company.* New York, 1922.

Ellis, Henry G. "Edmund Ruffin: His Life and Times," *John P. Branch Historical Papers of Randolph-Macon College,* III (June, 1910), 99–123.

Fields, Emmett B. "The Agricultural Population of Virginia, 1850–1860." Unpublished Ph.D. thesis, Vanderbilt University, 1953.

Frank, John P. *Justice Daniel Dissenting: A Biography of Peter V. Daniel, 1784–1860.* Cambridge, Mass., 1964.

Goodrich, Carter. "The Virginia System of Mixed Enterprise: A Study of State Planning of Internal Improvements," *Political Science Quarterly,* LXIV (September, 1949).

Gordon, Armistead C. *William Fitzhugh Gordon.* New York, 1909.

Gruchy, Allan Garfield. *Supervision and Control of Virginia State Banks.* New York, 1937.

Hall, Claude H. *Abel Parker Upshur: Conservative Virginian, 1790–1844.* Madison, Wisc., 1963.

Howe, Henry. *Historical Collections of Virginia.* Charleston, S.C., 1846.

Laing, James T. "The Early Development of the Coal Industry in the Western Counties of Virginia, 1800–1865," *West Virginia History,* XXVII (January, 1966), 144–55.

Lutz, Francis Earle. *Chesterfield, an Old Virginia County.* Richmond, Va., 1954.

Main, Jackson T. "Sections and Politics in Virginia, 1781–1787," *William and Mary Quarterly,* XII (January, 1955), 96–112.

Morton, Oren F. *A History of Rockbridge County Virginia.* Staunton, Va., 1920.

Nicholson, Edgar P. "James McDowell," *John P. Branch Historical Papers of Randolph-Macon College,* IV (June, 1914), 5–34.

Pendleton, William C. *History of Tazewell County and Southwest Virginia, 1748–1920.* Richmond, Va., 1920.

Peyton, J. Lewis. *History of Augusta County, Virginia.* Bridgewater, Va., 1953.

Porter, Albert Ogden. *County Government in Virginia: A Legislative History, 1607–1904.* New York, 1947.

Prettyman, E. B. "John Letcher," *John P. Branch Historical Papers of Randolph-Macon College,* IV (June, 1913), 116–37.

Rice, Otis K. "Coal Mining in the Kanawha Valley to 1861: A View of

Industrialization in the Old South," *Journal of Southern History,* XXXI (November, 1965), 393–416.

Risjord, Norman J. "The Virginia Federalists," *Journal of Southern History,* XXXIII (November, 1967), 486–517.

Robert, Joseph Clarke. *The Story of Tobacco in America.* New York, 1949.

——. *The Tobacco Kingdom: Plantation, Market, and Factory in Virginia and North Carolina, 1800–1860.* Durham, N.C., 1938.

Royall, W. C. *History of Virginia Banks Prior to the Civil War.* New York, 1907.

Schuricht, Herrmann. *History of the German Element in Virginia.* 2 vols. Baltimore, Md., 1898.

Shanks, Henry T. *The Secession Movement in Virginia, 1847–1861.* Richmond, Va., 1934.

Sanderlin, Walter S. *The Great National Project: A History of the Chesapeake and Ohio Canal.* Baltimore, 1946.

Scott, W. W. *A History of Orange County Virginia: From its Formation in 1734 (O.S.) to the End of Reconstruction in 1870.* Richmond, Va., 1907.

Simms, Henry H. *The Rise of Whigs in Virginia, 1824–1840.* Richmond, Va., 1929.

Squires, W. H. T. *Through Centuries Three: A Short History of the People of Virginia.* Portsmouth, Va., 1929.

Stoner, Robert Douthat. *The Seed-Bed of the Republic: A Study of the Pioneer in the Upper (Southern) Valley of Virginia.* Kingsport, Tenn., 1962.

Starnes, George T. *Sixty Years of Branch Banking in Virginia.* New York, 1931.

Strickler, Harry M. *A History of Page County Virginia.* Richmond, Va., 1952.

Sutton, Robert P. "Nostalgia, Pessimism, and Malaise: The Doomed Aristocrat in Late-Jeffersonian Virginia," *Virginia Magazine of History and Biography,* LXXVI (January, 1968), 41–55.

Swem, Earl G., and John W. Williams. *A Register of the General Assembly of Virginia, 1776–1918, and of the Constitutional Convention.* Richmond, Va., 1918.

Wayland, Francis Fay. *Andrew Stevenson, Democrat and Diplomat, 1785–1857.* Philadelphia, 1949.

Wayland, John W. *A History of Rockingham County Virginia.* Dayton, Va., 1912.

————. *A History of Shenandoah County Virginia.* Strasburg, Va., 1927.

————. *The German Element of the Shenandoah Valley of Virginia.* Charlottesville, Va., 1907.

Wertenbaker, Thomas J. *Norfolk: Historic Southern Port.* Durham, N.C., 1931.

Wingfield, Marshall. *A History of Caroline County Virginia, From Its Foundation in 1727 to 1924.* Richmond, Va., 1924.

Woodehouse, Edgar James. "The Public Life of George C. Dromgoole," *John P. Branch Historical Papers of Randolph-Macon College,* I (June, 1904), 260–86.

INDEX